ANDRÉ MAUROIS

MEMOIRS

André Maurois

MEMOIRS

1885–1967

Translated from the French by
DENVER LINDLEY

THE BODLEY HEAD
LONDON SYDNEY
TORONTO

PUBLISHER'S NOTE

The first half of these Memoirs was originally published
under the title *Call No Man Happy* in 1943. In his last
years, while working on the second half of his Memoirs, the
author subjected the first half to an extensive revision.

SBN 370 01312 3
Printed and bound in Great Britain for
The Bodley Head Ltd
9 Bow Street, London W C 2
by William Clowes & Sons, Ltd, Beccles
Set in Monotype Fournier
This edition first published 1970

CONTENTS

Preface, vii

PART ONE

THE APPRENTICE YEARS

1. The Earthly Paradise, 3
2. The Tree of Knowledge, 13
3. Paradise Lost, 22
4. The River of the Arrow, 31
5. Barracks School, 42
6. The Main Office, 51
7. 'The Practical Man Writes to Me . . .', 59
8. The Sylph, 68
9. 'For Better, For Worse', 76
10. O Time, Stay Thy Flight . . . , 86
11. British Expeditionary Force, 94
12. Colonel Bramble, 104

PART TWO

THE YEARS OF LABOUR

13. Home-coming, 117
14. Eurydice Twice Lost, 128
15. Life Must Go On, 137
16. The Walkyrie, 149
17. Climates, 161
18. The Twilight of the Gods, 174
19. My Dear Time's Waste, 181
20. The Ring of Polycrates, 192
21. The Last of the Fair Days, 208
22. The Kingdom of God, 213

PART THREE

THE YEARS OF MISFORTUNE

23. Sitzkrieg, 223
24. Blitzkrieg, 238
25. The Tarpeian Rock, 254
26. Amica America, 272
27. Pilgrim of the War, 283
28. Operation Torch, 293
29. Servitude and Grandeur, 303
30. From Corsica to Italy, 311
31. Return to America, 319
32. The End of Exile, 326

PART FOUR

THE YEARS OF SERENITY

33. The Return, 339
34. Back on Course, 350
35. Intermezzo, 359
36. The Big Biographies, 366
37. In Search of Time Past, 379
38. 1958–62, 390
39. Essendiéras, 399
40. Toward the Dénouement, 408
41. Annus Mirabilis, 417
42. Old Captain Death . . . , 426
    Index, 429

Preface

I beg the reader to bear in mind that these Memoirs are the personal recollections and story of a man, not an epoch. As it happened, I have been involved in the great events of my time, but I have endeavoured to evoke them as I saw and felt them and not as they appear to me today in the light of subsequent revelations. This is a rule I imposed upon myself in my biographies; I could hardly violate it in autobiography.

It is clear, for instance, that from New York City in 1940–41 I formed a very imperfect picture of what was going on in France at that moment. From the occupied zone I received no news at all; from the so-called 'free' zone letters reached me which had been written under fear of censorship and which distorted the facts. I had to make my decisions in the dark; I did so with the ardent desire of acting in the best interests of France. I hope that in this I often succeeded; others, pursuing different paths, were no less devoted to the same cause.

I have not wished to pass over the attacks to which I have been subjected on numerous occasions in the course of my life. They were unjust and often mendacious; they form a part of my story. On the other hand, I have taken the liberty of citing a small number of laudatory letters and comments. In justification I can say that this is not done out of vanity. Praises always surprise me. But to omit them entirely would be to falsify the perspective. Moreover they gave me pleasure at the time; everyone has need on occasion to warm himself in the sunshine of affection; I above all, who was by nature scrupulous and too much inclined to self-doubt.

Although I have known, sometimes intimately, many of the great men of my time, the reader will find in this book only a few conversations with them. Those that I had recorded were published in another work, *Choses nues*, where the curious and faithful reader will find a useful complement to these Memoirs. And now Godspeed! This, as Montaigne said, is a book of good will; may it be read with good will.

André Maurois
September 20, 1967
(before my visit to the surgeon)

PART ONE

THE APPRENTICE YEARS

I

The Earthly Paradise

For several weeks I have been teaching French in a California college. My window opens on a Spanish cloister planted with palms and cypresses, where pretty American college girls stroll. The sky has been blue since my arrival and will remain clear for the whole summer. How different this reliable climate is from the capricious valley of the Seine where I spent my youth, and what strange events have been needed to transform that adolescent, the heir to Norman spinning and weaving mills, into a quinquagenarian professor on the Pacific Coast!

From the music room rise the notes of a piano. I recognize a toccata by Bach and the playing of Miss Lowe, a tiny, exquisite and dexterous Chinese. Two nuns enter the patio. One of them, Sister Agnes Rita, handed me yesterday a brilliant and sound appraisal of François Mauriac; her face framed in a white coif gives her the appearance of a portrait by Philippe de Champaigne; her solid treatise seemed buttressed by centuries of theology and wisdom. The pretty blonde who greets the nuns with a smile is Marion Morris of Salt Lake City, daughter and granddaughter of Mormons; she spent some years in Paris and speaks lovingly of the Rue Jacob with its ancient courts and wrought-iron balconies. That brunette with eyes the colour of the sky is Bettina Schuster, an exile from Vienna, who learned the French of Rousseau and Amiel in Geneva. It would not surprise me if she possessed genius, but I am a professor who is passionately in love with his calling and is always tempted to believe he has discovered a masterpiece the instant he recognizes the accent of sincerity.

Yesterday I was fifty-six years old, and the girls of Mills College composed a sketch for this melancholy anniversary. The setting was a library. Midnight sounded. On the stroke, the heroes and heroines of my books—Colonel Bramble, Philippe Marcenat, Odile, Denise Herpain, Bernard Quesnay—suddenly came to life and spoke. 'There,'

I thought, listening to them, 'there you have what is left of a life and a life's work!'

A little later when I had returned to my room, it occurred to me that a legend sometimes survives as well as a surprising, unreal being whom I have called The Personage. The Personage is the man others believe we are or have been. He may be multiple. Two different Personages, contradictory and even hostile to each other, may survive us in the minds of our friends and our enemies and continue after our death a struggle in which our posthumous reputation is at stake. If we have been complex, reticent, mysterious, or simply honest, a whole army of Personages may carry on endless battles to obtain the right of representing us, and the combat continues up to the moment when impartial Oblivion puts these bellicose marionettes to bed together in the same box and locks it up for ever. 'In my case,' I thought, 'oblivion will come quickly. But today the clash of feelings is so violent that before eternal silence descends, there may spring from me several very astonishing Personages. Some will be better than I, others worse. If I am to be loved or hated, at least I should like the hatred or sympathy to be for the real man. Why don't I try to depict him as I think I have known him?'

At that moment, while the breeze from the Pacific swayed the eucalyptus leaves beneath the stars, I decided to write the story of my life in a direct, unromanticized fashion. Naturally, like every biographer, I shall make mistakes, some through fault of memory, others through fault of judgment. I hope, however, that if some leisured man of learning or some student in search of a thesis should ever attempt to disentangle the truth and poetry in this book, he will find few serious omissions or culpable complacencies. If I am conscious, with humility, of my mistakes and weaknesses, I remember, too, with pleasure those moments, of which there have been not a few in my life, when I have deliberately sacrificed my own interests for what I believed to be my duty. In choosing that duty I may have been mistaken, but that is not a mortal sin in the eyes of God or in those of a reader of good will. The man I am going to portray is the man I was or the one I believe myself to have been. Forgive him his trespasses, good people, as he himself forgives those who have trespassed against him.

My earliest memory is that of Sunday mornings in Elbeuf at the time when I was four or five years old and the town used to be awakened by the firemen's bugles. They would come down our street once a week, wearing antiquated helmets and hauling a hand pump in order to test the hydrant. They always played the same tune:

L'as-tu vue
La casquette, la casquette?
L'as-tu vue
La casquette au Pèr' Bugeaud?*

But this martial reveille gave me the same delight each time. My father would come in, pick me up in his arms, wrapping my long night-gown around my bare feet, and find a place for me beside him at the window. The fire chief, recognizable by his red plume, would shout to us, 'Good morning, gentlemen!'

To see the hose being unrolled, the powerful jet of water that rose higher than the house, the frail ladder that was hoisted, section by section, to the roofs, seemed to me the finest spectacle in the world. Then the ladder would be slid back into place, the hose would be rolled up again on its drum, the chief with the copper helmet would order: 'Fall in!', the firemen would form a column of twos, the bugler would play *La Casquette*, and the company would set off in time to the music toward the next hydrant.

'They manoeuvre like conscripts,' my father would say, putting the shivering small boy back into his still-warm bed.

This was the comment of an old soldier.

He had a passion for things military. A native of Alsace, he had seen the War of 1870 and at the age of seventeen had tended the French wounded on the battlefield of Froeschwiller. Later he had done military service in the infantry at Limoges, and had then become a scrupulous noncommissioned officer whose fine handwriting was the pride and joy of the sergeant major. As soon as my sisters and I could walk, he began drilling us and would make us keep step by singing marching songs. 'My tunic has one button, march!' he would commence, and we had to reply, 'My tunic has one button, march!'

'March briskly, march briskly, together we march briskly,' my father would go on, and we would thus get up to fifty or a hundred buttons.

The first book I learned to read was a history of the War of 1870: *Français et Allemands* by Dick de Lonlay. The names of Borny, of

* Have you seen the cap, the cap? Have you seen the cap of Pèr' Bugeaud?

Rezonville, of Saint-Privat, of Gravelotte used to evoke in my mind confused, sanguinary and tragic scenes: those of Chanzy and Gambetta, ideas of revenge and pride.

It is often said that those persons who remain optimistic all their lives and, in spite of trials and tribulations, maintain their confidence in life, are the ones who have had the good fortune to enjoy a happy childhood. My case would support this theory. Few men have felt a keener and more lasting admiration for their parents than I. Even today when I think about them and compare them with the thousands of persons I have known, I can see clearly that they were superior in point of moral worth to almost all the others. My father, an unselfish man, brave, discreet and appealingly modest, had four passions: France, Alsace, his mill and his family. As far as he was concerned, the rest of the universe hardly existed.

Scrupulous to a fault, he used to tire out the local tax commission and the customs authorities by the meticulous detail of his declarations. One of the lessons he taught me, as soon as I was able to understand, was respect for law and regulations. Later, when the income tax had been enacted and he would hear rich friends talk complacently about their ingenious and culpable evasions, he would become violently angry. His timidity, which was great and which made his conversation abrupt, nervous and difficult, would immediately vanish the moment his convictions were threatened. He had formed the most exacting conception of his duties and held himself responsible both for the quality of the products of the mill and the well-being of the workmen. If all captains of industry had lived and thought as he did, the bourgeoisie would have become a respected aristocracy.

My father, Ernest Herzog, was born in the Alsatian village of Ringendorf. He did well in his classes at the College of Bouxwiller, and then at the age of sixteen entered the mill belonging to his mother's brothers, the Uncles Fraenckel, at Bischwiller. This prosperous and well-managed business employed at that time four hundred workers and produced woollen goods. In 1871 the annexation of Alsace by Germany created a difficult situation for my family as for so many others. They had to make a choice. My great-uncles and my father of course chose France. A short exploration convinced them that Elbeuf, a small industrial town near Rouen, closely resembled Bischwiller in character and products; they determined to move their mill there.

My father, though still quite young, remained behind for a year in the Alsatian mill to complete its liquidation, and from that time gave evidence of his great capacity for work and management. He arranged, despite immense difficulties, for the departure and journey of the four hundred workmen. Then he too came to live in Normandy. But nothing ever consoled him for having had to leave Alsace. Our house was full of engravings showing the cathedral of Strasbourg, storks nesting on gabled roofs, and girls with straw-coloured hair tied with huge black ribbons. Every year the Alsatians in Elbeuf gathered for a big celebration at which they would sing their native songs and dance Alsatian dances. At such times I would see tears in my parents' eyes.

On Christmas eve we would go to the Protestant church whose pastor, Monsieur Roehrich, was an Alsatian, to join in a Christmas-tree party. The little red, white and blue candles, the tinsel, the gilded walnuts, the imitation snow, thrilled me. Everyone would sing, 'O beautiful pine tree, king of the forests, How dearly I love your greenery...' And on the way home my father would describe the pine forests of Alsace with their mantles of snow. It was at one of these Christmas parties, when I was five or six years old, that I learned from another child, who was beside me in the church, that my parents were Jews and that this was an astonishing fact.

For a long time I had recited every evening before going to sleep a prayer that began with unfamiliar and incomprehensible words and ended:

'God bless papa, mama, grandmother in Elbeuf, grandmother and grandfather in Paris, my little sisters, my uncles and aunts, my cousins, my friends, Marie and Emilie (these were the cook and chambermaid) and all those I love...'

I believed that other children prayed in the same fashion. In addition, my mother for a year had been giving me Bible lessons, but I never dreamed there could be any connection between me, a little French boy born in Elbeuf, and a people who had crossed the Red Sea in the midst of the waters, had seen their food descend from heaven in the desert, and had conversed with God on the fiery summits of mountains. On Christmas night, when I asked my father about my friend's comment, he told me that we were indeed Jews, but that Pastor Roehrich's Christianity was a beautiful religion too, a close relative and daughter of ours.

My mother brought us up entirely by herself and taught me to read at the age of four. Member of an Alsatian family like my father, she

[7]

had gone to school in Paris. Prize books with gilt edges proved that she had been a good scholar. She wrote and spoke a pure, classic French. While I was still a child one of my keenest pleasures was to hear *Maman* read poetry aloud, especially when the poem was sentimental, heroic and sad. I asked again and again for *Les Pauvres Gens* by Victor Hugo, and two poems by Déroulède which must be in *Les Chants du soldat*. One was *La Mort du clairon*, in which each couplet ended after the refrain, 'The bugle call sounded,' by a bugle sounding the charge, each time more breathless and abrupt. Of the other I remember only the beginning: 'He was a lad, seventeen at most, With long blond hair and clear blue eyes . . . ' Perhaps these poems were very bad ; I do not want to know and I have never reread them; they gave me my first literary emotions. I could not hear them without weeping. But these tears bore no resemblance to my tears of rage or fear; they were sweet and comforting and, I think, they made me better.

One remarkable characteristic of my mother was her exclusive and absorbing affection for her family. Her parents, her four sisters who lived in Paris, her husband and her children sufficed to fill her universe. She was inclined to be unsociable, not through disdain but through indifference. My father at the time of his arrival in Elbeuf had made a great many friends in the industrial world of Normandy through the esteem which his character immediately inspired. In his youth he had been very gay. Because he had a good singing voice he had been received into the small local society of amateurs that staged popular operettas: *Les Cloches de Corneville, Les Mousquetaires au couvent, La Fille de Madame Angot*. He knew them by heart, and I can still see that dear figure upright beside the piano whenever I hear: 'When you conspire . . . ' or 'Three times around the world I've gone . . . ' After his marriage he had little by little ceased to see his friends, and *Maman* never invited anyone to dine at our house except 'the family'.

My father had two brothers. My Uncle Edmond was a short, thickset, powerful and energetic man with walrus moustaches. He had been in the light infantry and always countered my father's military airs with the chasseurs' marching song, *Sidi Brahim*. Like my father, he had entered the uncles' mill and, as will be seen, played a role of first importance there. My Uncle Henry, who had a brilliant and paradoxical mind, had graduated with honours from the Polytechnique, and during the time of my childhood was State Civil Engineer at Guéret. From time to time he appeared like a brilliant meteor and was pointed out to me as an example. About 1895 he was named engineer at Dieppe quite close to us, and built there an ocean breakwater, pounded by the waves, of which his brothers and his nephews were very proud. Later he became Inspector General of Roads and Bridges and constructed part of the port of Toulon for the Navy. He was, like my father, an enthusiast for things military but in a quite different manner. It was he who first said to me: 'There's a man of genius in the French Army, Lieutenant Colonel Foch,' and who gave me *Les Principes de la guerre* the instant that book was published.

Uncle Henry loved to tell stories. His favourite was an Alsatian tale in which the Bad Wolf gains admittance to a house full of children in their mother's absence and devours them all except the one to whom the story happens to be told on that particular day. Toward the end of his life, after I had already published several books, my uncle hesitantly showed me the manuscripts of detective novels which he had been writing all his life. He had invented—before Conan Doyle but after Gaboriau—an amateur detective called Anthime Bonnardel who might have been the French Sherlock Holmes. I recall one of his ingenious inventions was a door latch held in place by a cake of ice. When the cake had melted it appeared that the door had been opened from the inside, a circumstance that altered by several hours the time of the crime and completely misled the police, but not the inspired Bonnardel.

My father and uncles, all three, had an exacting and lofty moral code. I have rarely encountered characters like theirs except among the Unitarians and the Quakers. They had had, as my father later told me, a Protestant grandmother, and perhaps they inherited from her the puritanism of which they were so proud. In their eyes the families which became allied with ours were unworthy aliens. They called their brothers- and sisters-in-law 'imported goods' or 'ducks' eggs' and treated them with condescension. Of their two sisters only one, Caroline, shared their cult; the other, my Aunt Marie, was an elderly maiden lady whose house fascinated and terrified me at the same time. She lived there with one of the uncles Fraenckel, Uncle Adolphe, who had had a stroke at about the age of fifty, had recovered, but had spent his time since then stretched out on a sofa from morning till night reading *L'Histoire de France* by Henri Martin and *Le Consulat et L'Empire* by Monsieur Thiers.

Aunt Marie was disfigured by a hare-lip which made her a kind of monster; she was so conscious of this fact that the shades in her house

were always drawn. Lithe forms glided about in the twilight—her cats.
She raised whole litters of them. Every floor was covered with saucers
of milk and skeletons of fish; all the rooms smelled of cat. That odour
made my gorge rise the minute I entered the house. At the same time
I was frightened because I knew I would be led up to Uncle Adolphe's
couch and that he would pinch my cheek, put down his volume of
Henri Martin and question me about the kings of France. For this
examination, which the darkness, the smell, and the disabled old man
rendered terrifying, my mother had prepared me as best she could.
Despite these many causes of fear, however, I liked to go to Aunt
Marie's house because of a certain inkwell in the form of a dog-kennel.
If one pressed on the dog's head the roof of the house flew open,
revealing the ink. This bit of magic filled me with admiration. I could
press the dog's head twenty times and always get the same pleasure.
Later on, when Uncle Adolphe died, an elderly cousin named Albert,
with whom the family did not know what to do, was ordered to go and
live with Aunt Marie. They detested each other, but dared not rebel
against 'a decision of the Uncles', and lived together for twenty years
with refinements of hatred that would have delighted Balzac.

These visits were brief and infrequent. We spent most of our time,
my sister Marguerite and I, alone with *Maman*, or left to our own
devices in the garden, which for me was the scene of varied and stirring
adventures. At the end of the garden was a lilac with a forked trunk,
on whose branches I read the tales of Perrault and Andersen, all of
the *Pink Library*, all of Jules Verne, and *La Guerre de demain* by
Captain Danrit. In one corner there was a rabbit hutch out of which I
made a fort and where I dug trenches and played war games all alone.
I was thinking of our garden in Elbeuf when I wrote in *Climats* about
the childhood of Philippe Marcenat. Once a week the laundress, an old
Alsatian woman, would come to boil the linen in a hot and mysterious
wash house, whose very name, *buanderie*, sounded evil to me. I loved to
see the deposits of soap that formed at the bottom of the wooden wash-
tub and to touch its soft and slippery sides. Sometimes, too, I would
work with the gardener who planted our flowerbeds with, as was customary in Elbeuf, a centre of begonias or geraniums and a border of
forget-me-nots or heliotrope. Toward the end of summer the sawyer
would come to prepare our winter supply of wood. His work
fascinated me. The noise of the saw, the clean, country smell of wood,
the sawdust which formed a thick, soft mattress on the ground, the

exciting instant when the log, completely cut through, divided and fell in two pieces, all this constituted a spectacle of which I never tired.

The events that interrupted the monotony of our days were minuscule. When there was to be 'company for dinner', we would lie in wait for the arrival of the pastry man who always brought the same vanilla and strawberry *bombe glacée* in the shape of a truncated cone surmounted by a rose-coloured ball, and the same plates of *petits fours*: glazed walnuts with pistachios, candied chestnuts, stuffed dates, and tiny chocolate éclairs. When my parents went to the theatre, which happened two or three times a year when a travelling company stopped at Elbeuf, they would bring us home a bag of candy to which we gave, as long as they lasted, the name of the play.

'The *Malade imaginaire* are good,' we used to say, 'but the *Demimonde* were better.'

One day my parents went to see *Les Surprises du divorce*, and the same evening a hairdresser in Elbeuf in a fit of jealousy shot his wife with a revolver. The two events became confused in my mind, and for a long time I believed that a divorce was a pistol duel fought on the stage of the Municipal Theatre. In a child's mind words are not clearly defined; they designate zones of emotion more or less extensive and not sharply bounded, and in this respect many adults remain children all their lives.

On Twelfth Night in Normandy groups of children with lighted lanterns used to come to all the doors and sing:

Bon Dieu, allumez du feu,
Donnez-nous la part à Dieu!
Il fait si froid dehors
Que mon camarade en tremble;
Bon Dieu, allumez du feu
Donnez-nous la part à Dieu!*

We would open the windows and hand them sous and cookies. I can still see those boys shivering and happy in the lantern light against the blackness of the street, which gave the scene the chiaroscuro of a Rembrandt. I envied them and would have liked to go about with them begging alms 'for the Lord's sake', but we were not allowed to do it.

Once a year, in September, there would be the opening of the Elbeuf Fair. How magnificent it seemed to me! We lived close by the Fair

* In the Lord's name light a fire. For the Lord's sake give us alms. Here my friend must stand and shiver, Unprotected in the cold. In the Lord's name light a fire. For the Lord's sake give us alms.

[11]

Grounds and in the evening a symphony of carnival sounds would pour into my bedroom. The calliope of the merry-go-round would blend with the clicking of the lottery wheels, the bells of the cake vendors, the cracks from the rifle gallery, and the roars of the wild animals. Each year it was a question of vital importance to know 'who was coming to the Fair?' Two large menageries, Bidel and Pezon, used to alternate, and we would talk about the great animal trainers the way music lovers discuss the merits of famous singers. We knew the names of Monsieur Bidel's children and followed, from one September to the next, their progress in the dangerous art of exhibiting lions and tigers. The circus brought with it its healthy stable smell, the girl horseback riders—and tightrope dancers who were my first loves. From the booths where gingerbread and nougat were sold, we would get unexpected presents and glorious cases of indigestion, especially when, stuffed with sweet-meats, we would clamber onto the giant wooden horses which careered forward at a slow and unnatural gallop. When later on I derived such keen pleasure from *Petrouchka* and from the *ritournelles* which, in Stravinsky's music, dominate the noises of the festival, it was because I remembered the Elbeuf Fair.

The Cattle Fair, also, was held below our windows in the same square, bordered by chestnut trees. On the morning of that day we would be wakened by the mooing of cows, the whinnying of horses and the bleating of sheep. We would run to the window. Peasants with sticks or whips in hand would be bustling among the animals. It was one of our rare contacts with country life. We knew scarcely anything of the fields, the farm's activity, or the tilling of the soil. Our walks as children were limited to the roads that led from Elbeuf toward the uplands and to the woods that bordered those roads. In the spring, the forests of Normandy were full of primroses, anemones, cowslips and periwinkles. We would make bright, delicate bouquets of them that withered in our hands before we got home.

'Throw away your flowers,' *Maman* would say to me as we came into town. 'You can see very well they're dead.'

But in those days my hopes were tenacious, and the sad fate of my flowers did not keep me next day from making new bouquets. When I try to recall the long-haired child who used to climb the banks and look for blackberries among the bushes, I find nothing but happy memories. What a peaceful life had been arranged for us, and how little we knew of the world and its ways!

2

The Tree of Knowledge

Whenever, in the course of our walks, we would catch sight from the hilltops of the town of Elbeuf, stretching along the bank of the Seine, I used to experience a sudden shock of joy. A line of chalk cliffs, topped by fields and woods, outlined the gentle and graceful curve of the river which was framed, on the farther side, by poplars and willows. From the town rose innumerable thin chimneys, slender pagan minarets of industry, from which ascended columns of smoke. Reservoirs of green water sparkled among the roofs of orange tile and bluish slate. We made a game of searching among all these houses and factories for *the* mill, my father's. Soon we came to recognize it by its long courtyard between two parallel buildings, one for spinning, the other for finishing, and by the huge weaving mill six stories high. It made us proud to see how big it was. At noon and at seven o'clock when the workers left, we would look with amazement at those floods of men and women that suddenly filled Elbeuf's usually placid streets. Another thing we loved to look at was the torrential streams of blue, yellow and red that flowed from the dye works.

Transplanted to the soil of Normandy, the Alsatian mill had not wasted away. Quite the contrary, it had grown with surprising rapidity. About 1890 it employed more than a thousand workers. When I used to spell out the gold letters engraved on a plaque of black marble in front of the main entrance, I was surprised and hurt not to find my father's name. The firm's name was FRAENCKEL-BLIN, and the other large mill in Elbeuf, which had also come from Bischwiller, was named BLIN & BLIN. 'F-B and B-B' was what the people of Elbeuf called them. In *Bernard Quesnay* I have depicted the fierce rivalry between the two firms. Nevertheless the Fraenckels and the Blins were cousins and outwardly kept up friendly relations. Actually they fought each other for trade with vigour and bitterness. The firm of Blin was the older by twenty years, having been founded under the First Empire, and con-

sidered itself superior in the industrial aristocracy to the firm of
Fraenckel. On the other hand, the latter was growing faster. Once
when I was looking at this plaque, I asked my father:

'But, Papa, why not FRAENCKEL AND HERZOG?'

From the look of suffering that came over his face I realized that I
had blundered upon a forbidden subject. Here is the story, which I did
not learn until much later. My father and his brother Edmond were by
unanimous consent the two most competent technicians in the mill.
My father managed the weaving with his characteristic thoroughness;
he knew each of the workmen, the performance of each loom; he was
constantly searching for ways of improving the product and reducing
the cost. My Uncle Edmond was the salesman; he went to Paris every
week and brought back the orders that enabled the mills to run. But
these two men were neither the founders nor the legal heads of this
large enterprise to which they devoted their lives, and they submitted,
my father with resignation and despair, his brother with indignation
and impatience, to a patriarchal tyranny, that of the 'Uncles'.

In my boyish eyes, the Uncles were awe-inspiring, mysterious and
sinister divinities. There had been five Fraenckel brothers: Emile,
Wilhelm, Adolphe, Louis and Henry. Emile and Wilhelm had died
before I was born. I have mentioned Adolphe reading Henri Martin on
his couch; 'Monsieur Louis' as he was called by the employees was,
during my childhood, absolute sovereign. He lived beside the mill and
had his house so constructed that his own apartment communicated by
an interior staircase with the offices. This architectural device was a
symbol. 'Monsieur Louis' had no private life apart from that of the
mill. Clothed perpetually in a black alpaca jacket, and wearing a black
silk cap, his chin framed in a little collar of bristly beard, he spent his
life in the warehouse where the finished lengths of cloth were stored.
He possessed no malice and even attained at times to the grandeur of a
textile Burgrave, but nothing in the world existed for him except wool
and cloth and machinery. When my mother used timidly to take me to
the mill, he would stare at the material in which she was dressed, would
finger it and say, 'This comes (or does not come) from us.' Then he
would pay no further attention to her. 'Monsieur Henry' was scarcely
more human. He had married one of my mother's aunts, Aunt Eulalie,
a fact that made him doubly related to us. This Aunt Eulalie was my
grandmother's sister and had acquired the same delightful culture, but
in the end she had accustomed herself to being regarded in the eyes of

the Uncles (her husband included) as an accessory not essential to the business and therefore of no interest, and led a completely vegetative existence.

The Uncles had promised my father and his brother that they would both be made partners as soon as the deed of partnership was redrawn. But one day my father discovered by accident that a new deed had been signed in secret and that his cousin, Paul Fraenckel, younger than he by some years, had been made a partner before him. It was a shock that made him ill for a long time. At home, for the first time, my parents' conversation was cut short when I entered the room. I still remember the tone of bitter censure with which my mother pronounced the words, 'Those gentlemen,' in speaking of the Uncles. She told me much later that she had advised my father at that time to resign from the firm. Such also was the counsel of my Uncle Edmond:

'Let's start a little mill together,' he proposed to my father when the latter told him of his discovery. 'In ten years we'll have more business than F-B.'

So proud and reserved was my father by nature that not only did he stay on but he said nothing. Nevertheless an essential mechanism, that of confidence, had been damaged, and from that day forward he was never completely well. When he told me the story himself, twenty years had passed, the injustice had been rectified and he had long since granted his forgiveness, but he still trembled when thinking of it:

'When I saw that deed with Paul's name and without ours,' he told me, 'I thought I should go mad.'

Too many bonds attached him to the mill for him to leave it. Many of the workmen were those very Alsatians for whom he had arranged transportation to France in 1871. In the morning when he made his tour of inspection, he would stop in front of each loom and exchange a few words, often in Alsatian dialect, with the weaver or spinner. He knew all their families, was consulted about their marriages, and was present at their funerals. His workmen loved him. 'Monsieur Ernest isn't easy, but he's fair,' they used to say, and they respected his extraordinary devotion to work. My father would never accept that an employer should arrive at the mill after the workmen or leave before them. When I was a child, work began at six-thirty; he would get up before six o'clock. He had learned how to perform himself each one of the complex operations that were under his charge, and without a moment's notice he could take the place of a weaver, or a spinner who complained of his task.

'This warp can't be woven, Monsieur Ernest. The thread's bad.'

'We'll see about that.'

And if the man was right, my father would acknowledge it. To be taken with him on his tour of inspection was a reward I eagerly sought. The din of the looms frightened me a little, but I loved the odour of the oily wool in the sorting room, the long twisted skeins turning in the vats of dye, the amazing silence in the drawing sheds, and the great steam engine with its brightly polished nickel work, whose connecting rods my father would touch with a friendly hand, like a trainer patting a favourite beast.

'Anything new?' he would ask the engine driver.

'Not a thing, Monsieur Ernest.'

The inspection tour went on.

When I was six years old, it was decided that I should 'take courses' in preparation for the Lycée. I should have preferred to continue working with *Maman*, but she arranged with an elderly spinster from Alsace, Mademoiselle Paulus, for her to give instruction to me and two or three other boys. She also had me begin piano lessons, at first with Madame Ritleng, an aged woman whose face was ornamented with long hairs which fascinated me, later with Monsieur Dupré, organist at the Immaculate Conception and father of the great organist Marcel Dupré. Monsieur Dupré was an excellent musician; he recognized very soon that I was not gifted.

'You understand music,' he said to me, 'but you haven't the hands for it.'

Usually he spent the lesson period playing Chopin, Schumann and Bach for me. If he did not make a pianist of me, he did teach me to love good music, for which I am grateful to him. Each year when the pupils' recital was held, I had to take part in order to reassure my parents. I always played a certain *Oriental Serenade* for four hands with Monsieur Dupré himself. 'Don't worry,' he would tell me. 'Just go *la*, then at the octave *la*, *la*, *la* and I will elaborate on it.' He elaborated so ingeniously that I used to be complimented afterward.

My parents also had me begin English and German. My first German instructor was Bertha Bussmann, a Catholic spinster, pious, massive and virtuous. She had been governess to a young lady in Elbeuf,

'Kleine Elisabeth', and had ended by staying on in town, where she was respected for her great piety. Fräulein Bertha talked to me constantly about one of her nephews, Heinrich Brüning, whose intelligence and abilities she used to praise. When Herr Brüning became Chancellor of the Reich, I wondered if by any chance this Brüning could be the 'Klein' Heinrich' whose praises I had so often heard sung. But Bertha was dead. Whom could I ask? A day came when, in the home of Colonel Roosevelt in America, I was able to put the question to the ex-Chancellor. It was indeed he, the nephew of Fräulein Bertha. Like his aunt, he was serious and pious. She was not really successful in teaching me German. Nevertheless with her I translated a play, *Thank God, the Table's Set*, and she made me sing:

> Ich hatt' einen Kameraden
> Einen bessern find'st du nit . . .

As for English, which was to play such a large role in my life, I studied it most negligently with a young and pretty Irish girl, Miss Lizzy MacAnulty, whose virgin beauty was fast fading in Elbeuf in melancholy loneliness because of some youthful indiscretion for which she had been exiled. She made me read *Little Lord Fauntleroy*, which I didn't much like, and *Treasure Island*, which frightened me. I remember that Miss Lizzy advised me for years to read a novel entitled *Thelma*. At the beginning of each lesson she would ask: 'Have you read *Thelma*?' 'No, Miss Lizzy.'

Almost half a century has rolled by and I still have not read *Thelma*.

My father wanted me to learn to ride horseback. 'You will be an officer in the reserves some day,' he said to me. 'Riding will be useful.'

There was a riding academy in Elbeuf run by a remarkable horseman, a former non-commissioned officer named Charpentier. He took a liking to me. My lack of aptitude for the piano was balanced by my natural aptitude for horsemanship. Charpentier handled me very roughly. He would start me at a trot without stirrups and keep me bouncing around for a quarter of an hour. Then he would give me stirrups, take up his long whip and send me off at a gallop:

'Your toes, Cossack! Sit! Sit! Sit! Glide in the saddle! Get your body back! Watch your toes!'

At first the smell of the stable, the cries of Charpentier, the long whip which frightened my horse, the rapid-fire orders bewildered me. But very soon I became a good rider. One of the horses had been high-schooled. I would do the Spanish gait, the trot, and change of feet in time to music.

'Right knee, left rein! Left knee, right rein!' Charpentier would cry. Then one day he said to me:

'Why, that's good . . . You'll be a horseman.'

At eight, I was entered in the Petit Lycée at Elbeuf. This was an annex of the Rouen Lycée. The classes were small in number, six to twelve pupils who, for that very reason, did excellent work. Our teachers were passionately devoted to their calling. My master in the sixth form, Monsieur Kittel, bald, thin, near-sighted, emotional and wearing a black goatee, had married a rich woman and taught by vocation and not from necessity. He loved to correct exercises, and he insisted that we fold our papers lengthwise and write on only one half the page. The other half he himself would cover in a long sloping hand that looked like him. Thursday he would take his pupils out bicycling and would treat them to strawberries and cream at one of the neighbouring farms and would quote verses from Virgil or La Fontaine in description of the country through which we passed.

It was Kittel who first said to me that I might some day write books. I was barely ten years old; he had given us an exercise: *The Story of a Cane*. This cane, cut in the woods of Saint-Pierre, was supposed to write its own memoirs. I no longer remember what sort of life I invented for it, but I do recall having composed with facility a long account which he read aloud to the class.

Another narrative, whose subject has remained with me all my life as a memory and a kind of warning, was *The Ring of Polycrates*. Polycrates, tyrant of Samos, having succeeded in all his ambitions and fearing that the gods may become jealous of him, decides to sacrifice a ring of which he is very fond by throwing it into the sea. Next day a fisherman, cutting open a fish he has just caught, finds the ring and returns it to the tyrant. The latter, terrified, believes that the time of misfortune is upon him, and presently indeed he is vanquished, ruined, banished, and dies. This pretty story troubled me.

'But,' I said to Kittel, 'since he sacrificed the ring, the gods should have allowed him to continue to be happy.'

'Ah!' Kittel said, 'he sacrificed nothing *but* the ring.'

Kittel also had me make my first speech. He directed us (at the age of ten) to talk for a quarter of an hour in front of our classmates. The subject of my maiden speech was: *A Comparison of the Esther of Racine with that of the Bible*. I prepared myself conscientiously, but a tragedy of vocabulary darkened my début. In telling the story of Esther I used, apropos of the proud Vashti, the word *concubine*. I did not know what it meant, but I loved its length and strangeness. Monsieur Kittel asked me to stay after class and was very severe with me;

'Why corrupt your classmates?' he asked me. 'If you have been reading the wrong sort of books, at least have the decency to keep it to yourself.'

I burst into tears. Somewhat confused, he comforted me, but repeated that *concubine* was a terrible word which no boy of my age ought to use. This episode left me disturbed and curious, and my teacher's emotion excited in me much more dangerous thoughts than the proud Vashti could ever have done.

But I owe a great debt of gratitude to Kittel. He gave me a taste for literature; he taught me respect for language; he instructed me so thoroughly in the rudiments of Latin that everything that came afterward seemed easy. Today, having travelled in many countries and observed many colleges, I can better realize the extraordinary good fortune we French students enjoyed in having as masters, when we were ten years old, men qualified to teach in any university in the world. These masters of secondary education were without ambition. They had no wish other than to mould to the best of their ability successive generations of young Frenchmen. To this task they devoted themselves with such passion that they suffered at the end of each academic year in losing their pupils. Kittel on the day before the distribution of prizes read us *La Dernière Classe* by Alphonse Daudet. He had great difficulty in getting to the end of it; he wept and his voice broke. We were touched, surprised and embarrassed. As a remembrance he gave me a book called *L'Ame russe* containing stories by Pushkin, Gogol and Tolstoy; in the front he put an inscription in which he asked me not to forget him when I became a writer. I have never forgotten him.

It was in the book I received from him that I first read *The Queen of Spades*, a story that made a great impression and inspired in me the desire some day to compose similar fantastic tales. Public speaking was another of my vocations. After attending a lecture given by Monsieur Ferdinand Brunetière at the Elbeuf Theatre on the comedies of Corneille, I decided to hold a series of lectures myself for which my sisters should be the captive audience. On several successive days I took my seat behind a table on which I had placed a glass of water, and these two unfortunates had to hear me talk about *Le Misanthrope* and about *Athalie*. They yawned, they wept, but I was adamant.

When I was twelve years old and in the fourth form I composed with great effort a verse tragedy in five acts. It was called *Odette de Champdivers*, and its heroine was the mistress of Charles the Mad. Why was I interested in this woman? I no longer know, and the play is lost. It was stolen from my mother's house by the 'occupation forces' in 1940. That is the least culpable of their crimes. However a new master, Monsieur Leroy, provided us with other models. Leroy, quite different from Kittel, was as much of a bohemian as the latter was upper middle class; he wore an immense, wide-brimmed felt hat, whereas Kittel dressed in a cutaway and high hat; Leroy was as untidily long-haired as Kittel was neatly bald, as easy-going in his ideas and vocabulary as Kittel was prim; but he was a great reader of Flaubert, Huysmans, Maupassant, and in the long run a useful influence for me.

Another of my teachers at that time exercised a great authority over me. This was Mouchel, who taught mathematics. This little man with moist and drooping moustache, his waistcoat always covered with chalk, was the son of a manufacturer in Elbeuf. At the outset of his career he had manufactured cloth like everyone else in town, but he was a theorist. He had developed some very subtle ideas about the weaving of wool, which was dangerous, had put them into practice, which was culpable, and had thus ruined his father and himself. Declared bankrupt, he had studied for a fellowship in mathematics, had passed the examination, and was teaching elementary algebra and geometry at Elbeuf. My father, who had a high regard for my other teachers, showed hostility and distrust whenever I talked about Mouchel. A business failure seemed to him a poor preparation for the high calling of teacher. A man who did not know how to make cloth could not be expected to know how to teach.

But my father and all Elbeuf were mistaken. Mouchel expounded the first books of geometry to us with admirable clarity.

'*Hein?* You understand? You understand?' he would ask us, his piece of chalk in his hand, and he would not let us go until we did understand. Thanks to him, I still know most of the definitions and demonstrations in Euclid. More important still, he gave us a method of procedure. He who goes steadily, step by step, finds everything easy; he who suddenly attempts, after squandering years, to make up lost time by frantic effort, finds everything impossible. The mind, like the heart, is formed early and many of us remain all our lives what our childhood made us. '*Hein?* You understand? You understand?' Thanks to little Mouchel with the moist moustache and chalk-covered waist-coat, we learned to reason.

What he was incapable of teaching was to challenge reason. But another and greater was to see to that.

3

Paradise Lost

At twelve I had finished the course at the Petit Lycée in Elbeuf, which went only through the fourth form. I was to continue my studies at the Lycée Corneille in Rouen. To me this was like entering a new dimension. I left the industrial city for the provincial capital. Before speaking of this new world, I should like to take my bearings by describing, insofar as I am still able, the sort of child I was as I emerged from the fourth form.

For my age I had done an immense amount of reading. My parents' library was limited but carefully chosen. It occupied the shelves of a huge, carved and gilded cabinet in *Maman's* drawing room, a room of state with shutters always closed, filled with furniture in white dust covers. Once a week, on Wednesdays, my mother, like all the ladies of Elbeuf, had 'her day' and received callers. The other women contended bitterly for the six possible days and considered it a mortal insult if a newcomer should dare to choose *their* day. But my mother was indifferent to these small worldly vanities and was delighted when calls were infrequent. No man ever called, and it would have been a scandal in Elbeuf if one were to have been seen outside the mills and offices before seven in the evening. At four o'clock the maid served China tea in rose-coloured porcelain cups. Even today the taste of China tea evokes for me *Maman's* day and the gilt bookcase.

On the other days of the week I was allowed to enter the darkened drawing room where I collided with the phantoms of chairs enveloped in their white shrouds. I used to open the shutters a crack—for to open them wide would have been a sacrilege—and I would rummage among the books. I first came upon all the classics (those of the seventeenth century; the eighteenth century horrified my parents); then the great romantics: complete sets of Hugo, Lamartine, Vigny, De Musset; *Le Mémorial de Sainte-Hélène*, my father's favourite book, in a de luxe edition illustrated with engravings; the plays of Augier, those of Labiche and those of Dumas *fils*. One shelf was occupied by the literary texts that had been used by my mother in her girlhood: Villemain, bound in brown; Nisard, in blue.

My parents used to give me as New Year's or birthday presents, in groups of six or eight volumes, Sainte-Beuve's *Causeries du lundi*, the works of Taine, Reclus's *Geography* and Michelet's *L'Histoire de France*. But most important of all, with furtive enthusiasm I used to select from the books in the drawing room the innumerable bound volumes of *Lectures rétrospectives*. This was a magazine, now defunct, which reprinted all the masterpieces of the French novel. Thanks to the *Lectures*, I read at that time, perhaps too young, all of Flaubert, all of Maupassant, the early novels of Paul Bourget, of Anatole France, of Marcel Prévost and of Maurice Barrès. I mixed the good and the bad, the serious and the frivolous, history and fiction. From good and bad alike I derived incredibly keen pleasure, literary delight and sensual feelings.

My sensuality awoke early, in ignorance and confusion. My parents' prudishness permitted no requests for explanations of those delicious and terrifying subjects. My father, who used to blush if his friends talked about a scandal or repeated a coarse joke in his presence, was far from imagining the seraglio where I kept for the delectation of my daydreams Mademoiselle de Maupin and Madame Bovary.

My true nature was romantic. I have described in *Climats* how I read in one of my prize books the story of a band of students who decided to form an army and selected a girl student to be their Queen. 'The Queen was called Ania Sokoloff. She was a girl of remarkable beauty, slender, elegant and graceful.' I loved the oath the soldiers swore to their Queen, the feats they performed to please her and the smile that was their reward. I do not know why this tale pleased me so, but thus it was, I loved it, and seated on the branches of the lilacs, smelling the perfume of the flowers as though it were that of a woman, I read and reread *Les Petits Soldats russes* and dreamed of a love that would be at once suffering, discipline and devotion.

To sustain me in this premature crisis of adolescence I had no religious faith whatever. I did not know the doctrine of the religion which by birth should have been mine. My father had a solid faith, but it was moral rather than metaphysical. In the domain of morals he was in complete agreement not only with Pastor Roehrich but also with Abbé Alleaume, superior of the Ecole Fénelon, a gifted priest who was our neighbour and with whom he often went walking. My father respected the traditions of his family and abided by them, but fasts and unleavened bread were in his eyes archaic curiosities rather than divine precepts. I believe if at the time I had met a cultivated rabbi who would have made me read the Bible and would have explained it to me, I should have appreciated its sublime poetry, the wisdom of the Kings and the Prophets, the solemn nihilism of *Ecclesiastes*. But my Bible studies were brief and uninspired and I did not get to know the Old Testament (which I read and admire so much today) until much later, and then through the English poets.

Like many children (and particularly Edmund Gosse, who has told about it in *Father and Son*), I had unfortunate experiences with the efficacy of prayer. One day when there was to be an examination in geography I prayed that our master would choose as subject the tributaries of the Seine, which I knew, rather than those of the Loire which I could never remember. He gave us the Loire and my faith was shaken. For some time my sister Marguerite and I had recourse to the practice of magic. We had invented a very powerful devil called Monsieur le Sort whose temple was in one corner of the hall. If one of us went to this corner and cried aloud: 'Monsieur le Sort, grant that we be taken to the circus on Thursday!' the prayer was sometimes answered. It may have been because *Maman* overheard it.

At Elbeuf I had stood first in my class with no great effort. The presentation of prizes, which marked the end of the academic year, was a pleasant and moving occasion for me. The Elbeuf Orchestra played the *Marseillaise*, and I still cannot hear it after all these years without seeing again the teachers, in their yellow or red robes with the narrow bands of white fur on the shoulders, the black and white robes of the judges, in short, the whole procession that approached laden with honours and importance to find seats on the platform. We would listen patiently to the heavily humorous discourse of some university Polonius, and then the Censor would read the names of the prize-winners. I knew that I would leave there loaded with green paper crowns and a gilded crown representing the prize for excellence, and with my hands full of books bound in red; but I understood quite well that in such small classes there was no great merit in standing first. The following year at the Rouen Lycée would be an entirely different matter, and I looked forward to it with trepidation.

There were two possible ways in which I could continue my studies, and between these my parents had to choose. They could put me in the Rouen Lycée as a boarder—it was thus that my Uncle Henry had prepared for the Polytechnique—or they could send me there each morning and have me return each evening. The daily trip would be tiring, for it would be necessary to take a train at six forty-nine in the morning, which meant getting up at a quarter to six, and at least two hours a day would be lost on the two trips. But my mother had an instinctive horror of my living away from home; and so, despite the fact that my health was not of the best, it was decided that I should return each evening to Elbeuf. There were, however, other young people, among them André Blin and one of Pastor Roehrich's sons, to accompany me. We were soon known at the Rouen Lycée as 'the Elbeuf train'.

Each morning—and in pitch darkness during the winter—with my schoolbag under my arm, I would walk through Elbeuf amid the labourers going to work. One could hear the machines in the factories slowly start to turn. The great glass windows would suddenly light up on the stroke of six-thirty. Presently in the smoky light of the railway compartment, seated on the dirty brown cushions, I would try to rehearse my lessons. How many verses have I recited between Elbeuf and Rouen! Even today I cannot think of those hideous stations, that charming countryside, those rivers and forests without seeming to hear the stanzas of *Polyeucte*, *La Jeune Captive*, *La Nuit de mai*, or perhaps: 'Sing, goddess, the wrath of Peleus' son, Achilles . . . '

The sequence of stations, their distance from one another, their odd, dissimilar names, formed a kind of musical phrase in my mind with a complex rhythm that I loved. First came Elbeuf-Rouvalets, a brief stop, a semi-quaver barely separated by a sigh from the point of departure. From there to La Bouille-Moulineaux was the longest run of the trip, an interminable interval punctuated by a noisy tunnel in the course of which one could shout without disturbing the other passengers: 'Eighteen-eleven! O year when the numberless nations . . . ' or: 'Waterloo, O mournful plain . . . ' Then came in quick, regular succession Grand-Couronne, Petit-Couronne, Grand-Quevilly, Petit-Quevilly, and finally Rouen. *Tac-tac . . . Tac-tac-tac-tac*. That was the rhythm of my childish thoughts on this daily morning trip, and when the exigent manoeuvres of a deputy resulted in establishing a station at Hêtre-à-l'Image in the middle of a wood, thus interrupting my longest interval by a short and wholly useless stop, it seemed to me that a strange and alarming dissonance had been brought into my life.

My first day at the Rouen Lycée was marred by a small but distressing incident that made so deep an impression that I should not consider it honest to omit it from this narrative. At that time it was the custom to begin the academic year by a mass called Mass of the Holy Spirit, celebrated in the beautiful chapel of the Lycée, which had once been a Jesuit college; the purpose of this mass was to invoke the benediction of the Holy Spirit upon the labours of the students. A few minutes before the ceremony the Head Usher called us together in the great courtyard and said:

'Dissenters, withdraw!'

The dissenters were the Protestants and the Israelites. About twenty Protestants and three or four Jews stepped out of the ranks.

'The others,' the Head Usher went on, 'will form in a column of twos and follow me into the chapel.'

There was the prolonged sound of tramping feet and the student body disappeared into a vaulted passage. Our little group remained alone beneath the trees, disconsolate and with nothing to say. From the nearby chapel rose the music of the organ magnificently played by my master Dupré, and the murmured responses. We strolled sadly beneath the chestnut trees of the courtyard. We felt no shame at being Protestants or Israelites, but we felt ourselves separated for an hour's time, on a solemn occasion, from a community which was, after all, our community, and we were unhappy, very unhappy, without knowing why.

Despite that one painful hour, I fell in love at once with my new school. The beautiful Court of Honour, framed by symmetrical grey buildings constructed by the Jesuits in the seventeenth century, the Latin inscriptions which ornamented the front of the sun dial and the pedestal of the statue of Corneille, the drum that rolled out from the head of the stairs at five minutes to eight, the ranks which immediately formed two abreast, this rigour, this discipline, gave me a joy I was to recapture later on with my regiment when we marched past the flag to the strains of a military band. Consciousness of belonging to a well-ordered group is an aesthetic pleasure which I believe musicians in an orchestra feel, as do students and soldiers.

At the end of a week our teacher, Monsieur Robineau, had us write a Latin composition. Thanks to Kittel, I knew how a Latin composition was made, and the text did not seem hard. Naturally I had no idea how I should rank in this class of forty students, none of whom I knew. A week later the Headmaster, Monsieur Desfours, appeared to read the marks. It was a solemn moment. The Headmaster, corpulent, bearded, businesslike, entered with his high hat in his hand, followed by the Censor who held a large sheet of paper. The whole class rose.

'Greetings, Monsieur Robineau,' the Headmaster said majestically. 'Sit down, gentlemen . . . Your marks are as follows . . . '

And the Censor read:

'Latin composition . . . First: Herzog, Emile . . . '

The Headmaster stopped him:

'Ah! I take occasion to congratulate Monsieur Herzog. This is a triumph for the Petit Lycée of Elbeuf. Gentlemen of Rouen, here is a challenge to do your best.'

Those who had been the leaders of the class the preceding year began to regard me with exasperation. A curvature of the spine forced me to wear an iron corset which made my movements slow and awkward. This object of ridicule, my unfortunate scholastic triumph, the renewed interest in the *Affaire Dreyfus* combined, for a number of weeks, to make me the victim of a number of conscienceless and cruel boys. It was my first experience of anti-semitism. I suffered frightfully, not having met, up to that time, anything but tenderness at home and friendship at school. Life at the Lycée, which I admired so much, would have become insufferable if I had not found support from potent avengers.

These were a group of sporting characters, dirty and high-spirited, with buttonless waistcoats tied together by pieces of string, who called themselves the Morin family. Blot, a star forward in rugby, was Father Morin; Loustaunau, Bouchard, Godet, Pagny and Patin (whom the Morins called 'Pascaline') completed the family. We took our meals in a refectory, eight to a table. The Head Usher would say grace or, more accurately, he would mutter: 'Sancti amen . . . Sancti amen.' Then we would sit down. The Morins, seven in number, as soon as they saw that I seemed unhappy, requested the Usher to put me at their table; and since they were the best fighters in the middle form, their friendship, added to that of Abbé Vacandard, chaplain of the Lycée, who enjoyed translating Cicero or Tacitus with me, quieted the brawlers.

From the beginning of the second form I could devote myself entirely to the joy of studying. The discovery of the Latin and French poets was an intoxication. My teacher in the second form, Nebout, admired only the romantics. He resembled his favourite authors in aspect, flowing hair, cape and vocabulary. Two plays written by him in the manner of Hugo had been performed in the local theatre. He taught us to love Villon, Rabelais, Montaigne, and to translate Lucretius. To him I owe the fact that I know by heart hundreds of verses of Ronsard, Corneille, Victor Hugo, De Musset. On the other hand, Texcier, the rhetoric teacher, a little man with a precise, delicate voice and a malicious smile, was a classicist. Through him I learned to understand Virgil, Racine, Mérimée, Anatole France. Every week he gave us a subject for a French composition: '*Letter from one of Racine's admirers to Racine after the uproar over Phèdre . . . Letter from Monsieur de Gourville to the Prince de Condé asking him not to lead an army against France . . . Letter of Conrart, Permanent Secretary of the Académie Française, to Saint-Evremond in defence of the Académie against that author's satire . . .* ' The research work, the arrangement of the material I collected, the imitation of the language of the time, gave me a delightful foretaste of the joys of authorship. From these years of study I have retained the memory of one long enchantment.

During my Year of Rhetoric I conceived an odd ambition. Each year the Minister of War gave a medal at the Lycée for the best of the whole school in gymnastics. I had just been relieved of my iron corset and I passionately coveted that medal. I asked Pichon, the athletics instructor, a former non-commissioned officer, lean and muscular, his hair *en brosse*, to give me private lessons; and I worked on the parallel bars, the high bar and the trapeze during all the recreation periods. As I had hoped, perseverance finally overcame my awkwardness, and Pichon taught me how to accomplish a thousand feats through limberness that I could never have achieved through strength alone. When I was master of my movements, I applied myself to improvement of form. With my body extended, toes pointed, muscles relaxed, I would swing about the bar in the sunlight, I would fly from trapeze to trapeze, and I would mount the parallels at a bound. Success in gymnastics, as in politics and in war, depends on precise timing. A certain release of the knees, which gravitation will regulate for you if it is begun at the right instant, becomes dangerous a split second later. When at the end of the year the contest took place among all the gymnasts of the Lycée, I got my medal. It gave me more pleasure than my diploma as bachelor of arts.

This baccalaureate was my first examination. It was given to the students of Rouen by the faculty of Caen, the ancient capital of Normandy, whose massive and beautiful churches are constructed like the tragedies of Corneille. The subject for the French composition was a sentence from Renan: 'To have had common glories in the past, to possess a common will in the present, to have achieved great things together, to be determined on further achievement, such are the essential conditions for being a people.' It pleased me so much that, in the delight of composition, I forgot where I was and why I was writing. The oral examination seemed easy. I was questioned about Descartes and his influence on literature; about Livy, an author beloved by candidates; and about a Homeric hymn that I knew by heart. Everything went as though on wheels except geography. An ill-tempered elderly man asked me the depth of the Rhône at the Pont-Saint-Esprit. I never knew any figures, and this one least of all. But despite this culpable ignorance, I passed with the honourable mention, 'Well done,' and the congratulations of the jury.

For several years I had spent my vacations in Paris with my mother's family, and there I found an atmosphere which was not very different from that of the Lycée. My four aunts loved the theatre and poetry. On Thursdays one of them would take me to the classical matinees at the Comédie Française. Before long I was commenting like a connoisseur on the Mascarille of Georges Berr, the Pourceaugnac of Coquelin the younger, or the Bérénice of Julia Bartet. To see Mounet-Sully in *Oedipus Rex*, Coquelin in *Cyrano*, and later Sarah Bernhardt in *L'Aiglon* was to me a solemn, almost sacred pleasure. When the exhibition of 1900 opened, the Comédie Française organized a series of afternoon poetry readings at the Trocadéro and my favourite actors and actresses took part, uncostumed, in reciting the poems of Chénier, La Fontaine, Hugo, Baudelaire and Verlaine. I could imagine in advance the intonations and rejoice in the happy inspirations of the actors. I lived in a wholly unreal world of poetry and passion.

These days in Paris intoxicated me all the more inasmuch as I was in love. I did not know with whom. I longed to die for a beautiful and unhappy mistress. I loved to read in the Greek and Latin poets the story of Perseus rescuing Andromeda. I repeated with delight the beautiful sonnet of Ronsard:

> 'Il ne faut s'étonner,' disaient ces bons vieillards,
> Dessus le mur troyen voyant passer Hélène,
> 'Si pour telle beauté nous souffrons tant de peine.
> Notre mal ne vaut pas un seul de ses regards . . . '*

* 'No cause for wonder,' those venerable elders said upon the walls of Troy, seeing Helen pass, 'if for such beauty we have suffered so much woe. Our ills are outweighed by a single glance from her . . .'

My Helen for several months was the youngest of my aunts, after that the sister of one of my schoolmates whom I had glimpsed at the gateway of the Lycée, and then the popular actresses on the stage at the Comédie Française to whom I sent letters in verse which were never answered. But did I even expect answers? My love was not of this world, and whether they wished it or not, these fair persons belonged to me in my dreams.

One day one of our masters at Rouen gave us as an exercise *The Palinode of Stesichorus*. 'The poet Stesichorus, having reviled Helen in his verses for the woes brought by her upon the Greeks, is struck blind by Venus and, recognizing his error, composes a recantation in which he expresses his repentance at having blasphemed against beauty.' Never had I written an exercise with more sincere enthusiasm. The theme of sacrifice for beauty awakened in me such profound echoes that despite my extreme youth I felt shaken, and I worked during those two hours with an almost painful ardour, as though I had a premonition of how often in the course of my difficult life on this earth I, too, should have cause to compose the Palinode of Stesichorus.

4

The River of the Arrow

The Year of Philosophy in the life of a young Frenchman was, at the time of my adolescence, the year of intellectual puberty. One can see in Barrès' *Déracinés* the significance in a negative sense for him and his friends of their encounter with the philosopher Burdeau, and in the biographies of Proust the positive role played by the philosopher Darlu in the formation of Proustian doctrine. For ten years all our attention, first as boys, then as young men, had been concentrated upon questions of form, grammar, style. Suddenly the background was illuminated. Epictetus and Epicurus, Plato and Aristotle, Descartes and Spinoza, Locke and Kant, Hegel and Bergson contended for mastery of our minds. The metaphysicians dissolved the universe into transparent clouds or dilated the individual until he became coterminous with the world. The moralists proposed conflicting doctrines to justify unvarying virtues. Dizzy and intoxicated, blind and drunk with power, the young man would allow himself to be deliciously borne along in the whirlwind of ideas.

My classmates and I at the Rouen Lycée in 1901 awaited our Year of Philosophy with all the greater impatience because our philosopher was a man who had already attained fame. His name was Emile Chartier. At the people's University in Rouen (these groups for mutual education had sprung up all over France after the *Affaire Dreyfus*), he spoke every week, and even his political adversaries admitted his lectures were original and eloquent. As for his pupils, our older schoolmates, they were like members of an esoteric religious cult, at once enthusiastic and secretive. Louis Canet, a close friend of mine who later became Director of Religious Affairs at the Quai d'Orsay, had received the Honour Prize in Philosophy the year before.

'You'll see,' he told me mysteriously, 'his class is not like anything you've ever heard before.'

We were not disappointed. The assembly drum rolled out. The

ranks defiled in front of Corneille and we proceeded to our seats on the benches of the philosophy classroom. Suddenly the door burst open and in came a big fellow with a youthful manner and a fine Norman head marked by strong regular features. He sat down at his desk on the platform, looked at us smilingly for an instant, then went to the blackboard and wrote: Σὺν ὅλῃ τῇ ψυχῇ εἰς τὴν ἀλήθειαν ἰτεέον.

He looked in my direction:

'Translate,' he said.

'One must go to the truth with all one's soul.'

He let us meditate for some moments on Plato's sentence, then began his lecture on perception.

'Consider this inkwell on my desk,' he said. 'When I say *this inkwell*, what am I designating? First of all, a black and white splotch which my eyes see; then a sensation of smooth resistance which my hand records' (he extended his hand and touched the inkwell). 'But how do I know that the sensation of smooth resistance and the black and white splotch are the same object? What is it in me that can discover an identity? My eye? Certainly not, since my eye cannot touch . . . My hand? Certainly not, since my hand cannot see . . . From this we perceive at once that when certain philosophers tell us that there can be nothing in the mind that was not first known by the senses, we must be on our guard . . .'

We had not been in class five minutes and already we felt ourselves shaken, provoked, stimulated. For ten months we were going to live in this atmosphere of passionate investigation. Chartier was a great admirer of Socrates and, like him, thought the best way of inducing men to exercise their judgment was not to offer them predigested doctrines but to stimulate their appetite and curiosity by constant surprises. Socrates liked to be called the Numbfish, from the fish that gives an electric shock to all who touch it. Chartier loved to shock us with paradoxical theses which he would support with all the trappings of specious logic. He would then sometimes demolish them himself, and sometimes leave us to find our way out alone.

Like Socrates, too, he loved examples and apologues. Some of his stories recurred constantly and they were famous among us. There was the one about a rabbi's maid who, when she was dying and delirious, began for the first time in her life to speak Hebrew; there was one about a sergeant, a veteran of the Colonial Wars, on whose legs a nurse put leeches, and he dreamed that he was amid the cactus in Africa; there was one about the Labrador duck which, when it is shut up, violently beats the cement slabs of its cage with its long, webbed feet, in the naive hope of making worms come out. The duck illustrated the lecture on instinct and habit, the maid illustrated the theory of memory, and the old sergeant that of dreams.

Chartier had narrow and strong political convictions, which he admitted. He was a radical, with some of the traits of Julien Sorel. But his radicalism was less a desire for reform than the perpetual vigilance of the citizen directed against the authorities. He held more strongly to freedom than to equality, and he believed that if freedom of the spirit remained complete it would suffice to maintain equality before the law, the only form of equality to which he attached importance. And so he was not a socialist, but this did not keep him from expounding the doctrines of that party to us with so much intelligence that he made me a socialist, as I shall recount, for several years. He was well pleased. 'Anyone who is not an anarchist at sixteen,' he used to say sometimes, 'will not have enough energy at thirty to be a fire chief.' But his political thought had another and quite different aspect. Devoted reader of Auguste Comte and Balzac, he believed in the need for ceremonials and in respect for customs. Chartier may have been anti-clerical but he was certainly religious. Few men could talk better about Christianity. In fact, it was he who first revealed to me the grandeur of the Christian doctrine and led to my accepting so large a part of it.

Chartier often quoted a maxim from *The Imitation of Christ*: 'Intelligence must follow faith, never precede it and never destroy it.' In respect to a doctrine like that of the Incarnation, he never said: 'Is it true?' but: 'It is true for faith; what does it mean for reason?' And this was his reply: 'Jupiter, the god of the Greeks and Romans, was neither god enough nor man enough. The god of the Jews was no longer man at all. Infinite and abstract, he remained cut off from man, as the authorities are cut off from the people, and did not manifest himself except through external miracles: columns of fire, celestial manna and the tablets of stone on Sinai. It was necessary for God to come closer to men again. And so religion incarnated him. To believe in the Father without believing in the Son is to give up knowing God. From this altar, the cradle, a religion arises and, examining this marvel, one finds the key. Look at the Child. This helplessness is God. This helplessness that needs everything is God. Such is the hope, by comparison with which even truth is an idol.' These intentionally obscure statements gave us glimpses into vertiginous depths. When I listened to Chartier, the

[33]

Voltairianism of Voltaire seemed almost as vapid as the Voltairianism of Monsieur Homais. 'Every proof,' our master would go on to say, 'is thoroughly discredited in my eyes.' Which put reason back in its place.

Chartier's influence on my literary tastes was as strong as his influence on my ideas. In the preceding years, under the reign of the delightful Texcier, I had learned to love Anacreon and Catullus, the poets of the Anthology, and the prose of Voltaire, Paul-Louis Courier and Anatole France. Chartier's diet was stronger meat. He admired *Candide*, but considered France no more than a good minor writer. He revealed to me Stendhal and Balzac. With the former he had natural affinities, since, like him, he had a love of liberty, a contempt for self-important people and a passion for naturalness. When he praised the description of the passions in the *Chartreuse* or the *Rouge*, we divined despite our inexperience that he had known violent ones himself. His almost unqualified admiration for *Le Lys dans la vallée*, a novel much discussed at that time by academic critics and in which we students of rhetoric found cause for ridicule, throws much light on his secret life.

Chartier was one of the most ardent Balzacians I have ever encountered. Not only had he read and reread *La Comédie humaine* a hundred times, but he cited it constantly and often used the characters of Balzac as examples in his lectures. It may seem surprising that this radical who was so bitter about reactionaries should choose as his favourite reading a novelist who was a Catholic and a Royalist. But this is one of those miracles of France. Chartier's Stendhalian passions made him distrustful and rebellious. His Norman-peasant instincts brought him back to the wisdom of Balzac. I remember that he especially admired *Le Médecin de campagne*, which might well be the political breviary of all French conservatives. Thanks to him, the work of Balzac has become a part of my life, and since my Year of Philosophy I have never lived without having *La Comédie humaine* within reach.

I have known few better readers than Chartier. He would get at the details of a text and savour their beauty. Also he was determined to remain a man of few authors. He believed that an ardent reader ought to have a limited library and reread the same books every year. If my memory serves, in addition to Homer, Balzac, Stendhal, his library consisted of Saint-Simon, Tacitus, Plato, Descartes, Spinoza and Hegel. He also used to read, like my father, *Mémorial de Sainte-Hélène*. Later on I persuaded him, I believe, to add to his favourites *Mémoires d'outre-*

tombe, Cardinal de Retz and Rudyard Kipling. Nothing was harder than to get him to read a contemporary author.

'It's better to wait,' he would say. 'If in ten years you still admire him, perhaps I'll try.'

Nevertheless he himself adopted Claudel and Valéry between the two wars and talked about them better than anyone else.

In our exercises he paid more attention to style than to content. 'This isn't *written*,' was a condemnation from which there was no appeal. The first thesis that he gave me was an idea from Plato: Μακρότεραν Περιτέον. 'One must take the longer road.' I still have one of my compositions at the top of which he had written in blue crayon: 'Compress, condense, and end with a bang.' He often put me on my guard against measured prose and against phrase-making.

'If you aren't careful,' he told me, 'you may become a distinguished writer of flowery prose. That's not desirable. Read the *Civil Code* and *Henri Brulard*. They'll save you from phrase-making.'

The subjects he gave us were designed to discourage rhetoric: 'A young woman is about to jump off the parapet of the Boïeldieu Bridge. A philosopher holds her back by the skirt. Dialogue.' Or again: 'Dialogue between a sacristan and a fire chief on the existence of God.'

If I try now to reconstruct the picture of the world which our master drew, this is approximately what I find. His course began with a long discussion of the theory of perception. He showed us that to perceive even the simplest objects requires very complex reasoning, and that this reasoning may go wrong, hence the illusions of the senses. How often he talked to us of the stereopticon which creates the illusion of depth and the straight stick that appears broken under water, accidents that reveal the weakness of our judgment. Then came the illusions of memory, of instinct and of reason. All of this made apparent the difficulties that beset the search for truth. Socrates and Descartes helped us at least to find a provisional method. Spinoza taught us to make our emotions serve us in our search. Kant kept us from pursuing the blind alley of metaphysics by showing us that we would find nothing in that direction except the laws of our own mind. Auguste Comte taught us to respect institutions and ceremonies. One of Chartier's striking characteristics was that when he was expounding the doctrine of some philosopher he would never criticize it, but would give us whatever truth there was in it. Refutation seemed to him a miserable game. 'It's a great mark of mediocrity to admire mediocrely.' He admired generously, and he even admired some of the writers whom at that time it was smart to ridicule, such as Victor Hugo and George Sand. He counted (rightly) *Les Misérables* and *Consuelo* among the greatest books. Furthermore, in class, he permitted hardly any discussion, holding it to be a waste of time. 'The master teaches, the students work,' he would say.

What I cannot convey in words is the enthusiasm inspired in us by this search, boldly pursued with such a guide; the excitement of those classes which one entered with the persistent hope of discovering, that very morning, the secret of life, and from which one departed with the joy of having understood that perhaps there was no such secret but that nevertheless it was possible to be a human being and to be so with dignity and nobility. When I read in *Kim* the story of the lama who sought with so much devotion for the River of the Arrow, I thought of *our* search. Chartier gave us not so much a doctrine (he would gladly have said with Gide: 'Free yourself from me!'), not so much a system as a method and a faith. 'One must go to the truth with all one's soul.' From his lessons I have retained a horror of hypocrisy, a desire to understand, and a respect for my adversaries. Like all human beings I have, in the course of my life, committed many faults; if I have occasionally acted well I owe it to the example of my father and to the teachings of Chartier.

At the end of the year, he entered me in the *Concours Général* in which all the colleges and Lycées of France competed. The examinations were given, with every precaution, at the Prefecture. The papers arrived from Paris in sealed envelopes. The Lycée gave the contestants elegant lunches, lobster and cold chicken. The mayonnaise was in a bottle and had turned. The preceding year I had won a prize for Latin composition and another for Greek in the *Concours* as well as first honourable mention in history. The subject in philosophy was: '*The Role of Habit in the Life of the Individual and in Society*.' For a pupil of Chartier's it was an easy theme. All we had to do was follow his method; a number of examples: the boxer, the gymnast . . . citation of authorities: 'Just as one swallow does not make a summer, so a single virtuous action does not constitute virtue.' "Ωσπερ ήδη ή φύσις ήθος . . . August Comte on social habits . . . Habit and instinct: the Labrador duck . . . ' We were allowed eight hours; I was finished in four.

A month later I was in Elbeuf, sick in bed with a sore throat, when I received a telegram from the Headmaster: 'Heartiest congratulations on receiving first prize in the *Concours Général*.' I had great difficulty in believing it, but it was true, and soon a splendid pile of books arrived from Paris. When the prizes were awarded after a brilliant rendition of the *Marseillaise*, the Prefect handed me my diploma. My schoolmates gave me an ovation, which was sweeter to me than the prize. Chartier, whose athletic body bulged his academic gown, had me sit beside him on the official platform.

'This is fine,' he said to me, 'provided you also understand that it is nothing . . . Now you must live . . . What are you going to do?'

That was a question I had been asking myself. I was devoted to this student life. It was delightful to attend classes conducted by a man of genius, to study, to pass examinations. Could not my whole life be one long cycle of studies extending from adolescence to the grave? This seemed to me not impossible. Why not enter the Ecole Normale? The life of a professor tempted me. I did not hope ever to attain in the eyes of my students the prestige of a Chartier, but I might become a respected professor, conscientious and perhaps beloved. Moreover I wished to write, and in some peaceful post in the provinces I should have leisure. I explained these plans to Chartier while the Censor was calling out: 'Class in Elementary Mathematics: . . . First Prize: Lefèvre (Henri) . . . '

'I don't agree with you,' he said. 'Not that you wouldn't be sure to succeed in such a career. I can see you being admitted to the Normale without any trouble at all. But afterward? There would be great danger for you. You have a terrifying facility. I am afraid you would write before you were mature enough to write. As a professor you would see almost nothing of the world that as a novelist you would have to re-create. While you were still too young, you would be taken up by little literary cliques. It was not thus that Balzac began, nor Dickens. The one was a notary's clerk and printer; the other a journalist. Isn't your father a manufacturer? I should much rather see you go into his factory. There you would see men at work. You will be David Séchard, César Birotteau and perhaps Doctor Bénassis. In the evening you will copy out by hand the *Chartreuse* or the *Rouge* in order to learn the technique of writing, as young painters copy the pictures of their masters. That would be a good way to start life.'

That evening when I had returned to Elbeuf on the usual train, laden with books, I repeated this conversation to my father. His kind face lighted up:

'I did not wish to oppose you,' he said, 'but since Monsieur Chartier has given you his advice, I am happy to be in agreement with him. I also believe you ought to come into the mill with us, or at least begin that way. If you continue to wish to write, your evenings will be free and, if you really have talent, no doubt in the end it will show. Besides, we must take into consideration that the workmen are attached to our family, that later on they would accept you as their head more willingly than a stranger, and that we have obligations to all these Alsatians. In the mill you will have a brilliant future. As for me, I have suffered somewhat under the tyranny of the Uncles in the past, but now they are old and the younger generation of Fraenckels will be like brothers to you, as they have been to Edmond and to me.'

I was not tempted. What would I, a reader of Plato and Descartes, be doing amid those piles of cloth, those oily machines, that greasy wool? Why should I embark on this arduous life, with practically no vacations, away from my beloved books, when nothing prevented me from leading the existence for which I felt myself made? However, when I heard the two men I admired most in the world, Chartier and my father, giving me the same advice, I could not remain indifferent.

In the end I got a reprieve. This is how it happened: At that time a young man could agree to take a single year of military service at eighteen in a special platoon called 'the exempt', provided he had gone through certain schools or had completed certain courses at the university, that is, held a master's degree. And so it was very much to my advantage to obtain my degree in Philosophy (Literae humaniores) when I was between seventeen and eighteen and to discharge my military service between eighteen and nineteen, so that I would find myself at the age of nineteen free of all obligation and master of my actions. My family approved of this idea and I returned to the Rouen Lycée the following year.

The dear old Lycée, on the day of my return, was no longer an austere and rather frightening edifice, but a familiar home which I entered with pleasure. I had decided to take my degree there rather than go to the University of Caen or to the Sorbonne, so that I might remain near Chartier. At the same time I wanted to attend classes in elementary mathematics since the preparation for my degree required little study. Unhappily Chartier was snatched away almost at once. In the *Concours Général* the year before, in addition to my First Prize, Rouen had received two other high awards in philosophy. It was a brilliant triumph for Chartier, and the lycées of Paris called him. One day in October Rabier, Director of Secondary Education, came un-expectedly to Rouen to see at first hand this amazing teacher who, despite his youth, seemed due for rapid promotion.

I have retained a very clear memory of that inspection because it gave me another occasion to admire my master's character. That morn-ing, as it happened, Chartier was delivering a lecture on morals and was starting to talk to us about our 'obligation toward prostitutes'. His thesis (which I do not dispute) was that the worst immorality was not the prostitution of the body but that of the emotions.

'For these women to render you a physical service,' he said, 'is the oldest profession in the world and I do not think they suffer from it, but they do have their pride. It would be distressing for them to prostitute their hearts. So take great care not to compel them to counterfeit passion they do not feel. You can in large measure preserve for them the dignity of human personality.'

He was at this point when the door opened and the janitor appeared carrying two chairs. We knew that this stage setting meant an inspec-tion. And indeed, a few seconds later, the Headmaster in cutaway and high hat introduced a thin man with a black goatee.

'Good day, Monsieur Chartier,' said the Headmaster in his guttural voice. '*Monsieur le Directeur de l'Enseignement secondaire* has made the trip from Paris in order to hear you. Take your seats, gentlemen.'

Chartier said to Rabier:

'What do you wish us to talk about, *Monsieur le Directeur?*'

'I wish you to continue the class,' Rabier said, 'from the point you have reached without paying any attention to me.'

We looked at one another. What would Chartier do? Perhaps at this moment his whole career was at stake. There was an instant of silence, then Chartier went on:

'I was in the process of explaining to these gentlemen their obliga-tions toward prostitutes.'

The Headmaster gave a start; the Director remained unmoved. Our eyes lighted with pride . . . Our hero remained intact.

It must be recorded to the credit of the Administration that it did not hold the liberalism of Chartier's lectures against him. Two weeks later he was summoned to the Lycée Condorcet in Paris and we lost him. I was inconsolable. I had sacrificed a year at the Sorbonne, which would have been invaluable to me, in order to work with him.

At that time one could substitute a short thesis for the oral part of the examination. I wrote one on: *Mathematical Demonstration according to Kant, Leibniz, and the Modern Mathematicians.* Recently I happened to reread it; since then I have learned a great deal, in particular to be less sure of myself and to suffer, but I would be happy to recover the vigour and precision which the study of mathematics had given me at that time.

The examination for the master's degree did not seem difficult to me. Because the foundation had been solidly laid long ago at the Elbeuf Lycée by Kittel and Mouchel, the edifice stood firm. There was on the faculty at Caen an aged professor of literature, Père Lehanneur, who had the reputation of being the most surly of examiners. He received me with ill temper.

'Monsieur,' he said, 'I do not much like to have children in swaddling clothes applying for the master's degree.'

Whereupon he grumblingly handed me a text from Tacitus. I did not acquit myself too badly and little by little his face lightened. It was he who read the results at the end of the examination. In announcing that I had passed he smiled and added:

' . . . with the excellent citation *Well Done* and the congratulations of the judges.'

His love of Tacitus had triumphed over his distrust of youth.

As a reward my parents sent me during vacation on a long trip with my Uncle Henry, the engineer. Afflicted with an insufferably boring wife, he was one of those Frenchmen who love war and bars 'because you go there without your wife,' and he profited by every occasion to flee the domestic hearth. Thus he had agreed to be one of the commission sent to study the progress of the work on the Simplon Tunnel, then under construction; he took me with him. I have a radiant recollection of those days. Some of the young engineers had brought their wives. We went into Switzerland and Italy. In the evenings at the hotels, little games were played; the young women would put on fancy dress. My uncle's conversation, full of mockery and poetic melancholy, delighted me. He understood better than anyone else the bizarre boy I was at that time, because he had gone through the same phases. My academic successes had, in spite of the wise advice of Chartier, given me dangerous self-assurance. Supported by philosophers, historians and scientists, I believed I was always right. With women I affected a high-handed manner; I behaved as though I were in a play by Marivaux or De Musset, by Dumas *fils* or Becque. My true character was that of my father, timid and affectionate, but youth and my little university triumph inspired me with a heady exuberance which was destined to be of short duration. In the course of this trip, in the shadow of an Italian station or hidden in the cypress trees on one of the Borromean Islands, I would succeed in slipping my arm around a waist, holding a hand or brushing the nape of a neck with my lips. My boldness went no further.

What did real women matter to me? At the bottom of my heart I still loved, as in my childhood, the Queen of the *Soldats russes*, who had become the Natasha of *War and Peace* and the Irene of *Smoke*. I loved a being made not of flesh and blood but of moonlight and crystal. At the instant that I was attracted by a young woman's beauty, I would lend her all the charms of my Sylph, all the wit of Sanseverina, all the boldness of Clelia Conti. Because her hair was the colour of ripe wheat and her eyes the colour of the periwinkle, I could not believe that she was not, like me, mad with poetry and famished for knowledge, and at a moment when she probably expected the silly traditional compliments of a young man I would talk to her about Spinoza.

5

Barracks School

'I have seen plenty of fellows work hard to keep out of the army,' said the surgeon major, 'but this is the first time I've seen anyone go to such lengths to get in.'

He was talking to me. I was standing naked under the measuring rod, thin as a starved dog. All the regulations were unanimous in ruling me out. I had neither the required weight nor chest measurement. My spine was not straight. My heart produced an abnormal murmur. But on the major's desk lay ten letters from doctors who were friends of my parents, requesting that he accept me. I wanted to be accepted more than anything in the world. Brought up by my father and my two uncles on army stories, an enthusiastic reader throughout my childhood of the war books of Danrit and, some years later, of Vigny, Stendhal and Napoleon, I should have considered it a disgrace not to be a soldier.

'*Monsieur le Major*,' I implored, 'take me. You'll see, I won't cause you any trouble . . . I know very well I don't look vigorous, but I am . . . At the Rouen Lycée I won the Minister of War's medal for gymnastics . . . '

This last was decisive, and I was authorized to join the 74th Infantry Regiment or, as it was called in Rouen, the Seven-Four.

Through the barracks I came in contact with a new Rouen. For a barracks extends far beyond itself. A whole military quarter surrounds it: cafés, bars, lunchrooms, furnished rooms, girls in kerchiefs; the small, low dwellings of sergeant-majors; the brick houses, three windows wide, of the captains; the four-window houses of the majors; bazaars where equipment is sold; restaurants almost like those of other neighbourhoods but nevertheless unmistakably soldiers' restaurants, just as soldiers' rooms are unmistakable. Rooms of young men harassed and pressed for time between supper and roll call; tired bodies, sleepy minds that can no longer judge or see but simply accept. Rouen contained several of these military zones. In 1903 we infantrymen knew only two: Zone of the Seven-Four, the Pélissier Barracks, and Zone of the Three-Nine, Jeanne d'Arc Barracks.

There was a lively rivalry between the two regiments. For me, a man of the Seven-Four, all men of the Three-Nine were badly groomed, all officers ignorant of tactics, all regimental customs ridiculous. It was a different world, almost unintelligible. They buttoned their capes to the right; their about-turn was slow, their drill absurd and their regimental singing frightful. In the evening our sergeant-majors and theirs would meet at the Folies-Bergère. The room smelled of cigars and absinthe. A revue we knew by heart would be played. The female lead was called Jeanne Paradis and she had fine legs. But we had spent the day on manoeuvres out beyond Saint-Sever, among the first fir trees on the road to Elbeuf, and we would be asleep in our chairs.

How far away my Lycée seemed! Just across the river, on the high point of the Sainte-Catherine bank—and I had no time to visit it. Nothing existed in the world except the barracks and the canteen. 'Sing, goddess, the wrath of Achilles . . . ' When sadness overcame me, I used to try to evoke that happy life: reveries in the study, Chartier's classes, philosophers' walks beneath the chestnut trees in the *Cours des Grands*. But I was surrounded by men I did not know, who talked an unfamiliar dialect and who, after their drinking bouts, vomited between our beds. Voices off key and dripping with sentimentality, the strong odour of twenty bodies in the steamy heat of a red-hot stove—ah, how sad their songs were.

'One year,' I would say to myself, 'still nearly a year. Three hundred days tomorrow morning.'

Suddenly the perfect notes of a bugle would sound lights-out beneath our windows. It seemed as if a chain of sound were being drawn across the unsullied night. I imagined it dancing above the houses of Saint-Sever, crossing the Seine and reaching (a hardly perceptible refrain of distant, martial music) the students in their dormitories. I would wait enchanted for it to come again, a little attenuated by distance, for the second and third battalions. Then silence once more.

'Out with that candle!' the corporal would say.

At the end of a month the platoon of 'the exempt' was assembled and we left for Eu. This was a small Norman town that re-echoed with the names of history; one of the seats of the house of Orléans, the scene of an interview between Louis-Philippe and Queen Victoria;

surrounded by hills and woods well adapted to manoeuvres. We were quartered in a country barracks, once a royal edifice on the bank of the Bresle, a charming trout stream overhung by willow trees and lined by poplars. We were a strangely assorted crowd. Many of 'the exempt' were graduates of law schools or MAs in literature or science, among them Etienne Gilson, later to become the great authority on medieval philosophy and now my confrère in the French Academy. At that time he was a bearded, good-natured, hairy and facetious soldier. There were many teachers, but they chose to keep to themselves. Finally there were 'the journeymen of art', almost all sons of manufacturers, who had taken this easy examination for no other purpose than to be admitted to the platoon; such was the case with my friends from Elbeuf: Legrix, Bernheim and Boulé.

Just as I had loved the life of the Lycée, I soon came to love that of the regiment. A large part of our existence was still that of college boys. Various officers gave us courses. One of them, Lieutenant Breynat, whom we called 'Chochotte' because of his pretty, womanish face, lectured us on military history and the War of 1870. Poor Breynat! He himself was not destined to survive the War of 1914. Lieutenant Isler taught us topography; thirty years later I found him a Colonel of firemen in Paris. Lieutenant Giraudeau taught us the duties of a section commander in the open field. It soon became a sporting and intellectual pleasure for me to participate in company manoeuvres. Each of us in turn had to take command of a section. 'Company left front into line!' Giraudeau would cry. It took quick reflexes to give the command immediately, 'Left by fours!' If one of those responsible made a mistake, two sections would be back to back or hopelessly tangled together. This human geometry amused me.

This military service in the country was mainly an excuse for agreeable walks. What could be more delightful than to find oneself in the spring on double sentry duty with a sympathetic friend at the edge of the forest of Eu! The anemones, the primroses, the periwinkles reminded me of the Sundays of my childhood. One lay in the grass watching the life of the insects. At the end of an hour the hoof-beats of a horse would resound from the distance along the road. It would be Captain Moulin, our commander, an excellent man, altogether lacking in eloquence, who had said to us on the day of our arrival:

'You have all . . . euh . . . but a single heart . . . euh . . . which beats under the same tunic . . . euh . . . '

[44]

We used to say that the reason the platoon was in Eu was that the colonel had asked Captain Moulin where we should be sent.

'Euh . . .' the captain had begun.

'Fine, the very place,' the colonel had said. 'They shall go to Eu.'

The captain approached our thicket:

'Euh . . .' he said to the two sentries. 'Have you seen the enemy?'

'No, *mon Capitaine*.'

'Euh . . . who is the enemy? Do you happen to know?'

'Sergeant Philippe, with Gilson and Boulé, *mon Capitaine*.'

'Euh . . . good. Have they got the white bands on their caps?'

'Yes, *mon Capitaine*.'

He would pass on. Once a week he had us capture by assault a little chapel situated on the summit of the hill that dominated the Bresle. Our one bugler would sound the charge. '*The bugle call still sounds*,' I would think as I ran. I was a long way from imagining that ten years later the Seven-Four would be rushing to attack real trenches. This training seemed to us at that time just one long, happy game. Soon the forced marches began, twenty kilometres with knapsacks on our backs; twenty-four kilometres; twenty-eight kilometres. All the marching songs were sung. We had an immense repertory, less delicate than my father's. *L'Artilleur de Metz* followed *Le Pou et l'araignée*, *Haton de la Goupillière*, and *Le Père Dupanloup*. During the hourly rest period Gilson would tell stories:

'The setting is an immense desert . . . To the right, nothing. To the left, nothing . . . In the centre a solitary date palm bows its head in melancholy. Seated beneath this palm there are three Bedouins . . .'

Captain Moulin rode up on his horse and addressed me:

'Euh . . .' he said. 'Why are you making this march? . . . Euh . . . You are down on the sick list. Euh . . . I gave orders that you were to be left in barracks.'

I got up and stood at attention:

'The sergeant did say I could stay in barracks, *mon Capitaine*, but I asked permission to come on the march . . . I can stand it perfectly.'

'Euh . . . But you are on the sick list . . . It's very irregular.'

This insistence annoyed me:

'It was the major who said I was sick, *mon Capitaine*. I don't feel sick.'

'Euh . . .' he said. 'I understand . . . You are the *Malingre malgré lui* . . .'

[45]

And he went on, much pleased with his wit.

I have always thought, with Disraeli: 'Either perfect solitude or perfect sympathy.' In the platoon I found this perfect sympathy. Jean Legrix, one of the noblest souls I have ever known, became a close friend at that time and remained so until his death which, alas, occurred during the War of 1914. My other inseparable companions were Demanche, son of a Paris lawyer, and Harlé, whose father was a manufacturer of electrical supplies in Paris. Elective affinities are inexplicable. I could not say what it was that drew us three together, for we were markedly different, but we used to find in one another's company a pleasure that was constantly renewed. For dinner, which we took outside the barracks, about thirty of us had formed a club which was presided over authoritatively by Jean Boulé, another native of Elbeuf.

We joked a great deal about military life, but if it were necessary, all these young citizens were capable of making strenuous efforts. I remember that toward the middle of June our strict and indeed ferocious sergeant-major, Sacams, announced with annoyance that we were to march in the review on the Fourteenth of July with the garrison of Eu, which was composed of a battalion of the 39th.

'It will be a disgrace,' he said, rolling his r's, 'because you "exempts" manoeuvre like tramps . . .'

It was true that we were negligent in drill. Our hundred right hands did not strike the slings of our rifles with a single thud; the butts of our rifles did not hit the ground at the same instant. The old sergeants who drilled us suffered, swore at us, but got no results. Suddenly Sacams' contempt piqued our vanity, and we decided that our parade on the Fourteenth of July should be a masterpiece of military art. I reminded my friends of a scene in Kipling's *Stalky*, and the stupefied sergeant-major saw us practising the manual of arms outside drill hours under the direction of one of our own number. Presently the platoon became a crack troop. This resulted in unexpected joys. Perfection, when it is collective perfection, brings its own reward. I retain from that review, held in the broiling sun, a memory of the same sort that certain fine concerts have left in my mind. This little experience helped me later on to understand the technique of military dictatorships and their fascination for young men. It also shows the value of close-order drill and the manual of arms in moulding a troop. From the Fourteenth of July on, in a battle we would have been good soldiers.

At the end of July the platoon was given its examination. This was conducted with great seriousness. Colonel Boelle of the 39th presided over the board of examiners; he had with him a commandant from the War College, an austere and brilliant Alsatian named Ringeisen, and our Captain Moulin. We were supposed to know all about troop movements in open country, formations in close-order drill, how to write orders, draw plans and expound the theory of war. I had the good fortune to be allotted the fine preamble to *Le Service intérieur*, which I admired as much as certain passages from Bossuet: 'Since discipline constitutes the principal strength of armies, it is imperative that every officer shall exact from his subordinates complete obedience and submission at every instant.' I repeated this with complete sincerity. My company manoeuvres went well, and I stood first in the platoon.

My return to Rouen was disappointing. The eight who stood highest were made corporals, and it happened that on rejoining the regiment I found myself in charge of a barracks room. It was a difficult assignment. A corporal was responsible for the condition of the room and the men. But since he slept among them he felt disinclined to punish his comrades, who on the day before had been his equals, and he could not obtain from his subordinates 'complete obedience and submission at every instant'. If he gave the order: 'Sweep out the room,' there would often be some drunken brute who would reply: 'Sweep it out yourself, you loafer.' What could one do? Give the oaf two days' confinement to quarters? For insubordination of this sort the captain was likely to hand out fifteen days in the guardhouse, and the colonel two months. Pretend not to hear? One would soon lose every vestige of authority. Nevertheless, if the barracks room was not swept out, the captain would come in and say:

'This barracks is a stable! Who is the corporal? . . . Confine him to quarters.'

For a whole month I was not able to go out. I paid dear for my humble rank. But living constantly with 'my good fellows', as they were called in those days, I learned a thousand character traits of the French workman and peasant. Up to that time, in the Lycée and with the platoon, I had mixed only with young men of the middle class, and I had had no opportunity of knowing the people. In the barracks of the Seven-Four I slept, I ate, I lived with them. What did I find? Much intelligence and shrewdness. My 'good fellows' formed opinions of their superiors that were seldom wrong. Our captain was held in contempt by them; ten years later the War of 1914 showed that he was unworthy of command. They adored our lieutenant, who in the same war died a hero. They entertained an invincible distrust of the powerful and rich. Patriots by instinct, they did not question their duty to defend the soil of France and they were ready to give up their lives for their country, always provided it was not to the profit of the rich.

At first, because they knew I was the son of a big manufacturer, they made life miserable for me. There was nothing easier for them than to get me punished. All they had to do was not execute an order, or else to execute it to the letter. Then, seeing that I was defenceless in the face of their malice and moreover full of good will, they adopted me with a strange, rough tenderness and from that moment did their best to protect me from Captain Pétry, a nasty beggar, who made it a point of honour to find reason for confining me to quarters. 'Being mess sergeant, he served thirteen portions to Squad Thirteen, which is composed of fourteen men, and fourteen portions to Squad Fourteen which is composed of thirteen men: Four days' confinement to quarters...' 'For not requiring his men to clean adequately under their beds: eight days' confinement to quarters.' This became intolerable. Then came the drama of general inspection. Pétry called together the sergeants and corporals:

'The general,' he said, 'has a horror of brooms. He believes that the dust raised by them spreads tuberculosis... He desires that the floors be cleaned with wet mops... and so mops will be distributed to you, and you will see to it that the brooms disappear until after inspection. Explain this to your men... Do you understand?'

I returned to my barracks and passed the word around. Two days later the general arrived. The mop was clearly visible beneath the rifle rack. The general stopped in front of one of my men, unfortunately an illiterate peasant, the stupidest of the lot.

'What do you use to sweep out the barracks?' he asked.

'A broom, *mon Général.*'

'And where is the broom?'

'It has been hidden, on your account, *mon Général.*'

After this incident Pétry began to hate me in earnest, and he spoiled my last months with the regiment.

Nevertheless I enjoyed rejoining the Seven-Four two years later. It was the rule that 'the exempt' who had seen only one year of service should go back to 'rejoin their class' which had served three. In the interval I had been made a sergeant, and I set off for the grand manoeuvres as a section leader. I had sworn to myself that I would serve at this trade just as well as I possibly could. Participating completely in the life of my men, I slept with them in barns, refusing the room 'with a feather bed' which the farmers invariably offered to a sergeant. Each morning I explained the manoeuvres for that day as well as I could to my section. Other nations fight tolerably well under mechanical discipline. Frenchmen have to understand. My men, once they had caught on, played the game with enthusiasm and intelligence. Feeling that I had established complete control, I was able to demand great exertion from them. Before long the colonel took notice.

'There's a fine section,' he said to my captain. 'The sergeant ought to be promoted to second lieutenant.'

But I forgot to make application, and the war, eight years later, found me still a non-commissioned officer.

I, who might very easily not have been a soldier at all if I had not wished to be, was destined to spend more than six years of my life in the army. I do not regret it. In the furious Europe of the twentieth century, a country was as strong as its army, and no one could say that he understood France unless he was well acquainted with the French army. I believe I was well acquainted with it, and I loved it deeply although I was sensible of its faults. It had fine traditions inherited from the Ancien Régime, the Empire and the Colonial Wars. It was one of the few institutions in France that had crossed the bridge of the Revolution. Educated in excellent schools, most of its officers attained in their youth a very creditable degree of intelligence and culture. Many of them entered the army, as Lyautey later informed me, full of a mystical loyalty that was almost religious.

The trouble was that in most of the corps there was too little nourishment for the men's enthusiasm. An army that has no well-defined task goes to sleep. In the colonies the officers worked. At the War College various enthusiastic teachers inspired the best of them. But in the garrisons routine gave rise to indifference. It was noticeable that little effort was being made to modernize methods or take advantage of scientific progress. Politics, especially after the *Affaire Dreyfus*, had crept into the army and divided it. The great service of Painlevé and then of Clemenceau among the ministers of war was to put military virtues above partisan passions.

As to the rank and file, they were the immemorial Frenchmen,

'Frenchmen, sons of Frenchmen, under the same oriflamme.' They were grumblers, always discontented and always ready to sacrifice their lives provided someone took the trouble to tell them why. A Frenchman has to understand. During manoeuvres I had been able to do with my men what I liked because I had treated them as intelligent, free human beings. The Frenchman asks nothing better than to work if the task seems to him worth while; if he gets the feeling that he is wasting his time he becomes embittered. In short, a Frenchman has a need of justice: promises must be kept and offences must be judged fairly. Such were the lessons I learned in the army; they were to stand me in good stead in industry.

6

The Main Office

It had been decided by my father, in consultation with the Uncles, that
I should enter the factory at the conclusion of my year in the army.
When the time came the Uncles had been reduced to 'Monsieur Henry'
alone, for 'Monsieur Louis' had had his second stroke and, with his
body half paralysed, was engaged in dying in that apartment above the
factory whence he had reigned over the family. All the Fraenckel
brothers had been stricken in the same way. They would work without
vacations and without recreation until they were sixty or sixty-five,
then one day they would collapse and lose consciousness; they would
revive with a twisted mouth, thickened tongue, and an arm and a leg
immobilized. Then would begin a life at reduced rate. One of the old
Alsatians from the mill would become nurse for his disabled boss. The
voice would come back, brokenly, the invalid would take a few steps
supported by a strong arm, or read stretched out on a couch like Uncle
Adolphe. All 'the gentlemen' would come in each evening, after they
left the mill, to spend five minutes sitting at the bedside.

'Anything new?' the living dead man would ask.

A brother, a son or a nephew would then give him the number of
pieces woven and sold, the price of wool, the results of the inventories,
and for an instant a brief ray of intelligence would light up the glassy
eyes. Thus it would be up to the moment of the second stroke, which
would precede the end by only a little.

In 1904 the general staff of the mill was made up of 'Monsieur
Henry', my great-uncle Henry Fraenckel, an old man whom I have
described as Monsieur Achille in *Bernard Quesnay*; 'Monsieur Paul'
and 'Monsieur Victor', sons of Louis Fraenckel; 'Monsieur Ernest' and
'Monsieur Edmond', my father and my uncle. Who was the head of
the business? By right of seniority old Henry Fraenckel, but he was a
modest and taciturn technician who, although he had a thorough knowledge of manufacturing, was wholly ignorant of the general business of

the firm. In all social contacts Paul Fraenckel took the lead. Cultivated, eloquent, a good Latinist, he loved all representative functions. It was he who represented the house in the Chamber of Commerce at Elbeuf and was later to become its president; he who would call at the office of the Prefect in Rouen when there was some labour question to be settled, and it was he who was to receive the Légion d'Honneur immediately after my Uncle Henry—an unvoiced, secret and humiliating sorrow for my father, his senior in years and in service at the mill.

These decorations succeeded one another in the family with the same regularity as the attacks of apoplexy. They were the occasion for great banquets which the mill gave to its fifteen hundred workmen, for it had once more increased in size. On the day when the news appeared in the Official Bulletin, a delegation from each of the workshops would arrive in the Show Room carrying flowers, and the personnel would present to the new chevalier a bronze by Barbedienne: *Le Travail*, or perhaps *La Pensée*. A month later the banquet would take place in the immense wool sheds which would be decorated with evergreens, red hangings and flags. Paul Fraenckel would assume the task of inviting the Prefect, a Senator, a Minister, or, if need be, an Under Secretary of State. There would be champagne and speeches. Then the Norman workers would sing, 'Viv' le cidr' de Normandie' the Alsatian workers would sing, 'Hans im Schnockenloch', and there would be dancing. Paul and my father would open the ball with two of the pretty girl employees. In Alsace my father had been a good waltzer and he had not lost his skill. These celebrations were gay and cordial.

But if you called the *head* of a business the one who controls production, then the real head of the Elbeuf mill was my Uncle Edmond. Each week on Wednesday evenings he left for Paris. He spent a day visiting all the big stores, all the wholesalers of cloth and all the clothiers, and returned Friday morning laden with orders or, in periods of crisis, with complaints. The report he made every Friday to the assembled 'gentlemen' was the high point of the week. The ceremony took place in the Main Office. This was an immense room hung with army-blue draperies over which were placed portraits of the dead Uncles. There a meeting was held every morning at seven-thirty to read the mail; an enormous rectangular piece of furniture with an easy chair at each of its four sides bore on its top the high pile of letters as yet unopened. The rule was that the first of the partners to arrive had the right to open the mail. But if while he was at work an older partner came in, the younger would get up without a word and the new arrival would proceed with the opening of the envelopes. I have seen on certain mornings four successive changes. Then the time came when, Death having carried off my betters, I myself opened the mail, an honour as prodigious as a stool at the court of Louis XIV.

On the morning of 'Edmond's return' the mail was relegated to second place. Of what importance were letters from the provinces when Edmond might be bringing back from Paris orders for a thousand, and sometimes for three thousand, pieces? Besides, he had the knack of giving dramatic form to the story of his day, always in chronological order, never spoiling his effect by announcing his successes at the start. If during the afternoon he had succeeded in snatching the Bon Marché order away from Blin, which was the supreme triumph, rendered even sweeter by the defeat of a hereditary enemy, he would not say so until the time came, and would begin coldly:

'At eight o'clock I went to the Samaritaine where I saw Mellino . . . He complained about the weave in the overcoats . . . '

For Edmond's report was often an indictment of this or that branch of the mill. When he had finished, my father, who was in charge of weaving, and Paul Fraenckel, who was in charge of the finishing, would explain the measures to be taken to fill the orders or to meet the complaints. If the discussion took too long, old Uncle Henry would begin very rapidly winding up an invisible machine. This was the signal that enough time had been spent in talking and that the moment had come to disperse to the workrooms.

My father, who knew all the techniques used in the mill, hoped to make me learn how to spin, weave and cut. But first of all I had to learn about wool. That was the most difficult of all the apprenticeships, for it required an aptitude of eye and hand which time and practice alone could give. It was decided that I should spend every morning with chief sorter Ursin, an old Norman, who worked with his daughter. Mademoiselle Ursin, a handsome and vigorous young woman, made me think immediately of Balzac's *Rabouilleuse*. She would stand facing her father in front of a large frame on which the wool to be sorted was laid. The fleeces came in the form of bundles of greasy wool that had been tightly compressed in ironbound bales, and these it was necessary to open up. Then one separated the wool from various parts of the animal: backs, flanks, stomachs, necks. If the wool came from Australia, the tufts were small and fine with black tips; if it came from

Buenos Aires, the tufts were larger; if from France or Morocco the staple was very coarse. Père Ursin taught me to take out the 'ganders', that is, the shiny hairs that will not take the dye and so would spoil the finished piece of cloth. Then he made me distinguish between first and second choice and separate them. At the end of a few days my father came to observe my progress.

'Is he getting on all right?' he asked Père Ursin.

'Faith,' said the old man, 'he has a good will, Monsieur Ernest . . . but he's not very intelligent.' A valuable lesson.

In the afternoon I would go to the spinning and weaving departments. The spinning mill with its silently turning carding machines and its winders drawing out the trembling tufts of thread twisted by the spindles, was a place of order and beauty. But I disliked the inferno of the weaving mill. The noise of the looms made the building tremble. In all the streets of Elbeuf you heard this harsh rhythm which was the heartbeat of the town. In the fulling mill I was the pupil of Père Fritz, an aged magician from Alsace, who taught me the art of 'teaseling', that is, of smoothing the wool in a rough cloth and making it shine. Wool workers were provided with natural thistles to perform this task. These thistles, sorted and classified into thirty varieties according to age and size of the spikes, played an amazing role in the perfection of this finishing process. Old Fritz examined the pieces to be treated with the authority of a great physician. He fingered them, tested their strength, and gave the prescription:

'No new thistles for this one,' he would say.

The mills in the north had adopted mechanical carding machines with steel spikes, but Père Fritz remained loyal, with reason, to the inimitable suppleness of nature.

Unfortunately, as I soon learned, these fine, heavy clothing materials of which my father was so proud were selling less and less. Men's clothes were changing. One seldom saw 'frock coats of Elbeuf cloth' except in old-fashioned novels. Even Brittany abandoned waistcoats of embroidered cloth for the republican jacket. The success of our mill had been based on the wearing of 'blacks', but the decent middle-class sadness of the nineteenth century was being supplanted by an appetite for colour and design. The women helped us to survive by wearing plain black cloth. But at the moment when I entered the mill, the gross business was slowly declining. It had attained ten million francs; now it was nearer to nine. Since the running expenses remained the same, this slight but steady decline presented grave problems. In all the departments in which I worked I inquired what the workmen earned. I was shocked and seriously disturbed by the low scale of the salaries. At that time a weaver received twenty to thirty francs a week; a carding girl twelve francs. This seemed to me altogether insufficient to live on.

'But what can we do?' said my father with whom I discussed the matter. 'We earn a bare three to five per cent on our investment. Even if you took no profit whatever, which isn't possible because the plant, the machines, have to be renewed, and if you divided the entire proceeds between fifteen hundred workers, that would give very little to each one of them.'

'Nevertheless it would give them something.'

'Not enough to change their standard of living . . . And how would *you* live?'

I asked: 'Couldn't you increase the sales price a little?'

'You know perfectly well our competitors would not allow it . . . The instant we increased the price of cloth by ten centimes we would be beaten by Blin or by the northern mills.'

'And if all the French manufacturers should get together and agree to increase prices simultaneously?'

'Then the foreign firms would monopolize the French market.'

'That could be protected by import duties . . . '

'Yes, but there is a limit that would be quickly reached in a country like ours that depends on exports. There would be immediate reprisals against our wines or our luxury products, and these industries would complain to Parliament.'

'But then what can we do?'

'I'm trying,' my father said, 'to reduce the cost price by improving the quality of the machines and increasing production . . . A mill that works under more favourable conditions can pay its personnel better. You have seen the new automatic looms? One woman can operate two of them. That means she can be paid more.'

'But it eliminates one employee?'

'Obviously.'

This labour question threw me into a distressing quandary. As I have said, Chartier, who was not a socialist, had talked to us about socialism with intelligence and understanding. Influenced by him, I was anxious not to make myself an accomplice in injustice or exploitation. Miserably I pictured a working woman encumbered with children and unable to provide them with decent lodging and food. When I examined the life of a man like my father I found him completely different from the cruel employers described by Zola in *Germinal*. 'If an ideal society,' I thought, 'was seeking a director for a great mill, a competent, just, hard-working, modest, frugal man of simple tastes, it could not find a more perfect one.' Moreover I saw clearly, since all the account books were open to me, that as my father had said, the profits of the mill represented a tiny percentage on the investment. And so what was one to think? And where did one's duty lie?

Mouchel, my former mathematics teacher, had become the socialist mayor of Elbeuf. I used to encounter him often on the streets with his moist moustache and his chalk-covered waistcoat. He would stop me and explain his projects:

'This unhappy city,' he would say to me, 'has been exploited by certain vested interests: the Gas Company and the Water Company. I have decided to get along without them, not to renew their contracts and to build a gas company of my own ... You understand? Besides, I'm going to build an incinerator for garbage, which will give me free power ... *Hein?* You understand? ... In ten years with the profits of these municipal industries I shall make this city the most advanced in social institutions in all of France.'

I submitted my scruples and distress of mind to him; he, naturally enough, was hostile to all forms of capitalism.

'The thing that's unjust,' he said to me, 'is that the united effort of the workers produces a surplus value, and this surplus value is confiscated under the name of profits by the capitalists ... You understand?'

No, I did not understand. I could not see that it was true to say, as Mouchel did, that the surplus value was produced by the workmen alone. Around me in the industrial world of Normandy I saw that two mills that were almost identical and employed the same number of workmen might make, one a profit, the other a loss, if the first was well managed and the second ill. Production itself could be increased or diminished by the methods of management. Nevertheless a certain form of socialism continued to attract me. I was ready to admit that my father was a Just Man. It seemed to me it was possible to go further and be a Saint, to turn over the mill to the workmen and continue to manage it for honour's sake. On certain nights of enthusiasm I proposed this sort of life for myself. In the light of dawn I realized it would not be easy to go into the Main Office for the morning conference and explain my plan under the eyes of the defunct Uncles.

My evenings were my own. I almost always spent them in my parents' house. To this provincial and retired life I owe the best of my reading. It was then that I read all of Saint-Simon, Taine, Sainte-Beuve (and in particular *Port-Royal*), Auguste Comte, Marx, all of Balzac, and many books on science. I made notes as I read and up to the time of the last war I still owned large notebooks in cardboard covers in which I had written down my impressions each evening. A theory of light and sound by Helmholtz would rub shoulders with an analysis of *Capital*; an emotional comment on *Déracinées* with a dry and precise note on Pearson's *Grammar of Science*; Henri Poincaré with Vilfredo Pareto. My intellectual appetite was voracious. However, for my own pleasure, I kept coming back to the same authors: Balzac, Stendhal, Tolstoy, Kipling. I loved the moral preoccupations of Tolstoy. At the age of twenty I felt very close to Levine in his discontent with life and his constant readiness to renounce the world and devote himself to austerity. Then I came to believe that Prince André in *War and Peace*, a disciplined soldier, silent and ready to submit to fate at his post without a murmur, was the finest human type. To this I added the thought from Marcus Aurelius that it is not difficult to be a sage in solitude, but it is a rarer and nobler thing to be a sage on the throne and in the press of great affairs. There, it seemed to me, lay the solution to my problem of conscience. It was not a wholly safe solution, for the Devil might choose this roundabout way of reassuring the Emperor or the Rich Man.

Meanwhile Kipling played a role of capital importance in my little spiritual drama. To the radical views of Chartier—that of the embattled citizen defying authority and fearing tyranny above all—Kipling opposed the idea of a necessary hierarchy. A society divided against itself will perish, the stories of Kipling said to me; a society that refuses to accept a leader will perish. Even the beasts submit to the laws of the jungle in order to survive. But, on the other hand, Kipling's leaders had to show themselves worthy of command through their courage and abnegation. I loved the type of Anglo-Indian he exhibited for our admiration: a good technician devoted body and soul to his task, mysterious and silent, loyal to his friends and severe toward rebels.

There again I found a picture of what a captain of industry should be. In my copybooks of that time I find impassioned dialogues between myself and myself, in which I defended by turns the thesis of Kipling and that of Chartier.

Every writer has his personal themes, the projections of strong sentiments that have forced him to write, and willy-nilly most of his books are built around these themes. Thus Stendhal, engrossed with the young man he would have liked to be, pictures himself under the names of Fabrice, of Julien Sorel and Lucien Louwen. Thus Dickens is obsessed with the idea of the child wife. Although I was not conscious of it, these interior dialogues were slowly forming in me a writer whose essential theme would be the opposition of two equally sincere sentiments and the necessity of reconciling these two halves of himself in order to go on living.

Little by little, through the daily contact with things and people that comes from working, I learned that abstract concepts do not exist in the real world, that the realities are quite different—human beings with their bald or well-covered heads, their myopic or long-sighted eyes, their thin- or thick-lipped mouths, their violent or lethargic appetites, their passions, their desires, their loves, their follies. 'What one must paint,' I said to myself sometimes, 'is not an abstract world in which words contend vainly with one another, but a universe of flesh and blood where bodies work together . . . In the mouthings of an orator, Catholics, Protestants and Jews may seem three hostile groups, but on the streets of Elbeuf the Abbé Alleaume, Pastor Roehrich and my father walking together make a single human group . . . What one must paint . . . '

During my sleepless nights I would outline magnificent novels that would be fair to both sides, and on awakening I found that I was, alas, totally incapable of writing them.

7

'The Practical
Man Writes to Me...'

During my childhood and adolescence I had always dreamed of being
a writer. My arduous life in the factory scarcely seemed to favour this
plan, but my hope persisted. During my last years at the Lycée I had
written a few stories; the army had inspired a long novelette, *Gaucher
Caporal*; from the life of Rouen and Elbeuf I had derived another, *Suze*.
All together there were enough to make a volume. I wished to publish
it. But how? I knew no one in the literary world. An editor in Paris
seemed to me a powerful and unapproachable divinity. I did not know
that every manuscript sent to a publishing house is given to a reader
and gets an honest chance. I hit on the scheme of taking my collection
to the printer in Rouen, my friend Wolf who had published the little
magazine of the Lycée, and asking him to print it at my expense.

Some weeks passed and then I received a batch of proofs. To see
my compositions in print was pleasurable for a moment. I reread them.
Alas! I had been too well nourished on good literature to preserve, after
that reading, any illusion of having written a masterpiece. One of the
novelettes, *La Dernière Histoire du monde*, was original, at least in idea.
I had imagined that through great advances in technology mankind,
about the year 10,000, had succeeded in getting along entirely without
physical effort either in work or in war. Then the women, little by
little, had gained control and, being conservative by nature, had con-
verted human societies into hives. Most of them, unsexed, had become
workers, always dressed in grey uniform, whose duty was to look after
the young of the hive or to accumulate reserves of food. A few queens
assured the continuation of the race. As for the males, drones clad in
brilliantly coloured doublets, they sat on the steps of the hive awaiting
the brief hour of the nuptial flight and playing on guitars or composing
sad poems. The women forbade them reading and writing on pain of

death, for they feared revolution. The man in my story, who wrote down these facts, was the last to know how to write and he went into hiding to do it; but probably he had been denounced, for suddenly he saw advancing toward him one of the Amazonian workers, brandishing a little poisoned dart—the sting. The story broke off abruptly in the middle of a sentence, and it could never be continued for, after the death of the narrator, there was no longer anyone in the world who knew how to write.

It was ingenious and, if not perfectly written, at least fairly well done. The story about the regiment was very Kiplingesque and it, too, had qualities; it illustrated a high but at the same time realistic idea of the art of command. But the rest were feeble, and the collection as a whole gave the impression of a work lacking in cohesion. Although the individual stories varied in quality, the volume itself lacked that unity of tone possessed by a collection of Kipling, or of Maupassant. I had the wit to realize this, and I went to my friend the printer and told him sadly that I had given up the idea of publishing the book and that he could distribute the type. He tried to dissuade me, but my critical instincts won out.

'Run off at least a dozen copies,' he said to me. 'That won't cost you much more . . .'

To this I consented, and of that first endeavour of mine all that remained to me was a dozen slender volumes bound in plain covers of pale blue on which was neither title nor author's name.

There remained, too, a feeling of despair which no one around me noticed, for I could be very secretive and I did not like complaining. 'Now,' I thought, 'it's over and done with. I shall sink little by little into this life of routine. For three years, five years, ten years, the impulse given by Chartier and Stendhal will still have some effect. Then inertia will win out. I shall no longer talk of anything but machines and cloth and salaries. Old and respected, I shall succeed Paul Fraenckel as President of the Chamber of Commerce. Each morning I shall make a tour of the workshops as my father does, until the day comes when I am stricken, having lived out in this sepulchre my brief and only life . . .' When I gave myself up to this reverie, I would spend dreadful evenings over an open book which I could not read, and for a while this despair turned me toward the frivolous social life of the community, which I had hitherto neglected in favour of my evening studies.

Elbeuf, like most small French cities, contained a number of cultured and agreeable families. My regimental comrade, Jean Boulé, had married a charming woman; my cousin Robert Fraenckel, a very intelligent man only a trifle older than I and enthusiastically interested in history, had married Olga Allatini, a beautiful Italian woman who shared my taste for music; a Blin household and a Bessand household rounded out a little group in which the women were pretty, the men gay, and the conversation lively and unconstrained. Soon I was giving up my evening work two or three times a week to join them. Since I could not get along without writing, I composed a revue for this group of amateurs, and then a comedy, and I tasted in this tiny society the joys of dramatic authorship.

I retained enough perspective to realize the futility of the kind of life I was now leading, and the miserable poverty, not to say blameworthy vulgarity, of the scripts that brought me this small local glory. But in my disenchantment and desperation, I took the same sombre pleasure in degrading the noble profession of authorship that women, disappointed in true love, take in throwing themselves into lives of dissoluteness. Only one man during this period understood what was happening to me: that was Chartier. Although he had left Rouen, he still remained for me, as for so many others, the Master. More so than ever, for he had begun in 1906 to write daily pieces for the *Dépêche de Rouen*, pieces that I greatly admired. The writer, like the runner, has his own distance at which he strikes his best stride. Chartier could make of a two-page article at once a poem, a lesson and a masterpiece of style. 'That's my acrobatic turn,' he would say. 'Besides, I only succeed once in a hundred times.'

He succeeded almost every day. The splendid thing is that Norman readers were able to see immediately that the *Dépêche* was offering them in these *Propos* something new and great. There were many of us who read them the moment the paper arrived, before the news. This was our morning nourishment, rich and strong. Many cut out the *Propos* and saved them. To tell the truth, there never had been journalism of this quality before and perhaps there never will be again. The fact that not a single reader complained about the difficulty of these articles or of their density is a tribute to the human spirit.

Chartier signed these *Propos* with a pseudonym: Alain (undoubtedly because of Alain Chartier) and later on as an author he was to be well known and then illustrious under this name. When I had the opportunity to spend a few days in Paris, which happened rarely enough, I went to see him. He had joined the teaching staff at the Lycée Condorcet and lived not far from there in the Rue de Provence in a little room furnished with a bed, a divan, a piano and that library of thirty volumes which he considered necessary and sufficient. Seated beside him on the tattered couch, I felt transported out of this world and free to express myself without reserve. He listened to my angry descriptions of the life of Elbeuf and what I called with adolescent hyperbole 'my spiritual downfall'.

'Frivolity,' he said, 'is a violent state.'

When he was talking about women Alain, like his favourite Stendhal, would alternate between adoration and cynicism. I have never heard anyone talk better about romantic novels such as *Le Lys dans la vallée* or *La Chartreuse de Parme*. But he used to say, too: 'Suppressed desire is a poison. If you want to see naked women, go to a brothel.' I believe he thought me dangerously inclined to romantic excesses, for he repeatedly commended cynicism to me. When I read Sainte-Beuve's *Volupté* I recognized myself in the hero, who is passionately in love with an unobtainable woman and on leaving her company goes to explore the disreputable quarters of Paris. In the evenings in Elbeuf, I would silently admire the young matrons of Elbeuf and write them verses which I would not show to them; Saturday evenings I would go to Rouen and with the help of an usher make a rendezvous with one of the obliging dancers of the Folies-Bergère.

When I observed in America and later on in France the freedom enjoyed by young men and women and when I realized the charm imparted to the first blossoming of love by a certain equality in culture and manners, I regretted bitterly the mediocrity and venality of the first women with whom I had been able to consort freely. In our small provincial cities at that time girls were so rigidly guarded and early marriages so cruelly discouraged, that a young man found himself forced willy-nilly to turn to the professionals. It was a sorry introduction to love and life. Body and soul acquired dangerous habits. When the soul could not find passions that would answer to its own, it sought refuge in fiction. The body grew accustomed to dissociating desire and admiration. Some even reached a point where they could feel desire only for women they despised. All this was unhealthy and disillusioning.

In 1906 the People's University at Rouen invited me to deliver a lecture. I accepted, and discovered to my surprise that I spoke easily.

Silent enough in everyday life, I felt no fear whatever once I was on a platform. Delivering these lectures in Rouen brought me back to serious work, for they required preparation. They gained me friends and a loyal public.

In those days the political life in Elbeuf was lively. Up to the time of the *Affaire Dreyfus*, Normandy had been conservative. Then the radicals had gained the upper hand and we had a deputy, Monsieur Maille, a worthy Norman with the face of a Roman senator, whose radicalism was so pale that even the most timorous of the middle class could support him. But at the next election Mouchel, my ex-professor of mathematics, who was already mayor of Elbeuf, had decided to be a deputy as well. Jaurès had come to make a speech on his behalf, and his poetic eloquence had swept our crowded stadium with beautiful metaphors. At the outset of the campaign the local political workhorses had laughed at a candidate without money and experience who delivered technical discourses to the voters and said to them; '*Hein?* You understand?' They forgot that Frenchmen love professors.

'That fellow,' Père Ursin, the old chief sorter, said to me, 'he's didactic . . . I like that.'

Mouchel promised that he would have the salaries of the deputies reduced, that he would remain poor, and that he would resist the temptations of Paris. People knew he was sincere and they found this touching. When the day came, he was elected by a large majority. I had campaigned for him.

From the very start he provoked some excitement in the Palais-Bourbon, where he dared to propose, as he had promised he would, a reduction in parliamentary salaries.

'Why,' he asked, 'should we deputies live better than the majority of our constituents?'

Unanimous murmurs silenced this trouble-maker. A little later he protested that the Chamber did not do enough work:

'Why not come at seven o'clock in the morning,' he said, 'and pass the budget on time?'

Right and Left treated him as a dangerous demagogue, but he was acting in good faith. I still used to meet him on the streets of Elbeuf.

'Our municipal works are in operation,' he told me proudly, smoothing his moist moustache.

This I knew, for the works functioned badly and a dreadful smell of gas had penetrated a whole quarter of the city. L'Allée des Soupirs

[63]

where lovers used to stroll on summer evenings had become unbearable. But Mouchel was in his seventh heaven.

'To be deputy and mayor!' he said to me. 'What a fine career! Each day brings some extraordinary incident. I believe you once thought of being a novelist? Oh, if you could only observe the incidents I witness! Listen, this very morning I was called to the municipal prison. A man had just hanged himself . . . He was still warm . . . It's perfectly fascinating. *Hein?* You understand?'

Some disturbing rumours began to circulate through the city. The municipal gas works, it was reported, were not meeting expenses. The unhappy Mouchel had unsuspectingly given jobs to all his campaign workers. A certain sly and artful Norman named D., who was a weaver in the Blin mill and one of the leading politicians, had been made director of the gas works in compensation for ill-defined services. He was incompetent, like most of those employed in the enterprise. There was no money in the till. The town had borrowed two million francs to pay the costs of construction; it would have to borrow anew in order to continue operation. Then the Prefecture protested; it could not authorize the new loans. Was the town of Elbeuf going bankrupt? One morning when we arrived at the mill the watchman said with great emotion to my father:

'Does Monsieur Ernest know that Mouchel has killed himself?'

I rushed to the town hall. The body was still on the pavement; the police were on their way. The deputy mayor had spent the night in his office bringing his accounts up to date, then at dawn he had got out his officers'-reserve revolver and put a bullet through his head.

His secretary, a nice young man who was devoted to him, told me with tears in his eyes that on the day before the mayor had said repeatedly:

'I made a mistake . . . I must pay the price.'

But the sacrifice of an honest man makes up for nothing. This death was a triumph for the local conservatives who had been predicting disaster from the beginning of the enterprise:

'Just see what socialism leads to!' they said.

Alain, in one of his *Propos*, wrote a beautiful eulogy on Mouchel: 'In this drama at Elbeuf,' he said in substance, 'we have nothing to regret, nothing to take back. To draw from the death of a Just Man arguments against his creed and faith, that is the sort of talk one might

expect to hear at the tables of the rich.' The article was admirably
written and it moved me, for I too had loved Mouchel with all my
heart, but for the first time I allowed myself to differ fundamentally
with my master. I wrote to him. My theme was: 'I mourn as you do
the death of a Just Man. But I do not think there is *nothing* to regret.
According to you, the desire that a business be well run, regret at the
bankruptcy of a town—these are topics for the tables of the rich? ...
You, Alain, are like a man off sailing in a yacht; it makes no difference
to you when you return. But I am a pilot aboard a merchantman; the
harbour lights alone spell repose for me.'

Two days later, to my great surprise, when I opened the *Dépêche
de Rouen* and turned as I did each morning to Alain's *Propos*, which
were its honour and its ornament, I saw that he had published my
letter. 'The Practical Man writes to me,' he said, and then quoted my
text in full. Next day in his *Propos* he replied. I rejoined in my turn.
'I have received,' Alain wrote, 'a new and striking letter from the
Practical Man about the sad occurrence at Elbeuf ... ' From that time
on it often happened that my letters and also my conversations with
him became part of his *Propos*. He loved to have me talk shop or
describe the Uncles whom he regarded, with reason, as similar to the
characters of Balzac. Based on them he created for his *Propos* a man
whom he called Castor who was a sort of industrial Grandet, narrow,
prudent and sensible. Some of Monsieur Henry's maxims delighted him:
'*All reports are false,*' Monsieur Henry would say; or: '*It's not enough
to give an order; you must also carry it out yourself.*' A remarkable
characteristic in the radical Chartier was that it did not displease him
to see me evolving a political philosophy different from his own but
one that was appropriate, he believed, to the role I was destined to play
as a leader of industry.

'I was afraid for a long time,' he said to me one day, 'that you would
become *too* intelligent. I am reassured.'

This pronouncement, harsh though it sounded, gave me a strange
pleasure. It came from a reader of Balzac and Comte, from a man who
used to say: 'In my eyes every proof is clearly discredited.'

During my student days he had feared I would develop the sort of
abstract intelligence that juggles brilliantly with words and doctrines;
the fact that I had become a 'practical man' seemed to him entirely
advantageous. 'Now you'll be worth more than all those jargon-
mongers,' he added affectionately.

My father had decided to give me a month's vacation each year. I spent the first one in England. For years I had fed on English poets and novelists; I felt a profound affinity with them and wished to become better acquainted with their language. I put an advertisement in one of the London papers asking for lodging in a private home for a young Frenchman. A hundred replies came in. I selected a widow who lived in Richmond on the bank of the Thames and who had three daughters aged sixteen, eighteen and twenty. My memory of this first month in England is a mixture of the Micawber family and Italian comedy.

My hostess, Mrs. D., was the widow of a dancing teacher of good Norman stock who had left an honoured name but no estate. At the time of my sojourn the only money there was in the house was the thirty shillings I paid each week for my board. On that they all had to live, and the meals consisted of such stuff as dreams are made of. But the three girls, Florence, Mary and Daphne, were ravishing. If I wished to take one of them to the theatre or out on the river, I had to buy her an evening dress or a hat, for they lacked everything. It made no difference to them. They were young and gay. In their company I saw the first plays of Shaw; musical comedies whose songs we sang on the way home; and the *Follies* of Pélissier which were then the rage in London.

At first I went out impartially with each of the three sisters in turn. Then Florence, the eldest, took the lead. Gentle, brown-haired, with the air of a Botticelli virgin, she had moments of great boldness. I used to go down to Richmond with her every day; I would rent a boat and take her out on the Thames. The islands in midstream were surrounded by willows. We would moor our boat to one of the trunks, stretch out beside each other on the bottom of the craft, and that day we would row no farther.

'Do you know,' Florence would ask, 'what in this country we call a butterfly kiss?'

I did not, but I was quite willing to learn.

'As for me, I have never liked French kisses,' Florence would say provocatively.

I would try to make her change her mind. Thus the hours fled. When evening fell, the prolonged sound of laughter, sighs and songs would rise from the innumerable boats that encircled the islands. What charming, irresponsible days 'written on water' I passed between Richmond and Kew beneath the willow trees of the happy islands!

These pleasures were not without danger. First of all, one had to be careful of the tide, which was quite strong in the Thames. Sometimes in the sweetness of the hour Florence and I would forget to let out the painter of our boat, and we would suddenly discover that the river had receded so far that the bow was hanging in mid-air. To avoid a catastrophe, I would have to clamber the length of the boat up to the bow and release the rope which would be jammed under tension and refuse to run. Nearby couples would be entertained at our plight and blonde heads would shake with laughter in the moonlight.

The second and more serious danger was love. Florence was engaged to a very rich banker in Riga who had been the boarder of the year before; she was to leave at the end of August to marry him. It was sad to acquiesce in losing her so soon. But what had I to offer? When the day came, I went to see her off on the boat in company with her mother and sisters. In travelling costume, she looked, as Stendhal would have said, divine. She took me to her cabin:

'Why don't you make the crossing with me?' she asked. 'You could return to France from Riga and we'd have a week more of happiness.'

It was a great temptation. But I had agreed to be back at the mill on the first of September and I had a fanatical respect for promises. I detached myself from her and ran all the way to the gangplank.

8

The Sylph

At the time I entered the mill, it was agreed by all 'the gentlemen', my father included, that I should spend a long time of apprenticeship in the different workrooms before being allowed to participate in the management of one of the departments. Events decided otherwise.

Every year at the end of July the ceremony of the Inventory took place. Theoretically it was the drawing up of a very simple balance sheet. In the debit column capital and debts were set down; in the credit column plant, machinery, accounts receivable |and the stock; the difference between the two columns was the loss or profit. But the evaluation of the stock in a large mill, an operation that today is simplified by new methods and new machines, remained at that time a painful task and the result was in doubt up to the very end, which made the Inventory an exciting drama with frequent crises. For two weeks all the employees were busy evaluating the cloth that was in process of being woven, the cases of thread and the thread on the looms. My father, surrounded by a whole staff, would call out:

'833,722 . . . Hannibal skin . . . Fifteen kilos of warp at 3 francs 50: sixteen kilos of thread at 3 francs 15 . . . 883,775 . . . Debussy Amazon . . . Six kilos of warp at 8 francs; eleven kilos of thread at 3 francs 50 . . . '

The calculators would send him the results of their multiplications. In the Main Office the department heads would bring in each evening the estimated results:

'Goods on hand will come to one million three hundred and fifty thousand francs . . . There are eleven thousand pieces on the looms and the average will be about 215 francs . . . '

But since each one strove to guard against excessive optimism and named a figure well below the one he actually hoped to arrive at, the advance estimates always seemed ominous. On the eve of the great day immense losses appeared certain. On the great day itself there would be a series of dramatic surprises, almost all agreeable, and in the evening the result would turn out to be what it had been every year since 1871: a modest and normal profit.

The second year I spent at the factory saw a break in this reassuring tradition. That year the nearer the hour of the decisive addition came, the clearer it became that the final result would be bad. When it was known, there was no escaping the fact that the year had been disastrous. This was grave. An enterprise that does not make a profit moves rapidly toward its death. What sickness had attacked ours? What cancer was gnawing at it? 'The gentlemen' had a clear conscience. They had done their best. There had been no shirking, no extravagant expenditures. The thing that had betrayed them was Fashion. The fine black cloth, those woollens of uniform colour at which they were past masters, were being more and more neglected. If they were losing money, it was because their gross business was diminishing while the operating costs remained the same. For several years Edmond had been saying to them in his Friday reports:

'If we persist in refusing to make fancy cloth, I will not be responsible for maintaining our sales volume.'

At first the Uncles had shrugged their shoulders. Patterns were not their stock in trade:

'A little flower reddish or greenish in colour . . .' Monsieur Henry would say disgustedly. 'Is that what you want us to make? No, we are manufacturers of Blacks . . . Each to his trade.'

But the disastrous inventory called for heroic measures. It was decided that a department of design should be created, and that a certain specialist, Monsieur Denis, should be engaged to manage it and that I should be put with him to learn this new trade.

Monsieur Denis was a big fellow, elegant, nonchalant, indifferent; he smoked cigarettes all day long and wore a flower in his buttonhole. 'A flower . . . In the office!' said Monsieur Henry with indignant contempt.

Monsieur Denis came from the Breton mill in Louviers, a small town near Elbeuf, and would have been able to teach us their secrets if he had known them. As a matter of fact, he knew nothing. The real creator of designs in the Breton mill was Monsieur Breton himself, and we were quickly forced to recognize that Denis was incapable of designing 'the lines' we lacked. Baffled and discouraged by the complete incapacity of my new master and stirred on by the anguish of my father in the face of diminishing orders, empty looms and the threat of closing, I finally said to myself: 'After all, what do we really need? To devise a few dozen new designs each season, to follow a certain trend in fashions and to discover the appropriate raw materials.' This seemed to me far less difficult than writing a Latin composition or solving a problem in geometry.

What I lacked for this task was technical knowledge. I knew only the rudiments of setting cloth. What I did possess was method, and a love of work. One morning when everyone in the office was aware of the complete checkmate of Monsieur Denis, I dared to speak out:

'Dismiss Denis. Hire a simple setter and let me try with his help to produce "a line".'

I was criticized for my audacity but I got what I wanted. The languid Denis with his flowery boutonnière was replaced by Martel, a vigorous technician in a blue smock, with whom I went to work. First, I had to know what the public wanted. What were these English and French lines that were so highly praised? Some old clients, friends of the firm, helped me out. They gave me samples. Martel unravelled them and pointed out the elements to me. My desk was covered with little bundles of thread of a thousand different shades. I saw with apprehension that to produce these all-important patterns hundreds of gradations and blendings were necessary. Would my elders, who were so habit-bound, so timid, consent to give me the necessary funds?

When Martel and I had drawn up a plan, I showed it to my father. He found it too ambitious. I reduced it. The sellers of samples who came to see me taught me that one could know in advance what designs and colours the English were going to feature the following season. It was like an incredibly well-informed secret service of the textile trade. On the themes indicated by them it was necessary to invent new variations. Here the general principles of the Fine Arts stood me in good stead: 'Beauty,' Alain had told me, following Kant, 'is that which is intelligible without reflection.' It was as true of a piece of cloth as of a monument, a painting or a poem. I set to work to have Martel produce designs that would be intelligible, simple and elegant. We made our experiments on little Jacquard looms, relics of an age that had disappeared, which old weavers used to manipulate by hand. Martel and I worked that winter as hard as men can work. Finally our first line was ready for the following spring. It comprised too small a number of series, but it had variety and grace.

'Now the thing to do,' Edmond said, 'is for you to come with me to Paris next Thursday.'

The Main Office sighed but resigned itself. A young man in Paris! What an innovation! Wednesday evening, in morning coat and high hat, for such was then the custom, I departed with Edmond. My reception was kind. All the old clothiers, the Dormeuils, the Pezés, the Chérets, who had known our firm for a long time, had been sorry not to be able to continue their orders. They inspected my poor efforts with generous tolerance. I returned that evening, having placed all my patterns and sold three or four hundred pieces. The only trouble was that my collection was now exhausted. I had not foreseen that each of the important firms would demand exclusive patterns, which made an immense variety necessary. Our preparations had been on much too small a scale. But this comparative success inspired my elders with confidence and I obtained more generous appropriations for the following year.

Three years later my department of design was manufacturing eight to ten thousand pieces a year, and the gross sales of the mill had passed by several million francs the high mark of the most prosperous years of the past. This was no special credit to me. The old factory was a robust and powerful organism ready for action. My role had been confined to evoking from it an effort adapted to the new times; it had immediately carried it out with traditional perfection. I was a little like the governor of a colony who has as support behind him the powers and riches of a substantial empire. But success sometimes gives an unearned prestige, and as it happened I found myself at twenty-three the independent and uncontested head of a vast, industrial domain. I had acquired some knowledge through experience. The Uncles' generation knew nothing of this new trade. They let me do my work in peace and, since they had great need of me, they treated me well. I had retained the memory of the injustice from which my father had previously suffered, and I promised myself, as soon as I felt I had more power, to see that the legal name of the firm should become: FRAENCKEL AND HERZOG. In this I succeeded a little later.

This power and responsibility transformed my life and to some extent my character. I now had so much work to do and so many daily decisions to make that I had hardly any time to meditate sadly about myself, or to analyse my scruples about the rights and duties of a captain of industry. 'Hamlet is a bad prince because he meditates on a skull,' Alain wrote to me. I was subject to the laws of action and the duties of one in authority. Now I dreamed of writing: *Servitude et grandeur industrielles*. For the desire to be a writer still preyed upon me. At the mill I had my own office full of thread, felts and fabrics. In a secret cupboard I hid some novels by Balzac, a Tacitus, the *Mémorial* and some large notebooks in which I continued to set down my plans and thoughts whenever I had a few free moments. Mixed with my lively pleasure in successful action was my regret for the books that would never be written and also for a way of life for which I felt myself made and which I would never know. At the Lycée I had dreamed of meeting Anatole France, Maurice Barrès, Rudyard Kipling. Now I was living in a world which had no point of contact with such men. How would this narrow, exacting life of a manufacturer ever bring me the opportunity of meeting them? When would it allow me time to write? I no longer saw any possibility of it, and this made me suffer.

Now that I had become master of my own actions, I went to Paris every week and I made Monday my business day, which permitted me to spend Sunday away from Elbeuf. I had discovered the Dominican concerts, and they provided me with constantly renewed delight. Father Dupré had already taught me to love Bach, Chopin, Schumann; Colonne and Lamoureux revealed Beethoven to me. It was an immediate communion. Everything that I had thought and been unable to say, everything I had hoped for and had not been able to express was sung in the wordless phrases of these symphonies. When that mighty river of sound began to flow, I let myself be carried on its waters. My soul was bathed and purified. The necessity of giving orders had tended to harden me. Beethoven called me back to kindliness, charity and love.

This lesson was especially necessary for me at that time. Preoccupied, overworked, harassed, I was becoming egotistical and authoritarian. In my eyes women were no longer what they had been at the time of the forked lilac tree, ladies to be attended by a respectful cavalier, but servants and instruments of pleasure. However, one of those whom I was seeing at that time was especially worthy of being loved. She was a student of medicine whom I had met on the train to Paris. Chance had led to a conversation. I had found my fellow traveller cultured and remarkable for the scientific turn of her conversation; since she was also very pretty, with the freshness of a Flemish blonde, I was eager to see her again. This was not especially difficult, although she was married, for she was studying to be a medical assistant and the courses, the hospital and, at times, a substitute for the night, gave her a great deal of liberty.

On two or three Sundays we dined together and then, wishing to receive her in my own establishment, I rented a ground floor apartment at the end of a courtyard in the Rue de Madrid. This was the time of bachelor apartments, of the novels of Bourget and of *Le Lys rouge*, and Madame N. took pleasure in covering her face with a thick veil and stealing into forbidden lodgings. Surely there was never a less exacting mistress. Twenty times Suzanne (this was her first name) said to me:

'Stay over in Paris Monday night.'

'What are you thinking of?' I would reply. 'I have to be at the mill Tuesday morning at seven-thirty.'

'Then let me have part of Monday afternoon.'

'You're dreaming, Suzanne. What about my work?'

Perhaps this professional conscientiousness was laudable but it was expressed ungratefully. I was becoming a puritan of industry.

When the time for my vacation came, I went mountain-climbing with a team of good alpinists in the massif of Vanoise, and on my way back stopped at Geneva. I had promised while there to call on an actress named Maggy B., a friend of one of my comrades, Claude Gevel. She was playing at the theatre in the Parc des Eaux-Vives. During the interval I went to see her in her dressing room. A girl was seated nearby. Maggy introduced me:

'Mademoiselle Janine Szymkiewicz . . .'

I stood silent, transfixed by the astonishing beauty of this stranger. How often I had dreamed of the perfect face in which the pensive gravity of the adolescent would be combined with the delicate grace of the woman. The countenance of my dreams was before me.

'Mademoiselle Szymkiewicz,' said Maggy, whom I barely heard, 'has come to ask my advice . . . She is thinking of going on the stage.'

I could not take my eyes away from this apparition which had suddenly fulfilled all the longings of my heart. The young woman was wearing a dress of tussore silk; it had a blue silk sailor collar trimmed with white beads and a belt of the same material. Her large straw hat was tied with a white ribbon trimmed with blue beads. She was looking at me, too, and, embarrassed by my silence, she smiled.

What did Maggy talk about that evening? I do not believe I ever knew. I remember my impatience for the interval to end and my tremendous desire to be alone with the stranger. Finally the prolonged, insistent ringing of the bell drove us out. As the door closed I said:

'Are you going back to the play?'

'No,' she said, 'I have no ticket . . . I just came to see Mademoiselle B.'

'May I escort you through the park?'

'If you like.'

When I recall that evening, the sentiment that I recapture is a mixture of admiration, enthusiasm and confidence. I fell in love immediately with her precise, slightly husky voice and the poetic sadness of what she said. And what did she say? She told me the story of her life. Her mother, a very beautiful woman from Lyon, had captivated a Russian gentleman, Count Constantin de Szymkiewicz. The latter had died very young, leaving his widow with two children. She had come to live in Switzerland and had put her daughter in a convent at Lausanne and her son in a boarding school at Neuchâtel. Janine, who had left school a year before, felt unhappy.

'But why?'

'Oh! It would be too hard to say . . .'

'Is it so complicated?'

'No . . . but it's painful.'

'Talking about painful things is one way of getting over them.'

A few minutes later we were seated side by side on a bench in the Parc des Eaux-Vives in the moonlight, and she was telling me why life in her home seemed insufferable to her. From the instant I first saw her the soul of the Knight of my childhood had reawakened in me. She was the Queen of the *Petits soldats russes*, the Natasha of *War and Peace*, the Irene of *Smoke*.

'It's strange,' I told her, 'but I have been waiting for you for twenty years.'

Our hands met in the shadows.

'You're like Reynolds' angels,' I told her.

'Don't put me too high,' she said. 'You'll be disillusioned.'

'I don't believe it.'

The moon disappeared behind the trees. My new friend got up.

'I have to go home,' she said. 'The Lions will be furious.'

'And who are the Lions?'

'My mother and grandmother.'

I accompanied her to the door.

[74]

'May I see you tomorrow?'

'Yes, come to the park at four o'clock near our bench. I will be there . . . We can have tea together.'

I walked back to my hotel along the shore of the sleeping lake. I felt joyful, light-hearted and confident. Suddenly all my cynicism had vanished.

9

'For Better, For Worse'

Next day I had lunch with Maggy at the Café du Nord and questioned her at length about the angelic apparition that had brightened her dressing room the night before.

'But, my dear,' Maggy said, 'you're not talking about anything except her. You're being almost rude . . . You didn't even come to see the end of my play. However, I forgive you; the child is unbelievably beautiful. What do you want me to tell you about her? I met her at the home of friends here in Geneva. They said she was charming and of a very noble Slav family . . . Her mother had left her Russian husband, who was the girl's father, for a Swiss diplomat who loved her, hence the residence in Geneva. Now the husband is dead; an uncle, Jean de Szymkiewicz who lives in Poland, contributes a small allowance for the education of the children. I have seen the mother; she is beautiful; she is gay and generous, but there is also great disorder in her affairs. The children suffer from the situation. You can well imagine how it is in this puritan city; they are not allowed to forget that, despite their excellent birth, they will never be received by the local aristocracy because of the liaison formed by their mother . . . hence the girl's desire to go to work, to earn her own living; in short, to get away from here.'

At the appointed hour I was waiting in the Parc des Eaux-Vives. An instant later Mademoiselle de Szymkiewicz arrived, and I was enchanted to find her even more perfect than I had remembered.

'*Bon jour*,' she said.

On her lips the syllables were smooth and long drawn out. She suggested that we hire a carriage and have tea at one of the farms near Geneva. Thus began a week of enchantment, understanding and tenderness. From morning till night we were together. Sometimes we took one of the steamers that tour the lake, and she showed me her convent at Lausanne and the beautiful cathedral from whose tower a watchman sings out the fleeting hours. Sometimes we wandered afoot through the old quarters of Geneva. She took me to see the ancient wall of the Escalade and hummed the song for me.

Finding as always an added pleasure in combining memories of my reading with my emotions, I determined to take her to visit the Château de Coppet, as a pilgrimage in memory of Madame de Staël, and the Château de Chillon in memory of Byron. 'How sweet are the first steps of love,' Goethe writes, 'when the young woman likes to learn and the young man likes to teach.' I do not know whether Janine liked to learn, but she wanted to please me and she listened patiently.

At that time I could not see a woman whose beauty I admired without immediately hoping to make her mind resemble mine. I used to like to quote Baudelaire's phrase: 'A man's mind in a woman's body,' and another from La Bruyère: 'A beautiful woman who has the qualities of an honest man affords the most delightful companionship in the world.' I did not understand that a woman of seventeen, however intelligent she might be, remains a child. To poor Janine, who had read a great deal for her age and who sincerely loved poetry and music but also loved the windows of jewellers and florists, I talked about philosophy and mathematics. With the tip of my cane I drew geometrical figures for her in the sand of the paths, and in the evening I named for her the constellations reflected in the waters of the lake. Then she would turn her head and look at me laughingly. And suddenly my pedantry would dissolve and I would be just a young man desperately in love. Time fled. I was already two days late in returning to the mill. I had sent a telegram saying I had been detained in Switzerland but giving no further explanation. Ah, how deeply in love I must have been, suddenly to show such boldness in wrong-doing!

What was to come of this romantic adventure? I had no idea. No doubt it would have been possible to ask Mademoiselle Szymkiewicz to marry me. But that seemed bold to the point of madness. Could I return to the Main Office and announce my engagement beneath the portraits of the terrifying Uncles?

'To whom?' I would be asked.

'To a young Russian girl who lives in Geneva.'

'A young Russian girl! How old is she?'

'Seventeen.'

'What do her parents do? ... What will the dowry be?'

'No dowry ... Her father is dead ... Her mother has nothing but debts.'

'Are you crazy?'

No doubt my father, who was also a romantic, in the end would have taken my part. But what sort of reception would the little industrial town give to a stranger from fairyland? Would she not be very unhappy? The answer seemed to me all too clear. Moreover, during a week of happiness there had been no mention of the future between Janine and me. She was afraid to think about it. Her own destiny seemed to her dark and full of obscure dangers. She often quoted a sentence from some novel: 'Beneath the sway of Mars, sentenced without reprieve, O maid of the golden tresses, beware . . .'

'Sentenced without reprieve,' she would repeat often, melancholy foreboding in her melodious voice, and for the first time in his life the self-assured, logical boy I then was understood that there were more things beneath the heavens than were dreamed of in his philosophy.

Janine's sorrows contributed almost as much to her prestige in my eyes as did her beauty. From childhood, the idea of love had been linked in my mind with that of devotion. To be the Perseus of some Andromeda, the Fersen of some Maria Antoinette had been my favourite dream. Life now imitated the dream.

'And the Lions?' I asked her. 'What do the Lions say about our daily excursions?'

'The Lions?' she said. 'They are speechless.'

She took me to meet her mother; I found a woman of jovial plumpness, still beautiful, and a little hostile toward me, which was only to be expected. The day after this visit a telegram arrived from Elbeuf: '*Fail to understand—designs held up by your absence—return immediately.*' However intense my desire to stay, I could not and must not disobey this order. I had to tell Janine about my departure. It was at Nyons beneath the trees bordering the lake, before the faint, reclining profile of Mont Blanc which dominated the flowery slopes. The sun was setting. I had waited until the last moment so as not to spoil our final day.

'I must leave, Janine, this evening . . . I'm going by the night train.'

I saw tears in her eyes.

'What will become of me without you?' she said. 'For a week I have been so used to having you always with me.'

'I promise to come back.'

She said eagerly: 'When?'

'Very soon. I won't wait for the Christmas holidays. I can always take a train from Paris on Saturday evening, spend Sunday with you, and be back in Paris at seven Monday morning to go on with my work.'

'Oh, do that!' she said. 'Swear to me that you will do that.'

I gladly took the oath, for I myself was very unhappy at leaving.

'I'm going to try,' I said, 'to spend five minutes without looking at you so that I can get used to it.'

I turned my head away; at the end of ten seconds our eyes met.

'I cannot do it,' I said to her. 'And in my turn I have to ask what will become of me without you?'

She sighed: 'Oh, you!... You will see other girls... You will forget me.'

'They will not possess your sweet moonlight radiance.'

She accompanied me to the Geneva station and at the instant when I had to get into my compartment she raised her lips to mine. We were both weeping, but we smiled through our tears.

'I have been too fond,' she said, quoting Shakespeare's Juliet. 'And you may fear that if you marry me my conduct will be too light...'

A sympathetic Swiss guard pushed me gently:

'Come, come!' he said. 'All aboard!'

I returned to Elbeuf transformed and distracted, but no one at the mill noticed it. I got through my work as usual. The coloured threads and the samples of cloth had piled up on my desk in my absence. The clients were clamouring for me to call. On the following Sunday I did not go to Geneva, but I did find in the Rue de Madrid my learned and voluptuous friend. She had a premonition of danger:

'What's the matter with you?' she asked. 'You are changed...'

I denied it, but in the second week I could not keep it up and informed Suzanne by telegram that on the following Sunday I would be absent. The night train took me to Switzerland; another brought me back Monday morning to Paris in time for my work. I then adopted the surprising, but for me delightful, habit of going to spend *all* my Sundays in Geneva. Janine would come at eight o'clock in the morning to meet me at the Cornavin station. As she was very pious and did not want to miss mass, she took me with her. She had been stupefied and disconcerted to learn that I was not a Catholic.

'I shall convert you,' she said.

I experienced an infinite sweetness in finding myself close to her in a church. The music and the singing were so beautiful, the Latin of the liturgy so sublime, and the lesson of the day, each Sunday, so perfectly and mysteriously in accord with our thoughts.

'How happy are they,' I thought, 'whose lives are framed by such a happy combination of religion and poetry . . .'

Janine had said to me one day at the beginning of our friendship:

'Promise me that you will never try to make me lose my faith.'

'Dearest, I would try rather to give you one if you were without it.'

This life went on until the beginning of December. Then one day in Elbeuf the doorman at the mill handed me a telegram: 'Arriving Rue de Madrid Saturday—Lions have become dangerous—Love—Janine.' This turn of events upset me. Not that I was any less delighted to see her in Paris than in Geneva, but what was I to do with her? To ruin the life of such a charming, proud young girl seemed to me horrible. Moreover, I was only spending two days a week in Paris. Could she live alone the rest of the time? Should I marry her? I was eager to do so, but I judged it impossible to talk to the family about it until Janine was at least twenty years old and my position more firmly established. I passed two sleepless nights thinking of possible solutions and arrived at a project which many will consider ridiculous and which only an academic mind like mine could have conceived. 'Since she is not happy at home,' I thought, 'and since I expect to marry her, why not take advantage of these two years to complete her education? . . . And why shouldn't I send her to England at my expense to spend a year at some young ladies' finishing school, and then another year at the university?'

When she arrived, artless and unconcerned, with her suitcase ('my light luggage,' she said in appealing tones, referring to *Manon*, no doubt) I informed her of my plan. She was surprised and a little upset:

'To England? But why? I shall never see you.'

'I shall do what I did when you were in Geneva. I shall come to see you every Sunday.'

'Is that possible?'

'Yes, by taking the night boat.'

'You'll die of exhaustion.'

'I am never exhausted.'

'But I don't know a word of English . . .'

'That's why you must learn it. Nothing will be more useful to you.'

After much weeping she agreed:

'On one condition . . . You'll take me there.'

'That's what I intend to do. I want to pick out your school myself.'

It took a little time to prepare for the trip, to provide her with clothes, to inform the Lions. Meanwhile I rented a room for her in the home of a friend of mine. Then during the Christmas holidays I obtained from my father under some pretext I have now forgotten three days' leave, during which I took her to Brighton, where I had discovered by correspondence a school that seemed excellent. I took great pleasure in shopping with her in the Paris stores. There was already a certain conjugal note in our friendship, and this seemed to me a propitious sign.

It was an odd feeling to receive each day from an English school the letters of a student who was at once my daughter, my pupil and my fiancée. I was amused to compare myself with the tutors in Molière and in Beaumarchais who educated their pupils in order to make them their wives. At Brighton and also at Clacton-on-Sea, where she went later, I presented myself to the headmistresses as Janine's brother. This explained my paying her school bills and enabled me to go out freely with her. At Clacton she formed a very close friendship with Louise (Loulou) Baumeister, an Alsatian girl to whom she told the story of our intrigue. So romantic a situation fascinated the bright and charming friend who was to be, as will be seen, of invaluable aid to us.

After a year of school Janine knew enough English to take courses at Oxford. There I boldly arranged for board in the home of Monsieur Berthon, one of the professors of French at the university. He had an English wife who was an excellent hostess and contributed a great deal to the formation of Janine's taste and taught her the art of running a household. Twenty years later the Berthons found out that we had played an innocent Italian comedy in their home and that their pupil's 'brother' had been in reality her future husband. They had the good grace not to harbour a grudge against me. Monsieur Berthon undertook to enroll Janine in the different courses at Oxford that a girl could attend. She happily followed those in literature but was bored with the classes in political economy which, for reasons that escape me, we forced upon her. I still own a notebook that she covered with humorous sketches alternating with scraps of a theory of wages.

In all the courses she attended, her beauty turned the heads of the young men. Soon she was besieged with admirers wanting to take her out on the river or to the theatre. When I came to see her and she described her popularity, with amusement but without vanity, for she was modest, I was inclined to be jealous. What would happen if one of these blond or redheaded young athletes offered to marry her?

'Don't worry. Several have already proposed. I replied each time that I was engaged.'

'So you are,' I said.

In her company I learned to know Oxford. She took me to see Magdalen, Christ Church, All Souls, and at University College the Shelley Memorial. Beneath the willow trees along the river we talked about our future. I was now determined to marry her. In the course of her year at Oxford she had acquired I know not what quality of assurance which inspired me with confidence in our plans. In Elbeuf my own authority was now great enough for me not to fear that my family would stand in my way, once they felt that I had definitely made up my mind. I knew that my father had thought of a different alliance for me, which would have brought together in my hands great industrial and financial power, but I knew, too, that he had a tender heart and that our romance would touch him.

It was a characteristic of my family that it was impossible for them to transmit a message that was painful or simply important to the person for whom it was intended. A telegram announcing a sickness, a death or an engagement had to be addressed to an uncle or a cousin who would then have the duty of 'preparing' the person concerned. Faithful to this tradition, I asked my sister Germaine, an energetic girl who was acquainted with the situation, to 'prepare' my mother. As almost always happens, my mother replied that this was far from being a revelation to her:

'I have thought for a long time,' she said to Germaine, 'that your brother was secretly married in England ... He has made so many visits there in the last few years. He gets a letter from there every morning and always in the same handwriting ... Yes, I was convinced that he was married ... But I have not yet dared to talk to Papa about it ...'

And so the problem remained unsolved. Loulou Baumeister, Janine's Alsatian friend, who had finished her studies in England and returned to Haguenau, suggested an excellent plan.

'Why don't you come,' she wrote to Janine, 'and spend your vacation at Haguenau? Your fiancé's family can become acquainted with you there. Since they are Alsatians, they will probably be happy to revisit their province, and this will dispose them favourably. As for my parents, to whom I have talked so much about you, they will be delighted to render you this small service. My mother's meals will sweeten all dispositions. Tell me when you will arrive . . . '

I believed with her that nothing could be more helpful to me in making my parents accept this 'exotic' and, in their eyes, wild marriage than the cordial and savoury atmosphere of an Alsatian household. How many times my father had talked to me of Haguenau! It was quite close to Bischwiller where he had had his first mill and to Bouxwiller where he had been brought up. He had never returned to Alsace after the war. I knew that he would feel freer there than in Elbeuf where the shades of the Uncles, harsh and sarcastic, wandered through the offices keeping censorious track of thoughts and working hours.

I have already said that my father and I had great difficulty in discussing with each other any intimate and delicate subjects. Twenty times I volunteered to go with him to the Caudebec mill or to the one at St. Aubin, determined to talk to him on the way. The curious thing was that he knew perfectly well what I had to say to him. But he was as timid as I, and we would return to the mill without having said a word. Finally an urgent letter from Loulou Baumeister, which showed me how painful Janine's false position had become, gave me the necessary courage. The news was received sympathetically but with some concern.

'Are you quite sure,' my father said, 'that you are not making a huge mistake in linking your whole life to that of a stranger who is so different from us?'

'But, Papa, I have known her for three years and I get along with her infinitely better than with the girls of Elbeuf or Rouen. Moreover, I am not asking you at this time to consent to our marriage, only to see her.'

'And who are these Baumeisters with whom she is living? Her relatives?'

'No, they are friends, but they treat her like a daughter.'

'I used to know a Dr. Baumeister,' my father said, 'prior to 1870 . . . '

And I felt that all was going well.

The trip to Alsace was a great success. My parents were delighted to see Strasbourg and Bischwiller again. The Baumeister family pleased them greatly. Their crusty forthrightness, their friendly familiarity, their Alsatian solidity brought back all their youth. The *Kugelkopf*, the mussel-plum tarts, the roast goose recalled the festivities of their childhood. Janine, pale, delicate and apprehensive, stood out from this robust background like a saint in a stained-glass window above the stolid, kneeling Donors. Her fragile beauty touched my father.

'I don't know whether you're right,' he said to me, 'but I understand you.'

The presence of this patriarchal Alsatian family around her reassured him. Unconsciously he forgot that she was in this house by chance and that it was the home of a friend. My mother, who was more critical, remained polite and reserved. I divined that she would have preferred to have for daughter-in-law Loulou Baumeister, who was as pretty, as poised and as brilliant as a soubrette in a play by Molière, and who had staged this whole pageant and was animating it with her spirit. But on the day of our departure when Monsieur Baumeister, admirably coached by his daughter, served us champagne for dinner and proposed a toast: 'To a happy event that is not far off,' my parents embraced us. The game had been won.

'And the Lions? What will the Lions say?' I asked Janine when we had left the table and were alone in Loulou's room.

'The Lions? They will be flabbergasted.'

She undertook the negotiations with her mother and the guardian-uncle who lived in Warsaw. All that Madame de Szymkiewicz asked was the promise that the children should be Catholic. The uncle approved. In Elbeuf the Main Office received the news of my approaching marriage, for which they had been prepared, with coolness. They dared not criticize; they needed me. And so there was no comment. Monsieur Henry put an end to an embarrassing silence by winding up an invisible machine with his hairy, bony hand.

We needed a house. I found one near the Caudebec mill that was modest but comfortable, surrounded by a fine flower garden. Janine went to look at it and loved it. On the other hand, she was terrified by the noise of the looms and above all by her silently censorious reception on the part of 'the Gentlemen'. After a few words Monsieur Henry gave a flip of the wrist, dismissing us to unspecified labours.

'Are you sure he's alive, that uncle of yours?' she asked me as we left the mill.

I felt that she was on the point of giving up our beautiful plan.

'I don't know,' she went on in a serious tone, 'whether I can live here. It seems so sad, so sad . . .'

'Not a bit of it,' I said. 'You'll see. The town is full of young couples. You'll find them little by little.'

The pleasure of buying furniture and a trousseau soon made her forget her dismay. Up to this time she had never had any personal belongings except a little ebony elephant with a broken trunk, which she solemnly brought me as her dowry. The marriage took place in Paris on October 30, 1912, at the Town Hall of the Ninth Arrondissement. Some months before, I had left the Rue de Madrid and had rented a small apartment in the Rue Blanche opposite the Church of the Trinity. It was in that church that an amiable, aged curé united us. To hold Janine's hand in mine, to slip the ring on her finger, was very sweet.

'For better, for worse,' she said to me gravely as we walked down the steps of the church. In Trinity Square, a flight of pigeons was circling in the sun.

10

O Time, Stay Thy Flight...

Our house in Caudebec was simple but charming. Janine's taste had worked wonders. Fresh from Oxford, she had selected English furniture at a Paris upholsterer's. Everywhere the rich brilliance of mahogany reflected vases of flowers. 'Doing her flowers' was one of my wife's greatest pleasures. She loved long, slender vases, Chinese vases with lustrous surfaces, Venetian glass, Wedgwood vases, engraved Lalique crystal. She would spend a long time studying the curve of a stem or a green cloud of asparagus fern. She knew how to thin out and lighten bunches of flowers that were too heavy. Our garden, like all those in Elbeuf, was an old-fashioned garden: beds of begonias and geraniums with borders of forget-me-not or heliotrope; but Janine quickly added a well-designed kitchen garden and a cutting garden crowded with a profusion of brilliant, variegated flowers like the high borders of the Oxford gardens. She proved to be a good housekeeper and kept up a correspondence with her grandmother, with her mother and with Loulou, in which recipes played a large part.

Was she happy? Certainly she found pleasure, after having suffered so much uncertainty and disorder, in being sure of her ground, mistress of her own little world and free from all material worries. We loved each other body and mind and heart, we had many tastes in common and the evenings we spent, while I read novels or comedies aloud or she played the piano for me or told me about her childhood, were charming. Desiring nothing more for myself, I believed with naive egoism that she too was completely satisfied. I learned long after her death, from letters she had written, that she had had great difficulty in acclimatizing herself to a family that was austere and ingrown. 'Our hermit's life,' she used to say. No doubt she had suffered in her mother's home in Geneva from an excess of caprice and from lack of foresight. But she, together with her brother, had acquired there habits of daring gaiety that found no scope in Elbeuf.

For me, who spent the whole day in an office between the blue smock of Père Martel and the grumbling of my partners, to come home at mealtime and find beneath a bower of lime trees a fresh and ravishing young woman in a bright dress, always ready to listen to me or to love me, was a delight. For her, these hours of intimacy were separated by the vast deserts of the days. What could she do? She did not get along with my mother as well as I had hoped. Janine admired her virtues and respected her, but she suffered from a feeling of being constantly supervised, and she sensed a steady, unexpressed criticism which disturbed and chilled her. Completely engrossed in her charities, my mother would have liked a daughter-in-law capable of helping her in managing them. Janine was too young, too lacking in patience. She liked my father very much and sometimes accompanied him on the piano in the evenings when he sang *Les Cloches de Corneville* or *Le Petit Duc*, but he was at the mill all day long, and moreover he was too old and too reserved to be her confidant. It took her a long time to form friendships with the young women of Elbeuf. Two of them, my cousin Olga and the wife of my friend Jean Legrix, could and should have been congenial. But beneath her detached and almost haughty manner, Janine was shy. She stayed at home and became bored.

If I attempt after thirty years to imagine what impression our family life made on Janine, I think she must have felt great amazement and, on some occasions, fright. All was honour, work and austerity, but we lived there, she and I, beneath the constant menace of Things Not Said. Mute monsters floated invisibly amid our vases of flowers and shelves of books. My bashful father and my mother who was so reserved surrounded us with melancholy reticences and unexpressed doubts. Repression, which in the Freudian doctrine serves principally to conceal impulses of sensuality, in our household also hid shades of feeling, wounded pride, conflicting ideas. Nothing was openly expressed and for that reason everything took on a disproportionate importance. Experience was to show the dangers of this attitude. For a long time I believed in the virtues of silence; I have come to understand the liberating virtues of confession.

Fortunately for Janine there was the trip to Paris that came each week to break the hold of Elbeuf and the monotony of our recluse life. I now stayed there two days in addition to Sunday, and we decided to rent a more comfortable apartment than my bachelor quarters at La Trinité; we found one in the Rue Ampère that was new and furnished with taste; and of this Janine made a thing of beauty. At the time we knew no one at all in Paris. I had a strong affection for my mother's family, and I found a subject worthy of Dickens or the Brontës in the four sisters who, in their fifties, came every day dressed in black to sit for hours around their seventy-year-old mother in the drawing room in the Rue de Tocqueville like almost silent statues of filial devotion, happy to waste stolidly away amid the family heirlooms. But if I admired the vigour of my grandmother's mind, her unimpaired memory, her sane and lively judgments on Anatole France, Romain Rolland, André Gide, and the prodigious prestige she retained in the eyes of three generations, I perceived that Janine was horribly bored by these collective meditations in the Rue de Tocqueville, and I rarely took her there. As for my clients, I was seeing them all day and had no wish to meet them again socially. And so actually we were very much alone, but we had no need of others. The theatre, concerts, museums and, for Janine when I was away, the dressmakers and milliners, sufficed to fill our lives.

The mill was steadily growing. It now employed almost two thousand workers. Monsieur Henry, last survivor of the Uncle's generation, had had his first stroke. One morning he had felt a tingling in his right hand, that hand which by winding up an invisible machine had so often cut short my proposals and ideas, and two days later paralysis had immobilized half his body. Now that man of iron was no more than a living corpse, watched over with insolence and devotion by an ancient Alsatian whom he would summon when he had need of his services during the night by pounding with his cane. Every evening on leaving the mill the three Fraenckel brothers and the two Herzog brothers would come to sit by his bedside.

'Anything new?' he would ask, moving his thickened tongue with difficulty.

They would answer him in figures: production, orders, prices of raw materials. There were, to be sure, certain events abroad that would have been certain to disquiet him—the Morocco campaign and the hostility of Germany—but no one ever mentioned these to him.

My father had finally received the Légion d'Honneur, after having been nominated by the Prefect with this handsome citation: 'For having, in 1871–1872, saved for France through his efforts and devotion four hundred Frenchmen. For having founded and supported numerous charitable institutions. For forty years of industrial accomplishment.'

The workmen greeted this award with a hearty, triumphant and tumultuous joy, which gave him the keenest pleasure. Not only had one delegation followed another into his office, bearing flowers and the classic bronzes of Barbedienne, but he received numerous letters from spinners and weavers all saying: 'Bravo, Monsieur Ernest, this time the government has done the right thing.' It was agreeable and touching to see that this unaffected man had been judged by those under him at his true worth, and that work, impartiality and justice retained their value in the eyes of the French workmen. My father, of course, held a banquet in the wool shed for the personnel, and opened the ball with Philomène, eldest of the Alsatian women, who had been brought to Elbeuf in 1871 in a wheelbarrow by her father. Some weeks later my father retired. His health was not good and, moreover, with his habitual generosity, he wished to give me his place now that I had a household of my own to support.

I myself was already becoming a senior. Two of my young cousins, Pierre Herzog and André Fraenckel, entered the mill in 1912, having taken their bachelor's degrees and done their military service. Both of them had taken the course for Cadet Officers of the Reserve, a new institution which had not existed at the time of my service. Pierre was in the infantry, André was a *chasseur à pied*. With them there, I was confident of the future of the mill. Together with Robert Fraenckel we made up a unified and enthusiastic young team imbued with the same theories. Like me, Pierre and André had the highest ideals of the duties of an industrialist, desire to get along with the workmen, innate respect for the interests of the nation and a sense of sacrifice. I was so happy to find them co-workers after my own heart that I forgot for some months the still bleeding wound of the literary vocation I had missed. Moreover, I was not writing any more at this time; I was too busy. All signs pointed to the life of a leader of industry for me, sovereign of his own little kingdom, and perhaps happy.

In May 1914, in the apartment in the Rue Ampère our first child was born; Janine was very ill, had a serious haemorrhage and remained weak for a long time. But she was happy to have a baby. An English nurse, an ageless person, red-headed and authoritarian, came into our house. We took her with us when we returned to Elbeuf at the end of June. In the train at the Saint-Lazare station, as I opened *Le Temps* which I had just bought, I read in the *Dernières Nouvelles* of the murder of the Archduke, heir to the throne of Austria-Hungary, and his wife at Sarajevo. I told Janine about it. She raised her head:

'Who has been assassinated?'

'The Archduke Francis Ferdinand.'

She pouted with indifference.

This news, this instant, marked the end of our peace and happiness, but how were we to have guessed it?

The whole first part of July was devoted to bottles of milk, charts of weight, which had become the sole subjects of conversation. Janine was suddenly showing herself to be very maternal, and this revelation modified the feelings of my family toward her.

'Up to now,' my Uncle Edmond candidly told me, 'I had considered her a stranger, an imported ornament, a duck's egg, or even a parakeet's egg . . . But now I approve of her.'

Meanwhile the mill ran normally, the collections were nearing completion, and we were all making plans for vacation. About July 20 the news became disquieting. There was talk of an ultimatum to Serbia, but the idea of a European war did not cross our minds. Two days later it was necessary to face that danger. I went to get my instructions for mobilization out of the bottom of a drawer. On the first day I was to go to the depot of the Seven-Four at Rouen. I was still a sergeant.

'How careless I have been!' I said to my wife. 'All I had to do was write a note and I would have been made second lieutenant, and now here comes the war and I shall have to go as a non-commissioned officer.'

'But you don't really think we're going to have war?' Janine asked.

'I don't know . . . Things are moving that way.'

'And what will become of me?' she asked in distress.

I myself was badly disturbed. Janine's life in Elbeuf was possible as long as I was there. Alone in the midst of a family that was not hers at heart, what would, in fact, become of her? I could not picture it. In vain I tried to make arrangements, to look ahead. Already I found myself caught in the teeth of huge gears that deprived me of all liberty. The headlines in the papers stretched to five columns; 'STATE OF ALARM IN GERMANY . . . GENERAL MOBILIZATION IN RUSSIA . . . WHAT WILL ENGLAND DO?'

On July 30 it was no longer possible, even for those who, like me, wanted to be optimistic, to preserve the slightest illusion. I went to the shop of Bonvoisin, the Elbeuf shoemaker, to buy military boots, distrusting the army issue. Then I went to look for a belt with a pocket for gold pieces, for I had been brought up on the stories of Captain Parquin, soldier of the Empire, who was always saved at moments of crisis by a napoleon drawn from his belt. My wife, despite her fatigue and weakness, went with me everywhere.

'I'm not going to leave you for an instant!' she said. 'As long as I can still hold on to you I don't believe that I am going to lose you.'

I had never seen her more beautiful or more touching since the day she arrived in Paris with her 'light luggage'. In the same tone, at once sad, childish, plaintive and imperceptibly mocking, she repeated:

'Poor Ginette! Poor Ginette!'

The streets of Elbeuf, ordinarily so empty when the mills were running, were filled from morning to night with distracted families. At our mill we cleared for action. All the young executives, Pierre Herzog, André Fraenckel and I were due to leave the first day. Robert Fraenckel, exempt from service because of his nearsightedness, refused to stay behind and went to Rouen where he hoped to enlist. My father, so recently resigned and in great need of rest, announced that he would take my place for the duration of the war and that he would refuse remuneration. Patriotism was in evidence everywhere. In August 1914 France showed herself marvellously united. Young workmen came to shake hands with their employers.

'Well, Monsieur André,' they would say to André Fraenckel, 'so you are in the *chasseurs*? . . . I'm in the *biffe*, Hundred Twenty-nine, the Le Havre regiment . . . '

Saturnin, the man who carried the pieces of cloth on his head in the storeroom like a drawer of water in an Oriental picture, a veteran of the African campaigns with a scar that bisected his face, told us about war:

'You'll hear the bullets, Monsieur Pierre; it's nothing much. You'll see . . . they go *psch . . . psch . . .* '

The Alsatians made an appointment with my father in Strasbourg:

'We'll get Bischwiller back for you, Monsieur Ernest . . . And you'll open a factory down there!'

Janine and I spent a sweet and melancholy evening. The weather was clear and warm; we went to sit in the garden beneath the trees. We held hands and hardly spoke.

'I hope you have not been too unhappy?' I asked.

'I have been so happy,' she said, 'that I wish now all my life had been like this last year . . . But I am so afraid of what is coming . . . '

Above us the stars were revolving, turning pale, but we talked on in the warm night until dawn. Very shortly after we had finally retired we were wakened by the drums of the mobilization. Only once when I was with the regiment had I heard the lugubrious 'beat to arms'. It overwhelmed me. From street corner to street corner the drum beats answered one another and re-echoed in our hearts. Then the bells in the churches in Elbeuf, in Caudebec, in Saint-Pierre fell to ringing out the tocsin. The die was cast.

I had to be in Rouen before evening. We spent our last morning in the garden. The nurse, silent and icy, as English women are in time of catastrophe, had come and placed the baby's carriage in front of us. After the rolling of the drums and the breathless summons of the bells, the calm was so complete that we seemed to be living through enchanted hours that could never end. Was it possible that such sweetness could serve as the prelude to so much horror? From the town, which was no doubt full of silent farewells, there arose neither songs nor cries. We could hear the bees, busy gathering honey in the lime trees of the arbour, and the quiet breathing of our daughter. This morning, which was one of the most tragic of my life, has left me with an impression of unbelievable beauty, of sweetness unbearable in its intensity, of sad and solemn communion. I felt that these hours, so cruelly and tenderly fleeting, were the last of my youth.

My parents, arriving to say goodbye, broke the enchantment. I went to put on my uniform which my father wanted to see. The infantry still wore blue tunics and red trousers. Mine had been got out of a wardrobe the day before and smelled of camphor. The puttees felt uncomfortable on my legs, used to the freedom of civilian clothes. My father, to hide his emotion, looked me over with the severity of an old soldier:

'You must polish up your buttons,' he said in a voice that trembled a little.

He was sad at my leaving but full of hope for France and happy to see a son of his taking part in the war of revenge of which he had dreamed all his life. Jean Boulé, who was to drive me to Rouen in his car, was announced. I had asked Janine not to go with me to the barracks so as not to weaken my courage. On the threshold she embraced me. Tears hung on her eyelashes but she did not cry. At the moment when I was getting into the car she rushed to the garden, returned with our daughter and held her up to me; terrified by the red cap, the baby began to cry. But the car was already moving toward Rouen.

'Poor Ginette!' I thought.

I I

British Expeditionary Force

The barracks of the Seven-Four in Rouen had taken on a warlike air. In the courtyard, behind a long table consisting of three boards supported by trestles, the quarter-master sergeants were seated, running through mobilization papers. Men in civilian clothes—bourgeois, workmen and peasants—were being checked in by the sergeants. When my turn came, an officer standing beside the table looked at my papers:

'Oh, no,' he said to me, 'you are not to go with the regiment . . . Special Mission H . . . Report to Building B, Room 52; you will find your friends there.'

In Room 52, Building B, I found Boulé who had brought me, Legrix, André Blin, some men from Rouen, and others from Paris with names like Marochetti and Breteuil . . . But what was this special mission? The better informed members of the group said that we were to be in charge of liaison with the British and that we would go with them.

'With the British? But I don't want to fight this war with the British! I'd rather stay with my own regiment.'

'Don't get excited,' they said to me. 'It's not even certain that the British will come. They haven't declared war yet.'

I went to see a major whom I had known well since the last manoeuvres.

'*Mon Commandant*, I do not know what this Mission H may be, but if it is really a matter of being an interpreter for the British, it seems to me absurd. I do not speak English at all well, whereas I think I would make a good section leader.'

'You are right, but there is nothing I can do about it. This mission was organized outside the regiment. General Huguet is in charge of it; he alone has authority.'

I learned later that Mission H had been got together very secretly. One day a *gendarme* had come to my parents' house and had asked my mother whether I spoke English. When she said yes, he put my name down. There had been no examination; no one of those concerned had been officially notified. My mother had forgotten to mention the visit to me. This *gendarme* had played the role in my life of one of those messengers incarnated in humble form which the gods in Homer made use of to accomplish the destiny of mortals.

When I returned to Room 52 I learned that we were permitted to go out. A huge crowd brimming with confidence and enthusiasm filled the ancient streets of Rouen. In front of the Café Victor, a band was playing the national anthems of the Allies: the *Marseillaise*, the *Brabançonne*, the anthem of imperial Russia and the Serbian anthem. Then someone shouted for *God Save the King*. The people of Rouen listened bare-headed. Near me an elderly Englishman with a red complexion and a white moustache was weeping:

'By God! I hope the boys will come.'

As the last notes died away, the crowd shouted: '*Vive l'Angleterre!*' I went into the café and asked if I might telephone to Elbeuf. It was permitted. I called Janine. To hear her voice was a delight.

'How wonderful!' she said. 'I'd already pictured you on the battle-field . . .'

'Oh no, I'm still here in Rouen. Come and see me tomorrow . . . What have you done all day?'

'Nothing,' she said in her *light-luggage* tone. 'I cried a little; I thought of you.'

Next day she came to Rouen with Germaine Legrix whose husband was also a member of Mission H. We now had a leader, Captain Ridel, an artillery officer in the reserve and a Parisian industrialist; he was a little man, lively, precise, epicurean, lovable and mercurial. He had brought with him to Rouen his wife, a beautiful redhead, warm-hearted and cultured. Our two families immediately became friends, a circumstance that turned out to be both good and bad luck for me. Good luck because the Ridels were to remain our friends for a long time; bad luck because Suzanne Ridel, touched by Janine's isolation, kindly urged her husband to keep me in Rouen as long as possible.

'When the British Army leaves,' he said to me, 'I shall have to stay here myself for some weeks, perhaps for some months, to organize the service of supplies and the bases. I shall need you.'

'But, *mon Capitaine*,' I said, 'I should prefer to go with the others; I want to see action.'

'You'll have plenty of time to do that. It will be a long war. And you must think of your unfortunate wife. She has explained the situation to my wife: she has no family in this country; she has not yet become a part of yours; she has not recovered from the nervous shock of her confinement. She is concealing her condition from you, but she is desperate.'

Later I often blamed myself for my blindness at that time. Men never understand the dreadful strains women are subjected to. The woman I adored was suffering from nervous exhaustion, and I saw nothing; I made her take a trip each day for the pleasure of seeing her for one hour; I thought not about arranging my life to make her happy, but about seeing that her existence was compatible with my duties as a soldier. Captain Ridel wished to do me a service in selecting me to stay in Rouen; I believe he unwittingly did much harm to our marriage. This is the reason.

Janine had married a young leader of industry, a power in his own domain and master of his actions. She suddenly found herself sharing the life of a non-commissioned officer, a tiny cog in a terrible machine, a small employee subordinated to innumerable superiors. At the moment when I left Elbeuf I had, in her eyes, the prestige that comes from danger courageously and sincerely accepted. At parting she had passionately embraced a warrior. What she recovered on the station platform was an unimportant functionary. I felt this contrast, and I suffered from it.

My regiment had set off with flowers on their rifles, accompanied by a throng of singing women, old men and children. How handsome it looked, how well they marched, and how much I regretted not parading with them! There followed two days of silence; the town, emptied of its youth, was waiting. Then one morning the captain sent me an order:

'Report at ten o'clock at Quai Cavalier de la Salle to meet Colonel Moore, and place yourself at his disposal.'

I have retained a splendid memory of the arrival of the first British regiments in Rouen in August 1914. The great transports loaded with soldiers in khaki, so closely pressed together that they seemed to form a single living mass, came up the Seine. On the bank French girls waved flowers and handkerchiefs.

'Hip! Hip! Hip! Hurrah!' the soldiers cried with one voice.

When they disembarked we admired their discipline, their numbers and the evidence they bore, in a thousand details, of the ancient tradition of a great people. For us foot soldiers of the Third Republic, the army meant an odour of coal tar, scanty coats, stiff boots. These British regiments had retained the elegance and finery of our armies of the old regime. Their beautiful drums painted with the royal arms, their horses in white harness, and the brilliantly coloured tartans of the High-landers filled me with admiration, surprise and misgiving. How would these bright paladins setting out for the Crusade receive us poor beggars of the French rank and file, jabbering a horrible English?

On this point we were quickly reassured. Not only did they receive us with courtesy, but they quickly became attached to us as though to mysterious, strange and useful animals which France had given them. Whether the man in question was Boulé, Legrix, André Blin or myself, in a week's time no English colonel could get along without 'his Frenchman' who, in this strange country with incomprehensible customs, had become a sort of Providence for him and his battalion. Colonel Moore, my colonel, was an Irishman, energetic, ambitious and anxious to astonish his superior, the quartermaster general, by the speed with which he carried out orders. In this I helped him to the best of my ability.

Organizing a military base is very much like any other job in civilian life. My days and nights were spent in renting stores, negotiating with the port authorities and military authorities. Because I spoke in the name of the British Army my modest rank was forgotten. Once more I dealt in large affairs. I got on well with my superiors and my comrades. But I was far from happy. The Germans were advancing. At Charleroi my unfortunate Seven-Four had lost half its men fit to fight. It was said that Rouen might be menaced from one day to the next. One night early in September Colonel Moore came to wake me up and said:

'You're leaving with me at once . . . The car is at the door . . . We're going to Nantes to establish a new base there in case Le Havre and Rouen become untenable.'

The Germans at Rouen . . . But what of my wife and daughter? I mentioned them to the colonel. He was sympathetic.

'Send word to your wife and advise her to leave for Nantes to-morrow, but do not tell her why nor that she will find you there.'

Poor Janine travelled for two days and two nights in a third-class carriage because the refugees from the north had crowded the trains and troop transports had overburdened the railways. When she arrived, exhausted and ill, the news of the victory of the Marne had just been announced.

[97]

'There's nothing more for us to do in Nantes,' the colonel told me. 'We must return to Rouen in all haste.'

Once more I had to break my wife's heart by abandoning her, worn out though she was, in this strange city.

Weeks passed. Everything was different from what we had expected. I had left Elbeuf to take command of a section, to manoeuvre and shoot, to risk my life. My desire for sacrifice had been denied and I had lost my equilibrium. After the Marne I hoped for a quick victory. But the armies had dug in and did not move. Now they required charcoal for their braziers, the only fuel that was not dangerous. There was hardly any left in France. Colonel Moore said to me:

'I need tons of charcoal . . . Produce it.'

With the aid of Captain Ridel I created a whole industry in the forests of Normandy. The braziers in the trenches did not lack for fuel. But I suffered from carrying on this overseer's task while my friends were under fire. I received sombre but courageous letters from my cousins Pierre and André. Both had been handsomely cited in the orders of the day. André, a lieutenant in the *chasseurs à pied*, had no doubt about his fate: 'The certainty of a fine death,' he wrote to me, 'leaves no place at all for fear.' At the beginning of 1915 he was killed by a bullet through the forehead while leading his company in an attack. I had loved him dearly, his death overwhelmed me. I said to Ridel:

'Don't make me stay in Rouen, sir, I implore you. I cannot bear to remain in safety when this boy has sacrificed his life for ideas I helped him to form.'

'But your wife?' Ridel asked.

'Do you think this life is making her especially happy?'

I knew that she was not happy. At Elbeuf she was locked in a silent but hopeless conflict with my family; in Rouen she complained that she never saw me except surrounded by tiresome majors and colonels. My departure for the front would leave her free to go and live in Paris in our attractive small apartment in the Rue Ampère. We did not lack for money, for contrary to my expectations the mill, which I had believed condemned to run at a reduced rate, was working at full capacity. Although it had lost a large part of its workers through mobilization, it had acquired hundreds of refugees from the north who had replenished the working force.

In March 1915 Ridel was appointed liaison officer with the Ninth Scottish Division and promised to have me sent to him at the front as soon as Colonel Moore consented. Colonel Moore, whom we called in the Hindu fashion 'our father and our mother', fought like a fiend when the Mission talked of suddenly taking away *his* Frenchmen and replacing them by strangers. Finally he himself was promoted and I was able to rejoin Ridel. Trips at that time were difficult and mysterious. A Railway Transport officer would give you a 'secret' route order which simply contained the number of your unit, then he would put you on a certain train with orders to get off at a specified station where another transport officer would shunt you on again.

After long hours of jolts, waiting and slow progress, I arrived at Béthune and learned that the Headquarters of the Ninth Division was located there. Gunfire was audible on all sides; part of the city bore visible evidence of bombardment; the train stopped outside the station because the latter was an enemy target. I found my captain in a little office near the station. He was the same as in Rouen, gay, mercurial, energetic, friendly:

'We're in luck,' he told me. 'This Scottish division is a picked troop ... With it we'll see things.'

Later he confided to me as a great secret that the British Army was preparing a gas attack in imitation of the one the Germans had launched at Ypres. This battle, the first I saw, was the battle of Loos. For the great day Ridel had put me at the disposal of the division commander, General Thesiger.

Several days before the attack Divisional Headquarters was moved from Béthune and installed in a small château on the road to Loos. The spectacle of the troops on their way to take up combat posts, heads bent before the passage of shells like wheat bowed down by the wind, shell-holes smelling of earth and powder, awakened in me a keen longing that I had not felt for a long time—the desire to write. The contrast between the calm of the khaki-clad soldiers, who stood at the crossroads directing the movement of traffic with the composed gestures of policemen in Piccadilly Circus, and the danger of their position seemed to me beautiful and worthy of being recorded; sadder but not less beautiful was the contrast later on between the appearance of the general on the morning of battle, very courteous and dignified, in uniform resplendent in red and gold, and the return that same evening of his corpse, stained with blood and mire.

My role during the battle was exactly that which I later assigned to the interpreter Aurelle in my first book. It was my duty to maintain liaison with the French batteries which supported the division. My promenade through the damp woods where lost soldiers wandered about seemed to me fantastic and romantic. I fancied I was Fabrice on the battlefield of Waterloo. I thought of nothing in the world except the proper execution of my minuscule role. Unfortunately this offensive at Loos was a complete failure. The wind changed and blew the gas that had been intended for the enemy back on our own troops. The losses in the Ninth Division were so great that after the failure of the offensive it was decided to send us back for a rest. Then it became necessary to reinforce the region at Ypres and GHQ sent us there. It was a harsh sector for weary troops.

All this Flemish landscape seemed strangely inhuman at that time. A house that was not disfigured by scars was something to look at. The little village of Poperinghe was cut in two, one half being in ruins while in the other prosperous shops survived where Tommies and Jocks purchased lace from young Flemish girls who were undismayed by the danger. Ypres was nothing more than a location and a name; Vlamertinghe, Dichebusch, Reninghels where our division was encamped, contained only the phantoms of houses where we found shelter for our sleeping bags. When I arrived in this sector I stayed with Captain Ridel in the Hoogegraef convent which was inhabited by six aged nuns and their Mother Superior. These good sisters had generously allowed us two beds in a room situated at the end of their own dormitory, on condition that we should come in after nightfall and wait before going out until they had gone to matins—stipulations which were, of course, always respected. Later I shared the tent of an English doctor in a field.

It rained. Oh, how it rained! The rich earth became a morass which was rendered treacherous by the beetroots over which we constantly stumbled. Since I had no rubber boots my feet were wet all the time. Sometimes rain squalls would upset our badly secured tent during the night, and we would have to crawl about in the mud under the wet canvas in order to get out. The British Army had given me a very nice horse and, remembering the lessons of Charpentier, I attempted to school him. But one day in jumping a ditch he slipped in the clay soil and fell on me. I can still see that huge mass plunging down on my chest and beyond it a livid sky traversed by black clouds. This accident sent me to the Divisional Infirmary where I found doctors and padres whose conversation was enchanting. It was while listening to them that

I had the idea of writing dialogues that would portray England and Scotland from the inside, without comment by the author, and I composed the first chapter of *Le Cheval et le faune*, based on an anecdote told me by Dr. James, a psychiatrist of brilliant and sarcastic intelligence, whose friend I had become.

Little by little there emerged from this arduous life a mad and melancholy poetry. At first it took a musical form. At the officers' mess, night after night, the colonel's gramophone ground out the same songs: *Destiny Waltz, We've Come up from Somerset, Pack Up Your Troubles in Your Old Kit Bag*; then came Kreisler's violin, Caruso's voice and that of Mrs. Finzi-Magrini, who was the colonel's favourite. Outside, the detonation of the cannon and the rattle of the machine guns provided marvellous counterpoint. From time to time one of the rough and gallant fellows would tell some story of India, Egypt or New Zealand. I would listen with a sort of rapture, as though some fine foreign book had come to life before my eyes. Then when the music alone traced designs in the silence, I would dream of Janine, of my parents. What were they all doing? I would summon up my wife's ravishing face bending over the cradle. Would she not forget me? Every day long letters came from her and packages of food, woollens and books. I sent her verses, written beneath the tent to the accompaniment of gunfire and wind.

What was she thinking about? Whom did she see? I asked her these questions constantly and complained of the lack of preciseness in her replies. That she should be living the life of Paris disturbed me. 'I'm taking lessons,' she wrote. 'I'm learning Italian. I'm riding horseback. I'm learning to drive in the Bois. I saw all the Aunts at the Rue de Tocqueville.' Her mother and brother had come from Geneva to live in Paris, and I was afraid their influence would be opposed to mine. Anyway, without having any specific reason, I was worried to the point of distraction. My acute anxiety cut like a melodious plaint across the harmonious exoticism of my comrades. A secret voice, hardly audible, kept murmuring within me: 'And this anguish, if you could describe it, wouldn't it, too, contribute to the beauty of such a book?'

Occasionally some officer would take me with him to Ypres. With an elderly colonel of the Medical Corps I went to take supplies to my friend Dr. James in Maple Copse, a little wood in the front line. At the entrance to the town a violent bombardment halted us in the middle of a military transport which was blocking the road. The shells came closer. Around us red explosions threw bits of machines, men and horses into the air. For the first time I knew the feeling of fear that twists your entrails and contorts your face. I had not experienced it at Loos because then I had a mission to fulfil, but in this crossroads of death we were immobile and useless. The colonel, seeing me grow pale, offered me his flask:

'Drink. Dr. Johnson said that brandy is the stuff of which heroes are made.'

He was right. A few swallows of good cognac brought back my natural optimism, and the bombardment became a spectacle.

Despite the way the days dragged, the weeks and months passed fast enough. General Furse had replaced General Thesiger, who had been killed at Loos. Furse was what the men called a strafer. As soon as he arrived in a quiet sector he would order bombardment and attack, and thus provoke the enemy to reply. Ridel had left us, summoned back to the artillery. With Georges Richet, who had replaced him, I translated a very good English book on the war, *The First Hundred Thousand* by Ian Hay who, under the name of Major Beith, was one of our officers. Nelson accepted our translation and published it. Another of our officers was Winston Churchill, a lieutenant colonel in command of one of our battalions, but I barely saw him at that time. When we left the Ypres sector, we were sent to recuperate at Outersteene in the rear of Bailleul. There I found a true French village, living and working as in time of peace, and I formed a warm friendship with the beautiful and sensible daughters of the local tavern keeper.

During this period of recuperation I became better acquainted with my Scotsmen. I had a chance to visit all the regiments with their diverse tartans: the Gordon Highlanders, the Seaforth Highlanders, Argyll, Black Watch, Cameron. Everywhere I picked up types and anecdotes which were to prove useful for the books I was dreaming about. I saw boxing matches in barns, football matches on muddy fields which were inaugurated by the solemn ritual of the bagpipes and drums. When Christmas came, I was requested to supply the division with turkeys and sage for the stuffing; on Saint Andrew's Day I saw the bagpipes precede the haggis into the officers' mess. Thus, little by little, was filled in the background against which I was to draw my characters. I began to see those characters as well, in obscure confusion, and I let their transparent shades draw nourishment from flesh and blood and from the conversation of my friends. I was in no hurry; I knew that one day, when the time had come, the ripe fruit would fall from the branch.

After the Bailleul sector, General Headquarters sent us to the Armentières sector. It was less dangerous than Ypres but, overworked and stunned by fatigue and nervous shock, I fell ill. The army doctors decided to evacuate me on Le Havre. On a card I was not supposed to see I read: 'Aneurism of the aorta'. Was it really so serious? In the hospital train that took me away, beautiful, rosy, blonde English nurses treated me like a fragile object. I let them do as they liked. Life had been so hard for ten months that a little feminine tenderness was sweet. And then I was going to see Janine again . . . To the devil with doctors and their diagnoses! My heart leaped, but with joy.

12

Colonel Bramble

From the British hospital train I was taken to the French military hospital at Le Havre where by good luck I found Dr. Leduc of Pont-de-l'Arche who was a friend of my family. He examined me and auscultated me with care.

'I solemnly assure you,' he said, 'that you have no aneurism of the aorta. What you have is an extra-cardiac murmur and incredibly violent palpitations. I am going to put you on the inactive list.'

I begged him to do nothing of the sort; I had finally been recommended for the rank of second lieutenant and I had set my heart on becoming an officer; this would not be possible if I stayed behind the lines.

'All right,' he said. 'I shall put you under observation for three months, during which time you will live here at the base. Then I shall examine you again myself and if it isn't too unreasonable I shall send you back into active service.'

The French Mission with the British Army, when it was informed of this decision, attached me to the staff of General Asser, Commandant of the British Base at Le Havre.

General Asser, a superb giant of a man, who had been Commander-in-Chief in the Sudan and whose eyes, beneath bristling brows, remained half closed from the Egyptian sun, was as Kipling said, 'a Presence'. A born commander, energetic, and even harsh when necessary, he nevertheless listened to complaints, knew how to soothe wounded pride and had formed a staff that was devoted to him to the point of self-sacrifice. His second in command, Brigadier General Welch, a little, dark, austere man with a hard face, served him like a faithful dog. British soldiers called them the White General and the Black General; in reality General Welch was as 'white' as his master and a perfect soldier, but he had assumed an implacable mask because his rapid promotion had given him as subordinates men older than himself. Fear secured respect; justice maintained it.

Before my arrival the liaison work had been carried on by Lieutenant Raymond Woog, a talented painter and charming companion, and by Sergeant de Chabaud-Latour, a courteous and meticulous elderly gentleman who served as the General's authority on protocol. Having some free time ahead, I rented a pretty, old house at the foot of the hill of Sainte-Adresse and had my wife join me. It was against the regulations since Le Havre was in the Army Zone, but all my superiors had become my friends and closed their eyes to it. In that small garden at Le Havre we spent hours that recalled the sweetness of the past.

Janine seemed contented. She had found friends in Le Havre. She loved the sea and the harbour and the fine pattern of masts and rigging against a dramatic sky that reminded me of Jongkind and Boudin. I believe she would willingly have stayed permanently in that lively city.

But in time of war nothing lasts. Since the British armies were complaining of poor organization of transport and supplies, General Asser, who had succeeded so splendidly at Le Havre, was suddenly made GOCL of C (General Officer Commanding the Lines of Communication) with the status of Army Commander and the rank of Lieutenant General and with residence at Abbeville. Lieutenant General Sir John Asser (he had received a KCMG from the King) took Welch, who had become a Major General, with him and requested the Mission to make me an officer and attach me to his staff.

Abbeville . . . A charming cathedral, surmounted by a graceful watch tower, dominated the town. Ancient wooden houses with sculptured beams surrounded a statue of Admiral Courbet holding out his hand 'to see if it's raining,' as the inhabitants used to say. The latter, shrewd and suspicious Picards, resembled the fifteenth-century burghers carved on the beam ends of their houses. Although the city was attacked nearly every night by German airplanes the tradespeople who were doing magnificent business with the British General Staff refused to be evacuated. Energetic girls braved death to sell postcards and beer to the Tommies. I had sumptuous lodgings in the home of Mademoiselle d'Aumale and took my meals with the General Staff, a group of officers to whom I became more attached than to any I had met up to that time.

The Colonel in charge of operations (G Branch) was Warre, son of the famous headmaster of Eton. Colonel Warre was an elegant little man celebrated in the British Army for having won the Kadir Cup, for pig sticking. This exploit of his youth conferred great authority upon his strategic views. His adjutant, Major Wake, also an Etonian, was a descendant of Hereward the Wake, the last Saxon who fought against the Normans at the time of William the Conqueror. Sarcastic, paradoxical, brilliant and highly educated, he became later on the Major Parker of my book but with a mixture of Colonel Jenner, Assistant Adjutant General and descendant of Jenner, inventor of vaccine. Douglas, the General's aide-de-camp, was a young artillery officer who had been seriously wounded and who shared my office; he played ragtime on my typewriter, tossed my papers about and gave voice to hunting cries whenever I was struggling with the telephone. Much simplified, he was the Childe Dundas of the book.

I had a great deal of work. General Asser was responsible for the defence and organization of an immense territory administered by French authorities. The relations with the latter were close and sometimes difficult. Often I would have to jump in a car and rush to make peace in some small village which believed it was insufficiently defended against airplanes, or in the heart of some French general wounded by a too-peremptory British order. My friendship with General Welch was invaluable. Every day I had tea alone with him and at that time could tell him frankly and unofficially a thousand important things. Even the British generals, knowing that he listened to me, would seek me out to explain ticklish cases:

'If you could say a word about it to Welch, it would help . . .'

I was the Grey Eminence of a Grey Eminence, a Father Joseph of the second degree. Moreover, now that I had become an officer, I was in command of a detachment of about thirty liaison agents and had to watch over them, pay them and keep an eye on their conduct. One of 'my men' was Jacques de Breteuil, a friend of the Prince of Wales, and another was the orientalist Eustache de Lorey. They all did their work well and gave me little trouble.

General Asser was much less intimate with me than General Welch, rarely descending from his Olympus to mix with mortals (except occasionally like Jupiter and for the same reasons) but he often made use of me in his work and on official visits. When Clemenceau came to the Somme front we went with him. Later President Poincaré and King George V were to meet at Abbeville, and I was instructed to go to the station and accompany the President.

'You will detain him for a quarter of an hour,' General Asser said to me, 'because the King wants to talk to some Kaffir chieftains and this will delay our schedule a bit.'

This curious mission earned me the imprecations of the French general who was accompanying the President and my first highly embarrassed conversation with Monsieur Poincaré.

'What's the meaning of this?' the General demanded. 'The King keeps the President waiting because he wants to talk to negroes? It's unbelievable!'

'But, sir,' I said, 'there is a reason ... These are the head men of the Kaffir workers who made an agreement for just one year and who now want to go home ... These workmen, however, are urgently needed to dig trenches, and it is hoped the King's prestige will make them stay.'

'All right,' Monsieur Poincaré said resignedly. 'But it is ridiculous to wait in this station. Can't the itinerary be extended a little?'

'Alas, no, *Monsieur le Président*, because police measures have already been taken along the appointed route.'

'Very well! Then we'll go slowly, but let's get off!'

The General seized me by the shoulders:

'Let's get off, for Heaven's sake! Let's get off!' he cried.

I had almost gained the prescribed quarter of an hour and we set off. Above us wheeled the Stork Squadron, on watch above the leaders of the two nations.

During the latter part of the war Abbeville was bombarded by German airplanes every night that was clear enough. We had anti-aircraft guns, but they never hit anything. Never were attacks more uniform. About ten o'clock in the evening a cannon would sound the alert. Twenty minutes later one heard the broken-winded whine of the German bombers. Flares illuminated the town and the nearby munitions depots. There would be a quarter of an hour of pyrotechnics. Then it was over for that night. People went to see the craters which were sometimes very large; the dead, few in number, were counted; and everyone went to sleep with his mind at rest. After the breakthrough in the Fifth Army front the attacks at times became heavier and we tried sleeping in the suburbs and returning to work in the morning. But this was exhausting and uncomfortable and the General Staff soon got tired of it. Surprise plays a large part in any fear of danger; as soon as it's well known, familiarity puts an end to fear and laziness to precautions.

I was entitled to a leave at regular intervals. I spent the first one in Paris in the little apartment in the Rue Ampère. It was spoiled by an indefinable and distressing feeling of uneasiness. As might easily have been foreseen, Janine alone in Paris and so beautiful had been discovered gradually by diverse groups whose life was not the studious, retired and modest one that I had planned for her. I was far away and, knowing that some of her new friends would displease me, she had never mentioned them in her letters. Now she found herself embarrassed and disconcerted by my return. Through the whole of that leave she made a kind and tender effort to make me happy, but I was not happy and I left with a memory poisoned by mysterious telephone calls and incomprehensible allusions. This she felt, and on the platform of the Gare du Nord she embraced me with solicitous and desperate tenderness.

Another of my leaves coincided with the first shots of 'Big Bertha'. When I left the station I could find neither a porter nor a taxi. Paris was in a state of alert. I walked through empty streets with my heavy suitcase in my hand. At regular intervals there was the sound of an explosion. This was a strange kind of raid. That evening the papers were still talking about airplanes, but in the course of my stay the truth became known and I advised Janine to leave Paris. She had spent the preceding summer at Bagnoles and at Deauville; from this time on she travelled, spending a few months in Brittany and then renting villas in the Midi. Her life and mine now contained, aside from our child and our memories, few common elements. The war had broken up our household like many others; and this was not the least frightful of its woes, this severing of so many domestic ties.

At this time I wrote my wife many letters in verse, but they were addressed to the Natasha and Irene of my imagination rather than to the real woman, homeless and unhappy, who needed a living presence rather than poetry. I remember two stanzas:

Ton coeur est transparent pour moi comme un ruisseau,
Comme des poissons d'or, j'y vois fuir tes pensées
Et j'y sais deviner, aux frissons d'un roseau,
L'invisible réseau d'actions effacées.

Si quelque jour, venant s'y refléter, une ombre
  Met notre bonheur en danger,
J'y verrai le premier, penché sur le flot sombre,
  Le visage de l'étranger.*

The end of 1917, for me as for everyone else, was unhappy. The war seemed endless, victory improbable. A vague shadow darkened my personal life. I sought refuge in fiction. For a long time, as I have said, the characters had been growing inside me nourished by my reveries. They were inspired in part by imagination, in part by the officers I had met in the Ninth Division and in part, too, by my friends and comrades on Asser's staff. A taciturn Colonel Bramble, made up from ten colonels and generals compounded and kneaded together; a Major Parker, who was a combination of Wake and Jenner; a Dr. O'Grady, who was in part Dr. James; and a padre whom I had met and learned to love among the Scotsmen, had little by little taken shape. During the nights in Abbeville, while I waited for the whine of the German planes, in order to escape my sombre thoughts, I set to work recording the conversations of these men.

Very soon the dialogues became a book. In my leisure moments I tapped it out on the staff typewriter while Douglas gave voice to hunting cries. Then I found a title: *Les Silences du Colonel Bramble.* What was I to do with this little work which I kept polishing and repolishing? I really had no idea at all. Publish it? No, that seemed too difficult, if not completely impossible. But I could give it to a few friends and, most important of all, I could record in it the fantastic duets of gramophone and artillery fire, the tremolo of the machine guns and the melody of anguish—and thus be delivered from them. When the book was finished, Raymond Woog, who had come to Abbeville to paint General Asser's portrait, read my manuscript:

'It *must* be published,' he said.

Such was also the opinion of Captain de Mun.

* To me your heart is like a crystal stream.
  I see your thoughts like goldfish dart and flash
  And from the trembling of a single reed
  I guess the vanished pattern of your acts.

  If ever shadow mirrored there should cloud
    Our happiness,
  I first, bent over darkened waters, will descry
    The stranger's face.

'But I don't know any publisher,' I objected.

One of my friends replied that nothing was simpler, and undertook to deliver my manuscript to a young publisher of whom he spoke very highly—Bernard Grasset.

Soon a reply came: Grasset liked the book and was ready to publish it. Since I was an officer on active service I had to have authorization from the Mission. The latter was very reluctant. Commandant de Castéja, who was our chief of personnel, summoned me to Montreuil:

'I find your little book very entertaining,' he said. 'But you can't publish it under your own name! . . . The British officers with whom you are living or have lived might recognize themselves and be offended. If there is the slightest complaint it will be this unhappy Mission that will be blamed . . . No, we give you our moral authorization, but you must use a pseudonym.'

This disappointed me, because as a young and unknown author almost the only readers I could count on were my friends in Normandy and my old comrades in the Lycée and the Regiment, who would not be able to recognize me under a pseudonym. Finally I resigned myself and selected the first name André, in memory of my cousin who had been killed in action, and Maurois, the name of a village near Cambrai, because I liked its sad sonority . . . André Maurois . . . How strange and new those syllables sounded to me then!

Meanwhile Grasset was printing *Les Silences*. He sent me the first proofs. They arrived at the time when the Germans were advancing on Amiens in March 1918. For several days I believed the war was lost. Long streams of refugees pushing wheelbarrows full of furniture, children's toys and potatoes, came through Abbeville. To establish and provision a new front we worked day and night. The bombings were redoubled. Thousands of trucks, rushing up French troops to seal the breach, maintained an uninterrupted rumble beneath our windows. I found reassurance in the calm of General Asser:

'It will be all right,' he said to me. 'We English have never lost a war. Why should we begin today?'

When my book appeared the battle was still raging and the fate of Amiens, where I often went, remained undecided. One day in Abbeville I received thirty small grey volumes printed on laid paper and with covers bearing the portrait of a Scottish colonel drawn for me by Raymond Woog. The hour was so dark that I got no pleasure from seeing my first book.

'Send these copies,' Grasset wrote me, 'to the critics you know.'

I didn't know any critics or, for that matter, any writers. I decided to send the copies to my friends and also to the men I admired. For Anatole France I composed an oddly archaic dedication in verse:

> Sans un regard de vous, ma Muse ira peut-être
> Dormir loin du séjour de vos belles amantes,
> Esclave dédaignée, mais encor frémissante
> D'avoir passé si près du Maître.*

And for Rudyard Kipling, I am not quite sure why, this adaptation of a little English poem of the sixteenth century (by Robert Herrick, I think):

> O mon livre, en t'écrivant,
> Je t'aimais comme un enfant.
> Comme un enfant, ô mon livre,
> Tu me fuis pour aller vivre.
>
> Aux demeures étrangères,
> Lors je t'abandonne, ami,
> Aux fortunes passagères,
> Mais tu demeures mon fils.
>
> Et mon paternel amour
> Indulgent donne toujours
> Un soupir à tes défaites,
> Un sourire à tes conquêtes.†

I sowed this poor grain hopelessly at the time when Ludendorff was attacking in Champagne. The harvest and the victory came with equal speed. Because this slender volume appeared at a time of anguish, because it shed a melancholy humour on our woes, because it opened the door to hope, because it portrayed our allies sympathetically, its success was immediate. From this circumstance I draw no argument in

---

* Without a glance from you, my Muse perhaps will seek a place to slumber far from the abode of your fair loves, a disregarded slave, but still a-tremble from having passed so near the Master.

† O book, while I was writing you I loved you like a child. Like a child, O book you leave me now to go out into the world.

Henceforth I relinquish you, my friend, to strange abodes and uncertain fortunes, but you remain my son.

And my paternal love, ever indulgent, will vouchsafe a sigh at your defeats, a smile at your triumphs.

favour of its literary merit. But it is a fact that the little pile of copies at the bookstore in Abbeville, which remained open despite the bombs, melted away like snow in the sun. The bookseller had at first ordered ten, then twenty-five, then a hundred. All of them went. At the end of ten days Grasset wrote me that it was the same in Paris, that he had been surprised and was caught unprepared by the sale, and that he was ordering a new printing of five thousand. Then it was ten thousand, then twenty thousand, then fifty thousand. The game was won.

More important to me than the numbers of my readers was the quality of the criticisms. My first reviews were delightful. Since I was completely unknown I had no enemies, I irritated no one and I could be praised without reservation. I was an officer in the army and this further entitled me to everyone's kindness. But above all there was in France, and there still is, a real generosity in the Republic of Letters which prompts men of established reputation to help new writers. Abel Hermant, Daniel Halévy, Pierre Mill and Lucien Descaves, who did not know me at all, spoke of *Les Silences* with a warmth that touched me. Kipling replied to me himself. Marshal Lyautey, to whom I had not sent my book but who had read it, wrote to me in care of my publisher a dazzling letter; 'My dear comrade, Good Lord! what an astonishing book!...' The leaders of the French Military Mission, who had hitherto treated me, naturally enough, as an almost indistinguishable part of the military machine, suddenly discovered my existence. The Commander-in-Chief, Sir Douglas Haig, when he came to Abbeville asked to see me and talked to me laughingly about Colonel Bramble, as also did Monsieur Clemenceau when, with his felt hat cocked for battle and cane in hand, he inspected our armies.

The tiger still roared, but the victory placated him. From the time that the German attack against Gouraud's Army was stopped, we went on from victory to victory. Beneath the blows of the French, British and American troops, the enemy line which had been so long invulnerable staggered and gave ground. One felt the end was near. I ought to have experienced an unmixed happiness—and naturally I was happy at the salvation of France—but by that time my personal life had suddenly been wrecked. Without warning a telegram, signed by a doctor, had summoned me to the Cap d'Ail to my wife who was very ill. I had great difficulty in getting permission to go there for two days. Her condition seemed so serious that I implored my superiors to allow me to remain with her. General Welch replied with friendly sympathy but with firmness that at that moment my post could not be filled, without preparation, by any other. I had to take my wife back to Paris and leave her in the hands of doctors, abandoning the being I loved most in the world at the instant when she had greatest need of me.

I was so worried that the victory itself seemed to me a distressing routine. On the day of the Armistice my British comrades, from General Asser to General Welch, from Colonel Warre to Childe Douglas, decided to give me a surprise. At the end of dinner they rose, forced me to remain seated and sang with great seriousness: *For he's a jolly good fellow, and so say all of us* . . . Then they presented me with a beautiful silver platter on which they had had their signatures engraved. I was deeply touched. Their affection, as I well knew, was sincere; for my part I had learned to esteem and love them. Our paths were soon to part. What would be left for me in the new world of the Peace? The mill? I felt myself very far removed from that calling. My cousin Pierre Herzog, after being wounded ten times and being cited ten times, had been killed at Château Thierry a few days before the Armistice. Thus the two brilliant and dependable young men who were to have formed a team with me were both gone. My family? I felt that even if Janine should recover, my home had been cruelly shaken by absence, by hostile influences, by Destiny.

No doubt I had found a new form of happiness in writing, but what does success amount to, even in a profession which one pursues with enthusiasm, if one has no one with whom to share it? My wife had seemed almost indifferent to this new aspect of my life. My dearest friends were dead. Almost nothing remained of the edifice patiently constructed in the first part of my life. On this evening of victory, when I found myself alone in my room, I felt exhausted and beaten. A few days later I developed a high fever. It was the famous Spanish influenza which was then ravaging the armies. An English doctor came to see me.

'I'm very depressed,' I told him, 'but on the whole I am not suffering.'

'I've seen more than one case like yours,' he replied, 'in which the patient did not suffer but died next day.'

This ominous prediction seemed to me at the time a very desirable solution of my problems. But the prognosis was in error. I did not die and, after a long convalescence, was demobilized at the beginning of

1919. I was thirty-three years old. In a few months my hair had turned white.

This was not the only change that had occurred in me. When I had left Elbeuf in 1914 I had been a provincial business man convinced that nothing in the world was more important than the happiness of my home and the successful operation of my mill. My little town, my little house, my little family seemed to me the centre of the Universe. I and mine were a part of an enduring and immutable system with established laws the knowledge of which allowed one to foresee events and to act wisely. The war had shown me that Empires under the impact of violence may fall in ruins in a few days, just as the noblest edifices of a great city may fall in a few seconds beneath the shock of an earthquake, and that the collapse of a state may bury beneath its debris the greatest fortunes and the happiest homes. To be sure, I had resolved to return to Elbeuf and take up the yoke there once more, but I prepared to do it without enthusiasm or confidence. I had lost my faith in all that. I had too clearly realized the existence of a larger world. I no longer believed in the eternal necessity, or even in the solid durability, of the machine in which I was a wheel, and already in the bottom of my heart I was forming, without ever putting it into exact words, a project that four years earlier would have been inconceivable—to leave my mill, my town, my province and go out and rebuild elsewhere, according to new plans, a life which the war had left in ruins.

PART TWO

THE YEARS OF LABOUR

13

Home-Coming

In the tumultuous brooks of Elbeuf still flowed the blue, green and yellow waters of the dye works. The loud, monotonous pounding of the looms made the air of the town tremble. In the long courtyard of the mill trucks loaded with bolts of cloth, barrels of oil and cases of thread, recalled the past. I breathed again the moist, vapid odour of steam and the heavy odour of greasy wool. But close to the main gate a second black marble tablet had been erected, bearing in gold letters the names of the owners and workmen who had died for France. It was a long list, beginning with these two names:

CAPITAINE PIERRE HERZOG

Chevalier de la Légion d'Honneur, Croix de Guerre

LIEUTENANT ANDRÉ FRAENCKEL

Chevalier de la Légion d'Honneur, Croix de Guerre

And so the young chiefs led once more and for the last time the invisible company of the dead.

Every morning when I arrived at the mill I would meditate for a few moments in front of that tablet covered with Alsatian and Norman names. All of us, both employers and workmen, now came to work later. Clemenceau had had the eight-hour day voted. The Uncles were no more than uncouth memories. We had trouble—after four years of surprises and dangers—in accustoming ourselves to a routine life. With the veterans, I preferred to talk about the war rather than the mill. Saturnin, our friend with the scarred face who worked in the warehouse, had come back a sergeant with the Military Medal, having campaigned in the Orient and later been a prisoner in Germany. He would discuss Cairo and Alexandria like an American tourist. In Bavaria a rich woman who owned a farm had offered to marry him. He had preferred to return to Elbeuf and, as formerly, carry on his head

[117]

pieces of black cloth and of Amazon blue. The workrooms were full of unknown heroes who feared nothing and were getting bored. I myself was amazed at my comfortable civilian clothes and at the fact that thenceforth I was answerable to no superior.

For the period of my wife's convalescence the doctors had advised me to live out of town and I had bought a house surrounded by a little park at La Saussaye, a pretty village near Elbeuf on the Neubourg plateau. No estate was ever more precisely laid out. The four hectares formed a perfect rectangle. The house, of brick and stone with a slate roof, was in the exact centre of the grounds. One quarter of the park was an apple orchard; one quarter a flower garden; one quarter a kitchen garden; one quarter a grove of fine lime trees. A garden of climbing roses, Dorothy Perkinses and Crimson Ramblers, adorned the central path that led down to the gate, through which a belfry was visible. The tiny village had been built in very ancient times by a chapter of canons whose little houses, decorated with sculpture, surrounded the church. Originally a fortified wall had protected the town. All that now remained of it was two gates with Roman arches which formed graceful and decorative boundaries. I at once fell very much in love with our house at La Saussaye. It was surrounded, as far as the eye could see, by fields of wheat sprinkled with poppies, cornflowers and daisies and one could recognize it from afar, when returning from a walk, by the three poplars which rose like masts above the lime trees where the bees hummed.

Did Janine become fond of her new home? I do not think so. She had returned from that other war, illness, bruised in soul and body. This was not visible to strangers because her beautiful face remained young and her smile sweetly childlike. But to her natural melancholy was now added a strange bitterness. Abandoned without a protector and without advice in a world rendered pitiless and perilous by the disorders of war, she had learned the meaning of treachery, perfidy and cruelty. From her brief encounter with life she had acquired a distressing cynicism which she hid by playfulness, by poetic gaiety and by a forced lightness, but which rose to the surface occasionally despite her. As at the period of our Geneva walks she would sometimes murmur: 'Beneath the sway of Mars condemned without reprieve,' and she would add: 'Mars ... the God of War ... You see, darling, I had cause to be afraid of him.'

She who had formerly loved solitude and put up with simplicity

now revealed an appetite for luxury, for gowns and for jewels, a taste
for dancing, for night clubs and jazz, which perhaps was natural but
which wounded the austere moralist that lurked deep within me. Observing her way of life, I thought of a comment by Alain: 'Frivolity is
a violent state.'

Perhaps I could still have made her happy if I had accepted her as
she had become and if I had given myself without reserve to the task
of reconciling her to life. I believed that I was full of good intentions;
I wanted with all my heart to sacrifice my desires to hers; I granted her
everything she asked: a fine apartment at Neuilly, a visit to Deauville,
trips, countless presents; but it was all done in a way that made each
gift a concession and a reproach. I would say to her:

'All right, but why don't you help my mother instead? There are so
many unfortunate people since the war!... Why don't you interest
yourself as she has done in the Wards of the Nations?... Why drag
me to Deauville when I could stay here and work on a book?'

When I reread, with greater maturity of mind, Claudel's plays and
in particular *L'Otage*, which gives such a clear statement of the doctrine of total sacrifice, I understood too late what had warped our
reunion after the conflict. In order to win back Janine I was ready to
make any concrete sacrifices but not the intellectual sacrifice that would
have consisted, I repeat, in accepting her as she was. The pleasures of
the artist which I had commenced to taste now attracted me more
strongly than those of love. The writer's egoism, more concerned with
his work than with the people who surround him, that strange combination of maternal solicitude and paternal ambition, grew visibly in
me. Our household, so peaceful in appearance beneath the beautiful
lime trees of La Saussaye, suffered from it.

This egoism became all the more exacting inasmuch as I was at that
time discontented with my efforts to write. *Les Silences*, with its wide
success, had proved to me that I could write a book and find readers.
And so as early as April 1918 I had begun a second novel. From the
time of my first visits to Oxford I had been thinking with eager interest
about a life of the poet Shelley. It seemed to me if I wrote that life I
could give expression to certain feelings that I had experienced and that
still troubled me. Like Shelley, I had become a doctrinaire under the
influence of my youthful reading, and I had tried to apply rational
methods to the life of the emotions. Like him I had encountered

material that was alive and sentient and did not yield to my logic. Like him I had suffered and caused suffering.

I was irritated at the adolescent I had been and also indulgent because I knew he could not have been otherwise. I hoped at once to expose him, to condemn him and to explain him. Shelley, now, had met the same reverses, with a hundred times more grandeur, but for reasons that were very much the same. Shelley's attitude toward Harriet, his inability to understand and to respect the frivolity of that child wife, his lessons in mathematics and lectures in morals, his Address to the Irish People, all these mistakes, I realized, were ones that in the same circumstances and at the same age I might have made and that perchance I might still make. To the pride and the certainties of adolescence there had succeeded in me a pressing need of pity and of humility, and here also I recognized traits of Shelley; those of his last days . . . Yes, in every respect, the subject seemed excellent.

But at that time I was living in Abbeville with no English library and no source materials, and as long as the war lasted it was clearly impossible for me to do the research work necessary for writing a biography. One day the idea came to me that perhaps it would be possible to make a novel out of this real life. Could one with any appearance of reality transpose the story of Shelley and Harriet Westbrook and Mary Godwin into modern life? Would that degree of romanticism be bearable outside the romantic period? The problem preoccupied me for a long time.

I was much attracted by the city in which the hazards of war had decreed that I should live. I loved its churches, the lovely paved courtyards of its mansions, and its houses with carved wood decorations. I began to read the histories of Abbeville and, among other books, the correspondence of Boucher de Perthes, a learned citizen of the town. He had an agreeable way of writing and his period interested me. It was the end of the reign of Louis Philippe, the Revolution of '48 and the beginning of the Second Empire. It seemed to me that 1848 was the epoch in France in which it would be appropriate to place a Shelley. His sentiments, his grandiloquence, his idealism would then seem plausible. And since I loved Abbeville so much, why not have him live in Abbeville? All this seemed fine. It remained to be seen what had happened at Abbeville during that Revolution.

I got permission from the Subprefect to examine the archives, and I became very much interested immediately in the file on Civil Engineering. There I followed the disappointments of an unfortunate engineer at grips with the sea, whose most carefully calculated works were being constantly destroyed by the waves. The symbol pleased me; thanks to my Uncle Henry I was familiar with the technique; I decided that my Shelley should be an engineer. From this moment my novel developed with a rapidity that surprised me. My hero, Philippe Viniès, was an earlier version of myself to whom I had become hostile.

The book was published in 1919 and had no success. One hundred thousand copies of *Colonel Bramble* had been sold; *Ni ange, ni bête* sold seven or eight thousand. Bernard Grasset blamed the title which he had always considered 'unpopular'. I condemned the novel. Nevertheless Alain liked it, a fact that surprised me and kept me from complete discouragement:

'You have thoroughly understood the lesson of Stendhal,' he said.

I had indeed understood it, but I had not been able to liberate myself from it sufficiently to express my own nature. It seemed to me, nevertheless, that I had something serious and perhaps important to say which should have been in *Ni ange, ni bête* but was not there and was linked obscurely but intimately with the character of Shelley; no doubt it would be better expressed if, instead of transforming Shelley into an engineer of 1848, I should write his life directly and openly. Hence sprang a keen desire to have time to read everything that had been published about Shelley, to reread his correspondence and his poems and to write a biography that would be, not the literary study of a poet, but the picture of a human conflict.

This desire, which became a need, made me impatient. Both the life in the mill and that at home seemed to me full of futile acts and words. Ah! To shut myself up to read, to write, no longer to have to listen to meaningless complaints, to live the life of a writer surrounded by creatures born of my imagination, such was now my dream. Later I gave it to Shelley himself: 'It seemed to him that in the crystalline mansions of his thought, Harriet and her daughter had fallen like blocks of recalcitrant living matter. In vain, with all the strength of his logic, he tried to rid himself of them; the ponderous reality was too much for his fragile arms . . .'

My work at the mill weighed heavily upon me. No doubt it was because other occupations to which I was better suited attracted me, but also because postwar industry no longer resembled that of the prewar days. Before 1914 if competition had been sharp and profits limited, at least a prudent man could pilot his ship with some intelligence. The costs of raw materials served him as landmarks, the value of currencies fluctuated only within narrow limits, salaries increased only by slow stages.

After the war all the compasses began to spin. Francs, pounds, dollars, marks, pesetas shot up and down without order or understandable rhythm. Immediately after the Armistice the needs of Europe were such that an unheard-of prosperity seemed to lie ahead of industry. Before 1914 clients had been heartless monsters, to be spoken of only with respectful dread, and they easily imposed their capricious demands on manufacturers who were disunited and always starved for work. In 1920 manufacturers, stuffed with orders, entered into agreements to deal with the buyers. The Brothers Blin approached us to form an alliance—a diplomatic revolution as astonishing as the one which at that time was bringing England and Germany together. When I went to Paris the triumph no longer consisted in bringing back orders but in cancelling them. On paper we were amassing fortunes; in reality, if one took purchasing power as the standard, the mill was growing poorer every day, but we were too ignorant of monetary matters to realize this.

The workers, seeing the factory gorged with orders and prices rising, quite naturally demanded their part in this prosperity; they hoped by some miracle to see their wages rise and the price of manufactured goods fall. Almost every week one trade union or another demanded ten per cent or twenty per cent increase. The employers agreed to everything. What difference did it make to them? Selling prices seemed to have no limits. They did not become hostile until professional agitators took over the question of wages in order to make it an instrument of domination. Then their pride as employers rebelled. Elbeuf entered upon a period of political strikes. In *Bernard Quesnay* I have described the most serious of them and the sadness of silent workrooms with their glittering and motionless machinery. Workers who wanted to keep on working and who were the honour of their class were few in number, were attacked, humiliated, beaten. This state of war between Frenchmen made me suffer more than I can say. Ever since I had been at the mill I had tried my best to be fair, but the adversaries in these two camps loved their prejudices more than justice. Who was grateful to me for my efforts? I was tired of this struggle in which I had no allies. I even missed the war. There if you suffered, at least you had the satisfaction of feeling yourself united with your comrades.

Soon the excessive rise in prices brought a crisis. It was sudden and terrible. Our clients, who had been purchasing madly, brutally applied the brakes. In a few days half our orders were cancelled. In a few weeks the strikes had been succeeded by unemployment. The workmen, haughty and hostile yesterday, were all of a sudden friendly and docile. Looms came to rest in the sleeping mill. The value of stocks in hand fell precipitately, and since the value had been assessed in a depreciated currency, we discovered that during these three years of folly we had lost our substance.

'We're children,' my cousin Robert Fraenckel said to me sadly. 'We should have done our bookkeeping in terms of gold. By measuring our stocks and our prices with an elastic standard we are running the risk of ruining our business.'

He was right, but when he and I insisted that a double bookkeeping system be installed, in francs and in dollars, our elders shrugged their shoulders:

'How complicated!' they said. 'And why do it? No one has done anything like that before!'

As for me, I was rapidly becoming more of a novelist than a manufacturer, and I consoled myself by deriving from our woes a short novel which I called *La Hausse et la baisse*.

In the spring of 1922 I received an invitation from Monsieur Paul Desjardins, Professor of Literature at the Ecole Normale in Sèvres, founder of the Union for Truth and estimable critic, to spend ten days during the summer at the Abbey of Pontigny. His gracious letter, written in a fine archaic hand, explained to me the nature of the Pontigny Conferences at which each year writers, professors and men of good will from all countries came together to discuss some literary or moral problem. That year the subject was to be: *The Sense of Honour*. André Gide, Roger Martin du Gard, Edmond Jaloux, Robert de Traz, Jean Schlumberger, the Englishmen Lytton Strachey and Roger Fry were to be present. The programme tempted me. Many of the names were those of people I admired and I felt a strong, almost morbid, need to hear conversations about ideas and books and not about strikes and sales. I suggested to Janine, who did not want to accompany me and did not want to stay at La Saussaye, that she go for a visit to Trouville, and I accepted Monsieur Desjardins' invitation.

The Cistercian Abbey of Pontigny is in Burgundy near Auxerre, not far from Beaune. In my compartment on the train from Paris were a couple who immediately attracted my attention. The man, hardly older than myself and almost bald, had deep thoughtful eyes, long drooping moustaches, and a waistcoat that was too big for him, from the pockets of which protruded innumerable sharp-pointed pencils; his wife was a fresh-looking, curly-headed blonde with timid childlike grace; their conversation, which I heard despite myself, interested me. Presently, seeing the label PONTIGNY on my suitcase, they introduced themselves:

'Charles and Zézette Du Bos.'

This mean nothing to me, and that was my mistake, for Charles Du Bos had already published fine studies of Baudelaire, Mérimée and Proust which were very highly esteemed by a small but discriminating group of readers. He spoke with extreme slowness; his choice of epithets was admirable. What he said was not only fair and true, it was the object itself miraculously transformed into words. When he talked to me about the writers we were going to meet, I was impressed by his seriousness, the minuteness of his character analyses and his constant references to the English poets. I had a feeling that I was simultaneously meeting a character from Proust and a hero from Dickens. I did not and could not foresee that this eloquent stranger was to become one of my most intimate and dearest friends.

We were met on the station platform in Pontigny by Desjardins and Gide. The Master of the Abbey looked like Tolstoy, the same unkempt beard, the same prominent cheekbones, the same faunlike look of genius. Though ceremonious and often meek, he was disconcerting because of his ironic manner. Gide, on the contrary, was reassuring. Wrapped in a great mountaineer's cape, with his Samurai's face framed by a wide-brimmed, grey felt sombrero, he made a startling first impression but quickly charmed one by the youthfulness of his spirit and by the immediate interest he took in new people. In this assembly, seething with talent, where I knew no one, I had feared I should be an outsider, but I quickly made friends. The rule of the house was monastic. We had our meals together beneath the Gothic vault of the old refectory of the monks, and Madame Paul Desjardins, stepdaughter of Gaston Paris, presided at them with calm dignity and seated the guests herself. She put me beside her daughter Anne, a wild young creature with black hair, lively, ardent and bursting with eagerness and intelligence. A whole group of youngsters, pupils of Monsieur Desjardins, surrounded Anne who, as daughter of the house, had great prestige at Pontigny and judged us with mischievous finality. She and I got on well together from the start.

The daily programme was simple. The morning was free and it was spent by some of us in walks to Auxerre, Vézelay, Beaune or along the river; by others in the library of the Abbey which Monsieur Desjardins, with feigned modesty, called 'the village library' and which was astounding in the quality of the editions and the choice of books. After lunch we sat beneath the arbour and the discussion began. Each day brought its own drama, for there was an immediate clash between the morbid susceptibilities of Monsieur Desjardins, the meticulous and desperate seriousness of Charles Du Bos, the diabolical maliciousness of Gide and the naivety of some of the strangers. Roger Martin du Gard, silent and with a sweetly impassive expression on his Norman lawyer's face, would listen and from time to time draw a notebook from his pocket in order to make a brief entry. The philosopher Edmond Jaloux waited in patient boredom for the moment when he could go to the Pontigny inn and drink a bottle of respectable burgundy. The Germans, Curtius and Grothuysen, enveloped the lucid ideas of the Frenchmen in profound and vague abstractions. Charles Du Bos (or rather, as all Pontigny called him, Charlie) who distrusted ideas that were too clear and would gladly have said of Voltaire, like the Empress Eugénie: 'I cannot forgive him for having made me understand things I shall never understand,' glanced approvingly at Curtius and Grothuysen. Lytton Strachey crossed one of his long legs over the other, shut his eyes in amazement at our lack of humour and went to sleep.

'And what in your opinion, Monsieur Strachey, is the most important thing in the world?' Paul Desjardins asked suddenly.

There was a long silence. Then from the sleeping beard of Strachey issued a tiny falsetto voice:

'Passion,' he said finally.

And the solemn circle, relieved for an instant, broke into laughter.

At four o'clock a bell announced tea. It, like lunch, was served in the refectory. After dinner we met in the drawing room to play subtle and learned games.

Portraits by Comparison:

[125]

'If it were a painting, what would it be?'

'A Venus by Raphael retouched by Renoir,' Roger Fry replied gravely.

Portraits on a Scale of Twenty:

'Intelligence?'

(The subject this time was Benjamin Constant.)

'Nineteen,' Gide replied.

'Dear friend,' Charles Du Bos interrupted anxiously, 'if you will permit me, I should say eighteen and three-quarters . . . '

'Sensitivity?'

'Zero,' Gide said.

'What?' Charlie broke in again in distress. 'But he is at least average, dear friend, or perhaps even twelve . . . or to be more exact twelve and a half.'

I was happy in this new world. Educated until I was eighteen among philosophers and poets in my old Lycée, then suddenly transplanted into a mill and cut off from my favourite occupations, I found again at Pontigny my true environment. At Elbeuf my extensive reading had served no purpose and I had to be on my guard against frightening people by my pedantry. At Pontigny all this reading became a factor in my success. I had been invited on the strength of Colonel Bramble as an amusing author but one not to be taken too seriously; what they found was a student of Balzac, which appealed to Gide, a man who knew Tolstoy by heart, which appealed to Martin du Gard. Charles Du Bos, put off by what seemed to him the levity of my first book and also by the fact that I had been one of Alain's students, for whose works and doctrines he had no great regard, remained aloof at first but our mutual friend, Anne Desjardins, seeing that I admired Charlie with all my heart, brought him to me in affectionate repentance before the end of 'the decade'. I made precious friendships that year at Pontigny. On the eve of departure, André Gide said to me:

'And what are you writing now?'

'A life of Shelley.'

'Why don't you come to my place in the country and show it to me? . . . I live not far from you.'

'But the book isn't finished.'

'Exactly . . . I'm not interested except in unfinished things . . . One can still mould them.'

I accepted. I had promised to join Janine at Trouville and spend some time with her at the Hotel Normandy in Deauville. I escaped for three days and went to Gide's home, which was on the other side of the estuary between Le Havre and Fécamp. Not knowing him well as yet, I expected to find the house 'artistically' decorated in the manner of *Paludes*, very Nineteen Hundred. I found an old Norman country seat, a long white house, elegant and unostentatious, and an upper middle class French household.

After dinner Gide asked me to read my manuscript aloud to him. 'It's dangerous for any script,' he said, 'but decisive.'

In my excitement I read very badly. But he listened to me with perfect attention well into the night. From time to time he made notes. When I had finished he told me that he had hoped for a more profound analysis of the poet Shelley and of his works. I replied that had not been my subject. Then he gave me certain detailed criticisms, all of them proper, about wrong words and superfluous ornaments. He advised me to sacrifice certain passages which were brilliant but in the wrong tone and which interrupted the action. Gide had the most infallible taste, and the lesson he gave me was useful to me for a long time. From this brief visit I took away friendly and grateful memories.

The sojourn at Pontigny was repeated each year, and the friendships that I formed there exercised a profound influence on me. The place was not without its faults. It was capable of producing pedantry, abetting the formation of little groups of literary idolaters and encouraging hair-splitting. But its virtues far outweighed its drawbacks, and the little groups were dedicated to great saints.

14

Eurydice Twice Lost

Through four years of war I had lived with the British. It would have been too bad if victory had broken the tie. In 1920 and again in 1921 my comrades of Asser's staff invited me to commemorative dinners. Some of them I entertained in Paris. General Byng (Lord Byng of Vimy), whom I had known in France and met again in London, said to me:

'Now you know the English army—good, but you don't know England. I am going to introduce the country to you. Come and dine with me at the Athenaeum.'

And he arranged an odd sort of dinner to which he invited a dozen Englishmen belonging to a dozen different professions and environments. I remember there was an admiral there, a minister (it was Sir Austen Chamberlain), a sporting bishop, a painter, a humorist (Owen Seaman of *Punch*), a manufacturer, a merchant, a trade unionist and a gentleman farmer. After each course I was told to change my place so that by the end of the meal, having talked to everyone present, I should know England. When the champagne was served Lord Byng made a little speech in the course of which he said to me:

'*We are all Brambles here . . .*'

It was true.

The army was not my only point of contact with England. When my book had appeared the novelist Maurice Baring, at the time Major Baring, was serving with the RAF in France; he had written me an amusing letter which served as the starting point of a friendship. When I went to London Baring always arranged a little luncheon in his picturesque apartment in Lincoln's Inn. He himself had charming and unusual friends. At his home I met Duff Cooper and his future wife, the very beautiful Lady Diana Manners; Harold Nicolson, Desmond MacCarthy, Lady Lovat and Lady Wilson, Hilaire Belloc and all the Cecils. A convert to Catholicism, Baring was ardently and sincerely religious. He had the gaiety of the saints, and their charity. The letters he wrote me (of which I had saved hundreds up to World War II) were typed in a bizarre mixture of black and red words in which whole lines were composed of w's or x's, alternating with scraps of poetic prose. The text was half French, half English, and the signature would be preceded by '*Amicalissiment*' or '*Votre vraiment*', a literal translation of *yours truly*. All this was a little mad, droll, full of delicacy and learning, with here and there a profound thought which would illuminate deep feelings. That was Maurice.

All England called him that. He was much loved there and with reason. He was consistently and unobtrusively generous. When I introduced him to the Abbé Mugnier, he was pleased by the Abbé's admiration for Goethe. Maurice owned a first edition of *Werther*. As soon as he returned to England he sent it to the Rue Méchain where the canon lived. He owned a collection of paintings by Carmontelle. One day a French friend said to him: 'There's a collection that ought to be in the Carnavalet Museum . . . '

'Really?' Baring said. 'I'll send them.'

He did so the next day. When the library of Ronald Storrs, Governor of Cyprus, was burned by the natives during an uprising on the island, Baring sent him this cablegram: 'Library on way. *Uno avulso*.' At the very moment he had learned of the catastrophe he had stripped himself of all his books.

Maurice also had a taste for the wildly imaginative and fantastic that was calculated to astonish a Frenchman. For many years he used to invite his friends to a dinner at a hotel in Brighton on his birthday, which fell in the middle of winter, and at the end of the meal would jump into the sea fully clothed. I have seen him with my own eyes, during a luncheon at his home, get up, strike a match and set fire to the curtains because the conversation was languishing.

One day when he was an undergraduate at Cambridge and was crossing the courtyard of Trinity, a Hindu student whom he did not know tapped him on the shoulder. Maurice Baring turned around.

'Oh, I beg your pardon,' gasped the student, 'I thought you were Mr. Godavery . . . '

'I *am* Mr. Godavery,' Maurice replied calmly.

These stories about Maurice amused me, but I much preferred his serious side and I kept urging him to write the serious, moving and profound novels for which he was fitted by nature. *Daphne Adeane* rewarded my expectations, and I introduced this book to the French public by a preface.

I was received in other homes in London. Lady Oxford and Mrs. Greville introduced me to men of politics; Lady Colefax to men of letters. It was at her home that I first met Rudyard Kipling whom I had admired so much. I was not disappointed. Kipling talked like Kipling. Kipling was a Kipling character. He was the first to put me on my guard against the optimistic pacifism which was then disarming England.

'Don't forget,' he said, 'that countries always end by resembling their shadows.'

This sentence seemed to me sybilline at the time; history proved it to be prophetic. Later in 1928 he invited me to come and see him at Burwash where he had an old house which had belonged to an Elizabethan ironmaster, and a wonderful garden. It was the country described in *Puck of Pook's Hill*, a book written for his only son who had disappeared in that battle of Loos which had been my baptism of fire. His death had stabbed Kipling to the very quick of his creative power and he was doing almost no writing. I found him discontented with his own country, uneasy about mine, excessively clairvoyant and prophesying misfortunes. But to see and talk with a man whom I had so long considered superhuman intoxicated me.

The most English of my retreats was Avebury Manor, a fine Elizabethan house with gables arranged in order of decreasing size and surrounded by prehistoric tombs, fields of dolmens and thousand-year-old yew trees. Inside it was furnished with canopied beds, huge fireplaces with open wood fires, tables set with bluish Waterford glass, and with rare and ancient collections of books. It was through my numerous visits to this Wiltshire home of Colonel Jenner that I came to know the county families of England, traditional, conservative and yet liberal. There I saw the life and way of thought of the country gentlemen who, together with the merchants of London, had so long constituted the backbone of the country and who still played such an important role in the Army, the Navy and at the Foreign Office. They had their faults, stubbornness and narrowness, and their virtues, courage and tenacity.

All things considered, I found them useful to their country and always ready to serve it. It was Colonel Jenner who first guided my readings in English history. He was well acquainted with it and would recount it from his viewpoint of Die-Hard-Tory, with vigour and sarcasm; but he made me understand why parliamentary institutions, which were being so much questioned in France at that time, had gained acceptance in England. It seemed to me useful and important to explain in our country these essential differences, and, from that moment, I formed the plan of writing a history of England one day. I was not to accomplish this until much later, and then under the urging of an energetic editor.

Finally in 1923 my life of Shelley was finished. I gave it the title *Ariel*. Charlie Du Bos, who read the manuscript, with a secret sadness because Shelley was one of *his* subjects and he himself was doing a book of a quite different sort, advised me to add an introductory note to indicate to the critics what I had tried to do. I listened to him and no doubt this was a mistake, for from this brief preface was born, much against my intention, the absurd and dangerous expression, *romanticized biography*. I had never used it; I had on the contrary said that a biographer has no right to invent either a fact or a speech, but that he might and should arrange his authentic materials in the manner of a novel and give his reader the feeling of a hero's progressive discovery of the world, which is the essence of romance. But few people take the trouble to read carefully, especially prefaces, and the success of *Ariel*, a success that astonished my publisher and me, gave rise to a whole series of *Romantic Lives* and *Private Lives* which were often very bad. For some time I suffered from the reaction against this avalanche of improvised and inadequate biographies and I took great care, when I myself returned to this type of book, to respect the legitimate phobias of meticulous, distrustful and jaundiced men of learning. Fortunately, to my great joy, Sir Edmund Gosse, the most eminent of the English critics, praised my *Ariel*, a fact that intimidated the malcontents. On the other hand, my master Alain was by no means enthusiastic:

'Why don't you write novels?' he said to me. 'Then you'll have a freer hand . . . I preferred *Ni ange, ni bête* and above all *Bramble*.'

He was now living in the Rue de Rennes. From time to time I would go to pick him up at the Lycée Henri IV, where he was teaching, and walk home with him. The war had changed him a good deal. Although exempt from military service, he had insisted in 1914 on enlisting as a private in the Artillery. From this experience of army life he had produced a cruel book: *Mars, ou la guerre jugée*. For a man so jealous of his independence the worst misfortune of war had not been death or danger but the suspension of civil liberties and public criticism.

'Who is in the right?' To find the answer to this question in the army you count the stripes or the stars of the interlocutors. It is likely that Socrates as a private would have suffered from this method. Hence in the case of Alain, veteran of the Great War, there had grown up a bitterness that he had not possessed when he was at Rouen. In the mud of the trenches he had contracted rheumatism which made him drag one leg, but he had acquired a better understanding than ever of Homer and Tacitus. He remained the man I admired most in the world. He had said kind things about *Bramble*:

'You don't tell the whole truth in it, but you don't lie; and that's a great deal. Your Colonel is massive, terrifying; he will last.'

After *Ariel* he wrote me: 'I know you well. You are a tender-hearted boy. Take care not to suffer too much.'

Ariel found in Janine an attentive, disturbed and surprised reader. Prior to this book my wife had not attached much importance to my vocation as a writer. *Bramble* had appeared at a time when she was suffering from a serious illness. The failure of *Ni ange, ni bête* had discouraged her. She had good taste, was a reader of Shakespeare and Swinburne and copied out her favourite verses in little classroom note-books. But in me she had married a manufacturer; she loved luxury and the pleasures that money provides; she now had three children: a daughter, Michelle; two sons, Gérald and Olivier; she had no desire to see me abandon a prosperous mill for labours the success of which was doubtful.

'Instead of scribbling in the evenings,' grumbled the red-headed nurse, 'Monsieur would do better to go out with Madame, and instead of scribbling during the day Monsieur would do better to look after his business.'

Janine repeated this comment to me as a comic example of the churl-ish English, but she herself was not far from sharing the opinion. After *Ariel* she was more indulgent and more respectful of my work.

'I should never have thought that you were capable of writing this book. In it you talk about women better than you've ever talked to me about them.'

'Who knows whether I didn't write this book just to tell you things I couldn't say face to face?'

She had read the manuscript. She reread the printed book twice. She searched it for allusions and explanations. She copied out passages from it. I discovered that she was surprised to see me criticize in Shelley precisely the same things that distressed her in me—the inflexible seriousness which she called my 'pedantry', the need to surround myself with professors whom she considered boring, the unconscious egoism of the artist. 'But since he understands so well,' she seemed to think, 'why doesn't he change?'

I had brought my new friends of Pontigny to see her. The meeting did not go off well. She considered them 'dry-as-dust pedants'. They found her beautiful as a poet's dream but frivolous, mocking and too well dressed. What they considered her 'coldness' was perhaps timidity in the presence of creatures of a different species from her own. Nevertheless Charlie, endowed with a mysterious sense of the tragic, had divined in her, beneath the ermine and the diamonds, what he called 'an authentic fatal being'.

At my request Janine had agreed to loan our drawing room at Neuilly, which opened on a beautiful garden, for a series of lectures that Charlie planned to give. Every Tuesday there met at the Rue Borghèse some thirty or forty persons to whom Charles Du Bos, carried away sometimes to the point of tears, talked about Keats, Wordsworth or Katherine Mansfield. These lectures were often excellent, for Charlie had prodigious learning. Since adolescence he had been reading all day long, underlining with one of those innumerable sharp-pointed pencils with which his pockets were always filled entire pages which thereafter he knew by heart. His great knowledge of music and of the plastic arts helped him to see analogies. He loved to point out subtle resemblances between Mozart and Keats, between a Chinese vase and a poem by Mallarmé. But the deliberateness of his speech, the unvarying tone of pathos and the multitude of long quotations discouraged his less serious listeners and we had great difficulty in assembling each week the reluctant members of the congregation.

Charlie and Zézette came to stay with us at La Saussaye during the summer of 1923. Du Bos had now a great deal of influence on me and I think it was good influence. He was a real spiritual director and his presence raised above themselves those who had the good fortune to be his friends. He lived in the highest regions of the spirit. The air that one breathed there was a little rarefied, but the light was brilliant and clear. He urged me toward greater profundity and toward the meticulous analysis of feelings. Others might have been in danger of going too far in this direction, as he himself did. But my natural tendencies were

[133]

rather toward rapidity, excessive clarity and simplification. By his example Charlie made me take a cure that consisted in complexity, slowness and obscurity. It did me good.

But this intimacy, which furthered my apprenticeship as a writer, was not good for my married life. Tired of my solemn friends, Janine accused me of imitating their faults.

'My, but you're getting hard to live with!' she said to me.

At this time I had some literary friends in Paris to whose homes I used to go occasionally without her in the evening. For her part, Janine went out a good deal with her brother, who had become a well-known couturier. He introduced her to a world I did not know. We both saw with despair the chasm, created by the four years of the war, growing deeper between us. Like a man whose feet are caught in quicksand and whose vain struggles only thrust him deeper into it, so our attempts at kindness, our little sacrifices, often unnoticed, misunderstood, ill rewarded, made us realize all the more clearly the danger of our position. Nevertheless between Janine and me there were so many happy memories, our love had begun with so much strength and assurance, that we could not accept the idea of a spiritual divorce.

During that summer of 1923 Janine, who had once more become pious, held long conversations with the Abbé Lemoine, curé of La Saussaye. He was a young and enthusiastic country priest of severe morals, who courageously endured almost incredible poverty in this country of rich farmers. I admired his disinterestedness and his faith; he exhibited great friendliness toward me. I do not know whether it was by his advice, but Janine tried, during that summer, to recreate the atmosphere of the first months of our marriage.

The three children in the garden were a delight to watch. Michelle rode proudly around the lawns on her new bicycle; the boys, whom their mother called *Topi* and *Little Man*, played with the flowers, the rabbits and the chickens. Janine, who loved them tenderly, was with them a great deal at this time, but she showed a foreboding sadness. Despite her youth, she talked constantly about death. One evening at La Saussaye she had a great open fire lighted in the library and burned many of our letters. This distressed me.

'But why, Janine?'

'I don't know ... I don't want to leave anything behind me ...'

'Why do you say behind you? ... You'll be here for another thirty or forty years.'

'You mustn't believe that,' she said, with a look that was filled with terror.

In October Charlie Du Bos resumed his lectures. He spent a long time discussing Browning who was one of his heroes. Janine, ill and in bed most of the time, seldom attended the lectures. Toward Christmas time she summoned up enough strength to prepare gifts and a tree. She was so fond of festivities and presents. As a gift for me she had had sent from London, in greatest secrecy, the sixty volumes of the *Dictionary of National Biography*, the absence of which from our library she had heard me deplore. I can still see her joy the day she led me to the shelves on which she had placed the 'surprise', I also see her face, thin but ravishing, as it looked through the glass door of the dining-room at the time when the children were having their meals.

At the end of December the doctors ordered her to spend some weeks in the south. She begged me to accompany her:

'Make the most of me . . . You won't have me here long to make you unhappy . . . '

She had adopted her 'light-luggage' tone which I was never able to resist. Although it was not vacation time, and despite the complaints of my partners, I abandoned the mill at its busiest season and went to live with my wife and the children in La Napoule near Cannes. Janine had a group of English and American friends there; the Henry Clewses and Winifred Mackenzie whom we both loved. We hardly went anywhere beyond our villa and the beach. We had long frank conversations; these weeks might have been sweet if the weather had not been so cold, the children sick and the nurse irritable. But various catastrophes so marred our vacation that at the beginning of February we decided to return. Janine was five months pregnant; she was sinking into despair.

We had barely arrived at Neuilly when she was put to bed with a violent fever. Her teeth chattered.

'But what has she?' I asked the doctors in alarm.

'Auto-infection,' they replied. 'Septicaemia . . . It seems to be extremely serious.'

They decided to operate. Janine agreed to the operation bravely but without illusions. She had asked to see her children again. The two little ones had been seated near her bed and had been playing at being doctors:

'*Mammy, we are two piggy goctors . . .*'

When the chloroform wore off and she regained consciousness, she suffered a great deal. I remained near her with the nurse. She talked like a person who was going to die and knew it. She declared that she was a true believer and asked me to have masses said for the repose of her soul.

Suddenly she cried aloud in terror:

'I can't see any more! . . . '

Her head fell back on the pillow. It was the end. I could not believe it nor accept it. At my insistence the doctor, who had been summoned back by telephone, attempted to revive her by injections of adrenalin near the heart, but in vain. I remained until morning kneeling beside the bed, holding her hand as it grew cold.

At the time when the noises in the street began and the screeching of the iron shutters of the shops, I went out to look for flowers. I returned with my arms full of lilacs and roses which I arranged around her. 'Poor Ginette!' I thought. 'This is the first time that you've not arranged your flowers yourself.'

I talked aloud to the body lying there. I could not imagine that Janine would no longer answer me. She was so beautiful, so calm. A vague smile was etched around the corners of her pale lips. The strong perfume of the lilacs filled the room. In my mind it evoked the forked tree of my childhood, my first reading and the Queen of the *Petits Soldats russes*. I had found the Queen in the wide, wide world; I had chosen her, won her and lost her. The penetrating and tender fragrance of lilacs was to bring back, to my dying day, the memory of that funeral bed, that icy forehead and my tears.

In the forenoon the first friends arrived. I left two nuns to keep watch in the room and received Charles Du Bos, who was gentle and compassionate. He volunteered to arrange everything with the Church of Saint-Pierre in Neuilly. I desired to have Fauré's beautiful *Requiem* played and Handel's *Largo*, which was one of Janine's favourites.

I feel an infinite gratitude to the Church for the poignant beauty of that mass. I was consumed with sorrow and love. The divine music of Fauré, the hieratic deliberateness of the evolutions, the solemnity of the absolution, comforted me. *Requiem aeternam, dona eis, Domine* . . . *Requiem aeternam . . . aeternam . . . aeternam.* It seemed to me that I could be at rest, and that if another world existed in which she whom I had so greatly loved survived, she would be happy and like the angelic, childlike and ardent girl whom I had seen in the moonlight that first evening beneath the trees of the Parc des Eaux-Vives.

15

Life Must Go On

The most terrible thing for the survivors in the death of a loved one is the feeling of irreparability. '*Nevermore . . .*' Nevermore should I hear that slightly muffled voice; nevermore should I see that beautiful thin face; nevermore would there be what she used to call a 'palaver', one of those long discussions, concerned sometimes with painful subjects, but now seeming so precious that I would gladly have given what was left of my life to talk to Janine for a single hour, a single minute. The weather, in that month of March 1924, was beautiful, and the sweetness of a premature spring, by its contrast, intensified my despair. Day after day the sun rose in a cloudless sky. I did no work. Each day I would go and buy flowers and arrange them as best I could, the way she would have done, moving a rose here, accentuating the curve of a stem, in front of the portraits I had placed in every room. Michelle, with a woman's instinct, would come and sit opposite me after dinner, and her grave sweetness re-established my connection with life.

Colonel Jenner, when he learned of my bereavement, wrote me; 'Do come to us in Avebury. The old house is very large. We will give you half of it. You won't even see us. The change will do you good . . .' I accepted this very kind invitation, but I did not find tranquillity of soul in England any more than I had in Neuilly. In vain I tired myself out with long walks among the upright stones and the turf-covered downs of Avebury. Each night in my dreams I found Janine again. Each awakening was a torture. When I returned to France the vault that I had had constructed at La Saussaye was finished and I had the coffin brought there. In front of the tomb I had placed a little semi-circular bench of marble, a willow tree and a large urn for flowers. I formed the habit of going every day to sit in the cemetery and dream of the past. We spent the summer at La Saussaye. The children in the garden were charming. Often they came with me to the cemetery.

'Let's take flowers to Mammy,' they would say.

Michelle had become serious, thoughtful, reserved. Although she had the grace and beauty of her mother I found in her, in a different form, my own scruples, shyness and reticence. The two boys, blond and rosy, looked enchanting on the green grass in their bright-coloured overalls. I loved to follow their simple and happy little lives. Each day they made a tour of the garden, as my father had formerly done of the mill, and with the same seriousness. They coveted the strawberries, looked at the sweet peas, admired the roses, counted the eggs that had been laid and went to visit the gardener. Then, as I had done at their age, they gathered wild flowers in the shadows of the trees and made fragile bouquets of them. Toward evening they would put on their tiny belted coats of pale blue and go for a walk on the uplands along paths that crossed fields of wheat, blond as their hair, in the midst of which their heads disappeared among the poppies and cornflowers.

As soon as I was able I forced myself to work. For a long time I had been thinking of writing *Dialogues sur le commandement*. On this subject there was a conflict of ideas that had troubled me since the time of Alain. The latter thought of himself as the Citizen on guard against the Authorities. He had taught me that the less a government governs the better governed a country is and that every leader is tempted to become a tyrant. But life had taught me instead (as had Plato's *Republic*) that for lack of leaders men fall into disorder and then into tyranny. Where did the truth lie? I hoped to put my thoughts in order and, as Renan says, make the two lobes of my brain argue it out.

In the preceding year at Pontigny, I had met a Lieutenant Blacque-Belair, son of the cavalry general who was commandant of the *Ecole de Saumur*. Aimery Blacque-Belair was a district commander in Morocco in the rebel zone. He was an earnest young man, a great reader of Gide and full of ardour for the profession of soldier. He became one of the interlocutors in my dialogue; the other was Alain. During the whole month of July the Lieutenant and the Philosopher carried on their argument inside me. My mind tried to be impartial; my heart was with the Lieutenant. Horror of disorder has always been one of my strongest feelings. Not that I love tyranny; I *hate* it because it, too, is a disorder and always ends by breeding anarchy. But I respect a just and legal authority. No successful action without discipline. Such was my theme.

The book was finished by the end of summer. The work had not been interrupted except by a visit at La Saussaye of André Gide, the Du Bos' and Anne Desjardins, with whom Michelle and I made a friendly and memorable trip to Chartres. My friends of Pontigny now replaced the friends of my youth who had died in the war.

My publisher, Bernard Grasset, was enthusiastic when he read the *Dialogues*; he said it was my best work. He would have liked a Greek title for it and proposed *Nicias*; the name sounded all right but the general had been mediocre; I refused. The *Dialogues sur le commandement* made quite a stir when they appeared. They were judged, very mistakenly, not as a literary work but as a political manifesto. As a matter of fact, I was not the advocate of any party. 'Not enough,' Alain used to say. I clung tenaciously to those essential liberties which seemed to me, and still seem, the prerequisites of man's happiness and dignity. But I believed that these liberties could not be maintained except by a discipline freely consented to, and that abuse of liberty always kills liberty.

Moreover I loved my country passionately; I desired its security and greatness. I saw that representative government which had succeeded in England functioned less well in France—for reasons I thought I could perceive. I wanted to attract the attention of the young people—the future leaders of France, in politics, military affairs and industry—to the rules of action which experience and history had taught me. Nothing more. The more fanatics of the Right and Left refused to believe that a dialogue could be nothing more than a dialogue and each tried to draw me onto their side. But certain distinguished soldiers like Marshal Fayolle and certain distinguished servants of the state like Jules Cambon, wrote me wise letters. Bergson, in a painstaking and profound analysis, praised me for showing the role of intuition in the make-up of the leader as well as of the artist. Alain, who recognized himself, appeared not displeased.

'Would you like to meet Marshal Pétain,' Grasset said to me one day in November, 'and discuss with him your *Dialogues*, which he has read? He is having lunch on December 2 at the home of one of my friends, Madame de Caillavet, together with Robert de Flers and Paul Valéry. She has asked me to invite you.'

'You know very well, Grasset, that I am in deep mourning and don't go out socially.'

'This isn't a question of going out socially,' Grasset protested, 'it is a professional luncheon. You are interested in certain ideas. Here's a chance to discuss them with remarkable men. That's all.'

I ended by accepting. 'Madame de Caillavet' was a name not unknown to me. It belonged to Anatole France's elderly friend, the mother of Gaston de Caillavet, co-author with Robert de Flers of *Le Roi*, *Primerose* and *L'Habit vert*. I expected to see a domineering old lady. I was delightfully surprised when I entered a ground-floor apartment in the Boulevard Malesherbes with Grasset to be presented to a young woman. My hostess was pretty and was handsomely dressed in a black and white gown. I do not know why, but she made me think of Janine, though she did not resemble her. She knew of my bereavement and talked to me with a compassion that touched me deeply. The marshal had been detained by some official duty and did not appear, but thanks to Valéry, Robert de Flers, Henri-Robert, Grasset and Madame de Caillavet herself, who knew countless anecdotes and told them wittily, the conversation was sparkling and the luncheon delightful. I left with Grasset:

'Now,' I said, 'explain this mystery. I expected to see a very old woman . . .'

He burst into laughter:

'You're dreaming! Madame Arman de Caillavet has been dead for fifteen years; this is her granddaughter, Simone de Caillavet.'

'Then why is she called *Madame* de Caillavet? Why not *Mademoiselle?*'

'Because she was once married. During the Peace Conference she married a foreign diplomat. After three years the marriage was broken, annulled.'

'She is unhappy?'

'I don't know at all . . . Her mother (the widow of Gaston de Caillavet) is remarried, to a cousin of hers and her name is now Madame Maurice Pouquet . . . Robert de Flers, who was Simone's guardian, takes the place of a father . . . Many writers and politicians come to her house, some because she is intelligent, others to see Robert de Flers.'

'Has she any children?'

'A little girl of four.'

'Is she a writer?'

'Some time ago she wrote verses and a few articles. I do not know whether she still writes. But she is much interested in literature . . . By the way, you're a great admirer of Proust; you must talk to her about him. She knew him very well.'

Madame de Caillavet had asked me to inscribe certain of my books for her. I took them to her myself; she was at home and received me; this was what I had hoped. This time I looked at her apartment more closely; it was darkened by tapestries of sombre foliage that were too high and appeared to have been made for a medieval hall. Our conversation was animated. Naturally we talked about Proust.

'For my mother,' she said, 'he had a childhood friendship, intermittent but strong . . . He drew from her (in part at least) the character of Gilberte Swann . . . And as for me, in his book I am Gilberte's daughter Mademoiselle de Saint-Loup.'

She told me how Proust had come, twelve or thirteen years after their marriage, to call on the Gaston de Caillavets one evening at midnight and had asked to meet their daughter.

'But she's been in bed for a long time!' Madame de Caillavet said.

'Have her get up, I beg you,' Proust said.

'He insisted so successfully,' Simone de Caillavet went on, 'that they got me out of bed . . . And possibly you remember the few sentences that were born of that visit?'

She went to find a copy of *Temps retrouvé* and showed me the passage about Mademoiselle de Saint-Loup which ends with these sentences: 'I found her very beautiful: still full of hope. Laughing, shaped by the very years that I had lost, she resembled my youth.'

I looked with emotion at the living woman who was in some measure Mademoiselle de Saint-Loup.

'Would you like to see Proust's letters?' she asked.

'He wrote to you?'

'Often.'

From a box she produced pages covered with that rapid handwriting which I knew well.

Marcel Proust to Madame de Caillavet: 'I found your hanging gardens, your antique columns and even, despite my pretended disdain, the signature of Napoleon, I found all this most agreeable. But even more, I like your daughter and the prodigious wealth of intelligence in a glance or exclamation of hers. "I do all I can!" (to be nice to you) was sublime . . . '

Marcel Proust to Simone de Caillavet: 'I was disappointed after your last *Dear Friend* to read *Dear Monsieur Marcel*. That's the way officers

[141]

in the army are reduced in rank ... Have you read *The Mill on the Floss*? If not, I beg you to read it ... How can you possibly write, or rather draw, whole pages of those little Chinese wands? You seem to produce a sort of strange painting in place of letters. It's delightful, it's more like water-colour painting or gardening than writing.'

I asked to see this writing that resembled a Chinese garden, and like Proust I found it 'delightful'. It had a deliberate, restrained grace.

Marcel Proust to Madame de Caillavet: 'Strange that one can love opposite physical types. For here am I in love with your daughter. How naughty she is to be agreeable, for it is her smile that has made me fall in love and that gives meaning to her whole person. If she had frowned, how completely at peace I should be. I am searching for the species of flower whose petals are exactly like her cheeks when she laughs ... I should like to see her laugh again.'

Bernard Grasset let me read a preface that Anatole France had written for a volume of verse *Les Heures latines* published in 1918 by Simone de Caillavet when she was quite young. France had drawn a curious portrait of her. He represented her as a girl who was 'mysterious, haughty, a little wild':

'At five years of age Simone was writing novels in a firm hand in school notebooks. One is surprised that she undertook them; the admirable thing is that she completed them ... One cannot will to will. Simone could use her will. She was born resolute. That can be seen from her firm little mouth, her determined chin, the way she carries her head and from her whole purposeful manner ... There is something predestined about a child whom a familiar spirit inspires, contending for attention with her dolls.' France found that resolute soul again in the form and substance of her verses: 'Stubborn, attracted by obstacles, she instinctively chose a difficult art. She liked to find resistance in the medium. She is, in the noblest sense of the word, a young craftsman. May she proudly accept this name. *Minerva the Craftsman*, thus the Athenians called their goddess.'

Proust has shown how all a man's tastes enter into the composition of his loves and how Swann, who was mad about painting, was captivated by Odette on the day when he found a resemblance between her and one Zephora, daughter of Jethro, as painted by Botticelli. I knew hardly anything about Madame de Caillavet; I was ignorant of all the details of her life, of her tastes, of her character; but a young woman who, as a child, had strolled through the museums of Paris with Anatole France and, as a girl, had been admired by Marcel Proust, seemed to me framed in precious imagery, adorned with rare and luminous words, and clothed in noble prose and wondrous legends. For the first time in a year I felt keen interest in a woman's presence, curiosity, perhaps hope. I asked her if her little daughter, who was the age of my sons, would like to come and play with them, and I took my leave.

Françoise came. She was a delicate child, overly intelligent, restless and sensitive. Her mother came to my house to take her home. She must have found a tragic atmosphere in those rooms filled with portraits in front of which stood arrangements of white flowers. (Arnold Bennett, who came to see me about that time, noted in his journal that the air of this house seemed charged with an almost morbid mystery.) Once more on this occasion Madame de Caillavet and I talked about poets and musicians. Next day I sent her *Le Vase étrusque* by Mérimée and Heine's *Intermezzo*. She expected flowers and was surprised, but I continued to be the man I had been at eighteen who delivered commentaries on the *Tractatus politicus* to young girls.

I had promised for a long time to go to Italy to see friends, and I left in January 1925. I was withdrawing more and more from the mill, and my cousins, seeing my indifference, had brought their sons-in-law into the business. I was still on the board but I planned to hand in my resignation as soon as the 'duck's eggs' had hatched. In Rome, Signora Paolo Orano (she was a French woman, Camille Mallarmé, niece of the poet and author of a good novel, *Casa seca*, whom I had met during the war) asked me if I wanted to meet Mussolini who was at the threshold of his power. I was taken to the Chigi Palace by Orano. I can still see that long feudal gallery, the little desk and the man with the out-thrust jaw who talked to me about *The Divine Comedy*. Next day I went to place violets near the Pyramid of Cestius on the tomb of Shelley. From the gardens of the Palatine I gazed at the Forum bathed in a light of dusty gold. I wandered through the Roman Campagna in pursuit of Chateaubriand and the night. In the shadow of the Colosseum I evoked the shade of Byron. A crowd of phantoms accompanied me, thronging so close that I hardly saw the living.

When I returned, the time of the first anniversary of Janine's death was approaching. I had an anniversary mass celebrated at Saint-Pierre de Neuilly; they played the same music as at her funeral. Fauré, Handel and the harmonious voices of the choir reawakened and then assuaged my grief. Madame de Caillavet attended this mass, together with my friends of Pontigny, my friends of the war and some writers.

Through Grasset I had become acquainted with Paul Morand, François Mauriac and Jean Giraudoux. At the Du Bos' I had met Jean-Louis Vaudoyer and Jacques Chardonne. Edmond Jaloux and his wife Germaine had become delightful friends. Germaine Jaloux, an excellent pianist, taught me at that time to love Wagner. In this field I once more encountered Simone de Caillavet, who was a devoted Wagnerian. She invited me to her home rather often, and there I saw Henri de Régnier, Gabriel Hanotaux, Paul Valéry and the dear Abbé Mugnier, an indulgent and romantic priest who was the first to make me love and understand Chateaubriand. Each time he saw me he would recite some beautiful phrases:

'Oh, Monsieur Maurois! Do you remember the moon of Combourg and "that majestic secret of melancholy which it loves to impart to the ancient oaks and to the antique shores of the sea?" . . . How beautiful it is!'

And his eyes would sparkle with enthusiasm, his white hair would form a hazy and poetic nimbus about his head. I loved him very much.

Simone de Caillavet's mother, Madame Maurice Pouquet—who was still young, celebrated for her beauty and possessed of a redoubtable and mordant wit—had revived in her town house in the Avenue Hoche the tradition of her mother-in-law Madame Arman de Caillavet, and there I met the Poincarés, great friends of the family, Professor Dumas, General Weygand, Admiral Lacaze, Anna de Noailles, Paul Souday and many writers of my generation. I was timid and rarely spoke in these assemblies, still being bewildered by the rapidity of Paris conversations. I preferred to see Simone de Caillavet alone and have her describe for me, with her relentless memory, this Parisian world of which I knew so little. From my province I had little realized the secret bonds that unite the political, financial, literary and social worlds. The role of an institution like the Académie Française had completely escaped me. I had never imagined the slow conquest of radical politicians from the province by the Parisian drawing rooms. Madame de

Caillavet clarified these pictures for me. But at the same time this young woman, who was so brilliant, let me catch sight occasionally of her own humility and this moved me.

It was evident that her marriage had counted for little in her life. She talked about it without bitterness, with surprising indifference. On the other hand she had retained a thousand memories of her childhood. She had been brought up by Miss Varley, an English governess, who still lived with her mother and to whom she was very much attached. From her she had gained a knowledge of the English language and literature which was another bond between us. Through the efforts of Miss Varley she had learned Shakespeare by heart before the nursery rhymes and recited: '*Most friendship is feigning, most loving mere folly*' at an age when she would have done better to be at play. Even her games had been Shakespearean. Her mother told me that as a child Simone had played at the 'marching forest' and had gravely made a circuit of the walks in their park at Périgord carrying an oak branch. When her parents, in order to strengthen her, had made her take baths in the river, the child had replied that she would only consent on condition that she be crowned with flowers and be allowed to wear a white nightgown 'to play the death of Ophelia.' Once when she was sent to wash ink stains from her hands she cried: 'All the perfumes of Arabia will not sweeten this little hand!' These stories could not but charm me.

In March 1925 I was due to leave Paris for a trip to Morocco. Marshal Lyautey, with whom I had remained in correspondence since *Bramble*, had invited me to attend the inauguration of the first railroad in Morocco, which ran from Casablanca to Rabat. I went with my friend Emile Henriot. In Casablanca Lyautey himself was waiting for us on the pier. There for the first time I saw his bold and tormented face, his warlike moustache (his teeth had been smashed by a horse's hoof), his hair that bristled straight up, his rapid stride, his explosive, restless and productive impatience.

The hazards of life have brought me into contact with almost all the great men of our time; few of them, on first meeting, have inspired me with the same admiration as Lyautey. Not that he was perfect; he had bizarre faults, affectations, caprices, rages. But he knew how to convert his weaknesses into instruments of his greatness. You respected him for his genius, loved him for his powers of imagination; and he made use of that affection to reinforce respect. He had at his disposal such a surplus of energy that he could animate not only his own life but that of thousands of other men and still retain enough vigour when evening had come and his innumerable tasks were done, to grow bored and disconsolate. He was the finest 'creature of action' that I have ever seen.

Lyautey showed us Morocco himself, entertained us in his home at Rabat and accompanied us to Marrakesh. Observing his work, I understood better than ever that action is possible and that a great man can do great things. The inertia of the universe is difficult to overcome, men are hard to convince, but the will, if it is united with patience, wins out in almost everything. Morocco was all order and beauty; fifteen years earlier it had been nothing but disorder and misery. A single man had performed this miracle.

In Fez the marshal lodged us in the beautiful palace of Bou Jeloud in rooms panelled in cedarwood with high sculptured doors. In the morning we would go out barefooted into a courtyard paved with sun-warmed tiles of white and blue faïence. Orange trees, planted amid the flagging, perfumed the warm air and a gentle Arabic fountain played in a faïence basin. The officer in command of Fez was General de Chambrun, whom I had known in Paris, and whose wife (née Clara Longworth) was an erudite Shakespearean. With them I went up on the hills beyond the gates of the city to see the evening shadows invade the white terraces and a little later to hear the shrill, sad singing of the women.

In the evening Henriot and I dined with General de Chambrun. Our host and his wife showed a forced gaiety, but we noticed strange, secret conferences, military messengers came in during the meal and whispered incomprehensible news in an atmosphere of apprehension and expectancy.

'Haven't you a feeling,' I said to Henriot, 'that we are in a house where someone is very sick and where, through courtesy, an attempt is being made to keep the news from the guests?'

'Yes,' Henriot said, 'there's certainly something wrong . . . I heard one of the officers say: "Is this post going to hold?"'

Next day as we were sitting down to dinner, General Heusch, the marshal's chief of staff, arrived. He was a witty Alsatian and was the life of the party. But the moment the last bite had been swallowed he shut himself up with General de Chambrun. Since they did not reappear, we took leave of Madame de Chambrun and toward midnight returned to our beautiful courtyard with its orange trees. At three o'clock in the morning we were abruptly awakened by dark shadows. We saw a sergeant-major and some soldiers:

'Messieurs, the general begs you to leave at once for Oudjda. The car is at the door.'

'A car? . . . But why?'

'The general desires you to reach Oran as quickly as possible. He has had rifles placed in the car.'

'Rifles? What sort of joke is this?'

We dressed grumbling. There were indeed three rifles in the car and a box of cartridges. Our chauffeur was a little soldier from the Midi, resourceful and intelligent. We got him to talk.

'What?' said he. 'You don't know? Why, it's war. Abd-el-Krim, the fellow who beat the Spaniards, has started an uprising in the Rif . . . All the tribes are revolting and going to join him . . . Look there . . . '

We were crossing a desert of white sand and we could see, riding along the crest of the dunes, handsome Arab warriors, with their long rifles slung over their backs. They were setting out for the Holy War.

'Do you think they are going to attack us?'

'As to that,' he said, 'I don't know any more than you do . . . But I'll be glad when we get within reach of Oudjda.'

As a matter of fact, we arrived in Oudjda without being forced to defend ourselves. The French Consul, Monsieur de Witasse and his wife, a cultured pair, gave us tea, comfortable chairs and *La Nouvelle revue française*.

'Ah!' they said. 'We were certainly glad to see you arrive. The general telephoned us three times from Fez about you. He was worried.'

When I saw General de Chambrun in Paris some time later he said to me laughingly:

'Well! Well! You know, when I made you leave Fez I wondered whether you were going to get through.'

'But why did you take the risk, general?'

'Because Fez might have been surrounded or even taken the following day . . . I gave you a chance to escape . . . But it was a relief to hear you had arrived.'

Just as I owe a group of friends to Pontigny, I owe another to Morocco. Commandant Cellier, Pierre Viénot and Lieutenant Blacque-Belair belonged to both groups. But this trip, and reunions later on in the Rue Bonaparte, introduced me to the whole crowd who had worked with the man they affectionately called the 'Chief'. Among them were Pierre Lyautey, nephew of the Chief, Vladimir d'Ormesson, Félix de Vogüé, Captain Durozoy. When the Chief returned to Paris at the end of the year, he often invited me to his house. I liked the spirit of his staff. These were men who thought of their work and of their duty ahead of themselves or of any party. In France, which was so badly divided, Lyautey was one of those rare leaders who knew how to make use of men of all opinions and all faiths and make them work together for the glory of their country. He was a monarchist, but he loved Herriot, the radical, because Herriot was a patriot. He was an ardent Catholic, but he had among his intimate friends Protestants, Israelites, Mohammedans and free thinkers. When Millerand, then President of France, came to Morocco, the Marshal said to him:

'*Monsieur le Président*, I know that in Paris you do not go to mass, but here I request you to go every Sunday because the Arabs are a religious people and they would not understand . . .'

And the free-thinking President respectfully accompanied the Catholic Resident to church.

'The Marshal, mighty ruler,' the natives said to me in Rabat or Marrakesh as they saw the Chief's car flash by at full speed. I thought so too.

16

The Walkyrie

On my return from Morocco I found my father about to undergo a serious operation. For two years he had been suffering from prostate trouble. A first operation had made it possible for him to go on living but at a reduced rate and with constant care, which irritated him. Although the doctors themselves had told him his general condition was not good and he would do better to wait, he decided to take the risk.

'Dying doesn't frighten me,' he said, 'and living like this is unbearable.'

And so he entered the clinic of the Brothers Saint-Jean de Dieu in Paris and resigned himself to Fate. On the day before the operation I went to see him and had a long conversation with him. He seemed happy and in good spirits.

'Whatever happens now,' he said, 'I have seen the thing I hoped for more than anything else in the world: the return of Alsace to France.'

Alas, from the first day after the operation it was clear that it had not been successful. He was seized by vomitings, complained of frightful pain and little by little fell into a lethargy which was the result of uremia. The following day the surgeon admitted to us that there was no longer any hope. A few seconds before the end my father opened his eyes and called me:

'You are there?' he said in a barely audible voice. 'Then it's all right ...'

After that he drew two or three breaths and appeared to fall asleep. The nurse held a mirror to his lips. He was dead. Never did purer heart cease to beat. For my mother, who had brought him there with so much confidence, it was a terrible blow and the end of her real life. But she showed great courage. The burial, which took place at Elbeuf, was just as he would have wished. From the cemetery, on the side of a hill overlooking the town, one could see the long orange roofs and the high chimneys of the mill to which he had dedicated his life. The workers all came. Many of the old Alsatian women wept. Bellouin, a weaver who had been one of his most loyal friends, gave a simple and moving speech. From Le Havre Monseigneur Alleaume wrote me: 'Your father was one of the most thoroughly noble men I have ever met. At the time when I was living in Elbeuf he did not have a single enemy.' This was the exact truth.

His death severed the last bond between the mill and me. I continued to go there, but each week I abandoned more of my prerogatives. Even when I was at La Saussaye I devoted almost all my time to writing. I had begun two books. One of them, *Bernard Quesnay*, was a novel of industrial life, an elaboration of the long short story I had published under the title *La Hausse et la baisse*. As Veronese did in certain of his pictures, I put myself in it twice: under the name of Bernard and under the name of Antoine Quesnay. Bernard was what I might have been if I had lived the *Dialogues sur le commandement*; Antoine what I might perhaps have been if Janine had lived. *Bernard Quesnay* is not a 'great' novel, far from it, but it is an honest book, and I believe a true picture of a world that is little known. My other and more important work was a life of Disraeli.

Where had I come upon that idea? First in a comment by Barrès: 'The three most interesting men of the nineteenth century are Byron, Disraeli and Rossetti.' This gave me the idea of reading the life and works of Disraeli. In him I found a hero after my own heart: 'I am,' he said, 'a radical in order to uproot what is bad; a conservative in order to preserve what is good.' And also: 'To conserve is to maintain and to reform.' This was the political philosophy that experience had taught me. The more I studied both history and men, the clearer it became to me that civilizations, as Valéry says, are 'edifices of enchantment'. The acceptance of conventions gives rise to a reign of order, and under the shelter of these conventions liberty flourishes. British conventions were among the most amazing of all, but because they were respected the country had been preserved from brutal shocks and, without a revolution, had become one of the freest in the world.

Since the war I had shared Disraeli's admiration for British tradition. Many of his sayings pleased me by their form and content. '*Never explain, never complain.*' '*Or perfect solitude, or perfect sympathy.*' '*Life is too short to be little.*' Phrases like these awoke an instant response in

me. His long devotion to his wife was the perfect image of the life I
had hoped for and that had been denied me. His influence on world
affairs, to me who had no such influence (nor wished to have), was a
vicarious compensation. I had never written a book with greater
pleasure.

Disraeli's high virtues reminded me that, in order to disarm millenary
prejudices, a Jew must make himself irreproachable in so far as that is
humanly possible. His honesty and his loyalty must be living refuta-
tions of the hostile legends. Disraeli's invincible courage had triumphed
over opposition. He had succeeded in making himself loved and respected.

As is known, he was baptized in infancy at his father's wish, which
relieved him of making himself a decision that faith alone would have
justified. As for me, I admired Christianity, as I have said, and considered the New Testament a sublime complement of the Old. Nevertheless I did not think that it was my duty to become a convert.
As long as my parents were alive, I knew that this would cause them
great pain. Though they were neither believers nor observers, they
clung to their family traditions. After the *Affaire Dreyfus* my father
considered that to be a Jew implied danger and that it would be
cowardly to evade it. I approved of his attitude and, despite strong and
affectionate urgings, I never took this step.

My best friends, Charles Du Bos and Maurice Baring, were devoted
Catholics. They said to me: 'You are in fact a Christian, *anima
naturaliter christiana* . . . Why don't you grant yourself the boon of
recognizing this?' But grace, that sudden illumination that Claudel
described and that Du Bos himself had known, was lacking in my case.
It was a painful situation. Having married a pious Catholic, I acquired
the habit of going often with her to church. I loved the church ceremony, the sacred music, the beautiful Latin texts of the prayers. To
look on from the outside as an involved spectator but nevertheless an
outsider at these rites that were so perfectly calculated to bring me
peace and guidance—this placed me in an ambiguous position, one
which seemed to me, however, the only honourable one I could adopt.
This will explain why writing the life of Disraeli was a delight.

In July I interrupted this work to go and spend some days in
Périgord with the family of Madame de Caillavet's mother, the
Pouquets. (The Caillavets themselves were from Bordeaux.) The
Pouquets owned the little château of Essendiéras between Périgueux

and Limoges. This ancient dwelling, adorned with feudal turrets, had been bought in 1794 by Maître Antoine-Chéri Pouquet, a lawyer in Angoisse. Beside it on the same hill a new house, more comfortable but without beauty, had been built by Simone's grandfather, a stockbroker in Paris, during the period of prosperity and bad taste. The tapestries, the overstuffed furniture, the thick curtains, the innumerable portraits and knick-knacks gave Essendiéras an air of Louis-Philippe.

To find there some of the same customs as at Elbeuf amused me. The employees of the Pouquet office had given Simone's grandfather, just as the workmen had given my father, a bronze representing *Work* by Barbedienne, with this inscription: 'On the battlefields of labour victory is fruitful.' But the photographs which covered the tables at Essendiéras, just as in Elbeuf, were more prestigious here. You saw Anatole France, now leaning against the shaft of an antique column, now in contemplation of the Pyramids. An adolescent Proust with velvety eyes; Victorien Sardou wearing a beret; innumerable pictures of Robert de Flers and Gaston de Caillavet in smiling friendship; and actresses: Jeanne Granier; Lantelme; Marie Leconte; and Eve Lavallière.

The view across the valley of the Isle was beautiful, embracing a region of tenant farms with lovely names: Brouillac, la Guichardie, la Cerise. Two long converging alleys, one of oaks, the other of chestnut trees, led from the road up to the château. A rushing stream, the Loue (or Louve), ran along the foot of the hills and nibbled at the Essendiéras fields.

In addition to Madame de Caillavet and Madame Pouquet, I found there the latter's husband, a mining engineer whose intelligence I relished; Simone's grandmother, a fine old lady, but a little confused; and Miss Varley, a super-English Englishwoman and passionate Victorian. To be honest, during these ten days, I saw hardly anyone but Simone de Caillavet, for she had undertaken to show me Périgord and we were on the go from morning till night. At Essendiéras I fell in love simultaneously with the landscapes of Périgord and with the woman who showed them to me. She passionately loved her province and talked about it with a profound and living knowledge of its ways that I found touching. Each village had its château, each château its legend. My companion told me the story of *La Fileuse* of Jumilhac and that of the châtelaine of Montal, the story of the château of Biron and of the château of Hautefort. She took me on literary pilgrimages in honour of Montaigne, Brantôme, Fénelon—and to Montignac where Joubert and

Eugène Le Roy had lived. She knew all about these men and their works, and I was struck by the invariable seriousness of her mind.

I went down into the chasm of Padirac; I climbed with her by precipitous roads to the tableland of Domme, whence one can see the lovely valley of the Dordogne framed by graceful fortresses and by serried rows of poplars. I sensed that my new friend was shy, reserved, almost unsociable. Although she had been married, she retained some of the qualities of a young girl. She had been raised most religiously, with a horror of sin and a fear of profane love. 'Apt at suffering and more fearful of joy than of sorrow,' Anatole France had written of her.

Later she admitted to me that she had been obsessed by the romance of her grandmother with Anatole France, and she had always hoped to devote herself, heart and mind, to an artist's work. She talked of 'going into literature as one goes into religion.' One evening as a result of a breakdown of the car which obliged the chauffeur to go back for repairs, we remained alone for an hour in the forest. The air was mild and caressing, the rays of the moon through the trees lighted the path we were following; the earth, covered with pine needles, moss and dry leaves, was springy beneath our feet. The simple beauty of sleeping nature put an end to our resistance. I dared say to her that I loved her. But I did not know how to reconcile this feeling, which was young, ardent and new, with a past whose funereal shadows still completely enveloped me.

The following winter in Paris I saw Simone almost every day. Together we went to the theatre and to concerts. Ardent admirer of Wagner that she was, she determined to make me love and understand him. In this she succeeded all the more easily because I myself was trying earnestly to understand her, and her Wagnerian reveries illuminated her character, which was far more that of Brünnhilde than of Isolde. She believed in the superhuman power of Parsifal because he was chaste; she felt a horror of the Flower Maidens, a physical horror that was almost hatred.

'Woe unto them through whom the offence cometh,' she would say when I reproached her for her extreme severity toward other women.

The music brought us together. Simone found in Wagner the symbol and perhaps the solution of her problems. And although I continued to prefer Beethoven I discovered profound lessons for the writer. The themes that illuminated and rendered intelligible that enormous cataract of sound seemed to me also appropriate to light up and arrange the

[153]

confused masses of fact in a biography or history. In Siegfried's Funeral March, in the conclusion of *The Twilight of the Gods*, I saw the inimitable model of what the end of a great book should be. I endeavoured to explain this to my beautiful concert companion and I led her by the paths of music to understand what in my eyes was the art of writing.

There was another bond which united us closely: that of work. She had told me at Essendiéras that her father had had her learn typewriting and that nothing would interest her more than to copy manuscripts for me. I had not taken her offer seriously. Nevertheless, as she continually talked about it, I gave her the manuscript of the beginning of *Bernard Quesnay*. I was stupefied when, after a period that was so short she must have worked all night, she brought me an impeccable text. The exactitude of the alignment recalled the amazing garden of little Chinese wands that was her handwriting. I entrusted her with other work. Then one day I said to her jokingly that if she also knew shorthand I would never want any other secretary. Without saying a word to me she took lessons in shorthand and a few months later asked me to dictate letters to her. Due to hard work and determination she had become in record time the best stenographer I had ever had. Anatole France had well described her as 'Minerva the craftsman', who performed her tasks with singular and meticulous perfection.

We found so much pleasure in being together that we paid no heed to the reactions of our families and our friends, who complained that they never found us free any more. Many of those around us understood more clearly than we ourselves that we were drifting toward marriage. Even my mother said to me:

'How can you live without a woman in your house? . . . Who will bring up your children?'

Yes, it seemed wise for me to marry again, and if I should do so, Simone was a companion after my own heart who was capable of taking a living part in my work and whom I loved. But her friends, like mine, tried to dissuade us from the idea. In the eyes of Pontigny, an alliance with the world of *l'Habit vert* seemed a frivolous contract and a danger to my work. Charles Du Bos, with his kind and touching gravity, put me on my guard against the 'salons'. Ah, if he had only known how little I liked them, how happy I was and what an ardent desire they inspired in me to find once more my solitude and work! To Simone people said:

'Marry a widower with three children, what a mistake! You will have endless conflicts with grandmothers and governesses!'

Moreover she had always said that she would never remarry. She had had brilliant opportunities more than once and had rejected them. In the independent life, which her inheritance from her father assured her, she had found peace, a little dull perhaps, but such as marriage had not afforded her. Her instinct prompted her to preserve it.

Nevertheless when it became evident that the manners and customs of our two families were such that the passionate friendship that united us could not continue except in marriage, our feelings were stronger than the objections of our friends. One evening we had a long conversation which lasted until dawn and in the course of which we decided to be married the following summer. Françoise was of the same age as my sons and got along well with them. Why not bring together the ravelled threads of two families torn by destiny and weave from them a single happiness? When we went to Elbeuf announcing this news to my mother, she received it with joy. It was decided that the wedding should take place in Périgord and that only the official witnesses were to be present.

I did not wish Pontigny to be sacrificed to Essendiéras, and at the end of August I went to Burgundy to attend a 'decade' and there encountered again, as of old, Gide, Charles du Bos and Martin du Gard. Then on September 4, 1926 I left for Périgord. There I found the Abbé Mugnier who had promised to marry us (he had married my mother-in-law and was to marry my daughter), Gabriel Hanotaux and Robert de Flers who were to be our witnesses. I had also asked Aimery Blacque-Belair, the lieutenant of the *Dialogues sur le commandement* and his wife, a pair for whom I felt a brother's affection, to come and join us.

For a year I had known Simone's family. Her mother, a vivacious and passionate woman, had a true talent as an actress which appeared in her way of telling stories. An excellent friend to those whom she liked, she was a redoubtable enemy to those she hated. But this authoritarian person recognized with naïve and touching devotion one authority herself, that of her husband Maurice Pouquet.

A native of Périgord, brought up on a country estate, graduate in engineering from the School of Mines, he combined the shrewd wisdom of the peasant with an astonishing and varied culture. He knew the most unexpected things, from the technique of industry to that of the fine arts, from the history of Egypt to that of Sweden; from the geology of Paraguay to the physiology of truffles. He seemed capable of managing a country estate, an industry, a bank, and during the war of 1914 he had systematized the technique of aerial photography for the French Army. When I came to know him better I discovered that his science was fairly superficial and that he managed the businesses entrusted to him quite badly. But at that time I admired him. How many happy evenings I have spent listening to him on the terrace of Essendiéras while the constellations rose slowly above the cedars, the shooting stars streaked the summer sky with their long trails of fire, the familiar owl quitted her tower to go hunting, and in the immense sleeping plain at our feet the night mists prowled.

It was a country wedding, intimate and charming. In the little town hall of the village my wife's uncle Pierre Pouquet, who was the mayor of the district, asked us the conventional questions. Robert de Flers made a lively and emotional speech in his best manner. He spoke very nicely of my parents whose pure and noble life Simone had described to him; of Simone herself who was so well prepared for the difficult task of being a writer's wife; then he said to me that he hoped some day to receive me in the Académie Française and, after having called me 'my dear André,' to refer to me for an hour as 'Monsieur'. The church was tiny. Abbé Mugnier officiated there and said lofty and beautiful things to us about fidelity and the relation between art and religion. Gabriel Hanotaux, a retired statesman and an active historian, astonishingly vigorous in mind and body, was the wit of the wedding breakfast which, as is customary in Périgord, was abundant and savoury. The omelette with truffles, the preserved goose and the cherry tarts, together with the maxims of Gabriel Hanotaux, made a thoroughly French mixture. Abbé Mugnier quoted Châteaubriand and Joubert as well as Goethe and Shakespeare. Simone, pretty and animated, sparkled, and I was proud of her.

In the journal of Mary Shelley one may read between two notes on her reading for the day, 'A wedding took place.' This dry discretion pleased me, and it seems that I had formed the strange project of making my second marriage slip into my daily life without causing any change in the arrangement of the latter. Simone, like every young woman, would have liked a wedding trip, a few weeks of solitude for two, in classical Italy or voluptuous Morocco. In this she was right, for the first adjustment of two lives is easier in a foreign environment which relaxes former ties. By a strange aberration I decided that we would do nothing of the sort but on the following day would join my three children and the nurse at the seashore at Hendaye. This is the explanation, though not a justification, of this absurd plan: I believe I had unconsciously found a sombre and bitter joy in being, in my own eyes and in those of my friends, the Inconsolable, and I had ended by indulging in a sentimental fetishism which was neither reasonable nor generous. Perhaps it had some obscure connection with the ancient cult of the dead and the need of appeasing their shades, which is as old as human society. Perhaps my white flowers, my sacred images and my commemorative services were nothing but attenuated forms of very ancient sacrifices.

At first this sentimentality had been the quite natural expression of an immense sorrow; then it grew unhealthy and, as Bennett wrote, morbid. The living should live with the living and for the living, and if it is laudable and pious to respect the dead, it is cruel to offer them human sacrifices. Worried, torn by memory and tormented by the chimera of an impossible posthumous loyalty, I had tried to make of my second marriage as small an event as possible with the obscure and naïve hope, no doubt, that the news, hushed, compressed into three words, would not penetrate as far as the dismal realms. For the same reasons, or rather the same superstitions, I refused under thin pretexts, to use the familiar 'tu' with my wife, though she wished it; I made her live in Neuilly in an apartment filled with memories of another woman, and when she tried to make my children hers, I rendered her attempted contacts with them more difficult by scruples and reservations which no reasonable being would have put in her way. My ill-considered refusal to authorize my sons to call her *Maman* was to create for a long time a source of embarrassment between them and her, a wall of words, transparent and impenetrable. But on this subject I was not a reasonable being.

The magic hold of the dead is strong and fearful. ' *Tel qu'en lui-même enfin l'éternité le change,*' the dead escape all accidents, temptations and errors. For two years I had been shaping at will a superhuman figure, retouching memories of the past, orchestrating a funereal hymn. I committed the error of trying to associate with me in this cult the woman I now loved. She was willing, but she suffered from it. The servants and the children's nurse contradicted her decisions with the wishes of 'Madame' and 'Madame' was a beautiful, impalpable phantom. The transfer of authority was accomplished with difficulty. The cook, the chauffeur, the latter's wife whom the children called 'Mammy Georges', stood upon privileges which they maintained they had received from the departed. I knew a long time later from Simone's confidences that during that first year, despite the deep love that united us, she had been unhappy to the point of desperation. I did not notice it. We are all blind when it is only the feelings of others that are at stake.

The adjustment of friendships in a newly formed household is also a delicate matter. My friends of Pontigny, the Desjardins, Charles du Bos, continued with affectionate persistence to put me on my guard against the people of society and their enchantments. Were they right? Society, in its best aspects, taught me a great deal, and in the time of my misfortunes I found it, on the whole, steadfast and dependable. It had no influence on my political ideas which remained what they had been made by Alain, my reading and my experiences. Its real danger is that it devours those hours which a writer should reserve for reading and for reverie. In society the novelist finds his models, but he loses there the leisure and also often the right to represent those models truthfully. The best solution is, perhaps, that of Proust: having known society, to escape from it through illness or withdrawal. Solitude is a difficult prescription in the life of any artist.

One of my great discoveries at that time was men of state. In my province of Normandy I had known the small fry of local political workers; party leaders, ministers and presidents retained in my eyes a legendary quality. I should have been as dumbfounded as Dr. Cottard if Swann had said to me, as he did to him: 'I had lunch at the home of the President of France.' Now at my mother-in-law's home Monsieur Raymond Poincaré, former President of the Republic and present Premier, was a guest like any other, human, ready to answer questions (like Monsieur de Norpois at the home of Madame de Villeparisis), and even strangely anxious to explain the part he was playing and to win approval. One day when an American magazine had asked me for an article about him, Simone begged him to tell us about his early life. He did so with an obliging, meticulous wealth of detail, constantly turning to his wife whom he treated with touching tenderness and attention: 'Isn't that so, Henriette? Surely it was in 1897 . . . '

That day I learned it was entirely by accident that he had got into politics and that he had not planned to. A surprising characteristic was that he continued to be shy, and this resulted in a certain brusqueness:

[158]

'Don't go abroad too much,' he said to me. 'As soon as one leaves the Place de la Concorde one ceases to make sense . . . '

Briand too had long been a frequenter of the Avenue Hoche, but he never came there at the same time as Poincaré. The two men were too different to understand each other or to take pleasure in meeting. Poincaré was a lawyer; Briand a poet. Poincaré loved the farmlands of his native Lorraine; Briand the seascapes of his native Brittany. Poincaré felt a need of facts and figures; Briand had a horror of figures, and if some inept person provided him with them he forgot them as soon as possible. Poincaré wrote out his speeches from the first line to the last in a neat, small, sloping hand and thereafter knew them by heart; Briand would prepare his while rolling one cigarette after another and trying out his arguments on whatever audience chance provided, and would then create his best effects from the reactions of these listeners. Poincaré's files were impeccable, aligned like the battalion of *chasseurs* he had formerly commanded; in the hands of Briand a file soon became so confused that he would discard it in disgust. Poincaré governed through bureaus, Briand through hearts. Poincaré from Lorraine and hence a neighbour of the Germans feared them; Briand, a Breton, did not fear them enough. Poincaré was painfully sensitive to everything people said about him; Briand did not read what was written about him and would cheerfully have said with Queen Victoria: 'The important thing is not what they think of me, it is what I think of them.' A wit declared that Poincaré knew everything and understood nothing; but this was not true, for Poincaré understood a great many things and Briand knew and read much more than he admitted.

Clemenceau, the remaining one of the three giants of the epoch, no longer came to the Avenue Hoche; nevertheless I was slightly acquainted with him. I had met him in the army at the time of *Bramble*. He had written me a lively and penetrating note about the *Dialogues*. I went to thank him and found him in his little apartment in the Rue Franklin seated in front of a semi-circular desk and wearing a forage cap on one side of his head and black gloves on his aged hands. His doctor was with him.

'The doctor here,' he said to me, 'has been assuring me that I have only a few months to live.'

'They've said that to me a number of times, *Monsieur le Président*, and I'm still here.'

'Ah, you are young . . . What are you going to give us next?'

'I'm thinking of a life of Wilson.'

'Don't do it! That man has done us a great deal of harm.'

Behind him was a canvas by Claude Monet depicting a landscape in la Creuse.

'Beautiful, isn't it?' he said . . . 'Those stones, I always have a feeling that if I struck them with my cane sparks would fly out . . .'

With a better knowledge of these great men, I found them quite different from the picture that rumour had drawn, and more human, infinitely more human, than the shadows they had thrown on the walls of my cave in Elbeuf. 'Hell must exist,' Abbé Mugnier used to say, 'since they teach us to believe in it; very well, Hell exists, but there is no one in it . . .' And Alain: 'As for Hell, the only people you consign to it are the people you don't know.' And so I welcomed the masters of France into the Purgatory of my judgments and, like Marcel Proust in his childhood before the belfries of Martinville, I felt growing within me the obscure but imperious desire to paint them. Beginning in 1927, in the 'Vivier' (fish-pond) where I keep ideas for books, plans and a programme of work, there stands on each page: *Political novel*. This novel was not written. It was transformed much later into a book of notes: *Choses nues*.

17

Climates

Personal friendships and reading, war and travels, had given me some knowledge of England, in so far as one can know a people, which is, alas, very little. Of America I knew nothing. It remained for me what it had been in my childhood, a mixture of Jules Verne and Mark Twain, to which there was now added Charlie Chaplin, Theodore Dreiser and the book by André Siegfried. But in 1927 James Hazen Hyde, founder of the Alliance Française in the United States and who now conducted that organization in Paris, proposed to me that I should be the official lecturer of the Alliance for that year. He explained the reasons for his choice. I was becoming, he told me, a pretty well known writer in America. *Bramble* had not been published in the United States but *Ariel* had had thousands of readers there; *Disraeli* had just been chosen by the Book-of-the-Month Club. In addition, I was now getting my start as a lecturer in Paris.

About 1925 a succession of accidents had thrust me into this new career. The *Vieux-Colombier* was arranging a series of lectures on the cinema and, because I had written an article on the subject, asked me to deliver one of them. Madame Adolphe Brisson (Yvonne Sarcey) who was president of the *Annales* Lectures, heard me and decided to give me a try. She proposed that I give one of a series of talks on the eighteenth century for her Society, a lecture on Horace Walpole and Madame du Deffand. The other important Lecture Association in Paris was presided over by René Doumic, Permanent Secretary of the Académie Française and editor of the *Revues des deux-mondes*, a great feudal baron of the realm of letters. He summoned me to the office of the *Revue des deux-mondes* in the Rue de l'Université and received me with his legs wrapped in blankets and seated behind a desk that had belonged to Brunetière and Buloz; he offered to let me give a 'little course' of four lectures in the Lecture Association in the spring of 1927. The 'big course' (of ten lectures) was, he told me, too heavy a responsibility for a beginner. Even the 'little course', he gave me to understand, was an honour of which I had still to prove myself worthy.

I accepted. There remained the problem of choosing a subject. Here Monsieur Doumic had very determined ideas. Sometimes they shocked authors and orators, but I think one could say of him what Lord Salisbury said of Queen Victoria, to wit, that it was enough to know her opinion on any subject to know that of the general public as well. Monsieur René Doumic had studied the reactions of his subscribers. When he said: 'For the French public there are only four English writers: Shakespeare, Byron, Dickens and Kipling,' he might dismay a lecturer who wanted to talk about John Donne, Keats or Swinburne; actually he was right, and the faithfulness of his subscribers testified to the accuracy of his judgments. My course was mediocre. But Monsieur Doumic continued to treat me with a mixture of esteem and brutal frankness, for which I was grateful to him. The esteem was proved by his confiding one of his precious courses to me; the frankness permitted him to tell me after the first lecture that I articulated badly, that the back rows had not heard me, and that I must not let my voice drop at the end of a sentence. I took this very seriously and with good results, I trust, for he said no more about it.

My trip to America was an important initiation. I made it alone, being too uncertain of the difficulties and fatigues to take my wife with me. On the *Paris* I learned about life on shipboard for the first time, the ephemeral intimacies it can create, the bracing air of the decks; the women stretched out on deck chairs with their legs wrapped up in blankets by deck stewards as a grocer wraps up a package; and the nightly conversations without end and without subject beneath the stars, while a reddish moon comes up, leaving a long luminous track upon the surface of the waters. For the first time I saw, on arrival in New York, the airplanes and the birds wheeling about the ship, the fishermen's boats, the noisy launches of the Health Department, the fortified hills which on nearer approach became skyscrapers, the pleasure resorts crowded with quaintly decorated buildings, the picturesque and singular animation of the Hudson River, then Pier 57 of the French Line, waving handkerchiefs, the mad confusion of the customs shed and finally the city, the city massive and geometrical and nevertheless monstrous, the city that is gigantic and yet human.

At the end of a few days I wrote to a friend: 'Come. Nothing gives one more of a zest for life than a morning on Fifth Avenue. Come. The air is intoxicating, the pedestrians hurry along. The crowds enslaved by the red and green lights, surge forward in waves like the sea. The churches have the appearance of children which other buildings lead by the hand. Come. The locomotives have little bells around their necks like the cows in Switzerland, and the Negro porters wear tortoise-shell glasses like young French women. Come. The valley through which this train is running is called the Naugatuck. It winds among the cliffs like the valley of St. Moritz. From each of the wooden stations one expects to see Charlot emerge dressed as a clergyman. Close to the tracks hundreds of cars are parked in a semicircle. Come. America is a vast desert interspersed with oases of Fords. Come, ready to believe in life and perhaps even in humanity. Come and try, for a few months, being younger by several centuries.'

Just what was it that I had loved so much? Everything—beautiful valleys, stately rivers, the blazing colours of the trees, the grace of New England villages. And then the youth and confidence. America in 1927 was not doubtful and cynical as it became after the Great Depression. In the universities, the ardour, the desire to learn and the faith in the future of humanity rested me after so much European negativism. Most of all I had loved the atmosphere of good will and comradeship in which the social life moved. No doubt there were there, as elsewhere, the hardheartedness of the wealthy, the enviousness of the unfortunate and the often sterile criticism of the intellectuals. But these reactions, which are native to every society, seemed to me tempered by a real desire not to inflict pain needlessly.

On the *Ile-de-France* which took me back to Europe I made this note: 'What have I gained from these two months? Is the memory of them pleasant or unpleasant? Pleasant, without question. I loved this country . . . Henceforth I shall remember that over there—quite close to us, only six days at sea away—there is an immense reservoir of strength and friendship . . . I myself, who am nervous and easily tired, have been healthy, alert and happy for two months, despite a frantic schedule. I felt younger in America. I found a youthful vigour in that fine autumn air that took me out of myself . . . '

From then on I was never to forget the existence beyond the seas of that 'reservoir of strength and friendship'. And a short time after my return to France I was to have need of this memory, for I suddenly found myself—I who in my provincial naïveté had believed I had no enemies—the object of an absurd and brutal attack which, however, was contrived with Machiavellian cunning.

My publisher, Bernard Grasset, had warned me in advance: 'During your absence a real plot has been organized against you. The crew at the *Mercure de France*—Louis Dumur, Valette, Léautaud have decided to destroy you. Why? They maintain that your success has been too sudden. *Bramble, Ariel, Disraeli . . .* these huge printings, your success with the critics, have exasperated them. They are going to try to prove that your books owe everything to English sources. This is absurd, but bitterness and venom are not subject to reason.'

Grasset was well informed. A search was made for an eminent English authority to attack me. Naturally none could be found. All of them, from Legouis to Koszul, were on my side. The role was offered to H. D. Davray. He consulted Wells whose translator he was. Wells replied: 'Have nothing to do with it. The accusation is stupid.' Whereupon Davray declined. Léautaud wrote to Arnold Bennett, whom he knew well, and was vigorously rebuffed. As a last resort, lacking any competent critic who was willing to undertake this base task, the conspirators chose a young man who contributed occasionally to the *Mercure* and who succeeded in inoculating himself with a hatred for me which was as violent as it was inexplicable.

The attack was brutal but totally unsuccessful. The unhappy young man juxtaposed texts in the most naïve fashion. Every time he found in my books and in earlier English works a fact such as: 'Little Ianthe, Shelley's daughter, had blue eyes,' he was noisily triumphant. What did he want? That, in order to be original, I should have said she had brown eyes? As for *Disraeli*, it was even more absurd. He reproached me for having imitated the work of Monypenny and Buckle! Buckle, however, was still alive and, far from complaining, had congratulated me. In point of fact, there was no literary resemblance between this excellent official biography in several thick volumes and the impressionistic and personal portrait I had sketched.

Every aspect of this attack was puerile, but it had been published in a magazine that had a reputation for seriousness. I could not ignore it. Being perfectly sure of my good faith, I went to see Valette, editor of the *Mercure*, who Grasset felt was an honest man, and I reproached him for the irresponsibility with which he had accepted a defamatory article without substantiation and contrary to the opinion of competent writers.

'None of this will hold water,' I said to him. 'If you had sent me a proof, which would have been the decent and courteous thing to do, I would immediately have shown you the baselessness of this accusation.' This sentence was to be later misquoted in the most improbable way by one of his assistants.

Valette replied, with a carelessness that surprised me, that it was customary for his magazine to welcome 'campaigns' and that he would be equally happy to publish my reply if I felt I ought to make one. My literary friends, who had had more experience than I, begged me not to do so: 'You will just be playing into their hands. What are they after? Uproar and publicity . . . Don't help them.'

I thought of Disraeli's motto: 'Never explain, never complain.' But I was too sure of being right to keep quiet. I replied at length. The most eminent English critics, among them Edmund Gosse, took up the question and wrote that they were unreservedly on my side. The conspirators found only a single English accomplice, and a totally discredited one at that, Frank Harris. The campaign misfired. It was to be resumed later during the occupation by those magazines that were subservient to Germany. Léautaud and Valette themselves came to regret it. When I published *Climats*, Léautaud said: 'He has written a fine novel. We were wrong to attack him.' He was not a bad man, but he had been very miserable. My obvious happiness had offended him. *Climats*, by showing him that I too had suffered, made him less hostile. For my part, I had pardoned him. This Balzacian episode and my lost illusions left me with the strange sensation of having been for a long time, without realizing it, the object of vigilant and systematic hatred on the part of a group whom I did not know.

Before this incident I had little idea of hatred because I had never felt it toward anyone. I was not jealous of my fellow writers, a fact for which I deserve no credit since I had always found the literary world cordial and on the whole fair. When Robert de Flers had said to me: 'I am going to have the Académie Française award you the *Grand Prix* for novels,' I pointed out to him a novelist I thought more worthy, and he was given the award. But our best actions gain us fewer friends than our omissions and forgetfulness earn us enemies. Without knowing it I had perhaps offended certain of my confrères by not naming them in a list of my spiritual mentors, others by neglecting to thank them for an article or for sending me a book. But I was conscious of my own good will, of the pleasure I derived from the success of writers whom I admired and of a sincere modesty in respect to my own work. Hence my amazement when faced with the hideous portrait of me drawn by this Zoilus.

It was because I had forgotten the Personage who had been constantly growing at my side from the instant I began to lead a public life and who had been eagerly fed by jealous and unfriendly hearts. What could this Personage be? A writer sprung from the business world who was interested solely in large sales (when, to the contrary, in writing the life of Shelley I had thought, and my publisher had agreed, that I was giving up all hope of large sales and that this book composed for myself would attract only a limited audience); a rich man surrounded by a crowd of secretaries who did his research for him (when I had no other secretary than my wife and my greatest pleasure was in doing my own research work); a man who was always in a rush and who dictated his books and threw them together hastily (when I wrote them all by hand, beginning them over again five or six times). If I had met this Personage no one would have detested him more than I. The Real Man was so passionately devoted to his work, he had so great a desire not to injure others, to be just, honest, and as Proust would have said 'gentil', that I believe Zoilus himself, if he had known him, would have judged him inoffensive and perhaps likeable. But Zoilus knew him as the Personage and that's why Zoilus was Zoilus.

When everything is taken into account, there is something to be said for enemies; they produce friendships by reaction. Writers who had hitherto seemed hardly friendly to me suddenly ranged themselves at my side because I had been ignobly attacked. Young men with more radical sympathies than mine, but of great talent, who had hitherto ignored me, expressed their sympathy: 'And so,' wrote Jean Prévost, the socialist, 'the most evident professional conscientiousness, the most perfect honesty of judgment do not make a writer secure from calumny.' This defence gave me more pleasure than the attack had given me pain. The appearance of my next book, which was a novel, *Climats*, was greeted by all the critics with a cordiality and a unanimous warmth that reconciled me to life.

The story of this book was strange, for I had produced it in spite of myself. The *Revue de Paris* had asked me for a story of four or five thousand words, and it occurred to me to recount in disguised form an adventure to which I had been by accident a witness. One of my friends while in Morocco had had a cardiac symptom and a doctor had brutally announced that the sick man had only a few hours more to live. Feeling himself condemned to death, he had summoned some of his intimate friends about his bed and had told them that he did not wish to die without leaving a true account of his life. Thereupon he had launched into a long public confession after the fashion of Russian novels. Emotion. Tears. Farewells. Then the vain wait for death. Death did not come, and the unfortunate man had to begin to live again among friends who now knew all about him and who henceforth refused to accept him as the Personage he had played all his life. I called the story *La Nuit marocaine*, or *Mort et résurrection de Philippe*. Philippe's confession was the story of his love for three successive women and the harm he had done to all three of them because of his weaknesses.

When Simone had copied the story and I had reread it, I observed that two of the three women (the first and the third) were very much alive, but the middle one, Jenny Sorbier, an actress, was completely unreal. The Moroccan setting of the beginning and the epilogue had not turned out very well either. By abolishing it, together with Jenny Sorbier, there remained the framework of a novel. Almost unconsciously I began to develop it and it 'came' with extraordinary ease. Was it because it was close to my life? Actually it was rather far removed, and those who read both *Climats* and the present account will see that in many points the divergence is great. Laymen ignorant of the alchemy of the novel look for an exact parallelism between the life and the work. It never exists. But I was able to nourish my imaginary characters on real emotions, hence the ease of composition.

In my first version of *Climats* Philippe Marcenat, after the death of Odile, made up his mind to take measures against romantic love by entering upon a conventional marriage. He married his own cousin Renée Marcenat, a mature young woman of sound character but no beauty. When I reread the book, however, I found strange discords. My Philippe of the first part who had found in Odile the incarnate Sylph of his dreams could not have agreed to the sensible marriage I planned to impose upon him. To induce Philippe to remarry it was necessary to give him the illusion of a Sylph lost and found again, to put him in the presence of a woman close enough to 'his type' for him honestly to believe that it was the reincarnation of Odile. Isabelle was born of the impossibility I encountered of making Philippe marry

[167]

Renée, and Isabelle in essence is Philippe himself transmuted into a woman, just as Stendhal's Lamiel is the female counterpart of Julien Sorel. What Isabelle brings to Philippe is less the image of Odile than the reflection of his own youth.

When this new version was finished I realized that the first part was moving; the second, painful. Why? Because in the first part the hero kept saying: 'I am in love and am not loved in return'; in the second: 'I am loved, I do not love,' which seemed insupportably fatuous. I decided to recast the second half of the book and to turn it into a confession by Isabelle. It was thus, and not by deliberate design, that *Climats* acquired that appearance of a diptych which some have praised for its originality and others criticized for its artificial symmetry. *Climats* is, of all my books, the one that has had the greatest number of readers, not in the Anglo-Saxon countries but in France, in Germany, in Italy, in Spain, in Poland, in Latin America and now in the U.S.S.R. Is this fair? And is the novel a true picture of love? 'I leave the decision to a lover and make no judgment myself.'

I finished *Climats* at Shalford Park in Surrey where we had spent the summer. In the spring of that year (1928) I had gone to Cambridge to deliver the Clark Lectures, an annual series of literary talks, which had been given in the preceding year by E. M. Forster and were given the year following by Desmond MacCarthy. Forster had chosen for his subject *Aspects of the Novel*; I chose *Aspects of Biography*, and I tried to give some idea of the biographer's technique. The series lasted for six weeks and during that time the lecturer lived in the Harcourt Rooms in Trinity College, imposing chambers, heavy with history, and took his meals at the High Table in the Hall beside the Master of Trinity who was the great physicist Sir Joseph Thomson.

'Why,' I asked him one day, 'does England produce so many illustrious scientists?'

'Because we hardly teach science at all in our schools,' he replied. 'Over here the minds that come to physics arrive in the laboratory with a freshness untarnished by any routine.'

I liked Cambridge very much, the ancient colleges of grey stone scattered along the river, the tender greensward of the banks, the willow trees leaning over the Cam, the old bridges beneath which passed the students' punts, and the room centuries old in which I spoke beneath the jovial but stern eye of Henry the Eighth painted by Holbein.

Besides Sir Joseph, two other famous professors attended my lectures: the poet Housman and the historian Trevelyan. It was the latter who said to me one day when I had been talking about Lytton Strachey:

'The most important event in the history of English biography in the twentieth century is not the portrait of Queen Victoria by Strachey, it is the conquest of Strachey by Queen Victoria.'

Trinity College where I was living had been Byron's college, and I often went to the little pool at a bend in the river into which he loved to dive and cling to a rotten log on the bottom. I was gathering notes at that time to write a life of Byron. In *Ariel* I had sketched his portrait but I was not pleased with it. It seemed to me that I had been somewhat unjust to Byron and that perhaps his apparent cynicism was more generous than the sensual idealism of Shelley. His correspondence, which I had annotated carefully, charmed me by its brusque and vigorous way of juxtaposing naked facts, just as certain painters juxtapose pure colours. In the course of the summer I made a pilgrimage to Harrow where I saw Byron's name carved by him in the woodwork, the tomb of Peachey to which he used to come limping in order to meditate there, and the rosebush planted above the ashes of his daughter Allegra. Then I went to the far north of England to visit Newstead Abbey, Byron's family seat. The monks' church was in ruins, the residential buildings, imposing and noble; seeing these Gothic arches, these cloisters, these forests and this lake, one could understand the feelings of the small boy who, after the meanness of Aberdeen, suddenly found himself lord and master of this magnificent estate. Rarely have I seen clearer proof of the necessity for a biographer to see with his own eyes the surroundings in which his heroes have lived. Newstead gave me the key to Byron's childhood: what the poet's enemies were later to call snobbery was the tumultuous surprise of the little Byron of Aberdeen faced by Lord Byron of Newstead.

At Annesley Hall, not far from Newstead, there still lived descendants of Mary Chaworth who had been Byron's first love. I asked to see the stairs, at the foot of which he had heard the girl say: 'How could I be interested in that lame boy?' and the door he had riddled with bullets when he practised pistol shooting. The owners of Annesley, Mr. and Mrs. Musters, did not know much about their ancestress. This was not the case with Lady Lovelace, widow of Byron's grandson, who guarded the family papers with vigilant piety. I knew that she owned a hundred precious documents and among them the Journal of Lady Byron which contained the answer to the difficult question of incest. It was impossible to write the book without having access to all these texts, the only authentic ones. Thanks to a mutual friend, Lady George Hamilton, I obtained permission to read them and went to spend two days at Ockham Park which was the manor house of Lady Lovelace. There, through whole nights, by the light of two candles I passionately deciphered an extraordinary document, the memoirs of a puritan who had been bold to the point of brazenness; they were so filled with life that I believed I could see Byron walking with jerky steps and crying aloud between those walls of grey stone.

When I returned to London I went to see old Lord Ernle who (under his original name of Prothero) had published Byron's correspondence.

'I am much embarrassed, Lord Ernle,' I said. 'You have always maintained that incest did not take place between Byron and Augusta. I have proof to the contrary and I have serious scruples in contradicting you . . . What am I to do?'

He laughed gaily:

'What are you to do? That's very simple. If incest took place, say so . . . As for me, I am almost eighty years old and at my age I am certainly not going to alter my opinion.'

To complete my Byronian researches I had to make Childe Harold's pilgrimage. During the years 1928–1930 this was an agreeable excuse for long trips across Europe. My wife accompanied me; we went from the charming women of Austria to the beautiful women of Greece, from the marshy pine forests of Ravenna to the palaces of Venice, from the Acropolis to the lagoons of Missolonghi. We little thought that ten years later this hospitable and diversified Europe was to become the domain of a single tenant, sown with hatred and misery.

When I returned, Harold Nicolson, author of the excellent book *Byron: the Last Phase*, entrusted me with a precious document—Tom Moore's book about Byron annotated by his best friend Hobhouse; and Lady Lovelace with numerous letters, among them those by Byron's father which were surprising by reason of the quality of style, reminiscent of that of the poet, and also for the very exact idea they gave of the pair who had been Byron's parents. Rarely has a biographer had at his disposal so many unpublished documents. Perhaps the book suffered from this, artistically speaking. I did not want to sacrifice anything. Hence the length of the work, which is a defect. But I think the picture of Byron is true.

Some critics accused me of having written, not a living biography like that of Disraeli, but a thesis for the Sorbonne. I have not reread the book for a long time and I myself no longer know its worth. Be that as it may, so far as I was concerned, it produced one useful result: it killed the myth of romanticized biography. Good or bad, this *Byron* represented an enormous amount of work. 'It must not be forgotten,' wrote the English critic Desmond MacCarthy, 'that this book is the most serious and most complete work we have on Byron.' This biography set the seal on my reconciliation with the scholars. Entrenched behind formidable parapets of notes and references I could henceforth await them without fear. They came, not as foes, but as friends. There, as elsewhere, preparedness assured peace.

I corrected the last proofs of *Byron* at Villard-de-Lans in the Alps at Christmas time, 1929. We had gone there to join my wife's daughter Françoise who, on doctor's orders, was obliged to live in the mountains. In the story of Byron there had been a person who had touched me very much; this was Allegra, daughter of Byron and Claire, who died alone and miserable in an Italian convent. To our great sorrow, for we loved her tenderly, little Françoise had somewhat the fate of Allegra. At an early age she had suffered from the results of being born in a broken home. She would have liked to grow up in the company of happy parents and to play with brothers and sisters. When she saw normal families she experienced a vague feeling of inferiority.

Our marriage filled her with joy.

'The good Lord is going to send me a big sister, two little brothers and a papa,' she announced proudly to the children in the Parc Monceau.

But she was not able to enjoy this new family for long. She had suffered from typhoid fever with hepatic complications and soon the doctors diagnosed a sclerosis of the liver. They did not conceal from us the extreme gravity of this disease. Only a sojourn at high altitude offered some small hope. And so Françoise spent the last two years of her life in the mountains and far from us. She did not suffer, but her extreme weakness and her little waxen face filled us with pity. Violent games were forbidden, for she was still in danger of a haemorrhage which might prove fatal. She read from morning till night and, at nine years of age, kept a diary. 'If God were really so powerful,' she wrote, 'there would not be any unhappy people . . . I have done nothing wrong; why am I being punished? Why have they sent me away from home where I was so happy with my brothers?' When her nurse read *Oliver Twist* aloud to her, she said: 'I do not understand everything but it is beautiful.'

The most harrowing thing was that, not knowing she was seriously ill, she believed herself unjustly exiled by us. Her grandmother, who adored her, made her long visits; we all went there as often as we could. But she suffered from that life and her mother suffered as well.

Finally on this Christmas in 1929 we had the feeling of having solved this insoluble problem. Françoise, touchingly delighted to see Gérald and Olivier again, was for some days exuberant with joy. I spent much time with the children and I wrote a story for them, *Patapoufs et Filifers*. This reunion of a family that was too often separated gave us great pleasure.

Alas, when Twelfth Night came we had to leave the mountains. Gérald and Olivier were to return to the Lycée Pasteur at Neuilly and I had engagements to fulfil. In despair Françoise saw the beautiful myth of her family vanish once more. She clung to her mother's coat:

'Stay, *Maman*, stay!'

Then she grew serious and brave. While we got into the car she stood stoically on the hotel steps. I looked at her white dress, her thin little arms and her eyes that were so intelligent and so tender, and I admired her silent courage. Poor Françoise! In her were the qualities of a charming and heroic woman which she was destined never to become.

We had barely returned to Paris when my wife had to undergo an operation. I had just left the hospital where I had spent two hours at her bedside when the doctor called me by telephone from Villard-de-Lans: Françoise had had a severe haemorrhage; she had lost consciousness. An oxygen tent and camphorated oil had been of no avail; there was no more hope. Toward eleven o'clock that evening he called me again to say that Françoise was dead. When they had put her to bed she had said:

'I want the photograph of my brothers.'

The nurse had given her a little snapshot of Gérald and Olivier both laughing, dressed in grey coats and shorts. Then the oxygen had produced a sort of intoxication and she had died without suffering.

One can imagine how painful and difficult it was to communicate this frightful news to Simone who had not yet recovered from the shock of the operation. Naturally she was too weak to travel. I went alone to the burial, which took place in Périgord. With my mother-in-law and father-in-law I escorted the little coffin to the tiny church where the Abbé Mugnier had married us. The countryside, which I remembered bathed in sunlight and laden with the harvest, was wrapped in thick and icy fog. In the little village cemetery the tenant farmers filed past the opening of the great vault where reposed four generations. I thought of the little girl in the white dress whom I had seen for the last time standing on the snow-covered steps, bravely trying to smile.

So many losses and misfortunes in the space of a few years had profoundly altered my outlook on life. I have shown how the too easy successes of my early years, followed by authority over a huge factory, had made me dangerously sure of myself. Until I was thirty years old I had not known failure in any sphere. For this reason I suffered from serious gaps in my spiritual education and a surprising lack of maturity. 'The feeling of awe is the best part of man.' I had lived too long unacquainted with awe. But the war, by suddenly reducing me to the lowest rank and seizing me away from all I loved, through anguish, illness and death, had given me an apprenticeship in sorrow. It was also an apprenticeship in patience and pity.

18

The Twilight of the Gods

In the course of my first trip to America I had greatly loved Princeton University, which I found not very unlike Oxford and Cambridge. No doubt the Gothic was authentic only in England, but Princeton could show very graceful eighteenth-century buildings, fine old lawns and a preceptorial system that recalled the Oxonian tutors. I had formed friendships: President Hibben, Dean Gauss; a young professor, Percy Chapman, one of the most cultivated Americans I have ever met; a charming Frenchman, Maurice Coindreau, were among them. When I received a letter from President Hibben in 1930 announcing the endowment of a new chair in French to be called the Meredith Howland Pyle chair, in memory of a Princeton student killed in the war, and asking if I would be the first incumbent, I accepted with joy. In my youth it had been my ambition to teach; in maturity, I was to have the opportunity; I was delighted.

As it was to be a long stay, Simone accompanied me and we decided to bring with us Emilie and Gaston Wolff, a young French Alsatian couple who had been in our home for a number of years and whose devotion and intelligence made them our friends. The university rented us a house that belonged to a professor who was taking his 'sabbatical year', an American custom which consists in giving professors every seven years an entire year's vacation, thus allowing them to read, to refurbish and enrich their minds and to escape from routine. It was a frame house, surrounded by maples and sycamores which the American autumn soon clothed in brilliant reds and yellows. Our lawn adjoined those of our neighbours; this country ignores the enclosures that are so dear to ours. Squirrels played beneath our windows. Our street, where only professors lived, was silent and provincial. My wife and I have retained limpid memories of Princeton. We found a full and tranquil happiness there which neither Neuilly, the country, nor our hectic trips had ever been able to give us because we had everywhere encountered excitement, professional duties or ties with the past. In that house in Broadmead we were alone together, bound to the world by no other tie than the work we had in common and that we both loved. Nothing spoiled these happy hours. My colleagues were courteous, helpful and agreeable companions, but they did not claim the confidential intimacy of our European friends. Almost every day we had at least one meal alone together.

'At last!' Simone said. 'I am having my wedding trip.'

In Paris those who did not know her well had believed she was infatuated with social life, formal dinners and receptions at the embassies, and she had played the role expected of her. Today I can very well understand the mechanism that moved her. Conscientious and hard-working, she wanted above all to fulfil her duties, whether toward God, toward her work, toward me, or toward the world and society. Her politeness was a form of devotion. 'To send regrets' after having accepted an invitation seemed to her a sin that only mourning or an illness could excuse. Not to reply to a letter, not to send congratulations or condolences at the proper time, these in her eyes were grave faults. Later on, when she had become a part of the political life of a rural community, she was to devote to public affairs the same effective interest that she formerly gave to social relations and the same scrupulousness, going to the same trouble for a municipal councillor as for a King. In Princeton she took pleasure in living a life of complete simplicity, doing her own marketing, going to the butcher and to the confectioner and serving tea to the students. In addition, eight hours of typing a day.

'I have never been so happy,' she said to me in rapture.

We began a new life, and it was the life both of us had always longed for.

My course was called: 'The French Novel from *La Princesse de Clèves* to *A la Recherche du temps perdu*. Fifty students had been admitted after an examination which had shown that their knowledge of French was adequate. Twice a week I gave a public lecture. On the other days students came to my house in groups of seven or eight, sat on the floor, smoked cigarettes and discussed with me the books of Balzac or Stendhal, of Flaubert or Anatole France that I had asked them to read. These conversations were pleasant, free and without strain. We talked about literary technique but also about history, morals and philosophy. I found a wholly new pleasure in being intimately associated with the life of the young and in becoming once more a student myself.

At the end of the semester President Hibben said to me: 'Your course has been a success; your students have made notable progress; would you like to stay with us and occupy this chair permanently? You would have to spend eight months of the year in the United States but you would have four months of vacation in France.'

I was sorely tempted, asked for time to discuss it with my wife and we hesitated a long while. We had been incredibly happy in Princeton. Moreover we realized that the Old World was heading toward ship-wreck and that it would be wise to provide a refuge for ourselves else-where. But to accept meant to leave France, to lose touch with our friends, to bring up our children in a foreign land. We believed we had no right to make that decision. I refused. Was it a mistake? It seems to me if I had said yes that day my life would have been much easier. Would it have been as full and as exciting? No one will ever know and I have formed the habit of considering that 'what did not take place was, so far as I am concerned, absolutely impossible.'

I returned from the United States certain that there was a duty to be discharged by a French writer who could speak English, which was to maintain, on every opportunity offered, a spiritual bond between France and America. This was certainly no reason to neglect my English friends, but at this time France and England were out of sympathy, and perhaps the key to these difficulties lay in Washington. During the war of 1914 when I had talked to the French about the English and to the English about the French I had found sympathetic listeners because their interests were identical. After the war these interests had diverged. France had asked for guaranties of security and, not receiving them, had carried on alone the policy of the Ruhr and that of Eastern alliances. England, frightened by old Napoleonic memories, had thereupon fallen back on an outmoded doctrine, that of the balance of power. Through fear of too strong a France she had favoured the rearmament of Ger-many. I had done my best to point out, in articles and in lectures, the danger of a rupture and even of a permanent disagreement between the two powers interested in maintaining the peace of Europe. At Chatham I delivered a lecture on England's foreign policy, a lecture that, alas, proved prophetic. But I sensed in each of the two countries a profound distrust of the other.

'We English,' Lord Tyrrell, the new ambassador to Paris, said to me, 'made two mistakes after the war: we thought that the French, because they had been victorious, had become Germans; and we thought that the Germans, because they had been defeated, had become Englishmen.'

I had met Lord Tyrrell (then Sir William Tyrrell) in London at the home of Lady Colefax. He was an Irish Catholic and less impermeable to French reactions than are many English Protestants. He had directed the Foreign Office for a long time as Permanent Secretary and had been appointed himself as ambassador to Paris. Subtle, witty and adroit, he was successful there in so far as that was possible. He did me the honour of inviting me to the first intimate dinner he gave. It was a strange occasion. Ramsay MacDonald, the Labour leader, was about to come into power, and Lord Tyrrell thought it would be useful to bring him into contact with some of the leaders of the French Left. So he had invited the two Sarraut brothers, Painlevé and Léon Blum. But since Ramsay MacDonald knew no French, the rest of the party was made up of bilingual Frenchmen and Englishmen who were to serve as interpreters. Hence my presence and, if my memory is accurate, that of André Siegfried.

As a matter of fact, one of the greatest dangers to Franco–English relations came from these meetings between statesmen who could not understand one another. France liked precise engagements. The English had a horror of them. Poincaré had irritated the English by his inflexibility. Curzon exasperated the French by his arrogance. The English loved Herriot because they found him like the traditional Frenchman of their imagination and also because he was very well educated and talked to them about their history. The French were fond of Austen Chamberlain because he had said: 'I love France like a mistress,' but that imprudent sentence cost him his ministry. Briand and Austen Chamberlain had been great friends. Both were men of good will; both had collided with the passions of their countries and had in the end been beaten. Political wisdom seldom finds its rewards in this world.

It has been said that ingratitude is the mark of strong nations, but that is false. Postwar France (I mean official France) was not strong but she was ungrateful. Who praised Briand for having tried to maintain the peace? Who gave a thought to Poincaré, that great servant of his country, at the time when he was dying, poor and paralysed, tenderly watched over by his wife in a villa in the Midi? Who rendered thanks to Lyautey who had given France an empire? No one save a small band of faithful friends to which I was proud to belong. I used to go sometimes and spend several days at his home at Thorey in Lorraine. The marshal's deafness made conversation difficult. But I loved to hear him tell of the great things he had done or to see him in his garden laying out a path with the same pains that he had formerly given to planning a city or mapping the course of a railroad.

Little by little, as a result of listening to him, the idea dawned upon me that there could be no healthier reading for the bewildered youth of France than a life of Lyautey. I was very familiar with it. He had given me a memoir about his youth which he had written himself with distinction, for he had the style of a gentleman, in the grand tradition of France. For the rest of his life I had his letters, his stories and many witnesses. The only obstacle was the difficulty I should encounter in writing for the first time a biography of a living man. Would the marshal respect a writer's liberty? I believed he would and I was right. From the moment I first spoke to him about this project he became fired with enthusiasm and gave me all his documents. When I started to write, he offered to read each chapter and for two years was a most active and, on the whole, most reasonable collaborator. He asked me to suppress certain anecdotes; they were of no importance. He made me work at hours which were not natural to me, for he hardly slept at all. But he helped me generously.

Up to that time many Frenchmen had not known what a great figure Lyautey was. The book earned him new admirers. 'You have invented me,' he wrote. That was only a witticism, but it showed that he was pleased. After that I was often asked to go and speak about him to groups of young people. It became the bond in common between me and Robert Garric's *Equipes sociales*, a movement of young intellectuals who were missionaries of culture among the French people, no longer in the too oratorical form of the People's Universities, but in the more human fashion of little circles of ten or twelve members which reminded me of my 'preceptorials' in Princeton. 'Not a day passes,' Lyautey wrote me again, 'when I do not receive from some stranger a letter that I owe to you.' If by this book I helped, however little, however inadequately, in surrounding his retirement with the thanks and the glory he had so amply earned, there is no work of which I am prouder.

Often he was sad. He had sudden lapses of memory which were frightening to his friends and which they tried conscientiously to hide from him. One evening when I was alone with him in his study in the Rue Bonaparte, he suddenly fell into a terrifying state of speechlessness and rigidity. I dared not say anything for fear of provoking an attack and I stayed close by, affectionately watching over him, for a period that seemed very long. Suddenly he looked at me and said:

'You are Poeymirau, aren't you?'

General Poeymirau had been one of his adjutants in Morocco twenty years earlier. I did not contradict him, and little by little he emerged from his dream. One day I heard the Duchess of York, later Queen of England, very charmingly draw him out of a similar reverie. It was at the Colonial Exhibition of 1931 over which he had presided with his customary skill. The Duke and Duchess of York had come to see it. He had taken them walking from the Pagoda of Ankor to the Algerian village and from Tahiti to Djibuti, and then had given them tea on the shore of the lake. Little tables for three had been set up. The marshal, tired by this long walk, appeared sombre. He invited the duchess to sit down at his table and then asked:

'To whom does your Royal Highness wish to give the honour of occupying the third place?'

The duchess who knew me and had asked me to speak for her charities in London, happened to notice me in the crowd.

'Mr. Maurois,' she said.

And so I was summoned, feeling much embarrassment at being chosen. The young princess addressed several remarks to me, and then turning to the marshal:

'*Monsieur le Maréchal*,' she said, 'you are so powerful, you created the beautiful country of Morocco and you have made this fine exhibition, would you do something for me?'

'For you, Madame?' Lyautey said in surprise. 'But what can I do for your Royal Highness?'

'Why this,' she said. 'The sun is in my eyes, *Monsieur le Maréchal*. Will you make it disappear?'

The marshal was looking at her in stupefaction when suddenly the sun went behind a cloud.

'Thank you, *Monsieur le Maréchal*,' said the duchess with perfect equanimity. 'I knew that you could do anything.'

He smiled and relaxed. In lowered voice the duchess said to me:

'I saw the cloud coming . . . '

After the conclusion of the Colonial Exhibition he suffered from the lack of an outlet for his energy which remained intact and young. For the man of action, as for Don Juan, old age is terrible. Born to create and to command, in the little Lorraine village of Thorey he was like the sovereign of a tiny kingdom.

'But good Lord,' he said to me, 'can't they see I am champing at the bit with impatience? Can't I still serve? Won't they give me some work to do? . . . No! . . . They think I am no longer good for anything . . . I have been written off as dead.'

'*Monsieur le Maréchal*, they can't leave a man like you inactive . . . The government will find something.'

'*Will find*, my friend! . . . *Will find!* . . . That's all very well, but I am almost eighty years old . . . If I am to make a career it's time for me to get started.'

When he died in 1934 I was in England. I returned immediately and rushed to Thorey, too late to attend his funeral. But he remains present among us and there are some of us Frenchmen on the earth who, in our days of despair and loneliness, feel ourselves united in hope by the memory of Lyautey.

19

My Dear Time's Waste

For a writer, the conduct of life is not easy. Should he encounter too many worldly disappointments, then he runs the risk of seeing his spirits dampened by anxiety and his heart invaded by bitterness. Should success make him a person of consequence, then social life engulfs him and his working hours are consumed by time-wasters. Celebrity, in a sociable country like France, creates duties he can hardly escape. The wisest deny themselves to the public; the others with great difficulty preserve a few months each year, and the best part of their lives is taken up with relatively futile tasks which they have not sought but have had the weakness to accept.

In point of fact I am unfair to myself in speaking only of futile tasks. Circumstance, my books and my friendships have made me the advocate and incarnation of a close *entente* between France, England and the United States. The moment a difficulty seemed to be dividing these three countries, the government asked me to write, sometimes in French, sometimes in English, articles designed to clear up the misunderstanding. At every Franco–British celebration, whether literary or sporting in nature, the anniversary of an important writer or the commemoration of some event, I was requested to be present and to deliver a speech. I might have refused? No doubt, but I deeply believed in the necessity of maintaining those always fragile bonds if one wished to save our liberal civilization. Now it is a fact that I was almost the only one to play this role. The time lost from my own work was put at the service of a cause I considered admirable. This justified me but did not solace me.

It was between 1932 and 1939 that I lost the chance to write certain big novels whose shadows I dimly perceived in the waters of my 'fish pond'. I wanted by my example to teach younger writers that they would only find salvation in solitude. 'O solitude,' Barrès had said, 'you alone have not debased me.' During those seven years I had too often agreed to become a sort of diplomat *in partibus.*

One winter we spent three months in Egypt because I had promised to give a series of lectures at the French Lycée in Alexandria. Egypt was beautiful and worth seeing; it was a good thing to be of help to the people there, whether religious or laymen, who were defenders of our culture; we enjoyed visiting the tombs of Sakkara and the mosque-citadel of Cairo, but day after day it was necessary to give talks, receive journalists and see various officials, French, English, Egyptian, Syrian, Coptic and Jewish. O vanity of vanities! In the spring we left for Malta because in a moment of weakness I had promised to write a little book about the island. The English critic Desmond MacCarthy gave us a letter of introduction to his brother-in-law Admiral Sir William Fisher, Commander-in-Chief of the British fleet in the Mediterranean, a great sailor and a great gentleman; suddenly we found ourselves guests of honour who went from party to party and from dockyard to cruiser.

Then, almost as soon as we had returned from our spring trip, we left for England where we spent part of the summer. Colonel Stirling and his wife, English friends of ours gifted with infallible taste, selected enchanting places for us to stay. It was necessary that our dwellings should be near London because I was working in the libraries there on my *Histoire d'Angleterre* which Fayard had commissioned. One year we rented Ormeley Lodge on Ham Common, a red brick house which bore, carved in an architrave of white stone as well as in many details of the woodwork, the three plumes of the Prince of Wales, for it had been given by the Regent to his morganatic wife, Maria Fitzherbert. From our garden we could see Richmond Park with its fine oaks and its copses stocked with deer.

'Ah!' we said. 'How wonderful it would be to live in Richmond Park!' But the park contained only three or four houses which belonged to the Crown. In 1934 the invaluable Stirling leased us one of them, Pembroke Lodge in which Lord Russell had lived at the time of the Reform Bill. In our drawing room a Cabinet Meeting had declared the Crimean War; from a hillock in the rose garden Henry VIII had seen the signal which announced the execution of Anne Boleyn; on our lawn was a little monument erected by Lord Russell to commemorate 'fifty years of conjugal happiness'. At night the whole of Richmond Park was ours and there we met, beneath the great trees, motionless and startled deer whose eyes gleamed in the shadows.

It was from Pembroke Lodge that I went one fine summer day to receive the degree of Doctor of Letters *honoris causa* at Oxford. Lord Halifax, Chancellor of the University, had chosen my name together with that of Lord Tyrrell, Sir Samuel Hoare, Arthur Henderson and Sir Maurice Hankey. In a long robe of black velvet embroidered in gold, his train carried by his son dressed as a page, he nobly presided over the ceremony in the Sheldonian Theatre. At the moment when each new doctor was presented to the assembly brief notices in Latin were read by the public orator. He had translated *Les Silences du Colonel Bramble* as '*Vepris illius, tribuni militum silentia.*' Arthur Henderson, who was called 'Uncle Arthur' by the English workmen, had become: '*Plebi laboriosae quasi avunculus.*' These learned jokes amused the English. For my part, as I bent down before Lord Halifax to receive the investiture, I was thinking of her who, twenty-four years before, had for the first time guided me so graciously and gaily among the grey stones of Oxford.

During this long sojourn we acquired many new friends and cemented old friendships. In Sir Robert Vansittart, who was now Permanent Under Secretary of State at the Foreign Office, I had finally found an Englishman who understood the danger of German rearmament and Great Britain's need to maintain an alliance with France. In his fairyland of a garden at Denham I was present at conversations between him and Charles Corbin, French Ambassador in London. Both took a clear-headed view of the situation; both were terrified by the blindness of the political leaders in the two countries. Lady Vansittart, standing on the bank of a pond dotted with waterlilies and surrounded by a white cloud of flowering bushes, looked like a Shakespearean heroine.

At Chevening Park, home of Lord Stanhope, we again met Kipling, who loved to lie on the grass and question the young men around him about the army and the navy. An immense park surrounded this beautiful house; in crossing it one came first to the Realm of the Sheep, then that of the Deer. Lord Stanhope, who was a descendant both of Pitt and of Lord Chesterfield, had a splendid library.

'What would you like to do this afternoon?' he asked me. 'Would you like to read the unpublished letters of Voltaire? Of Rousseau? Or the originals of Lord Chesterfield's letters?'

The Spencers lived at Althorp in a house full of memories of Marlborough. There we admired the family portraits painted in each generation by the best painters of the time.

'And whom have you asked to paint *your* portrait?'

'Augustus John.'

My old friends the Jenners were now living in Bath; I went there to see them and came to know one of the most charming cities in the world.

More and more the grace of England intoxicated me. Ah! how noble and charming this country was, and how I wished I could bind it more closely to my own. But what could I do and what were my hapless lectures, my poor articles, against the forces that Vansittart himself, powerful though he was, could not disarm?

After long hesitation on my part we had left, in 1931, the apartment in the Rue Borghèse in Neuilly, the haunt of beautiful and melancholy memories. My wife on several occasions had suggested houses which I did not like. Finally I had been seduced, not by a lodging but by an address. The new apartment was situated on the Boulevard Maurice Barrès; it was very close to the white house that had belonged to the writer and where his son Philippe now lived. Our windows afforded a sweeping view over the Bois de Boulogne and over Paris; as far as the eye could see stretched green waves of trees; to the left one saw the Arc de Triomphe always bathed in mist, grey or golden according to the weather; to the right, Mont Valérien was like one of the hills of Florence crowned by cypress trees. Soon I was very much attached to this new dwelling. I loved our white walls, our huge mahogany book-cases, which reminded me of my first house, and our pictures which were not numerous but had been lovingly selected (Marquet, Kisling, Boudin, Léger). The decorations were simple, a little bare and severe, but harmonious. We looked forward with pleasure to spending the rest of our lives there.

I had bought an apartment for my mother near ours so that she could spend the winters in Paris. As formerly, the five sisters dressed in black would meet every afternoon in the Rue de Tocqueville around the armchair of my grandmother, who was ninety years old and who remained as lively in mind, as curious about new books and as logical as ever. Simone, like Janine before her, had been surprised at first by these long séances in which gentle black-clothed priestesses intoned, as versicle and responsory, interspersed with religious silences, the daily catalogue of all the deaths, births, cases of scarlatina and chicken-pox, degrees, marriages, appendectomies and promotions in the Family.

But with her prodigious memory she soon became as learned in the genealogical and pathological mysteries of the clan as the Vestals themselves. With an indulgent and affectionate curiosity she breathed this strange, heavy and silent atmosphere which reminded her of the novels of the Brontë sisters.

Unhappily in Paris as in London 'duties'—articles, lectures, prefaces and talks—devoured my time. The only months of uninterrupted work were those I spent at Essendiéras. Périgord had captivated me and had taught me a good deal. In the army, and later at the mill, I had observed the Norman middle class and the workmen; at La Saussaye I had come to know the well-to-do farmers. In Périgord I had an opportunity of studying the gentry, descendants of the ancient landed aristocracy, a class that played a more important part in the life of France than the people of Paris, London and Washington knew, for it furnished the officers for the armies and the diplomats for the Quai d'Orsay; and on the other hand, I saw the tenants who were hardworking, economical, distrustful toward the Church and the Château, desirous of dividing up large estates and protecting small ones, socialists by fits and starts, radicals by inclination, conservatives by heredity and patriots to the core, because that was the way it was. There I recognized, in listening to the stories of political quarrels, the implacable division among Frenchmen and also as I looked at the Monument to the Dead, bearing more names than there were houses in the village, the solid unity of France always ready to arise again in the face of the enemy. Neither novelist nor historian can understand France at all unless he has an observation post in Paris *and* in the provinces. My knowledge of my country now rested upon Normandy and upon Périgord. Two strong pillars.

Our family life at Essendiéras was studious and monotonous. At eight o'clock each morning I would sit down to work in front of a window that opened on a wide horizon of hills, streams, villages and woods. No sound but the purring of the threshing machine, the humming of the wasps desirous of my flowers, the distant murmur of the Loue rushing over the stones of the valley and the clicking of the typewriter at which Simone in the next room was copying the chapter written the day before. At eleven o'clock I would join her and we would take the Tour of the Two Paths, the classic walk of Essendiéras, leaving by way of the oaks and returning by way of the chestnuts, the itinerary that Simone as a child had followed disguised as the forest in *Macbeth*. At La Guichardie farm we would stop to talk to the tenants about their children and their crops. In the fields or in one of the pastures the overseer Ménicot, a veteran of the wars and an excellent farmer, whose son was a great friend of my sons, would be superintending the work of harvesting, hay making or second planting, according to the season. We would confer with him about the small affairs of the estate.

On our return we would find a typical Périgord luncheon, always delicious and the result of careful thought, which was enlivened by the wit of my mother-in-law and the gaiety of the children. Then Simone and I would go back to work each in our own place. Toward five o'clock we would leave by the Oak Path or the Chestnut Path for a longer walk on which we would sometimes be gone two hours, discussing the progress of the novel. I would tell her about the new chapters. She would approve or criticize my ideas. When it was a question of the heroine she would often foresee better than I could myself what that rebellious spirit was going to demand of us. We got to the point, both of us, where we considered these characters real and, as in the time of *Climats*, they acted independently of me and sometimes contrary to my plans. In *Le Cercle de famille* which was finished at Essendiéras during the summer of 1931, I did not wish Denise Herpain to become the mistress of Jacques Pelletot before their marriage. But one day as we were walking along the Oak Path I had to confess the indiscretion they had just committed;

'I did all I could to prevent it . . . But he was a soldier and wounded; he was going away again; she had great need of sacrifice . . . In short what could you expect? There it is!'

'What will Monsieur Doumic think?' my wife asked.

The novel *Le Cercle de famille* was, in fact, intended for the *Revue des deux-mondes*. When it was finished, I was a little anxious about the impression that the sins of my heroine might produce on Monsieur Doumic and I read the beginning of my book to his son-in-law, my very dear friend, Louis Gillet. He encouraged me and I took the manuscript to Monsieur Doumic. A week later the latter summoned me and, in friendly sternness, received me with his legs wrapped up in a blanket.

'I am very sorry,' he said. 'I am even upset . . . I definitely wanted a novel by you, but the *Revue* cannot publish this one . . . No, indeed it is not possible. Our subscribers would protest.'

'But why, Monsieur?'

'Why? You ask that? These successive adulteries . . . '

'But, Monsieur, there is hardly one great French novel without adultery . . . *Madame Bovary* . . . *Le Père Goriot* . . . '

'Oh, to be sure, the *Revue* is obliged to admit adultery. But it only admits it when accompanied by remorse. At no moment does your heroine repent of her misdeeds . . . Madame Bovary died of hers.'

And so my novel was rejected. I felt no rancour toward Monsieur Doumic whose character I admired and who, I could not doubt, knew his subscribers better than I did.

The inspiration for *Le Cercle de famille* was a conversation I had with a young woman who described the emotions she had felt as a little girl when she discovered that a man used to come to see her mother without her father's knowledge. Her story was so poignant that I asked her how the incident had turned out. She told me and furnished me with many excellent details, but the actual romance stopped abruptly. I needed a conclusion. And then I remembered another person who might very well represent what Denise Herpain, married and unsatisfactorily married, would become. From a combination of these two characters with certain traits borrowed from other women *Le Cercle de famille* was born. I took pleasure in reviving some of the characters from *Climats* and *Bernard Quesnay*. Then in *L'Instinct du bonheur* which I wrote next, I made a point of establishing connections between the industrial Normandy of my first books and the agricultural Périgord of this. It was not a bad beginning and perhaps if the times had been different and my life more tranquil I might, in a series of novels, have been able to create a fresco of postwar French Society. This was what Alain advised; he, unlike most of the critics, considered me more of a novelist than an essayist. After reading *Climats*, he had written to me:

My dear friend, I refuse to compose a letter about *Climats*. There is too much to say. Having read it twice in quick succession, I have noted first of all that the interest is sustained, that it is absorbing, that, in a word, this is what I call *reading*. As to style, it is perfection; you have completely regained the grace of *Bramble*; and now you must bring a world to life.

There are no sentiments more familiar to me than those in which you involve us. I find tenderness here, which is the obvious thing, but also a fury which should perhaps be less restrained. (Reread the jealous Mosca. 'One must avoid blood,' in the *Chartreuse*.) I do not believe that feelings of this sort are lacking in *Climats*, but perhaps they are too much disguised by an exquisite courtesy. Should a writer be courteous? Our first impulse is to assassinate.

Naturally the second part, in which the woman speaks, was more difficult. But reading straight ahead, I found nothing there to criticize. Nevertheless I like *Quesnay* better, for there work and ownership are combined with feelings; but *Climats*, in its abstraction, is better made, perhaps because in it the feelings are reduced to their essence, something they always demand . . . There was more tragedy in *Quesnay* because it contained more about work and about oblivion. I believe that if you were ruined by a revolution, your labours would be more profound.

This letter gave me pleasure, but it awakened sharp regrets. 'And now,' Alain had said, 'you must bring a world to life.' That was indeed what I hoped to do, but was I armed for such a combat? I was not acquainted with all the aspects of French society as Balzac had been. How much did I know? The Norman industrialists, the farmers of Périgord, in Paris the literary world and the political world. 'If you were to be ruined . . . ' Alain had written. I believed that he was right. Ruined, I would have known Gobseck.

I told myself that for the making of a novelist in the grand style such as Balzac or Dickens, a picaresque life, at least in youth, was a necessity —and I had not had that. Would Victor Hugo have written *Les Misérables* if he had not had as mistress Juliette Drouet, a daughter of the people? Would Balzac have conceived César Birotteau if he had not himself experienced bankruptcy? Too well sheltered, I had been reduced to confidences and conversations as a means of exploring the society of my time. They are not the equivalent of a hard, hand-to-hand struggle with necessity. In art as in love, to reach a conclusion, one must come to close quarters.

Nevertheless I tried to do the best I could with what I had, and that was a fairly abundant provision. *Le Cercle de famille* was my first attempt after *Climats* to follow Alain's advice. I sent him this novel and wrote him with sincere humility that I did not think myself 'able to bring a world to life', as he had wished. He replied in a letter full of praise for the book and full of severity for my scruples. 'I am annoyed,'

Alain said, 'by your doubts about your own value; this is absurd. You have only to believe me on that point; I read only the masters and I cannot be mistaken.' He was not a man to lie. Moreover the critics were unanimous in their praise for *Le Cercle de famille*. Roger Martin du Gard wrote me: 'You have succeeded in what I try in vain to do.' Two novels, one sketched out, the other half written, awaited my own sweet will. One of them was entitled *La Race blonde*, the other *Les Oiseaux de feu*. 'And now,' I thought, 'I'm going to take my chance.'

Events decided otherwise. The political life of Europe was rapidly becoming so disquieting that it was no longer easy to find refuge in the world of fiction. In France Tardieu had been defeated in the election of 1932. We knew him well, for he too had been a frequenter of the Avenue Hoche. He was fond of good living, cultured and cynical, at least in words, for his feelings had their secret hiding place in his heart. He had kidney trouble and the doctors told him that if he went on eating and drinking so well he would never live to be old.

'I'm not concerned about that,' he would say. 'Short and sweet!'

While Tardieu was Premier I accidentally witnessed a tragic scene; the assassination of President Paul Doumer by the mad Russian Gorguloff. Every year a charity bazaar was held in Paris for the benefit of the widows and children of writers killed during the war. Many authors used to go there, together with pretty actresses, to autograph their books, and each year the President of the Republic would honour the gathering by a visit. In 1932 I was there as usual seated behind a table covered with my books; I was signing *Climats* for an old lady when I heard a prolonged uproar. The Chief of State entered. Two faint cracks rang out to which I paid no heed. But running feet, cries, and a sudden silence attracted my attention. I lifted my head and saw the president lying on the ground surrounded by kneeling men.

'What is happening?' I asked.

I left my table to find out. Claude Farrère, President of our Society, had thrown himself in front of Monsieur Doumer and had received a bullet in his arm. A doctor who had been leaning over the body got up saying:

'Messieurs, take off your hats ... The president is dead.'

He was obviously mistaken, for just then the wounded man opened his eyes and moved his lips. The doors of the hall were thrown open. It was Tardieu, wearing a coat with a fur collar and a high hat. I shall never forget the expression of despair and rage on his face.

'*Nom de Dieu de nom de Dieu!* But who did it?' he demanded . . . 'Why?'

Only then did I think of the assassin and saw a big fellow with the appearance of a stupid brute surrounded by policemen. Someone touched me on the shoulder. It was the old lady.

'Well, Monsieur?' she said. 'What about my inscription?'

Because Monsieur Doumer had been killed at a meeting of war correspondents, it was decided that four of them should stand guard over his body at the Elysée while he lay in state. And so I found myself standing at attention with three other comrades near the funeral bier on which the president lay in full dress with the red grand cordon of the Légion d'Honneur diagonally across his breast. The crowd filed past, sorrowful and respectful. As one couple was passing I heard the woman say to her husband, after looking for a long time:

'It is indeed he!'

After the election of 1932 Herriot, who had come to power, made an attempt at the Lausanne Conference to settle the question of reparations which was then poisoning France's relations both with Germany and with England. One morning Jean Giraudoux, who was an attaché in his cabinet, telephoned me:

'Would you like to come to Lausanne?' he asked. 'The Chief of State has authorized me to take you there.'

I accepted and had no cause to regret it, for I saw at very close range how an international conference functions. It was essentially a conflict of prestige between irascible experts whom uninformed but well-intentioned statesmen tried to placate. Herriot, generous and eloquent, rising above clouds of figures, would tell humorous anecdotes about Louis Philippe or discuss music with the Germans. The English delegation, knowing that he had written a *Beethoven,* had prepared themselves brilliantly on this subject, but he held forth on the poetry of jazz and took them by surprise. Ramsay MacDonald was there, accompanied by his daughter Ishbel, the Runcimans and the unfortunate Ralph Wigram who had been stricken by poliomyelitis but courageously continued his work. Every evening Paganon, Minister of the Interior and member of the French delegation, would receive the journalists:

'Today,' he would say, 'it would not be correct to say that we have taken a step forward, no, but it would be equally incorrect to say that we have taken a step backward . . . If you wish to give the public an exact idea of the situation say that, although we cannot indicate any actual change, the atmosphere, the climate (am I right, Monsieur Maurois?) is better . . . No! . . . Say: *imperceptibly* better . . . '

Net result: France gave up the reparations without any settlement of the question of the American debts. The delegates took a last dip in Lake Geneva. Giraudoux who, like his hero Jérôme Bardini, had disappeared for almost the whole conference, reappeared on the last day:

'Giraudoux,' Herriot said to him amiably, 'you are the most detached of attachés.'

20

The Ring of Polycrates

This is not the right place to recount the political life of France from 1932 to 1937. I have told in *Choses nues* about my acquaintance with all the leading figures of that period. What strikes me now, when I reread my notebook, is my intimacy with the men of every party. I talked freely and familiarly to Léon Blum, as I did to Tardieu, to Herriot and to Mandel. The British ambassadors, Sir William Tyrrell and Sir George Clerk, consulted me frequently. It was not my desire to play any role; I played one despite myself—on the margin of great public affairs—the role of conciliator and, as one critic said, of explainer. Having no strong political passions but certain firm convictions, I was able to understand, judge and unify. Almost weekly at our table, influential men who believed they hated one another met and came to feel esteem.

In 1936, at the time of the *Front populaire*, Léon Blum asked me to lend him the proofs of my *Histoire d'Angleterre* which I had just finished, and he talked to me about it with his customary intelligence. The book was published in 1937. I feared the judgment of the professional historians. They were generous. The distinguished English historian H. A. L. Fisher wrote me from Oxford: 'You have indeed rendered a great public service by giving to your countrymen so brilliant and just a picture of our English story. In its balance and proportion as well as in the uniform good sense of its political judgments, your volume seems to me entirely admirable . . .' The French historian Louis Madelin: 'Here, in its amplitude, is the history we have been waiting for and I am filled with amazement! . . . The ease with which you gambol through nineteen centuries appears to an old professional the summit of art.' And Bergson: 'Your history is a philosophy as well, for it is your interpretation of events, always present in the background, that permits you to enclose so many things *in a nutshell*. One understands England better after reading you.' The British prime minister

(Baldwin) and the leader of the Opposition (Attlee) both thanked me.

This game being won, I spent the year 1937 preparing a lecture series on Chateaubriand which I had promised to give the following year at the Société des Conférences and from which I planned to make a book.

My relations with Monsieur Doumic, president of that society, despite his rejection of *Le Cercle de famille*, became little by little very friendly. He had confidence in me because he knew I would do, not always well, but at least as well as I could, whatever I agreed to undertake; I had confidence in him because, again and again, I had found him fair, exacting and courageous. It was the third time he had asked me to give his 'big course' of ten lectures, which formerly he had considered too much for me. In the office of the *Revue* together we had settled upon the subject. He had suggested Shakespeare. I had replied: '*Domine, non sum dignus*,' and I had proposed Chateaubriand who had interested me for a long time. The Abbé Mugnier had been the first to reveal to me the human being in Chateaubriand beneath the theatrical Personage. I had devoted much study to him and I hoped to make him live again.

'I see only one objection,' Monsieur Doumic said, wrapping his legs in his blanket, 'that is, we have already presented a course on Chateaubriand at the Société by Jules Lemaître, but that is not a serious objection because Lemaître, who was excellent on Racine and fairly good on Rousseau, did a Chateaubriand that was unworthy of him ... and of Chateaubriand ... And so—go ahead ... '

Thereupon he added of his own accord that if the course was a success a membership in the Académie Française might be my reward. I thanked him without placing too much faith in what he said, for he had already on several occasions made similar remarks. It was the harmless, amiable and centuries-old custom of the Academicians to dangle this bait in front of their ambitious juniors. In 1925 Barthou had advised me, although I was very young, to present myself as a candidate for the Chair of Anatole France because he wanted a candidate against Léon Bérard.

As a studious child, raised in the shadow of the classics, the Académie had inspired me with the same sentiments and ambitions that the English Parliament inspires in the students of Oxford and Cambridge. To be chosen by one's elders and one's peers to sit in the company to which Corneille and Racine, Voltaire and Victor Hugo, Taine and

Renan had belonged, seemed to me a consummation devoutly to be wished. Later my friends at Pontigny, Gide, Martin du Gard, had inspired me with a profound distrust of any candidacy. Moreover at the time when I received Barthou's letter I had published only a few books which were not of sufficient importance to justify my being chosen. I replied that there were a number of very talented writers who had the indisputable right to be admitted before me, and despite his insistence, I held to my refusal. Eight years later Paul Valéry asked me: 'You or Mauriac?' I replied: 'Mauriac,' and to my great joy François Mauriac, who had many more titles and a much better chance than I, was elected. After Mauriac, many of my friends, Jaloux, Duhamel, Gillet, had been elected to the Académie Française. Then in 1936 Monsieur Doumic for the first time said to me:

'Your turn has come.'

I listened to the Sirens and for some weeks I thought, to my great surprise, that I, although I was neither a marshal nor a cardinal nor dying, was going to be successful in this first candidacy, which would have been contrary to the wise traditions of the institution. But Joseph de Pesquidoux, a good regional writer and an old contributor to the *Revue*, presented himself against me and Monsieur Doumic abandoned me, which immediately spelled my doom. When I next saw him he said to me, stroking his beard:

'Don't complain . . . Victor Hugo had three defeats . . . Besides, out of thirty-one votes you got eleven . . . That's a good trial gallop.'

Such was the traditional consolation.

But it was not the mirage of the Cupola that inspired me with the desire to write a *Chateaubriand*. My hero intrigued me: the women who surrounded him—Pauline de Beaumont, Delphine de Custine, Nathalie de Noailles, Juliette Récamier and Céleste de Chateaubriand herself—were a delight to draw; the epoch was one of the most dramatic in history and permitted me to sketch a picture of France; finally, to live in intimate association with the beautiful *Mémoires d'outre-tombe* was enchanting. I went to Brittany, and from St. Malo to Combourg, from Fougères to Grand-Bé, I tried to become thoroughly acquainted with the scenes in which Chateaubriand had passed his youth. Few writers today have so many faithful followers as he. The Société Chateaubriand helped me and protected me from errors. Countess de Durfort, née Sibylle de Chateaubriand, opened the Combourg archives to me. If my wife and irreplaceable collaborator had not been painfully ill I should have been happy in my work. But all that year was saddened by the dangers to Simone caused by a malady which was ill-defined but terrifying in its ravages.

The final touches on *Chateaubriand* had almost been completed, and with Monsieur Doumic I was searching for a title for the ten lectures, when he was taken ill with pneumonia. For a long time he had seemed to be growing feebler; it was a shock and a sorrow when I learned on December 2 that he was dead.

At this time I often saw Marshal Pétain, who was President of the French Information Centre for the United States, of which I had been named administrator. At the meetings of the Council he was friendly, exacting, punctual and precise. One evening as we were leaving a meeting he said to me:

'Why don't you present yourself as a candidate for Doumic's chair?'

I was astonished.

'I had not thought of it, *Monsieur le Maréchal* . . . And then a second defeat would give me more pain than success would give me pleasure.'

I consulted some of my friends, including Mauriac and Jaloux, who expressed themselves as favourable and confident, then sent off my letter of candidacy. It was addressed to the Permanent Secretary, and one had to weigh each word, for it was read aloud before the Académie and judged by severe critics. Austerity, simplicity, brevity are the rules. Then begins the period of visits. Many candidates retain a poisoned memory of this time. This is not true of me. To pay calls on thirty-nine men who are all, or almost all, very remarkable, some as writers, others as generals, prelates, admirals, scientists, ambassadors, is far from boring. Quite the contrary. Those who intend to vote for you say so, which immediately makes the visit happy and intimate; those who are against you have recourse to various tactics which are amusing to observe and which vary from brutal frankness to complete abstention. If a general talks to you for an hour about Frederick II or an archaeologist about cathedrals, you know that their votes have been promised elsewhere, but you have heard two brilliant lectures delivered to you alone by two eminent authorities, and you have had two lessons in diplomacy. That's not time wasted.

My shortest visit was the one I paid to Marshal Franchet d'Esperey. I knew him and relished his military brusqueness.

'I know what brings you here,' he said. 'You want to belong to the Académie Française ... That's perfectly reasonable ... Only I've made out a table of promotion ... You are Number Two ... Number One is Jérôme Tharaud ... And so if Tharaud presents himself against you I shall vote for him ... If he does not present himself I shall vote for you ... *Au revoir*, my friend.'

Tharaud did not present himself against me; my competitor was Paul Hazard, whose courtesy and perfect honesty guaranteed a chivalrous combat. We emerged from it closer to each other than ever. We had many friends in common so that certain men—such as Admiral Lacaze, Joseph Bédier, Louis Madelin—who would have voted for me against anyone else very loyally told me that they would begin by voting for Hazard. And so I did not count them in the score I was keeping, but even without them it seemed to me that I should have a majority in my favour.

'Don't have any illusions,' old experts like Abel Hermant told me, 'we've seen candidates whose reckoning gave them twenty-seven votes, unconditional promises, and who at the time of balloting received three.'

I followed my fluctuating prospects and the odd last-minute manoeuvres.

Chaumeix, accomplished electioneer, was hostile to me because he wished to present Henri Bernstein. Louis Bertrand, a convert to Nazism after his trip to Germany, carried on a savagely Hitlerian campaign against me.

Bergson, who kept me for more than two hours, said he would have liked to vote for me, but for several years had not been attending meetings of the Académie. He was in fact paralysed by arthritis deformans, and a meeting would have been torture. When I went to see him I knew he took no part in the elections and my visit was a pure matter of form. It turned out to be a delightful experience because of the importance of the subjects he discussed and the beauty of his language. Another memory left with me by that campaign was of the courage of Georges Lecomte, who was very ill and was supposed to enter a hospital but put off the day of the operation, against the advice of his doctors, in order to be able to vote for me. There is an academic heroism.

The day of the election, Thursday June 23, 1938, I went for a walk in the Bois with my three children. Simone, who was passionately interested in my success, had asked a friend to telephone her the results of the balloting and waited anxiously beside the instrument. The sky was clear, the air mild and our walk was delightful. We talked gaily of a thousand things and almost forgot the hour. At the exact moment of our return the telephone rang. It was a reporter:

'Please get off the line, Monsieur,' Simone said in exasperation. 'I am expecting an important communication.'

'Certainly, Madame,' he replied. 'I simply wanted to tell you that your husband has been elected to the Académie Française.'

My wife emitted a cry of joy and dropped the receiver. The noise attracted our attention. It was a happy moment. Ten minutes later the first friends arrived. The election had been quick and had been completed on the second ballot by nineteen to thirteen. I was, as Disraeli said, 'at the top of the greasy pole'.

That evening we kept with us for dinner some of our dearest friends. Their presence, their obvious pleasure, were sweeter to me than the victory itself. Not only were they my friends but they were all men I loved and admired. 'Oh, my friends,' I thought, 'how I thank you, being what you are, for being also my friends!' I had a fleeting impression, on that June 23 in 1938, that I had won my place in the world and that my old age would be, as befits that time of life, tranquil, respected, honoured. But in the far depths of my mind I heard, as in the *Ring*, the increasing roar of the Theme of Destiny.

Never in my experience had happiness been lasting or unmixed. In 1918 the joy of victory was blended with the anguish of illness. In 1924 at the moment when I believed that my marriage had been restored, death wiped it out. In 1930 a delightful and tender Christmas was followed by the death of little Françoise. In this year of 1938 my wife who had been ill for two years began to recover; my enemies seemed disarmed; my life was like one of those fairy stories in which a benevolent magician lavishes his gifts upon the possessor of some talisman, but I told myself with anxiety, as I watched the golden champagne froth within my cup, that the Gods are jealous and that the hour had come to cast into the waves the Ring of Polycrates.

There was one man I especially wanted to see after the election. That was Alain. He had often attacked the Académie in his *Propos*. For my part I saw nothing but good in this institution, which was one of the very few that had bridged the gap between the French Monarchy and the regimes that followed the Revolution. But I cared a great deal about my master's esteem and I wished to know how he felt. He had retired some years before and had left the Lycée Henri IV. For several winters he had continued giving an open course at the Collège Sévigné and this I had attended, happy to be a student once more, to sit at his feet and to listen to those splendid, those unique lectures. Then the rheumatism he had contracted in the damp dugouts in 1914 immobilized him, like Bergson. François Porché, who had gone to see him, had described him as 'a lightning-stricken oak'. I found him in a little house at Vésinet, watched over by a faithful woman friend. His face and head remained quite unaltered, and as soon as he spoke I recognized my master.

'Not only do I not blame you,' he said smiling, 'but I'm pleased that you should have had this joy.'

And he repeated the affectionate phrase he had used before:

'I know you well. You are a tender-hearted boy. Things that would be dangerous for others are healthy for you.'

But the 'boy' was now fifty-three.

Then we talked about Chateaubriand. I had brought him my book which was just out, and I had written in the front of it as we used to do in his classes: '*Lege quaeso.*' Alain knew the *Mémoires d'outre-tombe* as well as I did; it was one of 'his' books. We had a happy hour together.

The summer of 1939, which I spent as usual in Périgord, was devoted to my speech of reception at the Académie Française. It was my duty to deliver a eulogy of Monsieur Doumic. His son Jacques Doumic and his son-in-law, Louis Gillet, had loaned me his private papers and his journal; the man who emerged was, for all his eccentricity, lovable. Having known him well myself and having worked with him helped me in this task. I tried to draw a true picture of him. I was just finishing it when the first rumblings of an international storm were heard. Berlin was threatening Prague. The French government mobilized several classes.

EXTRACTS FROM MY JOURNAL

Essendiéras, September 10, 1938: I do not know what will come of this—peace or war—but I want to make a note of our anguish. For a week we have all been living in the shadow of the radio. Sometimes we get London, which is impassive and chilly: 'There has been a police report ... Weather forecast ...' and announces the most disturbing news as though it were a commonplace event. Sometimes one picks up Toulouse or Paris, less irritating but more disheartening. The only two consolations are work (I have finished my Doumic speech, but will it ever be delivered?) and music. Last evening, despite atmospheric and interior storms, the Franck Symphony remained wonderful. And even *Die Meistersinger*, which we had heard on the first evening of the Nuremberg Congress in company with the charming Peter Cadogan, was sublime.

We are returning to Paris day after tomorrow. The war? I am not afraid of death. On certain days I desire it. The world is too stupid. On other days I think the world beautiful, and my work consoles me for everything. Even in disaster, one can take pleasure in polishing a phrase, and at this very minute I find the slant of the sun on the woods and on Excideuil enchanting. *Resolution:* If war breaks out, I shall work without respite, both as an officer and as a writer, and I shall force myself not to brood on the unforeseeable future. This morning I am obsessed by four lines by Byron:

> Here's a smile to those who love me
> And a sigh to those who hate,
> And, whatever sky's above me,
> Here's a heart for every fate.

September 11, 1938: Last day at Essendiéras. One looks at this beautiful country, this valley fairyland, these brown tenant farms, and says: 'Shall I ever see them again?' This morning I worked as usual. Uninteresting mail. A medical magazine asks me for an article on 'Literature in the Year 2038.' I reply: 'By that time we will barely be emerging from the age of the caveman.' Numerous visits from neighbours in the afternoon. Pertinax and his wife. He is not as pessimistic as I am.

'One chance in a hundred of war,' he tells me. 'But how stupid French politicians have been for twenty years!'

The ex-Emperor of Annam and his daughter, the beautiful princess ... In the evening we listen to a speech by Benès on the radio, then search in vain for good music. On the BBC a humorist is telling stories. I fail to find him funny. Sleepless night.

[199]

Neuilly, September 12, 1938: We returned from Périgord through the Limousin, the Sologne, the Ile-de-France. The sunlight was soft, already autumnal, the colours muted. Villages and church towers, tiles and slate. Never has France been more beautiful. Along the roads the people seemed calm. Nevertheless each has a son called up, a husband in the reserve: in the fields the farmers were starting out on the hunt in parties, three or four guns, boys as beaters, reliable old dogs. Hitler would have been much surprised. Arriving in Paris, we went straight to *Figaro*. Saw Romier:

'Short of some act of madness,' he said, 'everything will work out.'

This was also the opinion of my friend Eric Phipps, British Ambassador to Paris. For a long time I had been acquainted with Sir Eric and Lady Phipps. I had met them after the war when Phipps had been appointed to Paris for the first time. Later he had been minister to Vienna, then ambassador to Berlin; but when he spent his vacations in England, I used to go and see him in his country house in Wiltshire. In the course of my life I have never met a woman more filled with kindness than Lady Phipps. A convert to Catholicism and very pious, she unostentatiously contrived material and moral good deeds that saved many unfortunates from misery and despair.

During all that year a great effort was made by the two governments to strengthen Franco-British ties, which had become much weakened. In July the King and Queen came to France and, as their grandfather Edward VII had done in his time, they conquered Paris. In November Neville Chamberlain in his turn was officially received; we dined with him at the Quai d'Orsay and afterward heard him tell about his interviews at Berchtesgaden and Godesberg, dominating the group with his small, birdlike head.

Neville Chamberlain, the most insular of Englishmen, had no idea what an Adolf Hitler could be like. One of my English friends had said to me that Chamberlain did not actually believe that Adolf Hitler was, like himself, a member of the Birmingham corporation, but he did believe that he was a member of the Manchester corporation.

At the Quai d'Orsay he described his reception in Berchtesgaden. He had been submerged by a torrent of words, which constituted the German Chancellor's 'conversation', and he had been discouraged by the impossibility of getting in the slightest reply. Then at the second interview, in Godesberg, he was met with declarations of such violence that he soon decided it was pointless to continue a conversation begun in that tone. 'Every five minutes (obviously following a prepared script) an officer entered and handed the Führer a dispatch. "Two more Germans killed by the Czechs!" Hitler would exclaim, his expression becoming terrifying. "All this spilled blood will be avenged! . . . The Czechs must be annihilated!" Seeing his fury mounting, whether simulated or not, I told the interpreter,' Neville Chamberlain went on, 'that I was going to return to my hotel. Since this was on the other bank of the Rhine, I had to cross the river in a ferryboat. As I was leaving, Hitler followed me onto the terrace, continuing to express himself with the same violence. There he suddenly stopped, the expression on his face changed with extraordinary rapidity, he looked at the river stretching at our feet and murmured in a soft, almost tender voice: "Oh! I am dreadfully sorry, Mr. Prime Minister . . . I would have so much enjoyed showing you this beautiful view . . . but it is lost in the fog . . . " Never have I seen a human face pass so suddenly from the most savage rage to the most poetic emotion.'

An official from the Foreign Office, who had accompanied Mr. Chamberlain to Germany, told me that the prime minister had been painfully affected by these interviews, that he was entirely unused to abuse of this sort, and that now, when the name of Hitler was mentioned in his presence, 'he made a face like a child being forced to swallow castor oil.' But Mr. Chamberlain considered it his duty to preserve peace and he still hoped to succeed in doing so.

In January 1939 I went to Great Britain to make an extended lecture tour which took me to every corner of the country. I discovered that public opinion was now ahead of the government. The latter hesitated to resort to conscription; the country was demanding it urgently. Everywhere English men and women of every class said to me:

'That man must not be allowed to dominate Europe; we must have a large army and a powerful air force.'

Returning to Paris, I wrote an article in which I predicted that England would announce conscription in the month of March; at that moment most of my French friends said that I was crazy, that Great Britain would never impose obligatory military service because there was a very ancient tradition against it. But in the month of March 1939 conscription was adopted.

This sudden re-entry of England into political co-operation with

Europe necessarily entailed a rapprochement with France. In June 1939 the *Association France–Grande-Bretagne* gave an official banquet in Paris at which were present Hore-Belisha, British minister of war; Georges Bonnet, French minister of foreign affairs; and General Gamelin. Hore-Belisha announced that if war came, the British armies would be under the orders of a French commander and that he would be proud to be able to say, '*our* General Gamelin'. The latter received the prolonged applause impassively. After the banquet we went with Hore-Belisha to the Polish Embassy where a great party was being given; he made a point of demonstrating by his presence the new closeness between England and Poland.

I have retained a tragic memory of that evening. It was a beautiful summer night. In the garden of the Hotel de Sagan (which had become the Polish Embassy) white marble sphinxes gleamed under the stars; an orchestra played Chopin waltzes; Roman fires threw their reddish glow. On the lawn women in crinolines, very beautiful (among them the two ravishing daughters of the German ambassador), danced with Polish and French officers. We all thought that war was near, that Poland would be the first to be attacked, and that this ball resembled the one Wellington gave in Brussels on the eve of Waterloo. The socially élite negligently sipped their champagne, chatting of frivolous matters. There was talk about the cruiser *Pasteur*, and some of those present dreamed of departing for South America.

A few days later Hore-Belisha returned with Winston Churchill for the Fourteenth of July review. Never had the French army been finer. In that parade we had combined everything that constituted our pride: the *chasseurs*, the Zouaves, the marines, the Foreign Legion, the infantry from the Maginot Line. Winston Churchill beamed. 'Thank God for the French army,' he said. We did not know at that time that men's courage, their military qualities and even the traditions of the finest regiments, are helpless when *matériel* is not worthy of the army. The parade of assault tanks reassured and enraptured the tribunes on the Champs-Elysées, but the latter were ill-informed and did not know that the Germans possessed more and better armoured tanks which our cannon could not destroy.

In the afternoon Hore-Belisha came to see me in Neuilly with a colonel who was his ordinance officer. He talked to me about the difficulties he was having in rebuilding the British army:

'Conscription,' he said, 'is all very well, but for the moment it is more a formula than a reality . . . I cannot call up all the eligible men because I have neither equipment to give them nor officers to train them.'

'And the officers of the last war?' I asked.

'They are not acquainted with the new *matériel*.'

'And if war were to break out tomorrow, how many divisions could you send us?'

'Right away? Not more than six.'

This figure frightened me. I was even more frightened when I learned a little later that our General Staff had asked from England, *for the whole duration* of a European war, only thirty-two divisions. I remembered that in 1918 we had had as many as eighty-five British divisions—and this at a time when the Americans, the Russians, the Italians and the Japanese were our allies; even so, we had only won the war by a hair's breadth. Here was cause for grave anxiety.

We were to leave in February 1939 for America where I had promised to make a long lecture tour. When we left Le Havre on February 15, Franco-Italian relations were strained. Were we going to be called back as soon as we landed? On the day of our arrival in New York the newspapers carried huge headlines: SIXTY-FOUR ITALIANS AND TWELVE FRENCHMEN KILLED ON THE BORDER OF TUNIS. Next day the news was denied. I found America irritated at France and England. All my American friends criticized the Munich agreement;

'Well and good,' I said to them, 'what would you have done to help us?'

'Nothing,' they replied with candour.

The truth is that the Americans' principal preoccupation in 1939 was not the European situation but the presidential election of 1940. The business world which was hostile to the president was isolationist at that time through fear of a third term. Meanwhile Roosevelt's partisans were behaving cautiously in foreign affairs in order not to compromise his chances. This was a situation very favourable to Germany's plans. I was surprised by the violence of feeling. To an old lady of Fifth Avenue who was sitting beside me at a dinner I said;

'Would you go so far, Madame, as to sacrifice your country and mine to your resentment against the New Deal?'

'Mr. Maurois,' she replied, 'I should rather see this planet blown into small pieces than have Roosevelt elected a third time.'

This seemed to me a perfect example of *dementia politica*.

My manager Harold Peat had arranged a long trip for me; Phila-delphia, Boston, Cincinnati, Columbus, Minneapolis, Detroit, Omaha, Tulsa, Chicago. In the last-named city friends had me to dinner with ex-President Hoover. He humorously described the amazement of men who in two or three thousand years would study our economy and discover that we had dug holes at great expense in Africa, found an ore there from which we extracted gold, transported this metal to America, dug holes at great expense in Kentucky and buried the gold there. Despite all our follies he retained his faith in democratic institutions;

'It's the only form of government,' he said, 'that makes it possible when things go badly to change leadership without violence. But for it to work, liberties must be respected, not only in theory but in fact.'

A little later I had lunch at the White House with a group of writers and was introduced to President Roosevelt whose lofty and gracious manner I admired. A patrician Whig and a plebeian Tory of the time of the Reform Bill, such were my impressions of Roosevelt and Hoover.

On March 15 when I was in Dallas, Texas, the Germans marched into Prague. Was this war? Many Americans seemed to hope so. But were they ready to fight? Quite the contrary; they were voting at that time for rigorous neutrality laws. Were we and England alone strong enough to win? I did not think so, and so it seemed to me my duty to counsel moderation at the Congress of PEN Clubs which was held in New York during the World's Fair. I have always had great respect for soldiers who sacrifice their lives, and little sympathy for bards who urge them on from afar with their songs. I made a point of saying this, although such a thesis cannot be very popular in a congress of writers:

'If men had a greater consciousness of the dangers that go with the use of certain words, every dictionary in the book shops would be wrapped with a scarlet band on which one could read: "High explosives. Handle with care." Military experts tell us of incendiary bombs which can set fire to whole towns, but we know of words which have set fire to an entire continent . . . We have anti-aircraft guns; we need anti-wordcraft batteries . . . Novelists, biographers, historians, it is our duty to draw of our little world as exact a representation as lies within our power. We have no axes to grind, no theses to prove, no election to win . . . During this difficult and perilous period, the greatest service we writers can render to the cause of peace is to hold explosive words under lock and key, to maintain a strict control over our emotions, and to tell our readers the truth, the whole truth, and nothing but the truth. So help us God ... '

The return trip aboard the *Normandie* over a sunny ocean with the slight feverishness of sleepless nights, the long political conversations, the sentimental badinage on deck, was a mixture of Watteau, Marivaux and Pontigny. I find this note which I made at the time, and published as soon as I had returned to France: 'What will the United States do if we go to war? Nothing for a year. After that it will give financial and industrial assistance. It will be at war at the end of two years ... ' A correct prediction. As we entered the port of Le Havre we saw with sorrow the wreck of the *Paris*, capsized and showing only her swollen belly. A mysterious fire had destroyed the beautiful ship on which I made my first crossing. Wasn't this, even now, the work of an enemy who chose this way of attacking our fleet?

We arrived just in time for my reception at the Académie Française. But before that ceremony there was another that moved me deeply. The headmaster of the Rouen Lycée had asked me to come and dedicate a new statue of Corneille in the Court of Honour. I had been overcome to learn that my dear old plaster Corneille, that of David d'Angers, past which I had so often marched, had been washed away by the Norman rains. The young cavalier who replaced him on the pedestal disconcerted me. But it was a great pleasure to deliver a eulogy of Corneille in this setting where forty years before I had started to read him. During the reception which followed, my old schoolmates presented me with a bronze plaque, the work of one of them who was a sculptor: it represented on one side the Seine with the Pont Boïeldieu, which I had crossed every morning in Rouen on my way to the Lycée, and on the other the cupola of the Institute in Paris.

To find my old friends of Rouen white-haired, some of them fat, and nevertheless so similar to the young men I had known, gave me much the same feelings that Proust experienced at the ball of the Prince de Guermantes. Yes, all these boys with whom I had played seemed disguised as old men. One was a prefect, another a senator, another a colonel of constabulary. Many had already retired. The elder Dupré, who had first taught me to love music, dragged himself about with the aid of two canes. My mother, who had come from Elbeuf as she used to do formerly 'for the prizes', was touched by the affectionate speeches in which reference was made to the child she had raised. I thought: 'The evening of a fair day . . . ' Alas, the evening had barely begun and the storm was gathering on the horizon.

A reception at the Académie is one of the beautiful French ceremonies. Everything contributes to its grandeur: the antiquity of the building, the strangeness of the procedure, the narrowness of the room, the quality of the audience, the prestige of the members, the military trappings, the traditional vocabulary and often the quality of the eloquence. Before being read at a public session, the speeches have to be accepted by a committee. I appeared before the latter and passed, with kind praises, this last examination of my life. The Duc de La Force said to me:

'You must remove the word *inlassablement* (indefatigably) which is not in the dictionary of the Académie.'

He was right.

After this test the newly elected member takes his seat. At the moment he enters, the whole Académie rises as a mark of courtesy; he bows, seats himself and takes part for the first time in the work on the Dictionary. The contrast between the simplicity of this ceremony and the majesty of the institution is not without grandeur and charm.

The following Thursday, June 22, 1939, the public session took place. The Secretary of the Académie gives only twenty seats to the newly elected member. I could only provide places in the Centre for my mother, my wife, my children, my mother- and father-in-law and a few of my intimates. But many of my friends had obtained tickets by courtesy of other academicians, and as I entered I saw the faces of all those who were dear to me. This entrance is made to the sound of rolling drums while the guards present arms and their officer salutes with his sword. Seated between my two sponsors, somewhat stifled by my green uniform, uncomfortable in my plumed bicorn hat, I looked at the two statues that stood on either side of the Desk, those of Bossuet and Fénelon. Seated exactly below me were General Weygand and Ambassador Paléologue; one of my great anxieties throughout my whole speech was the glass of water resting on the narrow shelf, which I feared I might upset upon those illustrious heads.

'Monsieur André Maurois has the floor for the reading of his speech of thanks . . . '

My heart pounded, but when I got to my feet the reception was such that I felt reassured. I do not know whether the heart of Paris has

changed; I do not think so; however that may be, the Parisian public
that day gave me one of the great joys of my life.

Monsieur André Chevrillon, who replied, graciously spared me the
customary strictures so that no bitterness spoiled that enchanted hour
for me. As I listened to him, I looked at the attentive and crowded
heads of the onlookers. At the foot of the Desk, perched on high stools,
sat some of the beautiful women of Paris: Edmée de La Rochefoucauld,
Marthe de Fels, Henriette de Martel. In the centre I discovered the sweet
face of Frances Phipps; then the bright eyes of Anne Desjardins which
brought back the evenings at Pontigny; Jeanne Mauriac and her
daughters; Blanche Duhamel and her sons; higher up the fourteen
grandchildren of Monsieur Doumic; a group of Norman students from
the Lycée; comrades of war; and a few old friends from Elbeuf who
evoked the pounding of the looms and the high chimneys with their
plumes of smoke. It was sweet on such a day to find this cluster of
friends come together from all the stages of my life ... But while
André Chevrillon talked about Byron, Disraeli and Lyautey, why
should a Greek verse, unsummoned, echo ceaselessly in my mind,
lugubrious and prophetic? Why should the sublime and bleeding face
of Mounet-Sully in *Oedipus Rex* haunt me on this day of triumph?
Why should I think so forcibly, the while a thousand faces smiled, that
Destiny remains as redoubtable as it was in the most ancient times, that
the sad wisdom of Sophocles is still true and that 'no man may be
called happy before his death'?

21

The Last of the Fair Days

The vales of Périgord, lined with poplars and willows, were more beautiful and peaceful than ever in that month of July 1939. The purple roofs of the tenant farm of Brouillac in the evening sunlight stood with their customary tranquil beauty in soft contrast to the green of the fields. Only the wasps, desirous of my flowers, in the mornings still disturbed my solitude. But this enchanted silence, this prodigious immobility of nature, seemed to me, as in July 1914, charged with mysterious menace. Each day when we opened the newspaper we expected to see in it the death warrant of our happiness. Poland, Danzig, the Corridor... When the terms of the Treaty of Versailles had become known, persons of intelligence had believed that from this bizarre map, from these impacted countries, the next war one day would come. After a thousand diverse feints it was on this vulnerable point that Mars once more seemed to fix his gaze.

At the beginning of August we learned of the death of Charles Du Bos. My sorrow was all the more acute because I had not seen him again. He had just spent two years teaching at the University of Notre Dame in Indiana. The tempo of American life had been too rapid for his feeble strength. In him I lost a friend who had guided me, uplifted me and often forced me to live, as he would say, 'at the extreme point of myself.' I, like all his friends, had often laughed at his gravity, at his masses of pencils, at his long quotations, at his carefully cherished maladies. Like so many supposed hypochondriacs, he had given irrefutable disproof to our scepticism by his death, and now we remembered nothing except his virtues. I saw again the affectionate softness of his eyes, the excited trembling of his long moustache, the thick coats which swathed his tortured body. From now on who would talk to me as he had done of Benjamin Constant or of Goethe? From now on who would talk to me with so much penetrating affection about myself? We were told by those who had been present at his end that he had died like a saint and a poet. Poor Charlie! For twenty years he had suffered, but he had been able to extract from the sufferings of the body the salvation of the soul. Might not the day come when we ourselves would need to remember his example?

About August 20 the political news became worse.

Worried, we decided not to stay in Essendiéras through September but to return to Paris by way of Malagar in order to pay a visit there to François Mauriac. The house was just as we had expected and as he had so often described it, a sunbaked white house, surrounded on all sides as far as the eye could reach by pale green vines dusted with blue sulphate; it had the fine, secret and intimate savour of an old liqueur. François and Jeanne were there, as well as their children and the Abbé Mauriac. As so often happens in the Bordelais, there was a storm in the air. The flies buzzed around us persistently. We took a long, melancholy walk beneath a violently hot sun and we talked about the dangers that threatened us all. At that time the peace depended on Russia, and England and France were negotiating with her. That evening after dinner, François read us his new play, *Les Mal-aimés*. He read well in his broken, muffled voice that added its own pathos to that of the characters. The play was a fine one; it had the same atmosphere of moral uneasiness and of restrained violence as *Asmodée*. Between the second and third acts we listened to the news over the radio:

'*Moscow announces a non-aggression pact with Berlin* . . . '

One of the children asked:

'What does that mean?'

I replied:

'It means war.'

We returned to Paris next day. Already troop transports were crawling along the railroads beside which we drove. When we arrived we hurried, as we had done the year before, to Lucien Romier's office, but this time our prophet did not reassure us. For several days we spent all our time hanging over the radio. The grave, sad speeches of Daladier were in consonance with the French people's desire for peace. But many were exasperated by the constantly renewed alarms.

'After all, *il faut en finir*!' said my barber who was leaving for the Maginot Line.

Almost every evening we dined with Pierre Brisson at some restaurant in the Bois, and then returned with him to the *Figaro* office to read the latest wires. On Thursday August 31 we thought the game had been won. It appeared that honourable terms had been offered to Poland. We returned home mad with joy. Next day the report was denied and Poland was invaded. Once more it was war, but war without Russia, with an America hobbled by neutrality, with an England ill-prepared, and against a formidable German air force.

Public opinion seemed surprised, hesitant. Soldiers in the stations did not leave with the same enthusiasm as in 1914. In an article in *Figaro*, the last I wrote before being mobilized, I tried to say why our war was a just one. This text is one of those that earned me the undying hatred of the German radio. Here it is:

WHAT IS IT ABOUT?

Dantzig? The Corridor? No, these are not the real objects of *our* battle. The truth is that for three years life in Europe and in the entire world has been rendered insupportable by a long series of aggressive actions. The recipe for them was simple. Among the states adjoining Germany one was chosen to be the victim. From the German minority in that chosen country, an ambitious and unscrupulous *Gauleiter* was picked. The German minority was declared to be suffering persecution. In Germany a violent press campaign was launched, soon followed by massive mobilization on the victim's frontiers. Once this was done, solicitous attention was paid to the other states of Europe; they were shown the most affectionate friendship; they were assured under oath that this would be the last act of the drama, the final course of the feast, that henceforth Germany would not covet any further territory; they were beseeched not to begin a European war on account of a miserable nation which, in any case, did not deserve to exist. Governments that have a horror of war and that are honest besides, have a tendency to believe in oaths; these gave in and with a sigh abandoned the victim to his fate. He was devoured. Next day the Reich would choose a new prey from among the nations so warmly loved when it needed their good will. The comedy would begin all over again.

This game succeeded in Austria. It succeeded in Czechoslovakia. It succeeded because Europe, barely convalescent, had need of peace. It succeeded because in the face of all experience, we hoped for a long time that the master of the Reich would one day keep his word. We have learned through hard experience to know the value of Nazi pacts. Each year we have seen the life of the world suspended, work brought to a halt, families torn apart, happiness destroyed, by the folly of a few men. We have had enough of it. We now know that to give in to the menace of Germany is to pave the way for a new swindle. We have had enough of it. We do not want violence, hatred and lies to be considered the highest virtues. We have had enough of it. We love life, to be sure, but we want to live in a world where one can raise one's children, carry on a life's work, form great projects, without being, twice a year, torn away from everything one loves by the caprice of an insatiable monster. We want to re-establish confidence and good faith in their place of honour. The free men of the entire world will help us to do this.

Although for a number of years I had not been of military age, I had made application to remain an officer in the reserves. And so, on September 2, I presented myself at the *Place de Paris* where I was informed that I had been attached, by the Ministry of War, to a Committee on Information of which Jean Giraudoux was to be the head and which was to be installed at the Hôtel Continental on the Rue de Rivoli. This was not at all what I wished: I had firmly decided to go to war, but it was necessary for the time being to accept the Continental. I went there. *Gardes Mobiles* were standing at the doors. The corridors were full of superannuated colonels, retired ambassadors and professors from the Collège de France. The conversation was brilliant, the disorder terrifying. The unfortunate Giraudoux had found himself suddenly, when war had already begun, forced to improvise a service of almost infinite complexity which, in Germany, had been functioning for years. It was an impossible undertaking.

As his second-in-command he had chosen an energetic and devoted man, André Morize, professor at Harvard and a friend of his.

I was in Morize's office at the Prime Minister's on Sunday, September 3, at five o'clock, when the ultimatum expired and the war began. When the five strokes rang out we clasped each other's hands.

'This is the first minute of the war,' Morize said. 'Let us never forget that we spent it together.'

I thought of the dramas I was going to see for the second time in the course of a short life: people fleeing along bombarded roads, cities and villages in ruins, families in mourning. All these miseries because a demoniacal corporal with a croaking voice had crystallized the Germans' need for revenge, because mindless and weak governments had neglected to arm the French in time, because the British and the Americans had refused to look at a future which nevertheless was clearly revealed by the sinister lightning of premonitory storms. We were to have the task of making good these follies. In this tragic moment I swore to do all within my power to destroy the monster and to unite those who were fighting against him.

That evening Giraudoux called me to his office. At his feet lay a beautiful dog which he was patting and to which from time to time he spoke. I looked at this elegant and charming man; I listened to his perfect phrases, ironic and gracious. Beyond this, I found in what he said the purity, the nobility, the love of a certain France which *is* France, and of a certain ideal of honour which *is* honour. It was strange, and a little frightening, to know that this great writer who had criticized the bellicose speeches of Poincaré suddenly found himself in charge of our war propaganda. To a superior officer who asked him, in an equally superior tone, what the French imagination planned to oppose to the inventions of Hitler, he replied: 'Cyrus the Great'. The reply pleased me, but were this fantasy and this flippancy on the part of the most French of perfect Frenchmen going to prove effective?

22

The Kingdom of God*

The Kingdom of God is within you.

Luke XVII: 20

This morning in the violet haze of dawn I seem to see an Italian city at my feet, bristling with churches and fortresses. In the distance the blue lake in Central Park, surrounded by pale foliage and wrapped in mist, recalls those tiny scenes almost lost in luminous confusion in the background of the paintings of the Primitives. Innumerable cars, yellow, grey and black, glide by even at this early hour, obediently following, on the checker-board of the streets, their precise ballet to the rhythm of the red and green lights. The pedestrians, seen from above, are no more than dark or brighter spots. Isolated on this peak I sometimes have the illusion of escaping like a lonely hermit on his column from the vanity and uproar of the city. These heights are favourable to contemplation. Let us take our bearings.

'Here below we are like spectators in a theatre,' wrote Chateaubriand. 'If we turn our heads away for a moment, a whistle shrills, the enchanted palaces vanish and when we bring our eyes back to the stage we find nothing but deserts and unfamiliar actors . . . ' For a long time on the stage of my own life I had seen a familiar setting which I thought was permanent. 'A view that cannot be taken away,' the architect had said when I bought my house in Neuilly. In this setting of the Bois, of Paris, of France, players whose lines and ability I knew had been enacting for twenty years a drama whose vicissitudes and dénouement I believed I had foreseen. The whistle of Destiny shrills. The view that 'could not be taken away' is struck. The Bois de Boulogne ascends into the flies; the Arc de Triomphe fades, the scene shifters

---

* This chapter is out of chronological sequence. It was written in 1941 in New York, high up in a tower that dominated Park Avenue. That was where the defeat had cast us, my wife and me. This text was to serve as the conclusion to the first volume of my *Memoirs*, which ended in 1939 and comprised: *The Apprentice Years* and *The Years of Labour*. The chronological account is resumed in *The Years of Misfortune*.

bestir themselves in the shadows. When the footlights come up again the spectator discovers a backdrop representing Rockefeller Center, the Empire State building, and on the stage are characters that had no part in the preceding scene and who do not even speak the same language.

'My life is like a story from *The Thousand and One Nights*,' I said to myself during the days of good fortune, 'in which the magician comes to seek a cobbler in his workshop and make him a caliph. My life,' I said, 'is a fairy tale. One morning I am living in a sorry province admiring from a distance great men whom I despair of ever meeting; that evening I have left my sorry province and those whom I idolized without hope have become my friends.' I forgot that often in *The Thousand and One Nights*, on the last page, the magician turns the caliph back into a cobbler again. This is also the ending of the strange story that I call my life . . . Friends, fortune, honours, home, I have had them all, lost them all, and now nothing remains except my workshop of public scrivener. More than ever my life is a fairy tale, but one in which the bad fairies seem to have had the last word.

Let us take our bearings. As in the photograph of an infant we find, to our surprise, the outlines of the old man's face, so in the heart of the man still burn the passions of the boy. The desperate need of devotion that I felt at eight when seated in the forked lilac tree in Normandy I read *Les Petits Soldats russes*, is the need which today still dictates for me a course of conduct that is so far from easy. The happiness I found in a well-turned phrase at the time when I was discovering the classics at the *lycée*, remains one of my greatest pleasures, and the first dollars I earned in this country went to collect around me once more Pascal and Bossuet, Retz and Saint-Simon. These scholarly virtues, this thirst for knowledge, this desire to teach, they were what made possible last summer those delightful weeks at Mills College.

Among the characters of fiction I find two brothers who help me to understand myself. One is Tolstoy's Prince André; the other is the Dr. Antoine Thibault of Roger Martin du Gard, both curiously moral without knowing why, through simple need of personal integrity. The Ethic of Engagement—I believe that is the definition of the personal code that controls my actions. It seems to me that in an indifferent universe man cannot rely either on nature, whose laws ignore our feelings, nor on the masses of humanity, whose actions are still natural phenomena, but that he must be able to rely on himself and on like-minded companions. The Kingdom of God can only be in the hearts of the Faithful. I have attempted all my life, by instinct rather than by deliberate choice, to be faithful to agreements, to the persons I love, to my country. Sometimes contradictory loyalties have made the choice difficult, almost impossible. I have done my best, not without anguish, awkwardness and mistakes.

I say: 'Faithful to my country, to persons,' not to a doctrine nor to a sect. Few men are less partisan in spirit than I. I do not like systems and I do not believe in them. I do not concern myself with factional disputes except, as Montesquieu has said, 'to bewail them.' I will accept tomorrow any form of government the French freely choose for themselves provided it assures their union, their independence and their security. But if in effort and in action I conform to the most exact disciplines, I cling tenaciously to liberty of mind. The scrupulous scholars who taught me physics, chemistry and history made me singularly exacting when it comes to determining facts. It is not enough for me to believe in its reality. I listen to an adversary with the dangerous desire to understand him. I have difficulty in imagining bad faith, deliberate ill will, Machiavellianism. Hence a naïve trust, countless imprudent actions, and the vain hope of converting fanatics by proving to them that they are wrong. That is to forget that they want to be wrong.

Are the fanatics mistaken? I believe so. But I know that others whom I admire hold the contrary view that these bitter and furious minds are the salt of the earth. 'You lack aggressiveness,' Lucien Romier used to say to me; and it is true that the moderation which is natural to me robs the mind of its mordancy. 'Truth is excessive,' our Alain used to teach, 'and one must go beyond, well beyond, the point of moderation if one wishes to understand even the simplest thing.' And Blake: 'The road of excess leads to the palace of wisdom.' I see clearly what they all mean by this, but excess is a climate in which I cannot live and in which I do not think wounded France has any chance of regaining her strength. Perhaps all sorts are necessary to make a world: the fanatics to shake the masses out of their lethargy and impartial minds devoid of bitterness, to appease, when dawn appears, the Furies, daughters of the Night.

Misfortune, which throws some souls into revolt, has cured me of certain prejudices. Because I began life in the camp of those who command, for a long time I had difficulty in understanding the grievances of those who are commanded. I would readily have said with Goethe: 'I prefer an injustice to disorder.' I would no longer say that today. Through my misfortunes I was to acquire, I hope, more tolerance, patience and pity. For a long time I believed, too, that every woman whose beauty enchanted me was intelligent, modest and good. Experience has not confirmed this agreeable belief and the cure has been painful. But the fundamental truth that misfortune has taught me is that sacrifice, when it is unmixed with pride, gives man incomparable joys. In fact, the greatest happiness of my life, the brief moments of ecstasy and rapture, have been those when I was delivered through love or charity from vain consideration of myself. To forget oneself is wonderful and in humility, if it be complete and freely accepted, there is immense security. According to the words of Sygne in Claudel's *L'Otage*: 'I am then seated in the lowest place, I can no longer be deposed.'

Night is falling. Shadows envelop the city while myriads of lights spring up. A long string of rubies mark out Park Avenue; then suddenly they are replaced by a long string of emeralds. In the direction of the East River the earth is more thickly sown with lights than the sky of Périgord was with stars. The nearest ones are steady; those on the horizon twinkle in the trembling mist, outlining unknown constellations. To the south towers and steeples glow. Illuminated by the white radiance of flood lights, pitted with dark holes, the giant figure of Radio City resembles a Brobdingnagian honeycomb raised against a stormy sky. The lines of the other buildings retreat and are lost in the night, but their bright windows rising skyward to the stars are like the stained glass of an immense cathedral, huge as the city. From these millions of faithful what prayer ascends?

Ah, I know very well what they would ask if they were wise, or rather what they would swear to keep. It is what they have. It is this liberty, this tolerance, these relatively gentle ways. Happy America, remember our mistakes and our anguish; do not believe that the future can be founded upon contempt for the past; reform and preserve; work; do not destroy. What have these many catastrophes taught us? That there is no justice without discipline. I was and I remain a liberal; that is to say, I believe men are happier and better if they enjoy the essential liberties. But I know today that there is no liberty without security, no security without unity. I know that if France wishes to remain a great country after this war she must fill in 'the bloody ditch' and reconcile the French.

Last summer when my students at Mills College brought to life some of my heroes I was struck by the predominance in my books of the theme of Reconciliation. *Bramble* was an effort to make the French understand the English soul; the English the French soul; *Bernard Quesnay* was an effort to show that good faith is to be found on the employers' side as well as on that of the workers; *Climats* was an effort to present fairly the woman's point of view and the man's point of view in a marriage; *Le Cercle de famille* was an effort to reconcile the generations. Always I have believed that words rather than facts pit men against one another and that in silence or in action understanding becomes easier. Even today in this chaos in which a civilization is dying I search anxiously for opportunities of conciliation, and frequent failures have not killed in me the persistent and perhaps absurd hope of seeing love triumph over hate.

Lack of realism? Not entirely, for love is a reality. But no one can bring it about that men shall be devoid of passions. The problem is to have them live under such institutions that these passions themselves will unite and reinforce society. I do not think this is impossible. More than once in the course of history a happy equilibrium has obtained. Never doubt that after this war a new equilibrium will be found. For a decade or a century it will seem stable. Then once more the fragile edifice will begin to tremble. 'What are the best laws?' Solon was asked. 'For what people and at what period?' he replied. Nations, like individuals, through all their lives ascend a steep slope, flanked by precipices, on which they are never permitted to rest. Each minute is a departure, each day a battle. Life is a game from which no one can withdraw with his winnings at any time.

News of the world still comes to me in my tower. A young man asks to see me. He has arrived from Elbeuf and hands me little photographs which show, reduced to powder, the houses that were the setting of my first years and the ruin of the fine quais of Rouen that I used to admire each morning with never-failing pleasure as I crossed the Boïeldieu Bridge. I question him and discover he is the great-nephew of the fire chief with the copper helmet and the red plume who is my earliest memory.

'And what became of the captain?'

'I only knew him,' he says, 'as an old family legend ... His son, my uncle, became a colonel and died several years ago.'

[217]

A telephone message informs me that the former headmaster of the Rouen Lycée has come as a refugee to his daughter's home in New York. I go to see him and am pleased to find an old and charming French scholar who in the time of disaster still wisely quotes the classics.

'How fine it was,' he says, 'that Court of Honour, the Corneille of David d'Angers and the noble chapel of the Jesuits in front of which I as an official of the Republic, had to restore the statue of Loyola . . . '

A letter from Louis Gillet, excellent and heroic, as befits that great-hearted man. Letters from André Gide, grave and affectionate, from Roger Martin du Gard, from Jean Schlumberger and from Anne Heurgon who is in Algeria and is bravely trying to supply my children with food, for France is famished and food occupies a pathetically large place in our correspondence. Gérald has found a position and is at work—wretchedly. Olivier, in bad health, is at school in the mountains. Of my daughter and mother I have no news except through my mother-in-law, but her letters, as is indeed necessary, are prudent, reticent, and often contrary to her thoughts, for she has everything to fear from the multiple censors. From these wounded envelopes, bandaged by the censor's stickers, there escapes a sadness. One dreams, one longs to see again those whom one loves and to say those things which letters must omit.

But it is time to get back to work. Already in the neighbouring room can be heard the clicking of my wife's typewriter. Occupied simultaneously by this book, by the lectures that must be prepared, by the war charities that are at present so difficult to support, we live almost alone and never have a moment's boredom. A happy marriage is a long conversation that always seems too short. Sometimes in the evening when the news from France has been better, when we have been satisfied by the day's work, when the lights of the city in the calm of night afford a sublime spectacle, we experience a fleeting, a culpable, a foolhardy feeling of assurance.

'Alas!' Simone says shivering . . . 'What more is going to happen?'

She knows now, as I do, that happiness like the pink and white anemones of my childhood is a flower that must not be picked.

Is she right? Will the whistle blast of Destiny in a few seconds wipe out this setting as it once caused the trees of the Bois to vanish? Will Rockefeller Center and the Empire State building ascend into the flies? Will the fragile and precarious existence that we have so painfully constructed during this year collapse like the one that formerly seemed to us so substantial? And what shall we see when the footlights come up again, if ever they do come up? No one knows. But timidly, anxiously, ardently we hope that it may be noble and lovely Périgord, a long valley lined with poplars, the red roofs of the tenant farm at Brouillac lighted by the setting sun, and when the night shall come, in a French sky above the plane trees and the cedars, familiar constellations which French voices will call by name in that most beautiful of languages.

PART THREE

THE YEARS OF MISFORTUNE

23

Sitzkrieg

I wrote the preceding chapter in New York in 1941 in a time of black distress. Everything was falling to pieces under me. In France my mother and my children appeared to be in mortal danger; the occupying forces had confiscated my mill, my house and my goods; my books had been banned.

In New York I knew that I was serving my country with fervour and efficiency. I had set myself two goals: to maintain intact an image of France worthy of love and respect; to convince the Americans that this war ought to be their war. Then I wished, as soon as the United States entered the contest, to enlist once more in the French army. But for a long time my political isolation had been growing intolerable and the calumnies to which I was subjected exceeded the imagination. I suffered from them to the point of thinking of suicide. From this I was saved only by attachment to a mission which I alone could accomplish, by the total devotion of my wife and by the fidelity of my true friends. Today, with the contest won on all fronts, I say to myself: 'Happy are they who, at a crucial moment in life, know how to rely on their conscience alone.'

And so I wrote a chapter, the final one at that time, in which I humbly offered up my sorrows to my duty and found in sacrifice my only joy. In concluding it I expressed the timid hope of continuing these *Mémoires* some day in sweet and noble Périgord, seeing from my window a long valley bordered with poplar trees, in the foreground our cedars and our cypresses and in the blue distance the soft beatitude of a sunny day in France. This wish has been granted. Twenty-five years later, in August 1965, I sit down to work this morning in my office whose windows give on our hills, our vineyards and our woods. The sky above the trees is 'so blue, so calm'. Today my wife reigns over this domain. She has made of it a thing of beauty. What a contrast, and what a contrast with our miseries during the years of misfortune!

In the outside world all breaches have been mended and, if long misfortunes had not taught me doubt, I could believe that my life was going to end in serenity. I have just become eighty, and all of France as well as many foreign countries have affectionately honoured my great age. Thousands of telegrams from New York and Moscow, from London and Barcelona, from Rome and Tel Aviv, have broken in a wave over Excideuil. My most recent book, *Prométhée ou la vie de Balzac*, has received the best press in every country that I have had in the course of my life. This surprised me—and delighted me. Shall I really enter upon my final sleep surrounded by this unanimous friendship which, after so many reverses, seems so sweet?

I dare not believe it. A quarter of a century ago one blast of Fate's whistle caused a whole stage-set which I had thought impregnable to rise into the flies. Everything, even the worst, can still destroy my fragile happiness. 'It seems,' says Montaigne, 'that fortune sometimes spies out the last day of our lives to show its power to reverse in a single instant everything she has built up through the long years.' I sometimes find myself repeating the lines from Sophocles' *Oedipus at Colonus*: 'Never to have been born, that is best of all. But once one has seen the light of day, the most desirable fortune by far (though coming later) is to depart whence one has come, as quickly as possible.'

I shall depart whence I came soon enough. What remains to me of life? One year? Three years? How is one to know? After a terrible illness (in 1961), my health has become excellent once more; my power to work remains what it has always been. Nothing proclaims the end of the spectacle. Nevertheless the hour is inexorable. Mortality remains at one hundred per cent. At midnight the curtain will fall. This certainty inspires in me neither fear nor haste. I should like to work up to the end and die at my desk, or in the course of some trip undertaken to continue the work of conciliation that has been my life's work. Most of all, I should like to finish these *Memoirs*. It is of little significance to me whether they appear before or after my death. The important thing is to leave a true picture of myself . . . And so I take up this story once more at the moment when, in 1939, a clock striking five times announces the beginning of the Second World War.

September 1939: *Le Continental*. This is what they called the General

Committee for Information because it was lodged in the old hotel of that name in Paris. I went there every morning at nine o'clock, in uniform. Giraudoux had asked me what I wished to do.

'Anything that you think proper,' I had said, 'but it seems to me that I could usefully maintain liaison with England, explain our needs to the British, urge them to increase their effort and to make known this effort to the French.'

He approved at that time, but he was submerged by the multiplicity of services he had to create, and when the list was posted, I found myself assistant to Monsieur Laroche, former French Ambassador to Warsaw, in an office charged with the duty of writing articles for French newspapers!

Rarely in the course of my life have I felt such discouragement and sadness as in the few days I spent at the Continental. As in 1914, I arrived full of spontaneous ardour. I wanted to go into battle. They said to me:

'See that articles are written.'

'Articles? But by whom?'

'By anyone you like.'

'But about what?'

'About anything you choose.'

'For what newspapers?'

'For all the newspapers that will take them.'

'And who will pay for the articles?'

'Oh, don't ask us for money; we haven't a franc.'

The most incredible thing was that the Commissioner General of Information of the French Republic in time of war actually had no funds. Also this organization, like the others, was immediately torn by political passions. The people of the Right said that it was the resort of communists; the people of the Left said it was a den of reactionaries. The Collège de France felt that there were too many diplomats; the Quai d'Orsay that there were too many professors; the Rue Saint-Dominique that there were not enough officers. For me, who hated quarrels, these discussions rapidly became so painful that I begged General Chardigny, who was in charge of army officers at the Commission and was therefore my commanding officer, to send me somewhere else.

'I'm not afraid of danger, *mon Général*,' I said to him, 'but I cannot stand inaction, disorder and feuds.'

'And where would you like to go?' this able man asked. 'There's not even a war.'

Occasionally some amusing episode would brighten for an instant the bureaucratic greyness of the Continental. Such was the case when Sir Eric Phipps, the British ambassador, and the most faithful of our friends, summoned me one day to meet a British naval officer who was to be in charge, together with myself, of a secret mission. I went to see Phipps who received me immediately, smiling with amusement. 'Have the secret envoy come in,' he said to his secretary. The door opened and I burst into laughter, for the messenger of the gods, most imposing in his naval uniform, was my friend Noel Coward. Sir Eric opened one of those red boxes in which the British carry documents of state.

'Here are your orders,' Sir Eric said to us. 'You are instructed to form a commission composed of you two, of German scholars of French birth and of two officers from the air force, one French and the other British. This commission will compose texts designed to wean the Germans from Nazism; printed on thin paper, your brochures will be folded and wrapped in bundles so that when they are dropped by our airplanes above Germany they will open and scatter our propaganda over a wide area.'

The strange commission began its sittings. A professor from the Collège de France pointed out to us what he thought were the proper arguments to persuade the Germans. Noel Coward and I plied our trade as writers and composed brochures to the best of our ability. Unhappily the practical results were discouraging. The bundles either did not open or fell into the water. After having laughed at this a bit, I felt myself close to tears. Wars are not won by methods such as these.

On several occasions Giraudoux asked me to talk on the radio; for example, to announce to the French the arrival of the British troops and to explain that Great Britain was at our side, just as in 1914–1918. This was necessary, for German propaganda showed itself much more active in France than ours in Germany, and already people were murmuring: 'The British aren't doing a thing.' As a matter of fact, during that 'phoney war' we ourselves did not do much.

I received many visits from writers. André Malraux came to tell me that he wished to enlist in a tank regiment. I talked about this to General Chardigny and Malraux got what he wanted. We were charged with the recruitment of war correspondents. Lazareff proposed Jérôme

Tharaud, Philippe Barrès and Joseph Kessel. I seconded these choices and Giraudoux confirmed them.

Every time I had the chance I told Eric Phipps how much I hated my life at the Continental and hoped to join the armed forces. Phipps must have acted vigorously in England, for suddenly, at the moment when I was in despair, I received a letter bearing the imprint of the War Office. Here it is:

Sir,

I am commanded by the Army Council to convey to you a most cordial invitation to act as French Official Eye-Witness at General Headquarters of the British Field Force, which has now arrived in France.

I am to inform you that, in the event of your accepting this invitation, our Military Attaché in Paris, Lieutenant Colonel the Hon. W. Fraser, has been instructed to make all the necessary arrangements for your reception with the Commander-in-Chief.

Finally I am to say that the Army Council fully appreciates the great service which a writer of your distinguished attainment and profound knowledge of the British character could render in maintaining these happy relations which have so long existed between the French people and the British soldiers, and to which your own writing has so largely contributed.

I hope you will find it possible to honour us by accepting our invitation.

I am, Sir, your obedient servant:

H.-J. Creed
Permanent Under-secretary for War

It is easy to understand that this letter gave me lively pleasure. It was my deliverance and it gave me the chance, despite my age, to follow the war. I rushed to show it to General Chardigny and André Morize, who both advised me to accept. They saw very well that at the Continental I was in a blind alley and without proper employment. I called upon Colonel Fraser, the British military attaché, who told me that British General Headquarters were located at Arras and that I was expected there and should ask for Colonel Reynolds. My wife, who was now my chauffeur as well as my secretary, drove me to Arras where, unfortunately, she was not allowed to stay. During the preceding war I had known this beautiful Hispano-Flemish city. I now found it teeming with khaki-clad soldiers and, for the space of a thought, I believed I had returned to twenty-five years ago.

Was this the same man who for the second time in the same uniform was joining the British army? Sometimes when I caught sight of my white hair in the mirror I experienced a shock of surprise and sadness. I felt myself still so young, so much a novice. And yet what differences there were from the soldier of 1914! The soldier of 1939 no longer expected much of life. He believed that the game was over, that his work had not been up to his youthful dreams, that doubtless he would never say what he had so much wanted to say. For a long time he had sought to discover the secret of the universe, the golden rule. He had come to believe that no golden rule existed. It will be seen that he was mistaken and that misfortune would reveal a happiness that good fortune had hidden from him.

The Official Eye-Witness ... such was my title, which I did not much like. The duties seemed ill-defined. Colonel Reynolds to whom the embassy had sent me was in charge of Public Relations, that is to say, the press, censorship, cinema and radio. This agreeable Englishman would listen with great courtesy to what you had to say, throw himself back in his chair, roar with laughter and immediately forget all about it. In his world I was a new and disturbing species ... The Official Eye-Witness ...

'Witness to what?' he asked me, laughing. 'Nothing is happening.'

I was required to present myself to the Commander-in-Chief. At that time General Gort was living in the Château of Habarcq near Arras. I was received there by his aides-de-camp, a magnificent Scottish officer in a kilt of the Gordon tartan, and the estimable Lord Munster, illegitimate descendant of William IV of England. In the little waiting room the Gordon and Munster gave me a strange and violent cocktail which they called the Harbarcq Horror, then they said:

'We are going to take you to the Chief.'

Never did a commanding general have a simpler office. On the door was a notice sloppily written and affixed by four thumbtacks: 'Office of the C.-in-C.' In the room, devoid of furniture, two trestles of raw wood supported a bare plank. This was Lord Gort's work table. The simplicity was intentional. Gort believed that a chief ought to live like his men. Very active, he had in time of war a single pleasure and sport

—walking. You would see him at dawn on the muddy roads around Arras, elbows pressed to his sides, head forward, his red and gold cap fending off the rain, followed by his panting aide-de-camp. Our first conversation was rapid and easy. Lord Gort began by talking about Hitler's plans:

'Will he attack through Belgium? . . . I believe so, because it is the only operation possible . . . You know Foch's rule: "In war you do what you can, making use of what you have." Only I do not see how Hitler can launch an offensive in winter in this Flanders mud . . . And if several months go by without battle, I fear boredom for our men. You know it's no fun when darkness comes at four o'clock to return to a wet barn with no light but a candle.'

'But in 1914, sir, we spent our lives in dug-outs and trenches . . .'

'That was different,' he said. 'At that time there was an enemy in front of us who managed to keep us busy . . . Here I am holding a line in front of Lille and Douai.' (He got up with a brisk movement to show me this line on the map.) 'I have nothing in front of me except Belgium, a neutral country. In these conditions, it is not easy to maintain a war-like spirit. No, if this inaction goes on, the men will have to be entertained. Lord Nuffield has offered me radios, but that's a problem in itself . . . Our soldiers cannot use the ones that plug in because they have no electricity in their cantonments . . . And so we have to have radios with batteries . . . But then the batteries have to be replaced . . . I'm engaged right now in equipping some trucks that will go from unit to unit providing this service. I'm not a general any more! I'm a repair man!'

After that he described for me the fortified lines which, according to information he had received from the Intelligence Service, the Germans had constructed in Poland against the Russians. And so that alliance was precarious. Then he told me what he had in mind for me:

'I would like you to talk to my men about the French army and to French civilians about our army. Also, occasions must be contrived for meetings between our regiments. Yesterday my lancers had lunch with your cuirassiers . . . That's fine . . . I myself often see General Giraud who is in command of your Seventh Army, on my left; a splendid soldier!'

The cigarette he had given me was beginning to burn my fingers and I looked about for an ashtray.

'Oh, throw it on the floor,' the General said.

For Lord Gort, who had eliminated all useless objects while on campaign, did not own an ashtray.

He had me provided with a car to get about in and an officer to accompany me. This officer turned out to be Captain Grant, an old peace-time friend of mine who had been the publisher in England of my little *Voltaire*. His regiment had been motorized and he himself classified as: *non-motorizable horseman*, which made him very proud. He did not have much of an idea of what we could accomplish together, but he was an agreeable companion and I liked him very much. We stayed together.

I needed lodgings. The hotels of Arras seemed noisy and mediocre. Grant and his friends did not have a mess. Just as I was beginning to despair, an opportunity presented itself. I had gone to introduce myself, as was my duty, to the French general commanding the Arras sub-division. Colonel Gillot, substituting for him, received me. Commander Poumier of the Engineers, who was Chief-of-Staff, talked to me about my books, about Mauriac and Julien Green, with obvious culture, and then invited me to lunch.

'We have a little mess in the Rue des Capucins,' he told me, 'the colonel, I and another engineer, Captain Puthomme.'

The conversation of these three men was of a high quality and their gaiety heart-warming. When they asked me after lunch if I should like to stay with them, I accepted with pleasure. Before long Colonel Gillot was retired and left us. His successor, General Hémelot, a married man, lived with his family, and 'the Capucins' were reduced to three, but they kept open house. How many charming boys—Pierre Lyautey, Jean Fayard, Simon de Peyerimhoff—frequented our mess! Coming from regiments or staffs near Arras, they would ask if they could lunch or dine with us. General Voruz and Colonel de Cardes of the Mission Française met with Lord Munster and Major Gordon at the Capucins' table. If military co-operation can be assured through personal friendships, then the Capucins of Arras were good liaison agents.

For friendship is needed to strengthen confidence. I found Franco-British relations in this war very different from what they had been in 1914. So far as the general staffs were concerned, understanding on the whole was better. But among the masses of soldiers and civilians distrust and sometimes even hostility were constantly inflamed by German propaganda, which was insistent, insinuating, sarcastic, tenacious and ingenious. It kept evoking the oldest grievances of the French: Jeanne d'Arc, Saint Helena. O the survival of archetypes!

'England will fight to the last Frenchman!' the Stuttgart radio proclaimed.

The smallest difficulty between the British soldiers and French villagers was exploited by the Germans, who would find out about it, I have no idea how, and give it vast publicity. General Brownrigg, Adjutant-General of the British Army, distressed by these difficulties, asked me to draw up the Ten Commandments of the British soldier in France. He had an enormous number of copies printed and distributed to the troops. These commandments were for the most part an appeal to mutual consideration and esteem, and are perhaps summed up in the Ninth: 'The task of our two countries is not only to win the war but to win the peace afterward. This they will be able to do only if they are united. They will remain united only if they understand each other.'

Meanwhile, General Voruz, in command of the French Mission of Liaison, had charged me with an analogous and complementary task, that of giving lectures to his officers about the English people and the British army. He had organized a liaison school at Auxi-le-Château and I went there from time to time to speak. Not long ago, in a lecture at the War College, Colonel Cailloux recalled the role I played at that time: 'Franco-British collaboration was given substantial support by a certain lieutenant (soon to be captain) who hid beneath his modest deportment a literary personality of the first order. The academician André Maurois had already played the part of Aurelle* ... Quartered at Arras, he regularly visited our allied units. At that time he was as remarkable an agent of rapprochement as he had been a wise interpreter in 1914–1918.' As a matter of fact, what I said was very simple, but useful.

Colonel de Cardes almost always accompanied me to Auxi-le-Château. I loved to watch this fiendishly clever Béarnais giving orders and straightening out a situation. Precision, rapidity, authority—he had the best qualities of the professional soldier. But at the meetings of the Franco-British General Staff which he attended, he was alarmed by the incoherence of the inter-allied plans. They were going into Finland; they were not going into Finland. They were not going into Norway;

* Aurelle is the name of the interpreter in Maurois's World War I novel, *Les Silences du Colonel Bramble.*—Tr.

they were once more planning to go into Norway. No master mind seemed to be guiding the coalition.

I got no better impressions from my observations on the Belgian frontier. The line seemed horrifyingly weak. The French Engineers, to be sure, had in 1937 built little concrete casemates which were supposed to be connected by an anti-tank ditch. But these casemates were few in number and the ditch would be effective only if it were commanded by anti-tank guns. Only the emplacements existed, however, not the guns. To complete the defences, the British dug trenches of the 1914 type, but in the mud of Flanders the parapets collapsed; and, moreover, what use were these miserable entrenchments against giant tanks or concentrated bombardment? My friends the correspondents of English and French papers, many of whom had fought in the last war, viewed the weakness of our defences with more alarm than did the generals. But what could they say and what could I myself write? The censorship did not allow us *any* criticism. Nevertheless, the facts were indisputable and were certainly known to the enemy: on the frontier a thin line, without depth, without the necessary armament; behind that line, nothing, no reserves, no mass of manoeuvre. *Quos perdere vult* ... Our leaders had long since reached the *dementat*.

The visits paid by General Gamelin to Gort's Headquarters were far from reassuring. I had known him well during peacetime and I hoped he would prove himself a brilliant strategist, for he was reputed to have been one of the inspirers of the Battle of the Marne in 1914. But I saw at Gort's table, and later at Vincennes, a burnt-out man, almost apathetic, overwhelmed by his responsibilities. Lord Gort, aware of the weakness of our line, said to him:

'Aren't your uneasy, General?'

'Yes,' Gamelin replied. 'The peasants in Lorraine continue to leave piles of manure in front of their houses in spite of my orders ... Yes, that disturbs me.'

Nevertheless from time to time the leader in him seemed to re-awaken:

'In this war,' he would say, 'the first to come out of his carapace will be lost.'

And again:

'Above all, it is necessary to keep from establishing a linear defence all along the frontier ... Napoleon despised that ... "What are you trying to do?" he once asked, "set up a cordon of customs men?" ...

The essential thing is to keep a substantial mass of manoeuvre which can be rushed to any threatened point.'

Alas! At the moment of truth one saw with despair that Gamelin had no mass of manoeuvre. He was more an intellectual than a soldier, thinking clearly but reluctant to act. A brain but no backbone. He meant well, however, and was attentive to details.

'What's this?' he said to me on his first visit. 'You are only a lieutenant?'

'Yes, *mon Général.*'

'That's ridiculous; I'm going to have you made captain.'

He did so.

Most of the experts (unlike General Gort) did not believe there would be an attack on Belgium. 'Why,' they said in their articles, 'should Germany add to the number of her enemies the Belgian army, which today is large and well armed?' Since, on the other hand, they affirmed that the Maginot Line could not be breached, 'there remains to Hitler only two possible avenues of attack: Holland and Rumania, but it is unlikely that he will choose either of these because Rotterdam is the *last lung* of Germany, and Rumania is already delivering to the Reich all the oil at its disposal.' The conclusion was that Germany would do nothing that summer, that it was a situation favourable to us because 'time works for us,' because by 1941 '*we* will have control of the air,' and, by 1942, enough heavy artillery and tanks to attack the Siegfried Line. How easy it is to believe what one hopes!

Hitler had said; '*I will rot their war,*' and, in the course of that long winter of inaction, he succeeded. The men grew tired of digging trenches in the rain to defend themselves against an enemy they never saw. One could have, and should have, taken the divisions one by one into the field and given them intensive training to prepare them for an entirely new kind of war, which could terrify them. All the experience of the campaign in Poland should have been put to use. But there was so little warlike spirit that the generals allowed themselves to be stopped by scruples, proper enough in times of peace. I remember asking one of them why he was not accustoming his infantry to seeing tanks with flame-throwers advancing against them, and to dive-bombers.

'If their first experience of this kind of attack happens on the field of battle,' I said, 'there is the danger of panic . . . If, on the contrary, they have been used to such spectacles, the novelty will have worn off.'

[233]

'You are right,' he replied. 'And I have asked for it several times . . . But the reply was that manoeuvres with tanks would ruin the harvest and that the civil authorities were opposed to it.'

No one behind the lines seemed to think about the danger of an enemy attack; everyone talked about the danger of boredom. At the beginning of the war the men had lacked blankets, sweaters, shoes, and committees had been organized: Packages for the Armies; Cigarettes for the Armies. The women at home made prodigious efforts and exceeded their goals. Soon the soldiers were receiving too many packages, too many gifts.

'With the best will in the world,' a British soldier said to me gravely, 'I *cannot* smoke two hundred cigarettes a day!'

Then the social élite of Paris and London founded new committees: Reading for the Army, Radio for the Army, Diversions for the Army, Music Hall for the Army, Sport for the Army, Art for the Army, Theatre for the Army. A witty lady, shocked by this frivolity, advised the creation of a committee of War for the Army. She was right, but such comments were frowned on.

On the British front, 'concert parties' composed of distinguished comedians and ravishing girls went about in military cars, solemnly escorted by officers. Maurice Chevalier sang with great amiability for the troops of both countries. His arrival at Arras made more of a sensation than that of President Lebrun. French and English soldiers acclaimed him. 'Maurice, sing *Valentine*!' cried the French. 'Maurice, the *Raindrop*!' shouted the English. When he left the stage he was besieged by autograph hunters: 'Maurice, it's for my kids . . . I'm a papa, you know . . . ' On the doorstep Chevalier would turn around and say to the soldiers: 'God bless you, boys . . . '

This was all very fine, but it hardly constituted an effective preparation for the German offensive. At a time when the country, at the gravest moment in its history, had at its disposal only a few weeks' respite to make up for errors of long standing, to complete its fortifications, to train its men, Frenchmen and Englishmen continued, except in a few sectors of the front, to lead the lives of functionaries subject to all the exigencies of military bureaucracy.

In that city of Arras where I was stationed lived some thousands of French territorials, old soldiers who had been mobilized, I do not know why, and of whom the army made no use. Their officers set them to making kitchen gardens, model poultry runs, and to raising rabbits and pigs. Laudable works, but possibly it would have been more urgent to fortify Arras and the line of La Scarpe. Commandant Poumier dared to say as much to his general; he was rebuffed.

'Fortify La Scarpe! But the enemy will never get that far. You have a defeatist attitude. Pay attention to orders.'

After one or two experiences of this sort, even the most zealous leaders returned to their routine. The soldiers, well nourished and little occupied, grew fat. The Tommies, as soon as night fell, wrote innumerable letters to their wives and sweethearts; the officers managed only with great difficulty to censor this monstrously huge correspondence . . . An unhappy captain would barely see one mountain of envelopes removed from his table when a new pile fell on it. Minuscule family quarrels, sustained and analysed from letter to letter, occupied the time of men who should have been reflecting that the future of liberty and the destiny of the world depended on their military qualities and their power of resistance. Hitler, just as he had promised, had rotted our war.

My impression changed in December 1939 when I visited the Maginot Line.

'I wish each British brigade,' General Gort said to me, 'to spend several weeks in Lorraine to get actual battle experience.'

And so I went to see the Scotsmen in front of Metz. The French liaison officer was Captain de Chambrun, son of the general who had entertained me in Fez. Attached to the Infantry of the Maginot Line, he had served in one of the forts of the Line and asked me to visit him there. I saw fine soldiers who inspired confidence. The armament of the forts, the perfection of the firing plans, the multiple observation posts, the large guns that flanked the anti-tank ditches, everything in Lorraine seemed as formidable as the line in Flanders seemed the reverse.

'In this sector at least,' I said to my guide, 'they will not pass.'

But I did not stop to consider that if the enemy broke through elsewhere and turned the Maginot Line, all this force would be useless and this magnificent army would become prisoners. On Christmas Day someone took me on a tour of the forts and villages of the front line. It was bitter cold. Snow and frost had enveloped the war in a glistening mantle. No countryside of Dickens was ever a more perfect Christmas setting than the one in which Lorraine entertained our allies that year.

It was beautiful to the point of unreality. A vaporous mist wrapped our countryside and clothed it in mystery. One could see barely fifty metres, but this small circle was a fairyland. Every tree, every frost-covered bush, was transformed into a bouquet of sparkling crystals ... The barbed-wire entanglements, like monsters touched by one of Shakespeare's fairies, resembled in their white sheathes the silver tinsel that glistens in the branches of a Christmas tree.

In the evacuated villages, the snow had brought the dead houses to life. Two laurel bushes in front of an empty inn, decorated with luminous crystal, looked like chandeliers. Each garden bush became a crèche, every forest glade a church of white marble. On the roads French and British soldiers, invigorated by the cold, slithered over the thin coating of ice and exchanged joyful greetings. Then as one approached the front line, the silence became intense; no gun spoke; no voice or cry broke the enchantment. On the deserted farms no dog barked, no cattle lowed. The mist enclosed each outpost, each sentry, in a silver ball decked with sparkling branches.

'There are mines all around here,' the Scottish colonel accompanying us said candidly, 'but I don't know exactly where.'

This speech made me think of my old Bramble, whom I had sought in vain in this new army.

On the day after Christmas I took my leave and went straight from Lorraine to Périgord. Our house at Essendiéras was sheltering more than sixty Alsatian refugees. They came from my father's country around Strasbourg, Bischwiller and Haguenau, and I listened with pleasure to their songs, which reminded me of the old workmen in our mill.

Simone and her mother had arranged a Christmas tree for the children and had postponed the distribution of presents until my arrival. I found once more, not without emotion, the pink, blue and green candles, the tinsel and the gilded chestnuts of Pastor Roehrich. As in the time of my childhood the Alsatians sang:

> *Mon beau sapin, roi des forêts,
> Que j'aime ta verdu-re ...

* O beautiful fir tree, king of the forests,
  How I love your greenery ...

A few weeks later I saw my son Gérald in uniform for the first time. He had just enlisted in the air force, at nineteen, and promised to become, so his superiors wrote me, an excellent pilot, though something of a daredevil.

'Here he is, a soldier,' my wife said, 'and we hardly know him.'

24

Blitzkrieg

Several war correspondents had, like me, visited the French provinces for Christmas and all were worried when they came back.

'People are listening to the German radio,' they said. 'It must be answered by precise facts; not pompous, empty phrases. Why not send us to England? Why not let us see the British war effort?'

Blaise Cendrars, a journalist and novelist of talent whom the English adored because of his picturesque, piratical air, his missing arm, his brick-red face, his military medal, talked about this project to the DMI (Director of Military Intelligence). The DMI, General Mason Mac-farlane, a Machiavellian and mysterious character, chief of the secret services, was thoroughly acquainted with the German army, admired it and feared it. Constantly followed by an enormous bulldog which lay down at his master's feet whenever the latter was talking, he used to come and deliver sombrely humorous lectures to the correspondents, and his remarks were often prophetic.

'You're happy about this lull?' he said. 'It foretells the storm. This phoney war will be followed by a phoney offensive. And then . . .'

He considered Cendrars' idea excellent.

'I shall arrange the trip,' he said.

And so some ten correspondents, whom I was to chaperone, crossed the Channel one sad January day on a darkened boat with all lights extinguished. Boulogne, enshrouded in snow, was sinister. On the other side we were welcomed at the pier by General Beith; this was my old friend Ian Hay of the preceding war, author of *The First Hundred Thousand*. He was now covered with red and gold, laden with honours, but he had retained the humour of his earlier years. In London the Minister of Information gave us a huge motor coach and we began to travel all over England in the bitter cold. The method of training pilots, the manufacture of artillery and the building of airplanes seemed to us intelligently organized. Nevertheless all my journalist friends, old soldiers themselves, looked sadly at one another each evening:

'The terrifying thing,' said the charming Lefèvre, 'is that all this is only a sample . . . The material is good, the methods are intelligent, but the quantities are inadequate . . . There are no men, no tanks, no airplanes. Tell me, *mon Capitaine*, have we so much as once seen a thousand men in a single group?'

'Just once,' I told him. 'The Canadian Division.'

'You can never make more than one division out of that! As for tanks, they haven't enough for instruction purposes . . . Have you heard anyone talk about combined operations—infantry, tanks and bombers? . . . Not a word. No, *mon Capitaine*, all this cannot be taken seriously. It is nice and well done, but when it comes to stopping the most formidable war machine, they are not ready . . . any more than we are.'

My impression was the same. I tried to reassure myself by remembering that 'the British lose all the battles except the last one,' that they never go to work until their backs are against the wall, that perhaps they were not showing us their larger units. At the bottom of my heart I knew very well that the British effort, like ours, was tragically inadequate. I found once more the qualities that I had always loved in this country: a sense of humour, discipline and courage, but I saw no trace of that state of mind, *My country's in danger*, that alone would have been effective at such a moment and in the face of such an enemy.

At the War Office I said to the British general who received me:

'You tell me, sir, that the active army, its reserves and the territorials, represent in the neighbourhood of 750,000 men, and that 600,000 recruits in addition are subject to call . . . Well and good . . . But then how does it happen that you do not already have thirty or forty divisions?'

'I know nothing about it,' he told me frankly, 'and the colonel who knows about the number of men fit to fight isn't here today.'

That evening in Parliament I encountered Hore-Belisha:

'What do you think of our new conscript army?' he asked.

'It seems to me to be made of excellent stuff,' I told him. 'But I am like Oliver Twist: I ask for more.'

In point of fact, aside from the Canadian Division, no one could show us a body of troops in training larger than a battalion. The instruction of the infantry was carried out by old sergeant-majors who taught bayonet fighting. This art was not likely to be of much use against Goering's airplanes. At the tank school the instruction was ingenious, but the tanks were few and superannuated. Nevertheless I had one consolation: that was the old chauffeur who drove our coach. Over icy roads, through ditches filled with snow, plunged from four o'clock on in the opaque darkness of the blackout, this little white-haired man carried on his difficult task. Twenty times we saw him covered with mud, numbed with the cold, and lost. Never did he lose his courage.

'Don't you worry,' he would say to us, 'it will be all right in the end.'

And in the end it was always all right as a result of his tenacity, good humour and patience. I encouraged myself to think at that time that he was an image of England; that she too would see herself, more than once in the course of that war, bogged down and apparently hopeless, and that perhaps, like him, she would get out of her difficulties and end by leading us to the Inn of Victory.

On ten occasions I was asked to lecture to officers and soldiers. As I was leaving one of these talks, made before the cadets of an aviation school, I overheard the conversation of two young people who were walking in front of me and who had not recognized me:

'Who's that old fellow who has just been talking to us?' one of them asked.

'I don't know,' the other replied, 'but I think he's a colonel named Bramble . . .'

On the boat that carried me from Southampton to Le Havre and which took twenty-four hours to cross because it had to zigzag to avoid submarines, I found Professor Langevin and a whole committee of French scientists who had just been conferring with British scientists about technical aspects of the war. From them I heard comforting news:

'What the British physicists have done since the beginning of this campaign is splendid,' Langevin told me. 'They have worked out a procedure to detect airplanes at a distance and a hundred other ingenious methods of defence . . . In the matter of magnetic mines, just see how quick they have been. In two weeks they analysed the nature of the mines, found a way of countering them and suggested simple and inexpensive means of protecting their ships. There you have efficient work. For my part, I am doing research on two or three fairly important matters . . .'

Thereupon he talked to me about the immense energy stored in all matter and about the possibility, if one could succeed in splitting the atom, of producing explosions that would destroy entire cities.

'We have made some experiments in southern Algeria,' he told me 'There lies the secret of victory.'

This was true, but we did not have the immense means necessary to wrest the secret from the atom. Nevertheless Langevin's conversation had opened vast horizons before me. Later, when I arrived in America, I met the great physicist Lawrence who, with a team of scientists, was working on the atom bomb. As we were analysing the means of winning the war, I innocently mentioned the splitting of the atom. He seemed terrified.

'Who told you that?' he asked anxiously.

I told him about my trip with Langevin; he saw that I was ignorant of the whole great plan and he unobtrusively changed the subject.

As soon as I returned to Arras, I was called upon by Captain Georges de Castellane, who was attached to the General Staff of the First Army Group and who came on behalf of General Billotte to ask me to give lectures to all the armies of the group. I was well acquainted with the general, who had been military governor of Paris. He was a brisk and brilliant man, competent in every way to command the best of the French armies. Unfortunately he was destined to be killed in an automobile accident at the beginning of the German offensive.

'I am going to have you visit all my troops,' he told me. 'Talk to them about the British army, about England and England's empire . . . I myself know the English well; they are slow, terribly slow, but in the end they get things done . . . And besides they hold on. That's what you must explain to our Frenchmen.'

That was the beginning of several weeks of active, nomad existence. Each morning a French military car would come to get me and take me to a new staff headquarters. I would have lunch with the general, and in the evening my lecture would be delivered before an audience of two thousand officers, NCOs and soldiers. Thus I saw a large number of our leaders. With the First Army at Bohain, I found General Blanchard, a smart and expert soldier surrounded by enthusiastic officers who planned and replanned the entry into Belgium in order to save half an hour on the timetable. He sent me to see a military review commanded by General Bougrain, and there I admiringly inspected superb regiments. In the following days I went to speak at General Altmayer's headquarters at Valenciennes; then to those of General de la Laurencie, whom I had known in Rouen just before the war, General Prioux and General Janssen, who were to become heroes in the defence of Dunkirk. (General Janssen, a man of dry humour, adored by his officers, met his death after giving the order: 'Die where you stand.')

It was hard, in March 1940, while you were lunching and dining so gaily in the various messes, to imagine that danger was so close. Nevertheless some of the generals saw it and when we were alone with them talked about it with anguish:

'My men are bravery itself,' one of them said to me, 'but they can't stop tanks with their bodies. Unless they are given anti-tank guns I won't answer for what may happen.'

In April I went on with my tour. I saw General Fagalde, crackling with energy, and, with the Seventh Army on the left flank along the sea, General Giraud. In physical aspect, in strength of character and in moral worth, he seemed to me a leader after my own heart. He was bitter about the inadequacy of our preparations.

'We shall not be ready before 1941,' he told me. 'Do you know how many airplanes I have at my disposal, I, the commander of an army? Eight! ... And how many flying officers for these eight planes? Thirty! That's our Air Force.'

The weakness of France and England in 1940 was not due to the quality of their armies but to the mad imprudence of those who, whether Conservative or Labour, men of the Right or men of the Left, civilians or soldiers, had sought secondary goals and partisan victory at a time when the security, indeed the very life, of the two countries was at stake. About the total lack of preparation on the part of the Allies, the most clear-sighted of the British commanders were in accord with General Giraud. Air Vice-Marshal Blount, who was in command of *Component Air Force* and whose melancholy distinction I admired, did not hide his anxiety:

'If we only had two hundred more bombers,' he said, 'I would be a little less worried.'

Paul Reynaud was now Premier. For a long time I had admired his intelligence and his courage, but what could he do? He himself said that he had found a horrifying situation: no tanks, no airplanes. Raoul Dautry, Minister of Armament, a stout-hearted man and a patriot, worked unremittingly, but one sensed that he too felt desperate.

'We shall begin to produce in 1941,' Dautry said, 'and we shall really be in full production by 1942. But what will happen before 1942?'

I was by nature so optimistic that these views expressed by well-informed men slid off my ill-founded confidence. Nevertheless at the end of April when I went to speak to the Ninth Army, General Corap's army close to Sédan, I experienced once more the feeling of anguish which the weakness of our fortified line in the north had given me. Behind the units holding Sédan there was nothing, literally nothing, and this gap at Sédan had already been, more than once, the route for invasions.

The Headquarters of the Ninth Army were situated in the little city of Vervins, an ancient market town with sunny streets, half-closed shutters, on whose rough cobblestones officers strolled by at fixed hours, putting in an appearance at their offices at the tranquil pace of bureaucrats. In a letter written to my wife on the evening of my arrival I said: 'I have found courageous people here, a little old and dusty . . .'

General Corap, a timid, intelligent man, not very military in aspect, had grown portly and had trouble getting into a car. His conversation was interesting, but one sensed a mind turned entirely toward the past. He told me how, as a young lieutenant, he had been mobilized in Algeria against England at the time of Fachoda; then how he had captured the rebel Abd-el-Krim in Morocco in 1925. The latter exploit had been the summit of his career and in respect to the task that now awaited the unhappy Corap, this summit seemed like a molehill.

I visited the troops in front of Charleville and was struck by their inadequate numbers. Returning to Vervins, I had the impression of crossing an abandoned country. I had to stop myself, as the car rolled through villages empty of soldiers, from thinking of an invading army. How little trouble it would have, once the frontier was crossed, in penetrating as far as Vervins! And what would it have found at the entrance to that city? Wooden trestles that a child could have knocked over, a sentinel with a bayonet on his rifle, and a brigadier of the *gendarmie*. No great obstacle to an armoured division.

Our best troops were on the frontier. If the enemy broke that line, the rest of the country would be hardly more than a military parade ground for him. No doubt he would encounter numerous cities on the way. But who would defend them? The idea of a frontal attack proceeding very slowly, at the rate of a few kilometres a day as had happened in 1914, and rather quickly forming a vulnerable salient, was so

[243]

strongly impressed on all minds that no one had even thought of worrying about the defence of Douai, of Vervins, of Abbeville and of Amiens.

The colonels and generals who commanded these places, which were, after all, close to the front, were amiable, aged men who had long since retired and who had been called up at the beginning of the war to take charge of what the army considered to be administrative sinecures. These honest bureaucrats, submerged under floods of papers, had never asked themselves what they would do if enemy tanks or motor cyclists armed with machine guns presented themselves at the gates of their citadels.

I returned on leave to Paris at the beginning of May and had lunch at the home of Paul Reynaud in the Place du Palais-Bourbon. Huge coloured maps on his walls took the place of wallpaper. As always, Reynaud was eloquent, dynamic. But one felt he was nervous. He was in conflict with Daladier on the subject of General Gamelin. His friend William Bullitt, ambassador from the United States, came to dine with us at Neuilly and brought Lawrence Steinhardt, ambassador to Moscow, who was passing through Paris. Both said that America was critical of us for not acting:

'You always leave the initiative to the enemy.'

'That is because the enemy can act without regard to international law . . . We are obliged to pay attention to public opinion, and in particular to yours.'

'Public opinion in our country,' Bullitt said, 'like all public opinion, is just waiting to be violated.'

During this same leave in Paris I received a visit from Dorothy Thompson, the distinguished journalist. She arrived from a tour of Europe, overwhelmed by the power of the Axis:

'All Eastern Europe,' she said to me, 'except Turkey, is in the hands of Germany.'

I was to spend the end of my leave in Périgord, and it had been agreed that my wife and I would start by car on May 10. That morning before setting out, I turned on the radio to listen to the news. I heard:

'Monsieur Frossard, Minister of Information, will speak to you . . .'

I trembled, for at that time our ministers never addressed us except to announce catastrophes.

'The Germans,' Frossard said, 'last night invaded Belgium, Luxembourg and the Low Countries . . . All officers on leave must rejoin their units immediately . . . '

This was the great offensive, predicted long ago by General Mac-Farlane. I had to return at once to Arras. Simone came with me to the Gare du Nord. There were so many officers crowding the platform that the trains had first to be doubled, then tripled in number. My comrades seemed gay and confident:

'At last,' they said, 'we'll have our chance to win this war.'

On that morning in a train full of military men I did not hear a single pessimistic comment.

On the platform at Arras Captain Grant was waiting for me:

'We're leaving for Belgium,' he told me.

'What part?'

'Brussels, Louvain . . . Plan D is in operation; that is, we British are to establish ourselves along the River Dyle close to Louvain . . . Meanwhile, on our left General Giraud will thrust forward toward the mouth of the Rhine in order to occupy the Dutch islands; on our right we will have the support of the Belgian army . . . Marvellous!'

He seemed altogether happy. To cross this frontier that we had so long contemplated from a distance seemed to him a great and splendid adventure. Would it turn out well? He had no doubts. Since the War of 1914–18 the French army had been in English eyes 'the strongest army in the world'. It would swallow the audacious Austrian corporal in a single bite. We did not notice that General Gamelin was taking the risk that only a short time before, at Gort's mess, he had said one should never run in any circumstances: he was leaving his carapace and dispatching his best troops, his few armoured divisions, on a thrust all the way into Holland.

But neither Grant nor I thought about the danger. We rejoiced in the spectacle, the game, the action.

Since morning the British army had been advancing in admirable order. The trucks were camouflaged with branches. Women and children along the road held out flowers to the soldiers. At the entrance to Brussels the columns moved off obliquely and swung around the city. Our car went straight in. To our great surprise, when we stopped in front of the Hôtel Métropole, we were surrounded by an immense crowd which cried: 'Vive la France! . . . Vive l'Angleterre!' Did the presence of two grey-haired captains warrant all this attention?

I went straight to the French Embassy. Monsieur de Bargeton, the ambassador, gave a cry of surprise when he saw me enter his office in uniform, flanked by Grant.

'What are you doing here?' he said. 'Don't you know that Brussels has been declared an open city to save it from bombardment? No allies in uniform may enter it. And so I must decline to receive you . . . Get out of the city as quickly as you can, you and your English friend.'

This was the explanation of our mysteriously enthusiastic reception by the crowd. Grant and I were the first officers that had entered Brussels. Naturally we escaped in haste from this illicit glory and were given orders to fall back on Lille.

I spent part of the night on the high tower of the Echo du Nord with Audra, Dean of the Faculty of Letters, and his wife, watching the bombardment of the suburbs. German airplanes seemed to be everywhere, and high flames encircled the city.

Next day we returned to Belgium. Everything was changed. No more offerings of flowers for the soldiers. No more cheers. Women and old men on their doorsteps were looking with dread toward the sky.

'But what's the matter with them?' Lefèvre asked. 'They look as though they had been stunned.'

They had, in fact, been stunned. All along the road we found evidence of German bombing. The destruction did not seem very serious. Here two houses had been blown up, there a railway had been wrecked, a little farther on a road had been blasted and a car reduced to fragments. But each village had had its bomb—that was enough to terrify the inhabitants. The killing of one little girl made all the mothers, through a natural impulse, take their children away. Soon we saw the first refugees. In the first wave the automobiles of the rich driven by impeccable chauffeurs; then the cars of the poor, stuffed with provisions and made ungainly by mattresses tied on the roofs; then the villagers on bicycles, with the curé at their head; then the sad procession of those afoot followed by a few barefooted loafers. A whole country was in exodus and this human wave, when it reached a village or a city, swept the entire population along with it.

Finally we reached a deserted region. Houses were closed, shutters barred; farm animals bleated or mooed. In the plain, some factories and convents were burning, red as stage fires. We were at the scene of the Battle of Waterloo. Leaving our car in the sunken road of Ohain, we went on foot as far as the line that the British army was to hold. Apart from occasional artillery fire, the front seemed quiet enough. But one asked oneself why we had left emplacements that had been prepared with so much labour during a period of eight months in order to come out and await the German tanks in the open field.

Two more days passed, and then I noticed grim faces among the Englishmen around me. I heard murmurs, reluctant phrases, and finally I learned of the rupture of the French front at Sédan. Colonel Cailloux of the French Military Mission has told how, from that moment on, everything was changed in the relationship, hitherto trusting and courteous, between the two armies. The French no longer encountered the eyes of their friends of the day before. They felt that the latter would have preferred them not to be there so that they might talk freely. 'Do you *really* believe that your troops will hold?' they were asked. And it was necessary to admit that, if the French army did not hold, the safety of the small British army would become an acute problem.

My impressions were about the same as those of Colonel Cailloux. I noticed mysterious conversations among the British officers. If a Frenchman, even an old friend like me, approached, an embarrassed silence descended on the group. Sometimes I caught a word, snatches of sentences: 'Evacuation.' 'Withdraw to the ports.' Our life took a disordered and unintelligible course. We received orders to return to Arras. The roads were now so choked with refugees that we could only advance slowly. The approaches to Arras were defended by barricades of sandbags hastily improvised. The Hôtel de l'Univers had been destroyed by a bomb. Part of the city had been burned. My friends Poumier and Puthomme of the 'Capucins' were still energetic and gay. I went to bed in our house, which was still intact, and all night I heard sirens and then the drone of German airplanes which evoked in my mind the nights in Abbeville twenty-two years before, and the wild cries of Childe Douglas.

On May 16, I wrote this letter to Simone:

My dearest one, We are living through days of terrible anguish. One must be calm and hopeful. Whatever happens, we love each other and that is indestructible. But we must foresee everything, the better as well as the worse. Here are my instructions for you:

(a) It is impossible for you to come here again, completely out of the question. Moreover I myself am ordered to leave.

(b) If things go well, it is possible that I shall be sent to Paris in the course of the next week, but naturally I shall have neither time nor means of letting you know in advance.

(c) If things go worse, I wish you to go to Essendiéras. I ardently hope that this will not be necessary, but I wish to have the assurance that you would be wise enough to make this essential retreat in time. Families are like armies: they can be saved by a prudent manoeuvre.

Since the beginning of this hard period, your wisdom and your tenderness have been my only reason for continuing to live . . . '

In the north, unverifiable rumours circulated. 'The Germans are in Cambrai!' The French Mission decided to withdraw and took me with it. Then it was learned that the news was false and we returned to Arras. 'The Germans are at Bapaume!' And Colonel Medlicott, head of the Public Relations, said to us: 'Reassemble at Amiens.'

On May 20 we found the city of Amiens overrun by refugees and stripped of its substance, like a field ravaged by grasshoppers. No beds available. I rolled myself in a blanket. During the night Colonel Medlicott had me called:

'The General Staff is leaving for Boulogne,' I was told through an English officer, 'but two of our cars have been destroyed, we no longer have room for you or the correspondents . . . The Germans are coming . . . Return to Paris.'

'And how?'

'By rail.'

'There are no more trains.'

'Then any way you can.'

He disappeared into the night. His brutal decision dismayed me. There were a dozen of us Frenchmen there, our baggage lost, without travel orders. Were we to be stupidly taken prisoner? We hurried to the station. The tide of refugees was beating against it in furious waves. An intelligent and kindly Military Commissioner understood our situation:

'There's only one way I can get you out of here,' he said. 'There is a baggage car full of gold belonging to the Bank of France that I am sending to Paris. You can get in with your comrades. Will that do?'

'Most certainly!'

It was a nightmare trip. German airplanes followed us and tried to destroy the tracks; the bombs fell close to the train; the engine proceeded at a walking pace, and at each level-crossing we found again the sad, rose-coloured tide of refugees which spread out between the rails and kept us motionless for hours.

Finally, after an interminable journey, we arrived in Paris. We were much surprised to find the city little changed. The shock of defeat had been so sudden and so violent that France, stunned into semi-consciousness by the blow, had not yet understood what had happened to her. My wife cried out when she saw me enter. Having had no news from me since May 16, she thought I was missing, a prisoner. She told me what people were saying in Paris: Weygand was now in command of our armies; the public was optimistic; they hoped for a Battle of the Marne.

Next morning I went to see my new French chief, Colonel Schiffer, and asked him what I should do. It was no longer possible to join General Gort. But I would not admit defeat. Could I not go to the RAF which had a base in the east? He gave me his authorization for a few days and I left for Troyes. There I found Air Vice-Marshal Playfair and visited his squadrons. The pilots were courageous, the planes excellent but, in the air as on the ground, we were outmatched by the infinitely superior numbers of the Germans.

It was at Troyes on May 28 in a café that I heard the radio announce the capitulation of the Belgian army. Returning to Paris, I went to report to Colonel Schiffer and found him with Captain Max Hermant of Weygand's General Staff. We talked about British public opinion, which did not seem to understand the desperate nature of our situation.

'Why don't you go to London,' Captain Hermant said to me, 'and talk in English on the BBC?'

'I have already agreed, at the request of the Ambassador, to give a talk on June 25 at the French Institute in London; all that's necessary is to send me a little sooner.'

'I will make the suggestion to General Headquarters,' he said.

On June 3, Paris was bombed by three hundred German planes. Despite the large number of dead and wounded, this raid made little impression. Like me, the French people refused to admit the idea of defeat. On June 5 the second German offensive began against our new lines on the Somme and the Aisne. At first the news seemed fairly good. At the Ministry of Information it was said that 'the line was holding,' that our airplane cannons were doing marvels against the tanks and that 'the German air force seemed out of breath.' This was the policy of an ostrich. But on the evening of the 8th the communiqué was dreadful.

There began to be talk of Forges-les-Eaux, of the region around Rouen. Would we have to submit to the Germans' entry into Paris? And would the city be defended? There were already a number of signs indicating that the government was thinking of withdrawing. In front of the Ministry of the Navy and in the courtyard of the Ministry of War trucks were being loaded with the archives.

'The heavy elements are being evacuated,' was the noncommital explanation at the offices.

On Sunday the 9th Colonel Schiffer told me that Captain Hermant had telephoned from General Headquarters that I was to leave immediately for London. He gave me a travel order with which to secure a seat in a British plane. I also had with me another travel order, signed for the Ministry of Foreign Affairs by Marx, Director of Cultural Affairs at the Quai d'Orsay. This second order directed me to go to Boston to give the famous Lowell Lectures in the autumn of 1940. This was a unique opportunity to talk to the American élite with the assurance of being understood.

I went to see the British Air Attaché and he said to me:

'Tomorrow at noon be at the Buc airdrome.'

Would it still be possible at noon on June 10 to get to Buc? I began to doubt it. Already it was said that German motorized divisions had reached Vernon, Mantes . . . Tanks had been seen at Isle-Adam. That was the suburbs of Paris. I begged Simone to leave for Essendiéras with my son Gérald, who had not yet recovered from an appendix operation he had recently undergone at the American Hospital in Neuilly.

'If the Germans, after crossing the Seine, cut the roads to Chartres and Orléans, you will be a prisoner.'

'I am not afraid,' she said.

'That's all very well for you, but what about the others? There is Gérald, who is a soldier and ill, whose incision has not yet healed . . . Emilie, whose husband is in the army . . . When the city is taken, if you are here you will have no way of communicating with me and we will be without news of each other for months.'

Finally she consented. We spent our last evening sorting out the things she was to take with her. She had so little space and we had so many souvenirs we wanted to keep safe that the choice was painful. From time to time we listened to the radio.

'The enemy is showing less initiative,' said the communiqué, optimistic to the point of lunacy. 'We are containing him at several points.'

But the names of the places mentioned proved that the invasion was proceeding rapidly.

Very early next morning we decided to go and say goodbye to our favourite places in Paris. My wife drove her little white car. The weather was glorious and a sunny, golden mist enveloped the city. In the empty streets traffic policemen were stopping the infrequent cars with pathetic and useless conscientiousness. Since I had left all my baggage in Colonel Medlicott's truck, I needed a raincoat and a suitcase. We went into several stores. The saleswomen were attending to their duties as carefully and as courteously as usual. Many of them had red eyes from having wept all night, but with one accord they kept silent about what was in the minds of all.

'The little people of France are admirable,' my wife said. 'So simple and so brave. How can men like this have been beaten? How can the Maginot Line . . . ?'

'Men can do nothing against machines . . . They were told: "Defend a line." They would have defended it. But it was never attacked. It was taken from behind and encircled.'

'I still can't imagine,' she said, 'that the Germans are going to enter Paris.'

A few days earlier we had had a long conversation about the entry of the German army into Paris with one of our dearest friends, the surgeon Thierry de Martel.

'As for me,' he had told us, 'my mind is made up: the minute I learn they are in the city, I am going to kill myself.'

Then he explained to us at length that most people do not know how to kill themselves and fail in the attempt, but that a surgeon holds the revolver as precisely as a scalpel and always hits a vital centre. Then, half seriously, he added:

'If you too are unwilling to survive our misfortunes, I offer you my services.'

On the evening of the 10th, when I was already flying toward England, the telephone summoned my wife who was sadly wrapping up the few objects she could take with her. It was Thierry de Martel.

'I wanted to find out,' he told her, 'if you and your husband were still in Paris?'

'André is on a mission to London. As for me, I am leaving tomorrow at dawn.'

'I too am going away,' he said in a strange tone, 'but on a much longer journey.'

My wife, remembering our conversation about suicide, realized that he was going to kill himself and tried to dissuade him:

'You can still do so much good. Your patients, your assistants, your nurses, they all need you . . . '

'I *cannot* go on living,' Martel said. 'My only son was killed in the last war . . . Up until this one I wanted to believe that he had died in order to save France. And now France, in her turn, is lost. Everything I have lived for will disappear . . . I cannot go on.'

And when she continued to plead with him he hung up.

On June 25 during a stop at the Azores, my wife learned from a bulletin in an American paper that Thierry de Martel had committed suicide at the moment when the German army had made its entrance into Paris.

In him we lost an incomparable friend, and France one of the noblest types of men that she has bred. This surgeon had been a model of chivalry. He had earned fortunes, and used them to support free clinics in which he had operated on thousands of unfortunates. I knew of one case in which he saved from death, by an operation that he alone could perform, a man who for a long time had been pursuing him with jealousy and hatred. He had proved on a thousand occasions his physical and moral courage. There could be no better measure of the immense disarray of the French in the face of this total disaster than the admitted inability of so brave a man to go on living.

During the retreat from Flanders on the road to Vimy, I came across an old French peasant standing on the threshold of his house and watching the crowd of refugees stream by. He said to me:

'The pity of it, *mon Capitaine*! . . . Such a great country . . . '

The pity of it, I thought in my turn, when I learned of the death of Thierry de Martel. It was crushing to reflect that such things (for France has produced more than a few) found themselves reduced to despair, and a great civilization found itself menaced because five thousand tanks and ten thousand planes which we could have produced with no difficulty at all had not been built in time.

When our purchases had been made my wife and I walked along the quais to the Invalides which we admired, among all the monuments in Paris, for the grace of its façade and dome, and then went on to Notre Dame and the Ile Saint-Louis. We returned by the Place des Vosges. Since the roads were certain to be filled with refugees, it was high time to start for Buc. From the balcony of the apartment in Neuilly, which we had loved so much, we looked for a last time together at the trees of the Bois de Boulogne, the Arc de Triomph and Mont Valérien, crowned with Italian cypresses. Then we embraced. We did not know whether we should ever see each other again.

To my great surprise I reached the Buc airdrome without difficulty. The myriads of cars that were leaving Paris that day were heading toward the south, not toward the west. At the entrance to the field a sergeant of the military police painstakingly checked my identity.

'The Germans are within thirty kilometres, *mon Capitaine.*'

That was not far, but he was calm, and like the little saleswomen in Paris, he was performing his duty to the last moment. The British airplane that was to take me had not yet arrived. I sat down on the grass and waited. The heat was stormy and oppressive. I fell asleep and dreamed of my childhood, of the forked lilacs of Elbeuf and of the white and pink anemones that faded in my fingers. A noise awakened me; it was a big Flamingo plane landing. Lord Lloyd got out. I knew him and went up to shake hands.

'I've come to see Reynaud,' he told me. 'Is he still in Paris?'

'Yes, I think so.'

It was his handsome plane that was to take me to London, but when the pilot tried to start it one of the engines refused to fire. After twenty attempts the young flyer said angrily:

'And that's how we're winning the war!'

At that moment another Flamingo arrived, a much less elegant machine, but it was in working order, and I was told to get aboard.

25

The Tarpeian Rock

But break, my heart, for I must hold my tongue.

Shakespeare: *Hamlet I.ii.159*

In the plane taking me to England, seated in the fuselage, watching the clouds and waves speed by below, I summed up the situation. It was frightful. France had been defeated and, unless America and England were in a position to furnish her immediately with aid in immense quantities, it seemed impossible for her to go on fighting. I had seen troops disbanded, roads blocked by civilians in flight. An implacable foreign power, then, was going to occupy my country. My wife and children were still there; I was to be separated from those I loved. All the ideas and all the sentiments that were dear to me—liberty, honesty of judgment, impartiality, generosity and charity—were going into a period of eclipse, and the defeat, exploited by enemy propaganda, could not fail to set loose evil passions. A world was coming in which I no longer saw any place for myself. 'If this airplane were to fall into the Channel,' I thought, 'it would be doing me a proud service.'

Since the pilot considered the usual course by way of Boulogne and Calais dangerous, we veered to the west, seeing beneath us on the Norman plain the advancing German columns, and left France in the neighbourhood of Caen. I recognized the mouth of the Dives and the beach at Cabourg on which I had so often played in my childhood. In the plane a Captain Crawshay told me of the death of Gordon, the handsome Scot I had so much admired at Lord Gort's on my first day there. He had requested permission to resign his post and take command of a battalion of Gordon Highlanders.

My moral depression was brief. From Hendon airport where we landed, I had myself driven to the French Military Mission which was under the command of General Lelong. He inspected my military directive and turned me over to Captain Bret, an old friend of mine,

[254]

who took me to the British Ministry of Information. There I met Charles Peake of the Foreign Office whom I knew.

'You want to explain the situation in France to the British public?' he said to me. 'You come at exactly the right moment. There is a press conference beginning in five minutes. You will talk to all our correspondents.'

I protested; taken unaware, I had nothing prepared, and to improvise on such a subject . . . But Bret, Peake and Sir Walter Monckton who had joined us dragged me onto the platform, and in torn, breathless and burning phrases I described the martyrdom of France:

'It is not in 1941 that you must help us, it is not next month, it is not tomorrow, it is today, it is this hour, it is this minute . . . '

When I had finished, to my great surprise the three hundred journalists stood up and applauded at length.

'You should be pleased,' said Harold Nicolson who was Duff Cooper's assistant at the Ministry. 'You stirred up those hard-boiled boys of the press.'

'I only said very badly what everyone knows.'

'Don't you believe it,' he told me. 'Our people are far from understanding the gravity of the situation. You must repeat these things on the radio for the whole British public, then for the Dominions, then for America . . . '

After this talk, Nicolson and Peake took me to Duff Cooper. It was agreed with him that I should repeat that same evening what I had just said, and that the BBC would give me its best time, that is, the 'Postscript to the News' at 9.15 in the evening.

It is not in 1941, it is not this autumn, it is not even next month that our friends can aid us; it is now. We know how courageously the British army and the Royal Air Force have fought, we know they have done all that was possible. The time has come to do the impossible. We have confidence in our British Allies. We know that they are ready to throw all they possess into the contest. What we ask of them is to understand the importance of Time. Remember the Spirit of Dunkirk. Before Dunkirk it was thought impossible to evacuate more than thirty thousand men in a few days from a half-destroyed port. The most optimistic said fifty thousand. In fact, three hundred and thirty-five thousand were saved. How? Who knows better than you who did it? . . . And if you show once more the Spirit of Dunkirk, you can also win this battle, and the war . . . For Dunkirk you gave all your boats. Now give all your men, all your airplanes, all your cannon. Let us together demand that America, who is so ready to help us, produce in two months what normally would take two years. All the experts will tell us that it is impossible in a few weeks to equip, train and transport a great army. Nothing is more true. It is impossible but it must be done, and it will be done . . .

The sentiment that inspired this speech was love of battered and violated France and the passionate desire to save her. But the British military leaders thought that to throw all their forces into this battle for France, already lost, would be to sacrifice the future without changing the present. At no moment did they risk their fighter planes which alone would one day assure the defence of England. They sent some troops, some squadrons, to France. It was a single straw to close a breach through which a torrent was raging. When I understood that the automatic reaction, *England first*, had come into play, I knew that for the immediate present France was doomed. At this I conceived a frightful sadness and for the moment some bitterness. *I was wrong*, and the British experts were right. Unable to save France, they felt capable of saving England, and the latter, later on, would re-establish France among the nations. This strategy, after terrible years, was to prove effective. To a Frenchman filled with anguish and with doubt, it seemed *at that time* egoistic.

The British people, less well informed, responded generously to my appeal. During the days that followed my talk on the BBC, I received thousands of letters. All of them said; 'We want to help France. What can we do?' The thing that struck me was the simultaneous desire to help, an unreserved generosity and a profound ignorance of what this war really was. When I described the suffering of the refugees, the ruined villages, the martyrdom of the army, I saw with surprise that people listened to me as though I were a being who had arrived from another planet. Public opinion would have wished the government to take much more radical measures to save France. But good will does not take the place of tanks and airplanes. 'These letters, these visits that I receive,' I said to Duff Cooper and Nicolson, 'are touching . . . But practically, what can you give us?'

Their faces became grave and sorrowful.

'Aside from the Canadian Division which has just left,' they replied, 'we have no more troops equipped for the war on the continent . . . We do not possess *matérial* to replace all that was lost in Flanders. We will send you some symbolic squadrons, but it is indispensable in the common interest that our aircraft factories and our ports remain well defended . . . If you can hold out until 1941 . . . '

Alas! I knew too well that we could not hold out, on the soil of France, until 1941.

To Charles Corbin, the French ambassador, whose attitude during this whole difficult period was wholly courageous and noble, I said; 'Just the same, it is strange that in the tenth month of the war the British do not have an army!'

'Yes,' he replied, 'but one must be fair. They have punctiliously kept the engagements that they made. The dates were fixed for the formation of the British divisions; these dates have been met. The fault was not to ask our allies for as many divisions as in 1914, but it is a fact that we did not ask anything of the sort . . . The myth of defensive strength and the myth of the fortified lines blinded our ministers and our generals.'

On the morning of the 13th, the press announced the arrival of the Germans in front of Paris. As I was sadly reading *The Times*, the telephone rang and a maid of honour told me that the Queen wished to see me at eleven o'clock at Buckingham Palace. My wife and I had frequently met the Duke and Duchess of York before they became sovereigns of England. I had seen them in London at the house of Mrs. Greville, and in Paris at the Phipps'. I had loved talking to the duchess who knew French well, had read all our books and judged them with taste and subtlety. She had had me invited to the Coronation and later, when she came on a visit to Paris, she had treated us on every occasion with affectionate consideration. But in these circumstances I could not imagine what the honour of this audience might mean.

Buckingham Palace, with its tall footmen dressed in red, its commemorative paintings and its bamboo furniture, remained very Victorian. Sir Alexander Hardinge conducted me to the Queen. She was, as always, beautiful and gentle. On the table stood an immense basket of red roses.

'Monsieur Maurois,' she said to me, 'I want you to know what sorrow I feel for Paris and what sympathy for the French in their misfortune . . . I love France *so much*. During our trip to Paris two years ago, I felt the heart of the French beating so close to mine. I would like to talk to them tonight on the radio. Will you write my speech?'

I replied that I was at her command, but perhaps the Foreign Office . . .

'No,' she said sharply, 'the Foreign Office would write a very good speech but a Queen's speech . . . I want to be a woman talking to other women. I will tell you what I would like to express, then you will return to your hotel, write the speech, and when it is ready you will bring it to me.'

My hotel, the Dorchester, was close to Buckingham Palace. An hour later I returned to the Palace with my text. Once more Sir Alexander Hardinge conducted me to the Queen's apartment. She read my composition and said; 'It is exactly what I wanted. Now we will rehearse it. You will read it aloud, then I will read it . . . And we will go over it again and again until it is just right.'

And so I read. In the speech was this phrase; 'A country that has such men to defend it and such women to love it can never perish.' When it was the Queen's turn, she read; '*Un pays qui a tel(s) hommes pour le défendre,*' omitting the *s*.

'I beg pardon,' I said, 'but the *s* should be pronounced; *de tels hommes . . .* '

'And yet,' she said to me, 'my French governess taught me that before an *h*, the *s* is not pronounced.'

'That depends,' I said. 'Before an aspirated *h* . . . '

And suddenly this scene, the red roses on the table, the portrait of Queen Victoria on the wall, the sympathetic face of the Queen, all seemed to be impossible. I thought: 'How can this be? My country has been invaded; my wife is in occupied Paris. Tomorrow, no doubt Nazi officers will be living in my apartment and will seize my papers; I am miserable to the point of tears—and here I am, talking to the Queen of England about aspirated *h*'s!'

Nevertheless I had to exercise control and go on with the rehearsal. The Queen's kindness helped me. When the speech was faultless, she asked me about what I had seen during the campaign, about my wife and my children. Her eyes, bright with tears, expressed so much human compassion that I was profoundly touched. 'Monsieur Maurois,' she said, 'I know that you have lost everything, but do you not find that when one has lost everything, almost everything still remains?' She was right. Faithfully at her post the little child Hope still remained.

In that interview with the Queen, at that tragic moment and in a historic décor I had so often described, there was a mixture of unreality and intimacy that overwhelmed me. Next day at the Dorchester I received a letter from the maid of honour. It contained the Queen's thanks and was accompanied by a little box—cuff-links of onyx on which the initial E (Elizabeth) was outlined in small diamonds. I treasure them lovingly.

At the moment when the footman dressed in red livery embroidered in gold showed me into the drawing room of Buckingham Palace, my entire possessions consisted of a uniform, two shirts and a few francs. In 1939, in answer to an appeal from the Minister of Finance, I had had all the money due me in England and America sent to France so that I no longer had any credits abroad. The news from France became worse and worse. I spent the weekend of June 15 to 17 at Marlborough, the home of my friends the Phipps'. There I found, as always, the most perfect confidence and understanding, but when on Monday the 17th the radio announced that an armistice had been requested I shut myself in my room, threw myself on my bed and wept like a child. In my diary I read:

'Frances' and Eric's tender friendship has relieved me a little. The news is frightful; the Maginot Line has been turned; Reynaud is resigning. June 18: One asks oneself each day how the news could be worse. And each day it is worse. Today Marshal Pétain asks for an armistice, and asks for it in the worst possible circumstances for this country—with no assurance about the departure of the British troops. It is sad.'

At this moment the British reaction was far from hostile to unhappy France. The Phipps' expressed their heart-felt sympathy. When I returned to London, Lord Winterton, Lady Diana Duff-Cooper, Harold Nicolson, the Amerys, Desmond MacCarthy and Raymond Mortimer, all were admirable in their kindness and tact. Since I was still wearing uniform, strangers would stop me in the street to express their sympathy. But doubt gave rise to embarrassment.

'And the fleet?' people would inquire anxiously.

What could I reply? I knew nothing. Then began an exchange of bitter and hostile communications between London and Bordeaux. I was deeply disturbed by this war of words, which seemed to me devoid both of dignity and discretion. There was nothing vainer or more dangerous for the two countries than to fly at each other's throat after a defeat for which they had been jointly responsible. To whom could their recriminations be helpful except to those whose whole propaganda had been calculated to produce just such a break? I understood very well that England had been painfully surprised by some of the clauses of the armistice (I had been myself), but the only attitudes that seemed to me appropriate to the extent of our common misfortune were, on the part of England, the affectionate deference of a warrior to the wounded comrade he must leave behind and, on the part of France, the sorrow of a soldier disarmed, his silent exhortation to his happier fellows able to continue the strife, and the hope of rejoining it one day at their side.

Charles Corbin, the French ambassador to London, and Roger Cambon, counsellor of the embassy, both tried and true friends of Great Britain, shared my feelings on this subject. As for me, at that time I was like a victim of torture torn apart by horses driven in opposite directions. At no other time in my life have I suffered such conflict and torment of mind. For twenty-five years I had been studying England and I had grown attached to its traditions and its history. I was not unaware of its political mistakes; I had spoken frankly of them in time of peace; but I knew its courage, its tenacity; I believed that its victory would assure the liberation of France. I still ardently hoped that the two peoples would one day find themselves united, but I had, alas, an agonizing presentiment that before this came about there might be—and that before long—agonizing and perhaps bloody quarrels.

At the last moment before the armistice, Winston Churchill had sought to aid Reynaud's cabinet to continue the battle by offering to combine the two empires under a single government. Each citizen of the two countries would have had a double Franco-Britannic nationality. All resources would have been held in common. It was an amazing proposal which, if it had been made a few weeks earlier, might perhaps have altered the course of history. It came at a moment when exhausted France asked only for *immediate* aid: planes, tanks, guns. But Winston Churchill, who believed he had made a prodigious offer to France, one that caused stupefaction in the British Parliament and even evoked criticism because of its magnitude, was wounded to see his declaration of union received with indifference. Many Englishmen shared his regret, and the best friends of France were perhaps the most bitter because they had been the most ardent.

'What a pity!' the distinguished English critic, Desmond Mac-Carthy, said to me, 'I would so much have liked to become a French citizen.'

I had just spent an intimate and melancholy evening with him and Raymond Mortimer, another author of talent, the first occasion for a long time when I had been able to survey the terrible events of our time and to talk about eternal things. Readers of Virgil and Horace must sometimes have spent such evenings in the fourth or fifth century in cities attacked by the invaders. We had talked about French poetry, which my hosts knew so well; we had recited verses by Mallarmé, Valéry, and by Malherbe and Racine as well. Then Desmond said:

'We know that we are menaced by everything: first of all, by death, which is not of great importance, but by tyranny too, which is more serious. Our duty is to save what can be saved and this depends only on us: the confidence we have in one another. For this two things are necessary: first of all, let us never forget the existence of our friends, their kindness and their affection. Even if we do not see each other for years at a time, even if people say to the French that we, the English, are monsters, or to us that the French have betrayed us, let us think of certain Frenchmen and certain Englishmen whose thoughts we know can never be anything but noble and generous . . . And then, when we have the chance, let us be very kind to one another, much kinder than usual. Today there is a great shortage of kindness in the world. The equilibrium needs to be re-established.'

That evening and also the days I spent at the Phipps' home and with Maurice Baring had revived in me the image of a better England. But often I felt the difficulties of the situation with painful acuteness. Relations between the two countries were growing more bitter. Sometimes the atmosphere in groups in which I was the only Frenchman reminded me of that at Lille at the moment of the débâcle. I would stumble upon mysterious colloquies which stopped at my approach. I would over-hear fragments of sentences: 'A blockade of France will enable us . . .'

I had no doubts whatever about the firmness of the English resistance. Churchill would never bow before Hitler. On the BBC he denounced 'this wicked man' and his accomplice, the 'jackal' Mussolini. He travelled throughout the island, preparing it for the struggle against invasion. Together with his military advisers, he settled upon a strategy. A new army, the Home Guard, was in training. On every beach I saw thousands of men digging anti-tank ditches and erecting barbed-wire entanglements. The few divisions that were well armed were kept in reserve to be rushed immediately into any breach and to close it. Churchill was not going to repeat the error of Gamelin by contenting himself with a linear defence of the coast and not retaining a mass of manoeuvre. Arms were lacking; he got them from Roosevelt; rifles, guns and American tanks arrived in immense shipments. I admired the fierce determination of a whole people and I knew that the invasion, if Hitler committed himself to that folly, would be repelled. But I would not permit people to make outrageous comparisons with France who, for her part, had not been protected by anti-tank ditches and the Channel.

General de Gaulle had just arrived in London. As early as the 15th, Corbin had told me that he expected him. Then the general had been delayed, possibly by a Cabinet meeting. I had admired him for a long time and had been one of the first French writers to comment in one of my books, *Un Art de vivre* in 1931, on the quality of his style and the firmness of his ideas. Daniel-Rops, who was editor at Plon of the collection in which *La France et son armée* had appeared, had noticed my praises and invited me to lunch with Colonel de Gaulle. I knew him slightly, very slightly, but I had a more than favourable opinion of him. I did not hear his appeal of June 18: I read it in the papers. I loved the noble sentence: 'France has lost a battle; she has not lost the war.' It was in accord with my thoughts. However, one will perhaps remember the fervour with which, in the regiment, I had recited: 'Discipline constitutes the principal strength of armies . . . ' While waiting until England and America were ready, was it not necessary above all to maintain the unity of the French? To be truthful, I think today that these scruples were vain. Discipline is necessary, but in the history of nations, in desperate situations, there are orders that ought to be disobeyed. Lyautey had run this risk. I was to run it myself later on when I left for North Africa. In June 1940 I sought agonizingly for the path of duty.

On June 21 General de Gaulle summoned me. His aide-de-camp, Lieutenant de Courcel, came to get me at the Dorchester. I was taken into a small office and found myself in the presence of a young general whose firmness of manner appealed to me. If he had asked me on that day to serve as an officer in the little army he was recruiting, I would certainly have accepted, but what he offered me was quite different. 'I am going to form a government mission,' he told me. 'I hope that you will be a member.' My role would have been to talk to the French, as I had already done on the BBC. This offer had much to tempt me. I found myself in London, demobilized by the French Mission, with no employment but eager to serve. Here was a sure way of getting back into active life—and at the top. To return to France, as most of our diplomats were preparing to do? There could be no question of that for me. In the first place, I would be subject to the Nazi racist laws; also I had conducted a violent campaign against Hitler; I had written a little book, devastating for him, on the origins of the war of 1939. My account would be quickly settled. A cable had just informed me that my wife, herself in danger, had not been able to stay at her mother's home in Dordogne and was trying to get to America by way of Spain.

'Yes,' I said to myself, listening to the general, 'there is the solution to my problem.' Nevertheless I saw equally strong reasons for not following what seemed to be the path of my own personal salvation. My dominant thought at that moment was that the *only* chance for France and England to vanquish Hitler was through the entry of the United States into the war. This also was the opinion of General de Gaulle who had talked about it in his speech of June 18. And this was a country where for a long time I had had a large audience. There I could render services infinitely greater than in England, where Churchill's support had already been completely gained. Opinion in America is formed by university professors, by writers and by women. It was precisely this public to which I would have access and over which, perhaps, influence. There and there alone, it seemed to me, lay the key to victory.

I reminded myself, too, that my aged and infirm mother was going to remain in Paris, and my daughter as well. They would be hostages who, if I continued to talk on the radio, might pay for it with their lives. My sons were in the so-called 'free' zone, but how long would their pseudo-liberty last? Moreover, what was proposed to me, to talk on the BBC, would certainly oblige me to take up the question of Marshal Pétain. I was aware that, enfeebled by age, he was no longer able to bear his great responsibilities. The talk I heard at that time in London made me think he would be attacked. Others would have the right and perhaps the duty of leading that campaign, not I. Here is the reason:

In the first place, I had known him for a long time and he had inspired in me a profound respect. In 1917 I had witnessed his efforts to end the mutinies; I could not forget that he had greatly helped to win the war of 1914–18. I had been a member of the Council of the French office of Information to the United States, of which he had been president, and I knew that he was a friend of America. In *Chose nues* I have reported some of my conversations with him. They had been numerous and friendly. Besides, I had a feeling of personal gratitude toward him. In 1939 at the time when I was a candidate for the Académie Française, I had been attacked with astonishing malice by Louis Bertrand, then a convert to Hitlerism. In a group of his cronies he had said, trembling with rage: 'We already have one Jew in the Académie —Bergson; it would be a scandal to elect another.' To this Marshal Pétain had instantly replied: 'Monsieur, that is not the question; the *only* question is whether Monsieur Maurois is a good French writer, and you yourself would not dream of denying that.' Georges Lecomte, who described the scene to me, added that this intervention had been decisive.

What was I to do? For a long time political action had tempted me. Now a chance was offered to take part, and in the service of a cause that was my own. And yet ... I asked General de Gaulle to allow me twenty-four hours for reflection. That night I did not sleep. My whole being, my mind, my hopes, cried out: 'Yes.' Then I pictured an officer in a high cap, wearing a swastika on his sleeve, entering my mother's apartment and saying to her: 'Follow me.'

Next day I went to the Embassy to ask for advice. Castellane, who received me, said: 'As for me, I'm going to return. I consider it my duty to share the miseries of the French and to help them in reconstruction. I recognize that your case is different. For you to return would be suicide ... Go to America where you are expected and where you will have a good influence. What's more, you have travelling orders from the Foreign Office. You have been mobilized. Your duty is clear.' Roger Cambon, who had joined us and who intended to remain in London, was of the same opinion.

At five o'clock I went to see General de Gaulle (despair in my heart) and told him, as he has reported in his *Mémoires*, that I thought I could be more useful to France and to England by going to the United

States. I believe in my soul and conscience that my choice in 1940 was a wise one and that, as I had hoped, I was able in America to render services to my country and to the Allies that no other available Frenchman could have performed at that time, but the decision had been painful and left me with lasting regrets. Our decisions are always made by a small majority.

From June 23 to 30 I was engaged in the intricacies of obtaining a visa and a ticket. There was no difficulty about the entrance visa for the United States. The consul said to me: 'We are happy to receive a guest who has always been our friend.' The authorization from the French Embassy was a matter of course; I had my travelling orders. I saw Corbin, the ambassador, who gave his approval. He was himself preparing to return to France. In the lower echelons of the English Civil Service I encountered more obstacles. The armistice had wounded people's hearts. At the passport office a peevish employee told me: 'We have no ruling for the French.' Thanks to Nicolson, I finally obtained passage on one of the ships that were taking British children to Canada. But I was required to pay fifty-two pounds for my passage. I did not have it. My publishers and my literary agent advanced the money.

My ship, the *Monarch of Bermuda*, was due to sail on July 4. I employed the last days in providing myself with civilian clothes and in saying farewell. With Frances Phipps and her son Allan, then on sick leave, I went to see Maurice Baring.

He had been stricken with Parkinson's disease and his whole body trembled so violently that the bed itself shook constantly. On his shoulder Maurice had an exotic bird, blue and yellow, which he loved. His trembling caused the colours to blend and turned the blue-yellow bird into a confused and iridescent image. Maurice, true to himself, said to me: 'This is a solemn occasion; let us have light-hearted conversation.' With Frances I went for a walk along the seashore. The beaches had become enormous workshops. Old England was preparing; I did not doubt her success. Alas! France, on the other hand, would not have this chance until after prolonged suffering.

The BBC asked me to talk to the French Canadians. I explained to the best of my ability the causes of our misfortunes—accidental, mechanical, local causes, a long series of blunders and catastrophes which altered nothing in the permanent virtues of France. These virtues, these cherished memories of France I recalled to the minds of my listeners, and I entreated them not to judge our actions too severely but to give France the affectionate understanding she needed more than ever at the moment.

During one of the last nights I spent at the Dorchester, the sirens woke me. Goering's airplanes were showering London with bombs. The instructions were, in case of an alert, to go down to the cellar. I was there, crouching in a corner, when the beautiful Diana Duff-Cooper discovered me. 'Why are you all alone?' She took me by the hand and led me to a group of men in dressing gowns and women in white and pink *déshabillé*. Her husband, Duff, was talking to a group of officers. 'Look what I found,' she said, pointing to me. Oh, how sorry I was to leave such companions.

I embarked at Glasgow. When I think of that ship crowded with children that took me to Canada, I feel as though I were remembering a dream. This enormous, floating nursery seemed unreal. On deck, hundreds of dwarfs with blonde or brown curly heads romped, laughed, cried, climbed the rigging, hoisted themselves onto the bridge, fell, wept and then laughed again. The smallest were harnessed like ponies so that one mother could attach to her chair or hold in her hand the reins of a foursome. My cabin was shared by Adrian, a boy of eight who was making this long journey alone.

During the whole voyage Adrian was full of reserve and dignity. Raised in an English school, trained from infancy to be independent, he was neither timid nor over-bold. He tried to do everything for himself, had learned to climb alone up to his bunk, which was above mine and very high, each evening he took his cold shower, each morning folded his pyjamas and put them under his pillow. He was clean, solicitous and brave. His parents lived in Siam. When his uncle had said goodbye to him in Glasgow, he had given him seven shillings and sixpence. This was his fortune. Mine was not much greater, but I was more economical. Adrian bought pencils, whistles and sweets at the ship's store. When he arrived in Canada he had only five shillings. His great sorrow was that he had been forced to leave his bicycle in Scotland, but he had brought its headlight with him and from time to time when he woke up at night he proudly illuminated the cabin.

A cruiser, the *Revenge*, and two destroyers escorted us, for the ocean was infested with enemy submarines. During the crossing I learned from a bulletin posted between decks of the terrible and deplorable affair at Mers-el-Kébir. Of all the misfortunes which for weeks had poured down upon us one after the other, this seemed to me the most awful. A Frenchman first of all, for twenty years I had been a warm friend to England; I was like the child of divorced parents who clings to his mother, but suffers. My heart said; 'My country, right or wrong.' My mind deplored this apparent rupture between two peoples who had, and would always have, great need of each other. Leaning against the railing, I looked out for a long time at the sea marbled with foam and at the great cruiser gliding silently at our side. The English passengers, respecting my sorrow, passed close by without speaking to me. Suddenly I remembered what Desmond MacCarthy had said to me that evening: 'Whatever happens, let us not forget that our friends, our real friends, have not changed.' And I fell unconsciously to murmuring the old Scottish song; *Should auld acquaintance be forgot* ... High up in a turret of the *Revenge* a light flashed; luminous signals, long and short, were sending out some mysterious message.

There were several Frenchmen aboard, including Alexis Léger, the ambassador and poet, and Henri Géraud (Pertinax), the great journalist, together with his wife. A British writer, Norman Angell whose books I esteemed, was on his way, like me, to lecture in the United States.

Sometimes I would get up at dawn and go on deck in order to stretch out and enjoy for an hour the silent beauty of the ocean before the flood of children arrived. The *Revenge*, black and active, would be chatting with us at that early hour in its language of lights. The destroyers raced around her like dogs around their master, and sometimes one of them would rush off a long way in pursuit of a phantom submarine. On one of these mornings Norman Angell came and sat down beside me.

'I knew you were aboard,' he told me, 'and I'm taking the liberty of speaking to you because, in this terrible catastrophe of France, there are many things I do not understand ... I am not talking about the military defeat, which can be explained by the lack of preparation on the part of both our countries and by bad strategic concepts ... It is the moral disaster that surprises me, and it is about this that I would like to ask you a few questions if it would not be too painful.'

'Ask them,' I told him. 'The subject *is* painful, but I do not try to escape my thoughts.'

He lay down on the deck chair next to mine.

'Does it seem true to you to say,' he asked, 'that the morale of the

French army and people was less high in 1939 than in 1914, and that the will to win was less vigorous?'

'Many units of the army fought well, but it is accurate to say that on the whole the army's will to win was less strong than in 1914.'

'And why? . . . The fate of France was at stake in both cases and the danger was greater in 1940.'

'That is true, but France in 1914 was a country relatively united; the France of 1940 was a country profoundly divided.'

'Hasn't France been divided since 1793?'

'Chateaubriand said of the Terror that that bloody ditch would never be filled up, and it is certain that memories of the Revolution for a long time dominated the political life of France. But in 1914 reconciliation in the face of the enemy was complete. For four years socialists and capitalists, radicals and monarchists fraternized. Peace put an end to that idyll. The Russian revolution inspired great hopes in the working class and great fears in the bourgoisie. One section of the latter stupidly believed that fascism and then nazism would be ramparts against communism. The authoritarian government in Rome and Berlin exhibited opposition to the government in Moscow while waiting to make an alliance with it. All of them expended huge sums for propaganda and exerted themselves to seduce the French masses. These foreign hands dug once more a deep ditch between the two Frances.'

'Nevertheless in 1914 . . .'

'In 1914 enemy propaganda did not exist; in 1939 it had been at work with diabolical ingenuity for five or six years . . . Now, democracies are regimes in which public opinion is all-powerful and without it nothing can be done. Examine the facts in France, in England, in the United States, and you will discover that public opinion in all three countries was wrong or was misled with surprising consistency. The public did not understand the danger and did not demand rearmament until much too late.'

'Their leaders could and should have guided the public.'

'Unhappily, the political leaders had acquired the habit of consulting it and not guiding it. You could see them relying on public opinion, consulting it, and asking themselves how they could please it and at the same time convince it that it was better for a country to live than to die. As for the military leaders, they were dependent on the political leaders and did not dare either to contradict them or to exert pressure on them. Lacking precise and definite orders, the agencies and the experts took their time. No one in our country prepared a schedule of action. In Germany Hitler said: "I wish to be in Paris on June 15. For that, I must begin the offensive at the beginning of May; I need the new tanks at the beginning of April." Thus he constructed his work plan, and woe to him who did not carry it out! With us what happened? The experts were asked: "How much time do you need to produce so and so many planes per month, or so and so many tanks?" The experts named a period at random and their dates were accepted. We made out our schedule in reverse. The war was supposed to take into account technical necessities, instead of the technicians being forced to take account of military requirements! As a result, we prepared for a battle in 1942 that was fought in 1940.'

Norman Angell lit a cigarette and smoked for some time in silence, looking at the seabirds that accompanied us, and now and then landed nonchalantly on the waves.

'In the end,' he said, 'what are the essential liberties that we want to safeguard at all costs? We want the law to be the same for all, which assures each one equality of opportunity; we want everyone to have free access to the sources of information (and this is the true meaning of freedom of thought); we want each one to be free to express his ideas so long as he does not preach the destruction of the State which gives him that freedom; and we want it to be possible to change the government if that is the freely expressed desire of the majority. That, it seems to me, is all.'

'That is all,' I said, 'and it does not mean that statesmen must each day before acting refer to public opinion and consult it like an oracle. A country can be perfectly free when its leaders, whom it has freely chosen, do not consult it on every individual point. If the British ministers in 1936 had had the wisdom to disregard public opinion and support France on the Rhine, we would have avoided this war.'

The sun was climbing in the sky. The curly-headed dwarfs began to invade the deck; their balls rolled among the deck chairs.

'Those balls,' he said. 'If we had only left them to the children, we would, perhaps, have paid more attention to the dangers that threatened us. It is a fact that for a long time our countries, rather than look at a painful reality that demanded work and courage, sought refuge in worlds of artifice. England has lived for cricket and football; the United States for baseball and the cinema; France for local politics and literary cliques. Sport and art are excellent supplementary activities when the requirements of security have been met; but to give them precedence over every other activity when vital problems have not been solved is an excess of political madness ... Politics itself became a sport. But when it is a question of saving one's hide, time becomes too precious to permit of these mass evasions ... While our children were rejoicing in the delightfully optimistic endings of Hollywood films, young Germans were at work modelling the real world ... The results of this are harsh.'

He got up.

'It's time for breakfast,' he said. 'Porridge and eggs and bacon are realities I do not scorn.'

Alone once more, I meditated for a long while on this conversation. I got out a pencil and, on the cover of the book which I was reading and which I still have, I wrote the following:

REMEDIES

Be strong. A people that is not ready to die for its liberties loses them.

Act Fast. Ten thousand airplanes built in time are worth more than fifty thousand after the battle.

Direct opinion. A leader leads; he does not follow.

Maintain the moral unity of the nation. Political parties are passengers on board the same ship; if they wreck it, all will perish.

Protect public opinion against the influence of foreign governments. To defend ideas is legitimate; to accept foreign money for defending them is a crime.

Act instantly against all illegal violence. Provocation to violence is a crime in itself.

Protect the young against any teaching designed to weaken the unity of the country. A country that does not seek to preserve its existence commits suicide.

Demand upright lives in those who govern. Vice of any sort gives advantage to the enemy.

Believe passionately in the ideas and in the way of life for which one is fighting. It is faith that creates armies, and even arms. Liberty deserves to be served with more passion than tyranny.

I was at this point when Adrian ran toward me holding out a bleeding finger.

'I have cut myself,' he said. 'Do you know how to make a bandage?'

I did so, to the best of my ability.

26

Amica America

'It is not for outward show that our soul must play a role; it is at home, within us, where no eye can reach but ours.'

Montaigne

On July 12 I arrived in Halifax and the following day travelled to Montreal by rail. On the station platform I was surrounded by reporters who greeted me in French, with that slight Norman accent which always gives me pleasure when I talk to French Canadians— and there I found my wife, whom I had left in Paris on June 10. Not having been able to inform her of my plans, I did not know she was in Canada. It is impossible to describe our joy; we had been so afraid we would never see each other again. She told me of her adventures.

Leaving Neuilly at dawn on June 10, she had found herself in a solid stream of cars on the Paris to Orléans road, moving at a snail's pace. Near Dourdan, German planes in three successive waves swept over the fugitives and fired on them with machine guns. Some gendarmes wisely forced my wife and her travelling companions to crouch in the ditches. Close to her, children were wounded in the shoulder and hip but none was killed.

She spent the night in her car at Vierzon among thousands of families who had no other home but their automobiles, and the following day reached her mother's house in Dordogne. More than a hundred refugees were already living in it. From there she attempted to get in touch with me in London, but her telegram went unanswered. Very anxious, she left at the end of five days for Bordeaux, and there found a depressing spectacle—the end of a society.

The administrative framework of France, which we had thought so strong, had gone to pieces under the bombs of the German air force. Because it lacked control of the air, the government had lost control of the ground. The police no longer attempted to maintain order. In Bordeaux people strolled unannounced into the office of the Premier or that of the President of the Republic. Ambassadors wandered about in the Lycée where a service had been installed that was supposed to tell them to which châteaux in the neighbourhood they had been assigned. Ambassadors' wives, perspiring heavily, decked with pearls, cooked on portable stoves in their Rolls-Royces on the Allées de Tourny. My wife encountered a minister we knew who told her that Paul Reynaud was going to resign and that the new government would ask for an armistice.

'I would hope,' she said, 'that the war would continue in North Africa.'

'That was Reynaud's programme,' he replied, 'but it has been defeated in the Cabinet by a vote of thirteen to ten. He is probably with Lebrun at this moment . . . I believe, moreover, that he is hoping the armistice cannot be concluded and that he will be recalled, but that's an illusion . . . The armistice will be signed and the Germans will be here within a week . . . You would do well to leave.'

'Where should I go?' Simone said. 'My husband must have been demobilized in London. Is it possible for him to return to France?'

'Obviously not . . . Communications have become difficult between France and England. And then your husband cannot really foresee what his fate would be under the Nazis . . .'

My wife knew that I had promised to give the Lowell Lectures in the United States in October and that I considered this engagement very important and had received travel orders from the Foreign Office. She told herself that I would try by every means to be in Boston in September. To get confirmation, she tried once more to send me a cable in London and, receiving no answer, decided to go and wait for me in the United States. Since she had letters from the Lowell Institute with her, she had no difficulty in getting the necessary visas. She was happy to leave Bordeaux, where she had been disheartened by the indifference of the people—far too many of them—who sipped ancient and illustrious vintages in the abandoned cellars of the *Chapon Fin* while France was in agony.

On the evening of June 17 at the International Bridge between Hendaye and Irun, she found the French customs men in tears.

'But why, madame?' they said to her, 'why have we been defeated? Could not this war be continued? . . . Will they at least leave us a little France? Is it true that the Germans will come this far?'

After the scenes of defeatism she had just seen in Bordeaux, the patriotism of these little people warmed her heart. Finally on June 25 in London, thanks to Cotnareanu (then owner of *Figaro*), she had been able to board the *Yankee Clipper*. As soon as she arrived in New York, she sent me a cable in care of the French Embassy in London. I had replied immediately to say that I was coming, but the British censorship had not allowed me to indicate the sailing date, the name of the ship or its destination. Finally American journalists had informed her and, realizing that I was on my way to Canada, she had been able to come and meet me at six o'clock in the morning on the platform of Windsor Station in Montreal.

Our happiness at being reunited was mixed with the dreadful sadness we felt at the miseries of France.

'Do you know,' my wife said, 'that this is July 14? . . . And do you remember? Last year in Paris . . . That splendid parade on the Champs Elysées . . . How happy and proud everyone was!'

It was indeed July 14. From the windows of Montreal tricolour flags waved. The French Canadians were loyal.

'May France in her turn,' I thought, 'be loyal to herself.'

We could not remain in Canada. I had no more money; my wife had only a few dollars, just enough to buy two tickets to New York. It was only there that I could earn a living for us. Our friend Robert Choquette had me talk on the Canadian radio, then we left for the United States. During the trip Simone managed a surprise. I had notes to prepare in English. She said to me:

'You can dictate them to me.'

'But you don't know English shorthand.'

'But I do . . . I have learned it during the war.'

To see New York once more sadly evoked the shining memories of the preceding years. To our personal suffering was added the sorrow of finding public opinion in large part hostile to France. With surprise we became aware of the development of a campaign, highly suspect in origin, that charged our soldiers with not having defended themselves. I, however, had seen our armies and and our leaders; I knew their faults but also their heroism; I knew the faults had been not a lack of courage but a lack of preparation and a faulty strategy, and if one were looking for those responsible, they were to be found in England and America as well as in France.

Fortunately my wife and I did not lack friends in New York. My publisher, Harper, immediately advanced me money on future publications. The president of the French Chamber of Commerce, Pierre Cartier, offered me his credit, which was great, but I did not want to incur debts. Clarence Dillon, the famous banker (father of Douglas Dillon who later was to become ambassador to France), sent me the day after my arrival a beautiful edition of Bacon with this note:

'The first book for your future library.'

We needed a place to stay. The strange thing was that, poor though we were, we had to choose one of the great hotels because we were known there. First of all, we went to the Plaza. Then the Ritz Tower at the corner of Fifty-seventh Street and Park Avenue put a little apartment on the seventeenth floor at our disposal. The management was incredibly kind. 'We know that refugees have no money. You can take care of the bill after you have made some. And if Madame Maurois wants to furnish the three rooms with French furniture she has only to pick it out in the antique stores; we'll pay for it.' I recognized American kindness, affectionate and inexhaustible.

An old friend, Mrs. Murray Crane, widow of a senator and powerful in political circles, asked us to come to her house in the country for our first weekend. (The second took us to the home of Clarence Dillon, the third to that of Eugene Meyer of the Washington *Post*.)

'Adolf Berle is coming to see us,' she had told me, 'the assistant to the president, who is being sent by Roosevelt to ask you about your impressions of England.'

Berle did indeed arrive, intelligent, brilliant and precise. The principal question he put to me was:

'What chance do you think the British have of resisting an invasion? The president has to form an opinion about this. The fact is, the British need destroyers; they are urging the president to give them fifty. This would be illegal (because contrary to the Neutrality Act), but possible if they were condemned as scrap iron. The only thing is, if the president agrees to this transaction, he wants to be sure that he is not running the risk of seeing his ships fall into the hands of the Nazis. He has official information from the Embassy; he wants to check this through private sources, you among them.'

I told him I was *certain* of the determination of the British, and that they would hold out, whatever the cost. Churchill was still indomitable. I had seen the immense labours performed by England in preparation for her defence. I knew the pilots of the RAF. There was no doubt in my mind about the outcome of an invasion. It would fail.

'The sequel,' I said, 'depends on you Americans. This war cannot be won except with your support. It is *your* war. A Nazi victory would destroy for a long time the civilization that Washington and Lincoln, Wilson and Roosevelt, fought for.'

'The president knows that,' Berle said, 'but he has to take account of public opinion which, in the Middle West and Far West, is still very isolationist. He is facing an election in November. I am sure he will give the destroyers and it will be an act of great political courage on his part.'

Roosevelt gave the destroyers, under the pretext that they were in exchange for military bases in eight British possessions, and they were of inestimable value in the battle against the submarines. Returning to New York, I received numerous visits. The one from Stefan Zweig troubled me; although he had recently married a young woman whom he loved, he remained crushed by his misfortunes. My own helped me to understand how he felt. In Vienna he had been the writer most highly acclaimed by discerning critics, one of a handful of great men of the country, surrounded with respect and affection; suddenly because that raucous and cruel corporal Hitler had proscribed the Jews and occupied Austria, Zweig found himself outlawed by a society of which he had been one of the most precious ornaments. This was justification for his despair. From that moment I sensed that this drama would end in suicide. I found myself in an analogous situation, but I preserved my hope and above all I believed that my French friends would not abandon me. There were some defections, but they were few and shameful.

In New York I had found again the Jules Romains, the Maeterlincks, the Thomas Manns. Romains, who did not have the same complex feelings toward Marshal Pétain that I did (gratitude, pity, apprehension), was harsher toward him than I, but each of us understood the other's state of mind and we got on very well together. At the home of Mrs. Lamont I met H. G. Wells, then on a trip to the United States, Poletti, a powerful New York politician, and Vincent Sheehan. All were critical of France and I had to speak daily in her defence. With success, for my interlocutors were men of good will.

From this came the idea that it was important to say, as exactly as I could, what I had seen of the war, to explain what in my opinion had been the causes of the disaster and above all, to prepare the way for

American intervention. Hastily I wrote a number of articles, which were later collected in a volume under the title *Tragedy in France*. This was in the month of August 1940. New York was sweltering under a wave of humid heat, and in order to work I had to live between two electric fans. When the articles were published, I received many moving letters.

'At last we can lift up our heads!' the sailors on a French ship, interned in the port of New York, wrote me.

'I have wept a great deal while reading you,' said a little French dressmaker, 'but you have restored my pride.'

As for the British readers, all those who knew the facts judged that I had been fair in what I had said about the relationship between the two countries. The English writer Granville Barker (at that time in charge of British propaganda in the United States) wrote to me: 'What a good book, if I may say so! . . . A fair-minded, fine-minded and essentially healing book . . . '

I take the liberty of quoting this letter from among so many others because later on the attempt was made, for reasons that were far from admirable, to distort the meaning of the book. General Gort's report was soon to show both the exactitude and the moderation of my account.

After this I was asked to talk at the Harvard Club, at Columbia University, at the Town Hall and twenty other places. This activity helped us to endure the agony that the news from France caused us at that time. Ah! but it was hard to substitute for the image of that rich, proud nation we had known, this picture of misery and feebleness! Soon, under pressure from the invader, racial laws were promulgated. They struck ancient French families, veterans of the two wars, admirable citizens whose sons had died for France. For me, they posed a problem of conscience.

'Don't go on making yourself the champion of France,' the cynics told me. 'What can she offer you from now on? A life of humiliation and poverty. Break with her openly. This will bring you a profitable popularity. And there is no risk! If the war turns out well, you will return to your home in triumph; if it turns out badly, you still have America and the Dominions, which are practically invulnerable. A child could see where your interests lie!'

Unfortunately duty almost never coincides with one's interests. My duty, it seemed to me, was to serve unhappy France to the utmost. In my lectures I took the position of defending *certainly not what seemed to me indefensible*, but French culture, the memory of our dead, the honour of our army, and also the children, the French prisoners, who had such great need of American aid.

At that time I lived for a number of weeks in a state of despair and exaltation. My country in chains had become for me the captive Andromeda whom, as an adolescent, I had so often hoped to love and to set free. Alas, I did not have long to wait for an occasion to prove that my personal wrongs would not alter my loyalty. A news story published in the American papers said that our old mill in Elbeuf was going to be taken away from us. My first thought on reading this news was: 'And so, if my father were alive, they would dare to say to him, to him who with his people had *made* that business and ran the greatest risks to see that it remained French, to say to him that he was not worthy to direct it!' Then I asked myself in bitter sadness whether the new management would tear down the plaque of black marble beside the gate:

MORTS POUR LA FRANCE

CAPITAINE PIERRE HERZOG

Chevalier de la Légion d'Honneur, Croix de Guerre

LIEUTENANT ANDRÉ FRAENCKEL

Chevalier de la Légion d'Honneur, Croix de Guerre

That evening an American journalist wanted to interview me about this act of robbery:

'It will do you good!' he told me. 'You can tell me what you have in your heart.'

'I have something in my heart, but it is not against France ... It is not she who committed these monstrous acts; they were imposed upon her. I am at peace; as soon as she is able, she will recognize her own.'

Nevertheless I thought that the marshal ought never to have signed those base decrees. Had he done it to avoid worse woes? Was he aiding the exodus of the most seriously menaced of the Jews? René de Chambrun, who was then in New York, assured me that he was. But I doubted it, and I suffered. Saint-Exupéry, who arrived from North

Africa, adjured me not to contribute to the divisions about the French. 'Defeat destroys what has been done,' said Saint-Ex, 'in that lies the threat of death.' In *Pilote de guerre* he expressed the idea that all the French had a share in the responsibility for the defeat and should assume it. 'Don't believe,' he said to me, 'that it was possible to continue the war in North Africa. I went there with my squadron with that in mind. But there was neither petrol nor spare parts, and the British swore they could not supply us with provisions. To continue in these conditions would have led very quickly to the occupation of North Africa by the Germans. That would have been an easy manoeuvre for them across Spain. By keeping Algeria, Tunisia and Morocco, we are preparing for the future ... As soon as the Americans understand ...'

About this time I received a visit from Mr. Polk (a distinguished lawyer of the firm of Polk, Davies, etc.), who had been in the State Department and remained an intimate advisor to Roosevelt. 'I know about your misfortunes,' he said to me, 'and the act of robbery committed against you, but don't be shocked because the president keeps an embassy in Vichy. He believes it would be a great mistake for America and England to fling captive France into the arms of Germany by useless sermons aimed at the French government or, worse still, by insults. The wise and effective attitude will be to provide food for the children and the French prisoners and to proclaim our aid. The tonnage? That amounts to nothing; a hundred thousand pounds.'

'And if the Germans should seize the milk intended for the children?' I asked.

'That's unlikely because the distribution will be entrusted to the International Red Cross and because it is not in the German interests to force the French population to the wall. Besides, if that should happen, the Red Cross would inform us and the shipments would cease. In short, the president wanted me to put you *au courant* with his ideas and he hopes that, despite your legitimate resentment, you will not oppose them. Remember that the president's private desire is to send American forces to the aid of France and England, but he *has* to wait. Remember, too, that an American embassy will be the best observation post from which to keep track of German intentions and inform the British of them.'

'I understand,' I said, 'but this will be very unpopular.'

'A president of the United States must know how to be unpopular,'

[279]

Mr. Polk said, 'when that is for the good of all. The day will soon come when we will be fighting openly.'

I said that I would continue my campaign for France and for the entrance of the United States into the war, which I confidently expected when the president judged that the hour had come.

'On his side,' Polk said, 'he will protect you, for you know that your speeches in favour of our entry into the war fall under restrictions of the law. Mr. Roosevelt will see to it that you can continue them.'

I did, in fact, have need of support. An America First Committee was campaigning both against Roosevelt and against any intervention in Europe. It comprised pro-Nazis, anti-English, Irish, Germans, Italians and also men of good will, apostles of non-violence. To counteract it, one of the best American journalists, my friend William Allen White, became president of a Committee to Defend America by Aiding the Allies. White did not yet dare to talk of military intervention by the United States: 'I favour aid to the British,' he wrote, 'because that is the way to keep America out of the war.' For him, this was only an interim policy.

I spoke in favour of intervention in the universities, colleges, in legal groups such as the Brandeis Society in Philadelphia. There I made precious friendships. Arthur Cowan, a loyal and trustworthy friend and an ardent francophile, introduced me to the judges of the Supreme Court, who were his friends. On November 5, I returned to New York to follow the returns of the presidential election with my wife. I was eager to observe the reactions of the American masses at the moment when a decision was being made on which depended the policies of the country in a crucial period. I knew both candidates slightly; I had been received by Roosevelt first in 1932, then in 1939; Claire Luce had introduced me to his Republican opponent Willkie. A liberal at heart, he had approximately the same feelings as Roosevelt. Professional politicians obliged him to condemn any war in Europe, and this in turn constrained Roosevelt to say to the same Americans: 'Your boys are not going to be sent into any foreign war.' He knew that this was untrue, but he believed that to defend a just cause it is first of all necessary to remain in power.

On the day of the election I was surprised by the general calm. From the moment when the first returns sped round the *Times* tower, the final result was certain. But the people near us, whatever their party, joked lightheartedly. Next morning I took a taxi and the driver turned and said to me:

'You saw the election? Fifty-five per cent of the country is for Roosevelt, forty-five per cent for Willkie. What does that prove? That we're almost evenly divided, that it's not possible to govern against forty-five per cent of the population, and that we have to find a meeting place halfway.'

I was struck by his good sense. When I discovered that this was widespread, I decided that American democracy was healthier than French democracy had been for a number of years. I was confirmed in this belief when I heard Willkie's speech on the role of a loyal opposition.

But the primary object of my trip to America was, as I have said, to give the Lowell Lectures in Boston. Possibly not all my readers know about this institution. In 1836 a member of the illustrious Lowell family, John Lowell, Jr., died leaving a large sum to found the Lowell Institute, an establishment for free higher education. Each year writers and scholars are invited there to deliver free public courses which are very widely talked about. Lawrence Lowell, president of the Institute at that time, had asked me to speak in French. When he had written to me in 1939, he was thinking of literary lectures, but when I arrived in New York he suggested that I talk about my memories of the war. This corresponded to my wish to make this series, which was going to be widely commented on in the press, an instrument of political action. To my great surprise, I discovered in Boston a faithful public of four to five hundred listeners for this series given in a foreign language. Some were Frenchmen, some professors, some musicians from the Boston Symphony Orchestra; others were Harvard students, Canadians, Belgians, Swiss, Russians, and also numerous Englishmen.

My host, Mr. Lowell, former president of Harvard University, was eighty-five years old and possessed an astonishing youthfulness of spirit. One day I had said that the United States was slow in making preparations, that perhaps it would be attacked before people expected and that it should exert its maximum effort not tomorrow but today.

'I don't agree with you,' he told me.

Surprised, I asked:

'And when do you think the United States should make this effort?'

'Yesterday,' said Mr. Lowell.

[281]

He took me to the Saturday Luncheon Club, to which Oliver Wendell Holmes and other illustrious Bostonians had belonged. On the day when I was there, the members were celebrating the eightieth birthday of Bliss Perry, former professor at Princeton, at Harvard and the Sorbonne, and one of them, Professor Rand, improvised during the toasts a very fine Latin speech, which showed me that the city of Boston was unlike any other in the United States—or in the world.

I loved the city of Boston just as it was. I loved its narrow streets, the square-cut English houses, the handsome Capitol with its gilded dome, the Common covered with snow.

I loved the schools around Boston: Andover, where I found at the head of the French Club the daughter and son-in-law of my old friend Alma Clayburg; St. Paul's, Exeter, Groton, so closely related to Eton and Harrow. I loved to watch the Bostonians who, modest in their way of life and proud in the tenor of their thought, economical and very rich, reminded me at the same time of the characters of John Marquand and the industrialists of Lyon. And so, combining work and social occasions, I spent two useful months in Boston.

On the subject of the Lowell Lectures, Brière, the French consul (today ambassador), wrote me later on recalling 'those days of anguish and sorrow which we lived through together with the comfort of your wise and steady patriotism, the patriotism of a Frenchman who surrenders none of his ideas nor of his old friendships. I shall never forget those lectures which contributed so much to rendering justice to France. You have no cause to regret the charm of beautiful past days, for your task in exile, thankless though it was, must give you the satisfaction of duty stalwartly accomplished in the face of ignorance, bad faith and hatred.' It is important to add that the letters from the British in Boston, and in particular from the British consul, thanked me with equal warmth for having treated England with so much fairness, friendship and admiration. My role as conciliator continued to be understood by those worthy of it.

Unhappily there were the Others.

27

Pilgrim of the War

Simone and I spent January 1, 1941, alone in a hotel room. American friends had invited us to a supper party, but the news we were receiving from France was so saddening that we shrank from any kind of gaiety. When the twelve strokes of midnight sounded, the radio brought us the joyous uproar of Broadway. We thought of Essendiéras and of the sorrow that would accompany this new year of defeat. Where now were the little Alsatians who had sung the Marseillaise on New Year's Day in 1940? A little later the uproar on the radio burst out again; a jazz band joined in; it was midnight in St. Louis, Missouri. What did people in St. Louis, Missouri, think about France? I was soon to find out, for I had promised to go there to give a lecture. We talked of our children whom we so much longed to see again, of our friends, of my courageous mother for whom life must now be so hard . . . Finally a new explosion of laughter and song announced that the stroke of midnight was sounding in San Francisco. Now all America had entered the year 1941.

Our own situation was more sombre than ever. Earning a living posed a grave problem. I could not manage it except by constant activity. I was, however, working in anxiety and despair. The news from France, fragmentary, confused and contradictory, did not enable me to form a picture of the realities. My mother-in-law spoke with respect of the marshal. Was she sincere, or did she dread the censorship? I could not tell. My mother and my daughter had succeeded once or twice in smuggling letters into the Free Zone; I trembled for them. We ourselves wrote with extreme caution. One of my sons was gravely ill. I had asked my parents-in-law whether they thought I could return, if only for a week, to see and help him. The marshal, to whom they had referred this question, replied: 'No! I would not answer for his life.' My friend Louis Gillet, an ardent anglophile, wrote to me: 'The old marshal is admirable; he offers as much resistance as is possible.'

I was sure of the sincerity of Louis Gillet, a patriot and hero of 1914–18. Nevertheless my son Gérald, and André Gide as well, seemed to be saying covertly that the regime was odious. I knew that all my possessions had been sequestered and that even in the Free Zone my books were still banned. In Paris a Captain Goering was occupying my apartment. What was it like in this captive France?

The visitors I received did little to enlighten me. Louis Rougier, who had arrived from London and North Africa, had seen Churchill and gave his impression that Pétain was playing a double game, only yielding on certain points in order to prepare for future re-entry into the war. I hoped that this was true. Paul Hazard, who was leaving for France and came to say goodbye to me, was confident of it. As for myself, I felt the frightful suffering of not understanding, of not being able to know what was happening in my own country. Saint-Exupéry, whom I often saw, said to me: 'We haven't the right, being here in security, to judge the unhappy French crushed beneath the boot of the occupation forces ... You and I at least came here poor, and determined when the time came to run all the risks of war again. But what is more ridiculous than to say like N.: "I am going on with the combat," when he is living here determined not to fight and comfortably supported by the millions he got out of the country in time?'

And together we recited the verses from *Tartuffe*:

> ' ... Aussi ne vois-je rien qui soit plus odieux
> Que les dehors plâtrés d'un zèle spécieux,
> Que ces francs charlatans, que ces dévôts de place
> De qui la sacrilège et pompeuse grimace
> Abuse impunément et se joue à leur gré
> De ce qu'ont les mortels de plus saint et sacré.*

Saint-Ex was right; at that time there were in every group of Frenchmen honest people and blackguards. We who hoped to restore unity in the face of the enemy thought of unity only as among heroes. Once a man acted in good faith, problems were resolved at once. I remember having a visit one day from a young friend, Etienne Burin des Roziers,

* Nor do I see anything more odious than the outward show of specious zeal, than these open charlatans, these worshippers of place whose sacrilegious and pompous affectation mislead with impunity and make a sport at will of what is most holy and sacred to mortal men.

who had resigned from the French embassy (where he was secretary) to join the Free French in Syria. 'I no longer want to be anything but a fighter,' he told me. 'I won't think about my diplomatic career until after the victory.' I replied: 'I approve with all my heart; if I were your age, I would do the same thing.' He asked me: 'What message shall I take from you to General Catroux?'—'My affection and my high esteem.' In the same vein I kept up an affectionate correspondence with André Morize who had become a militant Gaullist, with Louis Rouchard (brother-in-law of Pierre Brisson), with Charles Boyer and a dozen others.

But there were some who did not take this view. They thought only of preparation for vengeance. In the meantime they criticized, they denounced, they slandered. One of them above all, whom I do not wish to name because he is dead, pursued me for four years with ferocious hatred because I had wounded his pride one day by opposing his ambitions. 'I will pulverize you,' he had told me, 'I know how to hate. I will ruin you. I will isolate you. I will bring you to your knees.' It must be admitted that he did his best. At a time when I was giving my support (my moral support and, in the modest degree that my means then allowed, my material support) to all the efforts to defend the Jews, he accused me of being a racist! While I was campaigning for England, he wrote to London that I was anti-British! I showed him a thousand proofs to the contrary, letters of thanks which I had received from so many Englishmen, which Jewish organizations had sent me and which I still treasure today; hundreds of articles in American papers that proved the steady firmness of my attitude and the good effect of my lectures. Little did it matter to my persecutor. Truth was nothing in his eyes. 'Truth,' he said to me with a sinister laugh, 'truth is what serves my vengeance.'

Unhappily men accept without question whatever inflames their passions and their prejudices. 'Throw enough mud, and some of it will stick.' All these inventions were to melt away one day in the sunlight of the evidence, but for a time this adroit and perfidious Iago almost succeeded in his enterprise. He managed to sow doubt in the minds of some Englishmen (not, however, in that of the ambassador, Lord Halifax, who never ceased to show me his friendship). He contaminated a small section of the French colony in New York. He even poisoned from a distance the judgment of some of the French who had stayed in France or in London. Men who are today my best friends admitted to me when I saw them for the first time after the Liberation that they had taken me for an adversary, and they made affectionate apologies when I had them read articles, irrefutably dated, which proved the purity, the courage and effectiveness of my attitude.

Americans, in a better position to know the facts, almost all remained loyal to me. This is very much to their credit, for Iago neglected nothing. Was I going to give a lecture? He went to see the president of the university or the lecture manager and said: 'You're not going to receive that fascist!' One of them, nauseated, replied: 'Sir, before your visit I intended to ask Monsieur Maurois for one lecture; now I am going to ask for three.' Thanks to the fairness and friendship of Geneviève Tabouis, the Gaullist New York newspaper *Pour la Victoire* steadily rejected the diatribes of my enemies. I say this because at that time it took great courage to be fair and I remain grateful to Geneviève Tabouis and to her literary reviewer, Maurice Coindreau.

In Canada *Le Jour*, whose good faith had been beguiled, published under the guide of a review of one of my books an incredible mass of gossip. I replied: 'As for the rest of the absurd rumours which your contributor reports without a shadow of proof, I have already refuted them, but truth should be no less persistent than lies. Let it be said, then, once more: 1. That above all I desire the total liberation of France; 2. That this liberation is only possible through the victory of Great Britain and America; 3. That I ardently desire this victory; 4. That I admire the courage and tenacity of the British; 5. That I have praised them publicly everywhere; 6. That I admire the will to resist on the part of the French; 7. That I reject military and political collaboration with the invader; 8. That tomorrow France must be a free country governed by the will of the French people. Is this clear? And how often will it be necessary to repeat these things in order to discourage those who like your contributor impute to me ideas that I have *never had*, in order to condemn me.'

Le Jour had the probity to publish this reply entire, adding in a cordial note that they were happy to know that 'this excellent writer', beloved by all, shared the ideas of the paper and of its friends. Thus these attacks misfired. But rumours have a tenacious life and it can be imagined how great credulity could be in those times of passion and misery. I sensed it and suffered from it to the point of tears. In my *Vivier* for 1941 I find these notes: 'The honest man has trouble making up his mind to reply to calumnies. He knows they are so false that it is hard for him to think they might be believed by others.' And again: 'Public opinion is not *single*. There are those who talk and those who keep quiet. We have a tendency to take the volume of noise as an index to the number of those involved. But there are raucous minorities and silent majorities.'

The immense silent majority was favourable toward me. All the papers, all the reviews, all the magazines requested articles. I could only write a hundredth part of what was asked for. But I was now able to write directly in English, and this made the work go faster. The universities asked me for courses, the cities for lectures. I spent the year 1941 flying from state to state, to the four corners of the country. The classic airport with its baggage scales, loudspeakers, brilliant entry lights, rest rooms for the pilots, became as familiar and commonplace to me as the station at Elbeuf had once been. I flew principally by night, above a black gulf cut through at moments by the enchantment of cities, the green and red jewellery of signal lights. During these long trips, not being able to sleep, I read Shakespeare. *King Lear* and *Timon of Athens* echoed my sorrows.

I talked in Toronto and in Atlanta. There I lunched beside a Mrs. John Marsh, a modest person in glasses who said to me toward the end of the meal:

'You know, I write too . . . '

'And what do you write?' I asked with polite condescension.

'I've written a novel.'

'Ah, indeed. And what is its title?'

'*Gone with the Wind*,' she said softly.

In Texas I spoke in Houston, Austin and Forth Worth; then in Louisiana in New Orleans. I talked in Los Angeles and San Francisco, in Omaha and Denver, in Cincinnati and Baltimore. I spent the month of February at Knox College in Illinois and returned full of esteem for the good sense of the students and professors of the Middle West. In the traditions and customs of Knox there was something robust and healthy that seemed to me of great value for America.

In March and April 1941, I lived in Buffalo where the University had invited me to give a course in French literature. In New York I had been told:

'You won't like Buffalo. The climate is very harsh. There are only two seasons there, winter and the month of August . . . And the city is largely industrial.'

In point of fact I loved Buffalo. No city in the world has more beautiful trees. Above the broad avenues they form leafy, Gothic vaults. The sea of verdure that I saw from my window reminded me of our house in Neuilly and the green waves of the Bois. Even the cemetery had the grace of a park. The graves were arranged with calculated disorder along the sides of wooded hills which were ornamented here and there with flower beds of rose and pale yellow. On a pond splendid swans glided nonchalantly on their white wings. Wandering in this beautiful setting amid the shadows with some fair stranger, it occasionally seemed to me that I myself was a shadow or, as Lord Beaconsfield had said, 'dead, but on the Champs Elysées'.

Meanwhile our country was being accused of a thousand faults, often without proof. Deprived of information, I could hardly distinguish truth from falsehood. But when facts are lacking 'loyalty is the light of the mind.' I made a point of not judging from beyond the ocean a process the essential parts of which I did not know, and I continued to talk to Americans about the durable virtues of France rather than about her passing errors. The Red Cross and the Quakers were raising money for our war prisoners and our children. I gave benefit lectures under their auspices in Buffalo, Baltimore, Washington, San Francisco, New York and Philadelphia. Everything is surprising, However poisoned the political atmosphere, our meetings were enthusiastic, our halls were filled and our prisoners were succoured. I was to learn later that hundreds of children were saved through our shipments.

After each of these lectures (or after each of the courses) I received touching testimonials. The president of Knox College wrote me: 'It will be many years before Galesburg forgets your exalting visit. I am sure you felt the enthusiasm of your audiences. In the course of my long experience, I have never seen anything to compare with it.' From an Englishwoman in Toronto: 'My son, a soldier, wrote to me after Dunkirk: "It is the beginning, not the end. And as a great nation, we (England) must fulfil our destiny." Your sentiments are the same and a similar destiny awaits France, a destiny in which you will bear a part because no one can interpret your country to the world as you have done.' From Baltimore, Julien Green: 'I was too deeply moved last evening to tell you all the good things I thought about your lecture.

I felt, and this is what touched me most deeply, that you were fighting for France against all the evil forces here, against slackness, indifference and fear which are so cleverly sustained by our enemies' propaganda; what you are defending is our happiness, the happiness of all of us who turn toward Europe a gaze that grows more and more desperate.'

On my return to New York I was visited by a Monsieur Chapuisat of the International Red Cross. He explained that the hospital at Clairvivre, close to Essendiéras and staffed by doctors from Strasbourg who had fallen back into the Dordogne, was in need of medicine. He asked me whether I could send five hundred dollars to the Red Cross in Switzerland so that it could make the necessary purchases; he guaranteed that Clairvivre would receive the whole sum. At that moment five hundred dollars was a large amount for us. But the combination Périgord-Alsace went straight to my heart, and Clairvivre was supplied.

Our tiny apartment, through my wife's good offices, had taken on an air of France. She had had a photograph of the Angel of Chartres enlarged to the dimensions of the real statue. Hung above our window, it radiated peace in its beautiful smile. Between lecture trips I had got at my personal work again. I took notes for the first part of these Memoires. Lovingly I evoked my parents, my childhood, the Rouen Lycée. It was both poignant and needful. A writer has to press on sensitive nerves; the more he makes himself suffer the better his chance of uttering a true cry.

I was also making plans for novels. *Le Député de Pont de l'Eure*, a political novel, was to cover the period 1919–1940. *Le Soir des siècles* (or *Daniel*) was to have been the story of a young French Jew who has always felt completely assimilated and at home in a small city in the French provinces, who has married a Christian, found happiness with her, and who suddenly collides with Hitlerism and the hatred aroused by it. A final novel, the only one that was to be written, was called *Terre promise*. It was published in New York by Les Editions de la Maison Française (which also published Saint-Exupéry and Jules Romains) and in translation by Harper (*Women without Love*). Thanks to Simone, the decor in which I was working resembled that of my office in Paris. She had found a large Louis Seize table on which I spread my papers, and she had given me a big notebook bound in red leather with these words in gold letters: *VIVIER* 1941.

In this notebook I put down my ideas and my plans. It begins with:

Work Plan, January 1, 1941

Autobiography—or life of Bertrand Schmitt
History of France
History of the United States
Life of Victor Hugo
Life of Balzac
Literary studies (my lectures at Princeton)
Articles:
Philip (of Macedon)
Ahasuerus
Novels . . . (mentioned above)

Almost all these books (not the articles) were sooner or later to see the day. I also copied in the *Vivier* passages that I liked and that answered to my anguish. From George Washington: 'We must never despair; our situation has been compromising before, and has changed for the better; so I trust it will again. If new difficulties arise, we must put forth new exertion and proportion our efforts to the exigencies of the times.' Without any author's name: 'You are fully convinced of the purity of your ideals and the high virtue of your goals. But each man has the same conviction, with the exception of a few cynics who are convinced of the high virtue of cynicism.'

At the end of the last quotation I had added: 'This applies to present quarrels. What scorn answering scorn! The French who have remained in France despise those who are abroad and are not sharing the sufferings of their country; the French in exile despise those who, though able to leave, have been willing to live under the German yoke. And the truth is that there are honest and dishonest people in all camps. The criterion is disinterestedness. A young Frenchman who is fighting with De Gaulle is completely honest; an old Frenchman who, like me, speaks for France is honest too.'

In New York I was seeing principally the Saint-Exs, the Romains, Monica de la Salle, Rouchaud, Pierre Claudel, Robert Lacour-Gayet and many Americans. President Nicholas Murray Butler of Columbia University often invited us to dinner, one evening with Mrs. Roosevelt who talked to me about the happy effect of my lectures. At bottom she was in favour of American intervention in Europe. My English friend

Granville Barker introduced us to Sir Thomas Beecham, who had come to conduct a concert—a dictatorial and brilliant man.

But the time came to fulfil an important engagement: taking part in the French summer session at Mills College in California. We crossed the continent by plane. Nothing is more astounding than the immense wasteland that separates the Middle West from the Far West. As we looked at those dry, grey plains, cracked like the skin of an ancient elephant and extending as far as the eye could see, we were filled with admiration for the pioneers who had traversed them on foot or in their covered wagons. Ascending to four thousand metres to cross the Rocky Mountains and the Sierra Nevada left us short of breath, but the descent in Reno, that oasis of divorce, so rich and verdant, and the descent over beautiful San Francisco Bay with its globular islands, barren and volcanic, planted in blue water, repaid us for our mountain sickness.

'I can understand,' my wife said to me, 'how the migrants who paused at the summit of these mountains and after so much frightful aridity beheld so much beauty would have thought they were finally seeing the Promised Land.'

California remains in my eyes the country of happiness. It is not too densely populated; it enjoys the most constant and enjoyable climate on the planet; it is beautiful like Greece, sweet like France, picturesque like Spain and vast like Africa. The East is perhaps more alive; the Middle West more active; but California is the more primitive. The town dweller remains close to the pioneer.

I spent two days in Bohemian Grove near San Francisco, a forest nook with giant trees where five hundred business men, artists and professors from San Francisco and elsewhere, spend two weeks in the open air, sleeping under tents and eating together. In a central clearing an enormous bonfire blazed, the flames rising to half the height of the giant trees. On a platform on the side of a fern-covered hill, Lauritz Melchior sang and Irvin Cobb told stories. The floodlights were turned on me:

'Talk to us about France!'

I did my best. The trees surrounding me had already been there, I was told, when Christopher Columbus landed.

Mills College. A beautiful campus planted with giant eucalyptus. A Spanish patio where a fountain murmurs in the midst of cypress trees. We read and discussed the great books; in the evening the Budapest

Quartet played Beethoven; Darius Milhaud taught music; Fernand Léger painting; Madeleine Milhaud phonetics; René Bellé, son of my old headmaster at Rouen, poetry, all with ardour and talent. This Maison Française was a tradition of Mills College and, along with Middlebury, one of the centres of French studies in the United States. At the time of the disaster it had been feared that it would be wiped out by the débâcle. Then President Reinhardt and Mademoiselle Cécile Réau had had the courage to retain the session. We knew that on our success depended the future of the institution. In addition, we worked with an enthusiasm aroused by our mutual desire, stronger than ever in these dark days, to inculcate the love of our culture.

As had been the case earlier in Princeton, I felt the joy of fulfilling one of the vocations for which I had been born, that of professor. Often I would sit down on a bench and send one of the girls to the blackboard and together we would lay out the plan for a dissertation. It seemed to me that this labour of construction was one of the most urgent needs of these American minds, full of freshness and poetry as they were, but little accustomed to arrange their thoughts in an orderly fashion.

On the evening of July 14, the students gathered in the hall and asked me to say a few words to them. I took for my text a fine passage from Romain Rolland which one of them had pointed out to me the day before: 'How can it be permissible to slander a people who for more than ten centuries have been active and creative? . . . A people who twenty times have passed through the test of fire and been tempered by it . . . a people who, without ever having died, have sprung to life again twenty times . . . ' Then Madeleine Milhaud read us poems by writers who had been killed in one or other of the wars, we observed a few moments of silence, and then dispersed.

The heart grows accustomed to peace too quickly. Already on awakening each morning, I would think with pleasure of the beautiful, attentive faces I was going to see and about the emotions that would be evoked in them by some sentence of Stendhal, some letter of Flaubert. When the day of the 'last class' arrived, I remembered Kittel's last class in my childhood and how he had wept while reading us Daudet's story. If I had not warned myself in advance, I too might have wept, reflecting that this little group, now united by so much shared admiration, was about to dissolve forever.

28

Operation Torch

On December 7, 1941, Japanese airplanes attacked the American fleet at Pearl Harbor. The Americans, as usual on Sundays, were sitting by their radios listening to light music. Instead of songs they heard an unbelievable report: eight battleships sunk, three cruisers, three destroyers, two thousand dead. Was this some novel of the future or a bloody reality? A wave of stupefaction, then of fury, passed over the country. Next day the president announced in Congress that a state of war existed in fact. 'We do not like it,' he said, 'but now that we are in it, we are going to fight with everything we've got.' On December 10 Germany and Italy declared war on the United States. Churchill heaved a sigh of relief: 'The Lord hath delivered them into our hands,' he said.

Yes, the Lord had delivered the Nazis into the hands of the Allies and henceforth their destruction was certain. It would take a long time, very long. But the decision for which I had so constantly pleaded, the entry of the United States into the war, was finally a fact. It was often said: 'Without Pearl Harbor this decision would never have been made.' That is false. The president had made up his mind long since, as I knew, and I felt month after month his people coming closer to him. Since October I had encountered after my lectures many fewer objections from isolationists. From now on my task was going to be a little different. It was no longer necessary to recommend solidarity to the free peoples. That had been won. Now Roosevelt must be given the means to carry out his policy. John W. Davis, former candidate for the presidency, who was president of the committee for war loans, begged me to talk to the country at large about them. Later the Canadian government asked me to carry on a similar campaign in French Canada. I knew that this sort of lecture could have no literary value, but this was a time to act and not to shine.

This is not the place to give a detailed account of my lectures in

1942. Almost every month I was gone for fifteen or twenty days. When I could stay in New York I was doing research at the Public Library for a history of the United States. My wife who had always had the instinct of an archivist helped me. She suffered more than can be described at being away from France, from her dearly loved Périgord and from Paris, but she bravely acclimatized herself. All the shop-keepers in the neighbourhood knew and loved her. 'Mrs. Maurois is democratic,' they would say. Sometimes we allowed ourselves a week-end in Princeton. Our sojourn in 1931 at that old university had remained one of our dearest memories. Those well-kept green expanses reminded us of France and England. We would dine with our friend Coindreau at the house of the Casadesus', with the Girards (relatives of Daniel Delorme). Then we would go to spend Sunday at the home of Allen Tate in a delightful Alpine countryside on the bank of a torrent.

At the beginning of 1942 *The New York Times Magazine* published an article of mine, *The Undying Spirit of France*,* which I had written in 1941 at Mills College. After reviewing previous instances when the French national spirit had asserted itself in the face of a foreign conqueror, 'No,' I concluded, 'the spirit of France has not changed. The conqueror cannot prevail upon it. He has no more illusions now on the subject. He knows that, though France understands the necessity for European co-operation in a free Europe, there will be no French acquiescence in a European order founded on a foreign domination of France. "To have had common glories in the past, to have a common ideal in the present, to have achieved great things together, to be determined to achieve more, that is what makes a nation." That Frenchmen have achieved great things together—museums, monuments, empires all over the world proclaim it; that they are determined to achieve more, any young Frenchman will tell you. Therefore they are a nation and will remain a nation. The French spirit is today what it was at the time of Joan of Arc, though it cannot assert itself in the same way. It is a spirit of resistance and of confidence. It is the eternal story of France; it will have the same dénouement.

'"Do you hate your enemies, Joan?" asked perfidiously one of the judges of Joan of Arc. "I do not know," she said, "but I know they

* Copyright 1942 by The New York Times Company, reprinted by permission.

shall be turned out of France, except those who shall die there." Such was and is the Spirit of France.'

The news from France remained fragmentary and far from reassuring. Marshal Pétain had met Hitler in Montoire. After this conference, was it still possible to believe in a double game? Later, when Admiral Leahy returned from his mission, I got a number of detailed facts from him. Pétain, clear-headed in the morning, toward the end of the day became a prey to dangerous counsellors. Leahy had found him sentimental, pro-American and determined never to abandon his Frenchmen whom he called 'my children'. When the Germans had demanded the recall of General Weygand who had closed North Africa to them, the marshal declared that he was unable to protect him. 'I have no troops,' he said to the ambassador, 'and you know, Mr. Leahy, when one has no troops, one can do nothing.'

In July 1942 I returned once more to Mills College in California where I was to give a two-months' course. My wife remained in New York because she was undergoing prolonged and urgent dental treatment. At Mills I was delighted to see again President Reinhardt, my dear friends the Milhauds and my students, but now I was waiting with impatience for the chance to get into uniform again and go to war. Where? It was not exactly known what the plans of the combined chiefs of staff were. An immense army was in training in the American camps. What would its first objective be? I did not know.

In October I spent some days on Long Island in a large country house which the Saint-Exupérys had rented. Denys de Rougemont was there and the conversation was lofty and grave. At midnight Consuelo Saint-Exupéry and her guests would go to bed and St. Ex (whom Consuelo called Tonio) would remain alone working on *Le Petit Prince*. Toward two o'clock in the morning, Tonio's voice would awaken the sleepers: 'Consuelo! I'm bored; come and play a game of draughts.' When the game was over, Consuelo would return to her bed and Tonio to his book. Toward four o'clock in the morning: 'Consuelo! I'm hungry!' A moment later Consuelo's steps could be heard on the stairs going down to the kitchen.

My books were selling well in French and in English, in Canada as well as in the United States. And so we did not lack funds. But we were living in a constant state of agony and expectation. The present seemed empty and unreal. We were waiting for a future of victory. Finally one evening in November, toward midnight, we learned when we turned on the radio that the Americans had landed in North Africa. This operation, if it were successful, would furnish a springboard for a subsequent drive into Sicily and Italy. What would the French troops in North Africa do? I ardently hoped they would join the Allies. This in fact is what happened, after a certain amount of friction. The United States government had tried to get Marshal Pétain (or General Weygand) to go to North Africa and take command. Then General Giraud, consulted in advance, had accepted.

Little by little more precise news filtered out. The landing, well prepared by a small group of Frenchmen and by General Clark who had arrived secretly in a submarine, had not encountered any serious resistance in Tunisia or in Algeria. General Juin had been in communication with Murphy, the American consul. In Morocco, the fighting had been heavier. General Béthouart, chief of the pro-Allied forces, had been arrested, condemned to death and then saved by the arrival of the Americans. The French army in Africa did not whole-heartedly recognize the authority of Giraud. He himself complained of being under the orders of Eisenhower when he had been promised supreme command. Many of the generals and officers considered themselves bound by the oath they had sworn to the marshal (wrongly, since the oath had been exacted from them). Roosevelt was compelled, unwillingly, to accept the aid of Admiral Darlan, who was then in Algiers with his sick son, in order to obtain a 'cease-fire'. This choice greatly surprised me. Darlan, especially since Mers-el-Kébir, had been vituperative on the subject of England. Would he sincerely agree to work with the Allies? I preferred Giraud whom I knew slightly, having spent a week at his headquarters in 1940. I knew he was a competent and brave soldier. 'This may work out very well,' I thought, 'with De Gaulle head of government and Giraud commander-in-chief.' The idea that these two men could be in disagreement did not occur to me. Their goal, the liberation of France, was it not the same?

As soon as the clouds of battle disappeared and one could glimpse the new Algeria, Saint-Ex and I sent a cable to offer our services as officers. We were immediately accepted; a mission was to be sent from Algiers to Washington; we were told to get in touch with it.

My wife was in despair when she learned that the Germans were entering Dordogne. What would her mother do? What would become of the Alsatian refugees with whom she had been so much occupied at

Essendiéras in 1940? What would become of the manuscripts and paintings that she had saved with such difficulty by taking them to Périgord in her car? Nothing is ever the way one pictures it. In the first place, the danger had been greater than she imagined. Her parents had agreed to hide an arms cache for the secret army in their garage. My mother-in-law, who had been so ambiguous in her letters, had revealed herself courageous in action. She was questioned by the SS who were threatening to set fire to her château: 'Where is your son-in-law? We have orders to arrest him.' To this she replied with all the talent of an actress: 'What do you mean? You are the Gestapo, a police force that considers itself omniscient, and you ask me where my son-in-law is when all the world knows he is in America! Is this a joke?' Apparently the SS officer recognized that he was being ridiculed and admired this staunch old lady, for he dismissed his men but not, alas, before having Eugene Ochs, one of the unhappy Alsatians, shot—a man whom everyone loved and who was condemned as a deserter. We learned later that a whole group of the FFI had secretly camped at Essendiéras for two years and that my parents-in-law had fed them.

As for me, I was experiencing my first days of resurrection and I had ordered a French captain's uniform from an American tailor. I could not find a *képi* anywhere except at a theatrical costumer's. I find this note:

December 31, 1942: Worked on the history of the United States. Received a visit from Pierre Claudel and his three charming daughters. Dined at the Gides' with Level and Rouchaud. Then we welcomed the 'New Year of Victory' at Edwin James', editor-in-chief of *The New York Times*. Istel, an important civil servant to whom I said that I believed the unity of the French who were hostile to Nazism had now been established, replied: 'Don't believe it! Of course they are hoping for liberation. But each of them is playing a game, the object of which is to be sure of his position in postwar France. It's important to know *who* will hold the first elections, who will get the posts, the honours, the power.'

January 1, 1943: Worked all day. Toward five o'clock Pierre David-Weill came to see us. He explained very lucidly the plan for the push into France. Dined with Simone and the Milhauds at Fernand Léger's; he prepared a French *pot au feu*. This great painter is a great cook. The conversation bristled with projects and with hopes. A marvellous opening of the new year.

January 2, 1943: The French Mission from Algiers has arrived. It is led by General Béthouart, the hero of the Moroccan affair, and by Lemaigre-Dubreuil. The latter is an industrialist and was one of the leaders of a little group of plotters who negotiated the tactics of the landing with General Clark. Lemaigre-Dubreuil whom I found sympathetic reminded me a little of François-Poncet. His story: from 1940 on, he had had conversations with Bob Murphy, the Consul General of the United States, and had offered his good offices to prepare for an Allied landing. His numerous factories had given him an excuse to travel. Weygand shut the Germans out of Africa. Little by little Lemaigre-Dubreuil and his friends established liaison with Giraud. When J-Day came, the Vichy officials in Algeria were arrested by four hundred young civilian conspirators and in Morocco by Béthouart's sharpshooters. A delay on Giraud's part almost spoiled the whole affair. 'At last it has been accomplished,' Lemaigre-Dubreuil told me. 'Your first mission will be to help Béthouart in America; he has come to ask Roosevelt for modern arms for the French African army. We do not know anyone in the United States; you are the friend of American journalists and politicians; arrange the first meetings. Béthouart is at present in Washington; the president fundamentally supports us, but we need the concurrence of the New York press with its great influence on public opinion . . . As soon as General Béthouart returns, arrange a press conference.'

'You know that I want to enlist and leave for Africa,' I said.

'Of course! You will arrange that with Béthouart, but meantime your task is here.'

The first tangible sign of France's re-entry into the war was the appearance in New York Harbour of the French flag on the battleship *Richelieu.* It was Pierre Claudel who announced this to me in a voice trembling with emotion: 'Come,' he said to me on the telephone. 'Come and see the tricolour.' The sight of that blue, white and red flag snapping in the sea breeze brought me the wildest, liveliest and purest joy that I had felt since 1940. The three colours sang a sparkling Marseillaise within me. Presently the commander of the ship invited me to lunch aboard and I had the pleasure of seeing my books in the library. 'I thought they were banned,' I said to him.

'Never with us,' he replied proudly.

General Béthouart returned from Washington. What good fortune! He turned out to be all that one could have hoped; a great soul, an energetic leader, and politically objective, he had proved his courage with his Alpine troops at Narvik and later with his sharpshooters in Morocco. There to his great regret he had been forced to fight against the French; a secret telephone, of whose existence he was unaware, had enabled the Resident General to have him arrested. But as soon as he had been liberated he had asked his adversaries of the day before: 'And now when do we march against the Boches?'

At my apartment I arranged for him the press conference he desired. My friend Edwin James of the *Times* sent us his best reporter, Anne O'Hare MacCormick. All the journalists were charmed by Béthouart's frankness and objectivity and they promised their support. Many asked: 'And what will become of the Gaullists in all this?' 'No problem,' Béthouart said. 'There can be only one French army.' It was not as simple as that. The president and the State Department had been greatly in the wrong in not maintaining any contact with General de Gaulle. Cordell Hull, a violent man under his sage appearance, retained a grudge against Free France for having seized Saint-Pierre and Miquelon after he himself had guaranteed the status quo of those French possessions. This insignificant pinprick to his self-esteem had become infected. Roosevelt, for his part, refused to take this minuscule incident seriously, but he had made plans for Operation Torch (North Africa) without consulting General de Gaulle. This was a serious mistake. It was painful for the Gaullist soldiers who had taken a stand at the time of the armistice to see new leaders appear on the scene. 'And what about us?' they asked.

Darlan had been assassinated in December. There remained De Gaulle and Giraud. Eisenhower informed Roosevelt that the majority of the army in Africa preferred Giraud but that the civilian population warmly supported De Gaulle. Bob Murphy wrote to the president that Giraud was ready to work with De Gaulle. Harold Macmillan, who represented Great Britain in Algiers, proposed that General de Gaulle should play the role of Clemenceau, Giraud that of Foch. In January in Morocco Roosevelt and Churchill succeeded in having the two generals issue a conciliatory communiqué and exchange a handshake, which was recorded in a 'historic' photograph. As it turned out, this spectacular reconciliation could not produce lasting results. Giraud, an excellent military man, was in no sense a statesman. Nor did he wish to be. He was interested in one single thing: driving the Germans out of France. General de Gaulle saw further into the future and was intent on keeping France among the great powers. He alone could succeed in this tour de force. As for me, I clung tenaciously to the hope that the French would become united and I requested Béthouart to let me enlist. 'You are too old to be a captain of infantry,' he told me, 'but you can be a liaison officer. Later, when you have seen some of the operations, you can return and tell the Americans how the French are employing the arms that are going to be given to us.'

And so I went to Washington to complete the formalities of enlistment. General Béthouart asked me to stay a while longer in America where I could be of service to the French Mission. After that the Americans undertook to furnish me with transportation to Algeria. My happiness at rejoining the French army was mixed with a great sadness at leaving my wife. What would become of her alone in New York? She had come so as not to be separated from me; I could not abandon her without remorse. To be sure, we had dear friends in the United States who would look after her, but what was she to live on? For two years my lectures and articles had assured our existence, but when these resources were exhausted? The Mission told me that I could make over to my wife a large part of my captain's pay. 'And I will work,' she said. 'I will do translations.' Our friend Tom Kernan entrusted to her his novel *Now with the Morning Star* which he had written in English and which the Editions de la Maison Française had accepted for publication in French.

This time of waiting was at once sweet and painful. Sweet because we were together and enjoyed each instant of reprieve; painful because the hour of separation was approaching, as it had formerly in Paris. Once more we were entering a future full of menace. What would I find in Africa? Rommel was threatening Tunisia. The French African army equipped by the Americans was going to be an essential factor. In New York the news of my departure had spread. It exasperated my irreconcilable enemy because it proved the falsity of his accusations through an action of which he showed himself incapable. Others who had in some measure betrayed me came back with extraordinary effusions of friendship because they believed I was going to become a power in Algeria, something very far from my wishes. I re-read once more *Timon of Athens* and was not surprised to find human nature invariable.

Frank Polk who had on several occasions brought me messages from Roosevelt asked for a meeting: 'The president knows you're going to North Africa,' he told me. 'He has asked me to inform him about your intentions. Do you plan to engage in politics?'

'Certainly not. I shall be only an officer and that is all I wish to be.'

'Too bad,' he said. 'The president would have liked you to defend his ideas on France. He thinks that after the Liberation, of which he is confident, it will be necessary to call the National Assembly, excluding only those senators and deputies who collaborated with the enemy. The others will be useful because they are experienced in public affairs. In a time of crisis it is impossible to recruit or create a whole new political personnel. The president believes that Herriot could achieve a union.'

I repeated that I did not intend to meddle in politics and that it was the right of the French to make a free choice of their destiny and their leader.

Finally the French Military Mission in Washington sent me my orders. I was to take a train at six o'clock the next morning for Lee Hall, Virginia, whence I was to be taken to Camp Patrick Henry to await embarkation. My wife accompanied me to the platform in the Pennsylvania Station. She has said to me since that when she saw my train plunging into the tunnel, reminding her of the Metro in Paris, she asked herself once more: 'When shall I see him again? . . . And will I ever see him again?' She slowly climbed the exit stairs and found herself alone in that immense awakening city.

From the camp I wrote her a letter (in English since the army censor had to be able to read it):

'What I want to say is that I never loved you more and that, whatever happens now, this last year has been, thanks to you, and in spite of exile, the happiest in my life. Never were we more united, never did we work better together . . . And yet, feeling as I do, I leave you to go to the wars when naught compelled me to do so. That is because I feel, and believe, and hope that, by doing so, I prepare our future happiness. When we go back to France I want to be amongst those who fought for her to the last . . . '

I made the crossing on a troop transport. A cabin had been assigned to me and three American captains. An hour after we sailed, a young naval officer came to see me.

'Sir,' he said, 'is it true that you are only a captain?'

'It's true.'

'But how is that possible? You are old; you are famous; you have the highest French and British decorations . . . In our army you would be a general.'

'No doubt, but in the French army I am a captain.'

'It's very awkward,' he said. 'The captain would like to put you with the generals.'

'Don't let it embarrass him!'

Kindliness won out over regulations, and I left for Africa comfortably installed in a general's cabin.

29

Servitude and Grandeur

Here I begin the account of a period that seemed to me both grand and melancholy. Grand because I came in contact again with the French army and was overjoyed to find it fiery and confident after all its misfortunes. Melancholy because I was to be faced in this temporary capital with the image of a France still divided. The troops in the field behaved in the tradition of Vigny and Péguy; the miserable squabbles in Algiers recalled Saint-Simon and Retz.

To be fair, one must explain the origin of these painful misunderstandings. After the landing, General Eisenhower, learning, as I have said, that General Giraud could not rally around him the whole of the army in Africa (some of them considered themselves bound by oath), had had recourse to Admiral Darlan and had formed an 'Imperial Council' in which Giraud participated but which also comprised certain men whom the French in London called 'the vassals of Vichy'. It was an expedient that could not prove successful. When General de Gaulle had agreed, after Darlan's death, to co-operate with Giraud whom he esteemed, he had demanded the removal of this Imperial Council and the establishment in Africa of a central French power, the National Committee of Liberation, which would be presided over alternately by De Gaulle and Giraud. A frail compromise which could not but engender conflict.

I suffered bitterly from these conflicts at that time, though I was completely innocent, having arrived without knowing about them and with a passionate desire for unity. I wish to say at once that the reader must not forget, in considering these disquieting facts which were true in their time, that after the end of the war the clouds very quickly dispersed. Ink fades fast in the chronicles of Time. 'Wait,' says an Arab proverb, 'and stay at your window; you will see your enemy's corpse pass by.' I am not a man to harbour grudges and I prefer to say: 'Wait, open your door and you will see an old enemy come in who has become your dear friend.' But in memoirs such as these one has to follow the chronological order of events. We must return to Casablanca in 1943.

It was a joy to take my place again at a mess table with French officers. To my great surprise, many of them knew of my role in America. One said to me: 'It was an article by you in *The New York Times*, reprinted in a Swiss paper, that for the first time gave me the certainty that France would free herself.' Another: 'In 1940 I heard your speech to the Canadians. It did me good.' In Casa I met Christian de Fels (son of my friends André and Marthe) who was getting ready to leave for the United States where he was to be trained as a pilot, and Pierre Lyautey, nephew of the marshal, who invited me to come and stay with him, an invitation I thankfully accepted. Pierre described to me the end of the campaign in Tunisia. 'What a pity you missed it! It was sublime. The French army played a decisive role. The stratagem that brought the victory was devised by our General Juin.'

Letter to my wife: Here I am on French soil. It gives me a strong feeling, perhaps not altogether as strong as I had expected because this city holds so many Americans, Arabs and other nationals that the French are a bit diluted. But just the same it is delightful to hear French spoken again in the streets by the children, to encounter the old turns of speech, to enter libraries which, poor though they are, are French in appearance, atmosphere and smell; to talk to French officers who are at home here, being the managers of the city.

In Morocco the populace was not in need of food. 'But wait till you see Algiers!' people said to me, sighing. Nevertheless I was in haste to get there; it was necessary, however, to find a seat on a plane and this seemed very difficult. However, the order that assigned me to the Headquarters of the Commander-in-Chief gave me priority and three days later I landed at the airport of Maison Blanche. Captain de Clermont-Tonnerre was waiting for me there on behalf of General Giraud and had reserved a room for me at the Hotel Aletti. He was the bearer of an invitation to lunch next day with the Commander-in-Chief.

Another officer was waiting at Maison Blanche—Saint-Exupéry. He accompanied me to my hotel and when we were alone he said to me: 'Ah, my poor friend! What sort of wasps' nest have we fallen into? You will very soon find out what the political atmosphere is like.

[304]

Unbreathable! Two Courts reign over this city, two rival factions. Both you and I believed that from now on there would be a single French army, one and indivisible. That is not the case—at least not yet. I am very unhappy, and you will be too.'

Nevertheless during the first days there I believed that Saint-Ex had been mistaken. I was so happy to see my old friends that everything seemed fine. At lunch at Giraud's I met General Mast, Resident General in Tunisia; Joxe, Secretary-General of the government; Henri Bonnet; General Devinck, Chief of the General Staff; General Chambe, one of the great aviators of the 1914–18 war. After lunch General Devinck told me what use he expected to make of me: 'General Béthouart has written us that in order for the Americans to understand our role it is essential for you to follow the military operations and write the history of the re-equipped Army of Africa. After that, in six or eight months, we will send you on a mission to the United States to describe what you have seen in articles and lectures. Then you'll return to be present at the outcome which, we are convinced, will be victory.'

There is no reason to be surprised at this blithe certitude. Rommel's defeat in Tunisia had been, as Churchill had said, 'not the beginning of the end, but the end of the beginning.' The Axis had lost two hundred and fifty thousand men, more than two hundred and fifty tanks and two thousand three hundred airplanes.

'At this moment,' General Devinck continued, 'no operations are under way. But don't worry; the Allies will carry forward the attack; the French army will take part in it and you will accompany it. In the meantime Captain de Clermont-Tonnerre will take you to our newly equipped divisions and also to the battlefields of Tunisia. You will be our historian—and later, when the operations are resumed, our liaison officer.' This programme pleased me. It was all I had hoped for.

Letter to my wife: My dearest, I have just spent five days on the road visiting the regiments and the Headquarters of the new French army. Five hundred kilometres a day, the sirocco—that is, a furnace of sand—scrambling among the rocks to follow the manoeuvres, little sleep because we start at five in the morning ... It is good training for following a campaign when the time comes ... My reception everywhere is fine. Naturally there are all kinds here: enthusiasts and those who are lukewarm, moderates and those who are violent, but it seems to me that the good outweigh the bad. You will say that this is my eternal optimism. Perhaps. Nevertheless when I observe men like my companion Clermont-Tonnerre, like General de Monsabert, I cannot keep from admiring our Frenchmen. This combination of culture and courage is unique in the world. General de Monsabert went into battle during the Tunisian campaign at the head of his troops, cane in hand; the same general quotes Caesar and can decipher a Latin inscription; he knows history and is making it. Clermont-Tonnerre prepared for the landing of November 8 by re-reading the Odyssey in Greek ... '

I saw the possibility of a book, *Victoire en France*, which would be the sequel and counterweight to *Tragédie en France*. And so the first weeks were happier than I could have dared hope after St. Ex's warnings. Captain de Clermont-Tonnerre conducted me on long trips to the large units newly equipped by the Americans. Everywhere the morale was splendid. I was received by life-long friends like Durosoy, whom I had known as an artillery officer under Lyautey and who was now commander of a tank regiment. I spent pleasant hours with General de Monsabert and General Henri Martin, both highly cultivated men. General and Madame Catroux, our old friends, had thrown open their house in Algiers to me. When I stayed in the city, which was seldom, I took my meals sometimes at the mess in the Hotel Aletti, sometimes in the handsome Arab setting of the Cercle Interallié, which was managed by Monsieur de Witasse, the diplomat who had received me so kindly at Oudja in 1925. But almost always I was invited out, sometimes by Bob Murphy, the minister from the United States, sometimes by Lord Duncannon, sometimes by Lemaigre-Dubreuil who lived in a splendid palace, sometimes by my dear Anne Heurgon in whose house I finally went to live.

I had quickly realized that to live at the Hotel Aletti in the lower part of the city when the Headquarters' offices were at the top of the Rue Michelet was impossible. I had no car (except, of course, when on duty); I was very poor, having consigned the larger part of my salary to my wife and, crippled by rheumatism, I struggled through the broiling city dragging one leg. The climate affected me very badly, the food even worse. To be closer to my office I first went to live in the home of an engineer, Monsieur Thomas, whose wife rented me a room. The Thomases were a harmonious and sympathetic family and did their best to make me comfortable. The day after my arrival I had gone to call on Anne Heurgon (Anne Desjardins from Pontigny). Gide was a lodger in her house. The reunion was cordial. Gide seemed in fine form, gay, playful and curious about everything. His youthfulness of spirit astonished me. Anne, whose hospitality was infinite, immediately offered to take me into her home (I accepted after Gide's departure), but she had in her apartment in addition to her husband, a professor of Latin who had been mobilized with the rank of captain, her children and soon some young officers who had arrived from New York: Christian de Nicolay, Michel Porgès, Christian d'Aumale. It made a crowded household. I dined there frequently. There would be ten or twelve at the table. Anne succeeded, I do not know how, in giving us couscous and date desserts. I believe she got up at dawn to stand in queues in front of the stores to get supplies.

For a long time I was without news of Simone. Then the American army invented a system of microfilm and I received minuscule missives, photographs of the originals. 'Ah, who can say what will be invented next—such joy to receive a letter.' These miniatures were my only connection with my wife, who was my only connection with life. Through them I learned that General Béthouart and Commander Pilot of the French Mission had been very kind to her and were helping her send me the medicines I so much needed; that the Claudels often invited her to visit them; that she was at work. Sometimes a friend on his way to America agreed to take with him a longer letter. Philippe Soupault, among others, did me this service. At such times I wrote volumes and relieved my heart with greater freedom.

For the misery one suffered in Algiers at that time was lack of freedom. A paper, the TAM (Tunisia, Algeria, Morocco) had asked me for some articles which I wrote with the authorization of my superiors; they were of the purest patriotism with no shadow of politics. Some occult power informed the publisher of that journal that, if he published me, he would get no more paper! Many similar episodes astonished me as much as they saddened me. Was my savage enemy in New York pursuing me across the ocean? I did not know, I did not understand, and my state of mind affected my health, already undermined by heat, humidity and strange food.

A dreadful piece of news came as a final blow. My mother had been arrested by the Nazis. This was reported in the American papers, and I was informed by people in New York. She had not been sent to a camp but to a hospital which served as a prison for the aged and infirm. (She was suffering from an arthritic hip and could not walk.) On top of the sorrow of knowing that she was a prisoner and perhaps ill treated, I felt a vague fear. Had my enlistment been the cause of her arrest? I was to learn later on that it had had nothing to do with it. A woman who coveted her apartment had denounced my mother, who had hitherto been overlooked, in order to get it! Moreover, the woman had succeeded. What could I do to help? Alas, nothing! Later I learned that a former deputy from Elbeuf had interceded for my mother in Vichy but to no avail. From the time that Dordogne had been occupied, I had no way of communicating with my parents-in-law. A note from them reached me through the Red Cross, asking if my wife were in New York and if she were well.

Letter to Simone, July 22, 1943: In the intervals between my trips the people I see most often are naturally Gide and Anne Heurgon at whose house a place is set for me whenever I am not engaged elsewhere; Captain de Clermont-Tonnerre, my constant companion whom I like so much; General Chambe whose books you know and who is kindness itself; our friend Georges-Picot; the Catroux; the United States consul ... And then there is the huge Arab population whom one encounters in the streets, enigmatic, reticent and better informed than we know. This morning on the tram I heard two young Arab girls talking—in French, of course. As good Moslems they were veiled. One said to the other: 'My mistress is unbearable. She runs her finger over the furniture to see if there is any dust. There is no dust; I work well and willingly. If she would only leave me alone! She has the habit of talking about me to her husband at the table and doing it in Spanish. I said to her: "Be careful; I know Spanish, and French, and Arabic, and American!" ... Besides, I don't like her to call me Fatma; if she calls me Fatma I shall call her Marie.'

August 1: A great piece of news; Olivier is in Madrid; he crossed the Pyrenees on foot and is going to join me here. It was Monseigneur Boyer-Masse in Madrid who sent me word by telegram. I was surprised and overjoyed; this proves resourcefulness and courage on his part ... I spent the week making the rounds with the General Staff, and this filled me with enthusiasm. We have a fine, a very fine, army, well equipped by the Americans and composed of excellent men who are delighted with their equipment. I shall try to say this in an article which I will send you. Everywhere I run into friends. This would be fascinating if the climate did not make me so ill. What heat! What humidity! Crippled by rheumatism, I drag one foot; my liver which I can ordinarily ignore is manifesting its discontent brutally. To follow a manoeuvre in this state is not always easy, but enthusiasm triumphs over fatigue . . . I have just been told that Minou is here. Perhaps she has news of you. I shall try to see her. You cannot imagine how difficult it is when one is poor and without a car in this furnace of a city where all the streets are perpendicular.

August 5: Hervé Alphand who is leaving for the United States has agreed to take this letter . . . I am about to go to Morocco where I will be living at the home of the Resident General [Puaux whom we knew when he was ambassador in Vienna] . . . This evening I am dining at the Cercle Interallié. There you meet the two hundred people who 'because they go to bed late believe they are the leaders of Algiers— and the world.' The two 'courts' are represented although the two consuls never put in an appearance. In the patio with its decorative tiles people sit on cushions in Oriental fashion and talk very late into the night, which is always starry.

I dined there last evening with Gide; Warburg, an American; and an Englishman, Lord Duncannon. A life of waiting. And then, as soon as one leaves Algiers and gets into the open country and sees the soldiers, it is like a bath of innocence and patriotism—a renascence.

As I had written to my wife, a telegram from Monseigneur Boyer-Masse, chaplain of the French Embassy in Madrid, had informed me that my second son Olivier was in Spain. As soon as he had heard (on the radio) that I was in Algiers, he determined to join me. A first attempt to cross the Pyrenees has failed. The Germans arrested him in the forbidden zone and interned him at the fortress of Ha, close to Bordeaux, where he was maltreated. Very fortunately, since he had made numerous visits to Hendaye, he had known for a long time through mutual friends the Spanish military commandant at Irun, one of my faithful readers, and the latter, having learned of the sentence, had taken active measures and succeeded after three months, first in having my son released from prison and then in getting him across the frontier . . . Olivier hoped soon to get authorization to come to Algeria and join me. My elder son Gérald was in hiding in France, waiting for the moment when he could enlist, which came for him at the time of the landing.

My work at General Staff remained the same: to prepare for publication the archives of the operations in Tunisia, to traverse the whole country for the purpose of reconstructing the battles, and most important of all, to maintain liaison. The British and Americans asked me to give numerous lectures to their troops. The purpose was partly to occupy their minds during this period of inaction and partly to explain France and North Africa. I spoke in English almost every day. General Eisenhower became interested in this project and came to attend one of my talks. The lady who commanded the corps of French women attached to the army also took me with her on a number of tours. General Devinck sent me for a week in great secrecy to a camp commanded by Commandant Gambiez (now a general) where commandos were being trained by the methods employed by Lord Mountbatten. They were taught silent surprise attack and individual combat; they were trained in parachute jumping. I followed the first stages of this training, but the army doctor would not let me jump from an airplane; I was too old. I admired Commandant Gambiez who inspired limitless affection and confidence in his men. He was training elite troops and shock troops. General Devinck said to me mysteriously that they would very soon find their employment. 'And so will you,' he added.

3o

From Corsica to Italy

I believed that my first expedition would be to Italy. After the victory
in Tunisia the Allies had occupied Sicily and had just landed at Naples.
General Juin, whom I knew well, was to command the French divisions
and I thought I would leave with him. But suddenly an unexpected
event took place in Corsica. The island had been occupied for a long
time by the Italians. And what an occupation! Eighty thousand
Italians, presently followed by twenty thousand Germans with tanks,
guns and airplanes. Hitler understood the importance of this platform from which one could leap either into France or Italy. Corsica,
with three hundred thousand inhabitants, could hardly muster thirty
thousand fighting men; now it found itself policed by a hundred
thousand. This was a tribute to the military virtues of the Corsicans.
A merited tribute, for they had immediately organized a resistance
force.

The French General Staff for its part was making preparations for an
expedition to Corsica. To succeed, the operation required the support
on the island of armed and organized resistance units to aid the Allied
air and sea forces at the moment of landing (which would be difficult).
First of all, it was necessary to arm the Corsican patriots. This was
done both by parachute and by submarine. Commander Lherminier
made several trips with the submarine *Casablanca* to the shores of
Corsica. The officer who was directing the resistance forces on the spot
was Commander Colonna, a hero of the antique mould whom his men
in their secret code called Hannibal because he was fighting against
Rome. I saw him later, on a hospital bed, exhausted by nine days of
fighting, feverish, emaciated but very handsome, with the clear eyes
of a mystic.

'Above all, do not say that I was the soul of the uprising. Each man
put his soul into it. My role was to arm the partisans, to form them
into regiments and above all to make them understand that, if they

[311]

rose up too soon, they would be massacred in vain. The British radio was to give the signal when everything was ready . . . It was a hard task. Remember that a hundred thousand enemies had divided up our island into squares, that you had to have a passport to leave your village, that every partisan caught in the act was tortured, then killed. And nevertheless we were able to accumulate tons of *matériel*. Sometimes, when I would arrive in the submarine with arms, my men were not there on the shore at the rendezvous. In that case I had to unload the arms with the help of the sailors and hide them in the brush. But in the end everything was arranged. I had ten thousand armed and disciplined men, with a leader in each village.'

At the beginning of September 1943 came the dramatic change. The King of Italy dismissed Mussolini, and Marshal Badoglio signed an armistice with the Allies. For the Corsicans, this changed all the aspects of the problem. They had prepared for a struggle of harassment against the Italians; now they were going to have to fight an open battle against a heavily armed German force which occupied not only the port of Bastia but a whole corridor along the east coast, thus permitting them to control the shores and the landing fields from Boniface to Bastia. Nevertheless since incidents kept breaking out almost everywhere between Italians and Germans after the armistice, the patriots believed that on September 9 the favourable moment had come to begin their uprising. The spontaneous outbreak was both military and political. Ambushes wiped out German convoys and emergency municipal councils were set up. The Germans reacted rapidly. An armoured brigade and a division of infantry arrived from Sardinia. The partisans found themselves in great danger of being overwhelmed and sent an appeal to the French armed forces.

For the Commander-in-Chief this appeal posed a formidable problem. The Americans and British in Italy were at grips with a still powerful German army in entrenched positions. They needed all their means of transport by air and by sea. And so the plans that had been made for Allied support to a landing in Corsica had been cancelled for lack of *matériel*. In view of this, was it wise to throw French troops, necessarily limited in number, into the assault on the island? The venture seemed hazardous. But could one fail to respond to the appeal of Frenchmen who had courageously undertaken to secure their own liberation? If we did nothing, it seemed clear that the Germans were going to gain control of the whole island, thus depriving the Allies of that precious stepping stone. Giraud made his decision. He summoned General Henri Martin, who had just been named commander of an army corps, and said to him: 'I'm going to send the shock battalion, the Moroccan troops and the mountain division to Corsica at once. You will command these troops and you will take Corsica.'

The enterprise seemed daring. For naval transport we had at our disposal only two old steamers and the submarine *Casablanca*. It would be necessary to cross the Mediterranean at a time when the Germans had many submarines and airplanes in that area. A ship like the *Ville d'Ajaccio*, which had for a long time provided a service between western France and Corsica, had no anti-aircraft defences. It could, if need be, transport fifteen hundred men, but it ran the greatest risk of being sunk.

As soon as I heard of this expedition, I was drawn to it both by this opportunity of seeing action at once and by the chance of being one of the first to set foot on French soil. I asked General Devinck to assign me as liaison officer to General Henri Martin. He began by saying no. 'This is more than dangerous. If you are sunk or killed, I shall be blamed for having sent you on the expedition.' Admiral Lemonnier, who was present at our embarkation on the *Ville d'Ajaccio*, told me later in Paris: 'I did not think you would ever return from that adventure.' To tell the truth, at that time I held my life cheap. To die was to escape from the torment of Algiers.

Contrary to all expectations, the crossing on this old ship crowded with soldiers was without incident. By a miracle, which even now I cannot explain, we were not attacked. The *Casablanca* had preceded us with elements from the shock battalion; they were to spread the rumour that they constituted the advance guard of an immense army. Ajaccio was still in the hands of the Italians, but they respected the armistice and did not oppose our landing. The populace gave us an enthusiastic welcome. General Henri Martin invited me to take my meals at his mess with his General Staff plus a young British general, Peake, and an American colonel. But we were not there often. Sometimes with the men of the shock battalion, sometimes with General Humbert who had become military governor, I crossed and recrossed the island and witnessed the first engagements. The shock battalion performed marvels. At night the German airplanes would bomb Ajaccio. I have retained a strange and beautiful memory of an evening spent in a park with General Humbert; while the bombs fell, we talked metaphysics. The starry sky, the whistle of death around us, my interlocutor, the subject, combined in an exciting effect. It reminded me of certain conversations in *Bramble*.

We had brought with us a government commissioner named Luizet who later on was to become Prefect of Police in Paris; for his chief assistant he had chosen Filippini, a young Corsican engineer who had formerly worked with my father-in-law Maurice Pouquet. The head engineer of public works was called Lehanneur. 'I took my master's degree at Caen,' I told him. 'An old and very strict Latin teacher there had your name . . . ' 'That was my father,' he said. Destiny weaves its tapestry skilfully. A bookseller in Ajaccio came to see me; he wanted to show me that he kept all my books well hidden in a cellar beneath his bookstore. 'The Germans have banned them, but they are much in demand and I sell them. The Italian officers used to buy them out of hatred for their allies, for there was no love lost between the two armies.' Our chief, General Henri Martin, had gone to the Italian Commander-in-Chief, General Magli, and, although he had not persuaded him to fight against his former allies, he had secured the loan of trucks.

The astonishing thing is that the Germans, who were infinitely more numerous than we were, did not throw us into the sea, something they could easily have done. But they decided at the end of a few days to evacuate Corsica. However, in order to carry out their embarkation in good order and load their tanks and guns, they needed to hold onto Bastia to the last moment. This is the best port on the island and relatively easy to defend because the approach on the land side is commanded by the high pass of Teghime. I went and installed myself in Saint-Florent at the foot of the pass with the native troops under the command of Colonel Boyer de Latour, which were to take the defile by surprise. The Germans fired on Saint-Florent but without doing much damage. Finally the pass was cleared and we took Bastia. I was lodged in the home of the headmaster of the Lycée. We had hardly arrived when a terrible bombardment, far more effective than the earlier one, took a heavy toll. The Allied squadrons, coming from Egypt, had delivered this fine stroke in order to help us, not having been informed in time that the city was in our hands! 'That's the army,' Doctor O'Grady would have said.

A letter to my wife gives some idea of this expedition:

October 8, 1943, Somewhere in France: My dearest, Obviously you know where I am and what campaign I have been involved in and why I could not write. This was a daring and hazardous move. We were a handful of French on an island occupied by a hundred thousand foreigners. The success was rapid. I believe General Béthouart has shown you my reports. I have seen everything from close up, I have seen it well and I have been everywhere. We have an excellent leader who treats me as his friend. A happy interlude in the sorrows to which I must return.

If you were present, I could live here. It is a rustic island, mountainous and of incredible and constant beauty. I have not found a single spot in it that is ugly. As for the landscape, at times it reminds one of Scotland with its thistle-covered moors, at times of Italy from Florence to Siena, at times of the Alpine torrents, at times of the bays of Provence. The villages are of stone, and very poor, but the hospitality is generous. Very little work is done; people love to hunt, they love cafés and long political conversations. Everyone is in the street at all hours of the day.

In addition to the natives we have here our army, which I love more and more, the Moroccans who feel at home as they do everywhere and drive jeeps along impossible paths, innumerable sad Italians—ah! so sad one is tempted to comfort them—and then the impeccable English (it has been a pleasure to have them again as comrades in arms) and some Americans who help us to survive in this war-stripped country with their rations.

I have the impression that at the time of the return to France food will be the great problem. You cannot imagine the joy that a bar of chocolate gives to these people who live on beans and chick peas. The season of chestnuts is about to begin, and this will be a precious resource. What has become of those times at Essendiéras and the blanched chestnuts in cream? Have I told you that Essendiéras wrote me (through the Red Cross) to ask news of you and that I was able to send them word? As for young Olivier, I am still expecting him; he writes from Spain that he is awaiting sailing orders.

As for me, my dearest, I have but one dream: to take up our studious life together with you, to see only few and loyal friends, to live very far from all public life. The crowd is mad, inconstant, easy to win, easy to lose. In that direction lies neither security nor any true honour. I would still like to write a few vigorous and lasting books. What will be the best retreat for this work? Neuilly? Périgord? The Midi? I do not know . . . Here I am out of the world. If I had been well and if I could have seen you sometimes, I would have been happy, but alas ! . . .'

General de Gaulle came to congratulate the troops and was acclaimed by the populace. Luizet said to me: 'This leaves no doubt about the return to France. De Gaulle alone will count.' Since October 1 General Giraud had no longer been co-president of the Committee, having been forbidden the combination of civil and military functions, but he remained Commander-in-Chief. The liberation of Corsica being complete, he ordered me to return to Algiers by air. There General Devinck received me: 'Now,' he said, 'you have a fine story for the Americans. Just one more little campaign in Italy and I will send you over on a mission.' Upon my return from Corsica, I had found Olivier, whom Anne Heurgon had installed in her home. He had suffered a great deal during his internment in the fortress of Ha. For anyone as nervous as he, so many shocks and excitements were dangerous. But he insisted on enlisting and was accepted for the transport service. Since he could speak English, he was sent to Bari in southern Italy to join the British troops there.

I myself left for Italy toward the end of November by army airplane. After a landing in Sicily, I proceeded to Naples. I was lodged in the old French Institute, much damaged by bombs. The stairway had crumbled and you climbed to the second story on a fragile plank. The city retained its character. In the evening officers from all countries dined on the harbour Chez Zia Teresa and beautiful voices sang *Santa Lucia*. The programme assigned to me called for a stay with General Clark, Inter-Allied Commander-in-Chief at Caserta, ancient seat of the King of the Two Sicilies. The American army had installed its GHQ in a splendid park there, a baroque Versailles peopled with giant statues. I spent several very interesting days with the Chief of the General Staff, General Gunther (whom I was to see again fifteen years later at SHAPE, when he was in command of the Allied Armies in Europe). He showed me the American lines and then sent me on to General Juin.

The latter first had me visit several French divisions. I already knew their commanders. The morale of these troops seemed very high. The messes were very gay and brimming with hope. Then General Juin himself took me on a tour of inspection of the French armies at the front. 'This is going to be difficult,' he told me. 'The Germans are entrenched in those mountains. Monte Cassino will be hard to take. But it will be done.' He spoke to me of Giraud with affection and respect. I made a note of some of his remarks: 'The Army of Africa cannot forget that Giraud obtained for it a modern armament and it is this that allows us here in Italy today to play the major role that you are observing. Moreover we owe him wise and important decisions during the campaign in Tunisia and the liberation of Corsica. That was a noble chase. On the military level there is no more glorious leader. That he has been eliminated from the political sphere is hard but after all natural. In the face of Vichy, which continues to vegetate with its impotent chief of state, there is no place for any political organization except one embodying the Resistance. And there De Gaulle has the right of priority.'

When I left Juin, I returned to Naples. After that I was to go and spend a week with the British army, whither I had been summoned by General Alexander, and I expected a great deal from these contacts. Suddenly during the night of my return to Naples I was seized by vomiting and dreadful intestinal pain. This lasted several days. Had I been poisoned by the food at the messes or was I exhausted by the endless tours along the entire length of the front? I do not know, but never in my life have I felt so ill. An army doctor who was summoned ordered me evacuated by air to Algiers as quickly as possible. This doctor advised me to go to a hospital as soon as I arrived. But I was careful not to do so. The day was approaching for my departure on the mission to the United States and I did not want to run the risk of being delayed for a moment from seeing my wife. Moreover I could not be of any further service in Algiers (now that the army had left) while in America an account of what I had seen would be useful. After that, I would return to be a witness of the re-entry into France.

I thought I would get my travel orders soon after my return. But it was more complicated than I had imagined. The order had to originate at Headquarters of the Allied Forces, that is to say, with Eisenhower. Since my mission had to do with Information, the American Services demanded authorization from the State Department. Alerted by my wife, my friend Denny, manager of Town Hall in New York where I was to speak, undertook to obtain clearance. Finally I received a document:

[317]

AG 201–AGP–Maurois, André (off)   20 December 1943
SUBJECT: Travel Orders

TO: Captain André Maurois (Fr)

1. You are authorized to proceed on or about 26 December 1943
from this station to Washington, D.C., in order to carry out an
assigned mission and upon completion of temporary duty return to
proper station.

2. Travel by military aircraft rail and/or surface transportation is
authorized.

By command of General EISENHOWER:

Only then did Devinck give me my French travel orders:

Office of the Commander-in-Chief
Special Headquarters   Algiers,
Liaison and Information   December 27, 1943

TRAVEL ORDERS

Captain Maurois of the Special General Staff of the Commander-in-
Chief, engaged on a mission to the United States, is authorized to take
with him photographs, drawings and documents for the performance
of that mission.

Civil and Military Authorities are requested to accord him all aid
and assistance within their powers to permit him to accomplish his
mission.

GIRAUD, General of the Army
Commander-in-Chief

P. O. General DEVINCK
Chief of the Special General Staff

I embarked on December 28 at Maison-Blanche in an American
aircraft. The passengers were numerous and I had to make the flight
seated on the ribs of the plane. We made a landing at Casablanca and
then at a camp in Brazil. I was exhausted by dysentery and fever, but
the idea of being with my wife for the New Year sustained me.

31

Return to America

My airplane landed at the airport in Washington on December 31. The trip into the city and the search for a room took time. It was two o'clock in the morning when I finally got to bed. I did not want to phone Simone in the middle of the night, since she was certain to know nothing about my return. The mails were still very slow and the decision had been a sudden one. But as soon as I woke up I rushed to the telephone and called her. She was still half asleep.

'Where are you? Are you talking from Algiers? I thought . . . '

'I am in Washington and I will be with you in a few hours.'

She gave a cry: 'What a joy! You are going to spend New Year with me? It's a miracle! I was so sad last evening at the Claudels' . . . What time are you arriving? I'll come and meet you at the station.'

To return to my wife again, to our minuscule but charming apartment, to the Angel of Chartres, all this gave me a happiness impossible to express in words. It would require the pure notes of *Parsifal*, mounting endlessly to transcendent heights.

'But just look at you!' my wife said.

As a matter of fact, I felt very ill. I weighed myself, which I had not done for six months; I had lost over twenty pounds! I made an appointment with our physician, Dr. Kling, who subjected me to a complete medical examination: analyses, X-rays, blood count. The results were disturbing.

'I barely recognize the man I sent overseas six months ago in good health,' he told me. 'You have dysentery, which I hope is not amoebic, cardiac arythmia accompanied by tachycardia . . . And then this dreadful loss of weight. You need six months of complete rest.'

That was easy to say . . . I had a mission—to talk to Americans about the reconstituted French army—and I was determined to fulfil it. Immediately, moreover, the Alliance Française and various American groups (the American Legion, the PEN Club, several universities) arranged lectures for me. On these occasions I described what I had seen with an emotion that proved contagious. In Washington and New York, in Chicago and Boston, my reception was unforgettable. Now I no longer had to say to our friends: 'France will arise,' but instead: 'France has arisen.' I find a clipping from an American paper and quote it here because I want to give some idea of the climate of this return, so as to be able to contrast it with the renewed descent into misfortune that was to follow.

SPONTANEOUS TRIBUTES—In earlier days, when he went from lecture to lecture, André Maurois received warm ovations. But now that he has returned from North Africa, Corsica and Sicily with a marvellous account of French, American and British troops fighting side by side, he awakens depths of emotion never reached before. Without even touching on politics, he brings his audience close to the men themselves and compels recognition of the greatness of their leaders. It seems to be a spontaneous impulse on the part of his hearers to rise at the end of his lecture and sing the Marseillaise. Rochester and Chicago set the example. Now it is like an established custom.

Being an officer, I had naturally asked the French Military Mission in Washington for permission to give lectures and publish articles, and I had received it without difficulty. General Béthouart had left for Algiers where he was to be Chief of the General Staff. General Beynet, who had taken his place, put me in the hands of Colonel Pilot, an officer of high intellectual and moral worth. For several weeks all went well, aside from my deplorable health which was further undermined by these trips. Then came an unexpected and inexplicable blow. Monsieur Le Trocquer, Commissioner for War in the government in Algiers, cabled me orders to return immediately. What had happened? General Beynet sent a cable to point out that I had travel orders signed by the Commander-in-Chief and that my mission was far from being completed. Le Trocquer replied that the Commander-in-Chief had no right to sign such an order. This was untrue, though he had just been deprived of that right. A new and regrettable episode in the strife between the two French General Staffs.

'And what are you going to do?' Colonel Pilot asked me.

'What can I do? Obey.'

'Then you'll have to go through the whole business of vaccination: yellow fever, tetanus and the rest.'

'Very well. I'll ask my physician to see to it. In my precarious state of health I'll have to be attended by him during this series of shocks.'

When I told Dr. Kling that I was going back again and asked him to vaccinate me, he was indignant: 'This is madness,' he told me. 'You are much too sick to stand the injections and the military life. I *absolutely* refuse to send you back there; I'm going to give you a certificate.'

'I want to go.'

'And I'm against it! I'll ask for a consultation with the president of the American Medical Association.'

This prominent physician made a thorough examination and concluded that I had, in addition to the cardiac trouble and a disturbing cachexia, chronic appendicitis. (His diagnosis was right, for I had to have an operation later on.) I was broken-hearted because I had been determined to prove to Le Trocquer that I was still a disciplined soldier. Colonel Pilot, whose advice I asked, said to me:

'I'm going to have you examined by a commission of army doctors. Then you will see.'

The army commission confirmed word for word the opinion of the New York experts. After this verdict Le Trocquer left me in peace. Ten years later I was to meet him when he was President of the National Assembly, at a festival in Saint-Malo where he was presiding and in the course of which I was to give a speech on Bernard Shaw whose *Caesar and Cleopatra* was being played in the open air. Le Trocquer introduced me to the audience with high praises for me as a writer, a man and a citizen. During dinner I sat next to him and I could not help saying:

'Why the devil did you persecute me in 1944 when I was working for our country?'

'I persecute you?' he said. 'I had no such intention, but several cables from a Frenchman in New York asked me to recall you. I did so. That was all.'

I returned to work. During the intervals between my trips I wrote a novel, *Terre promise*, and I did research for an *Histoire de France*. I was aware that there were many histories of France, but Americans hardly read them at all and it seemed to me useful to show them the role France had played in western civilization. Also I hoped that this

[321]

history would be different from those that had preceded it. I was not going to limit it to narration; I would try to give explanations, sometimes through great movements, sometimes through great individuals.

I have said that it had been my habit for a long time to make out a work plan every six months. Here is the one I find in my *Vivier* for 1944.

Work Plan

Histoire de France
Lives?—Tolstoy, Balzac, Constant, Lamartine, Sand, Browning
Literary studies: Baudelaire, Verlaine, Rimbaud, Mallarmé, Valéry
Novels:
Bertrand Schmidt en exil (novel in the form of letters)
Les Oiseaux de feu
Solange en guerre

Novel about musician: Central idea: artist who lives to express something that is his alone. (In the case of Debussy, nature freed from conventional forms.) The legitimate egoism of this type of man who must safeguard his work. For him love is only a means. Model my hero partly on Debussy, partly on Wagner. Story told by a witness: 'At first I thought of writing his biography, but . . . '

Essays:
Ce que je crois
Les Illusions
Monologues des morts (in the manner of Browning and of Claudel's Pontius Pilate)
Short Novels: Put the characters of my novels in the setting of the present war—Send Alain Marcenat, Isabelle's son, to New York—Make Bernard Quesnay an officer in the FFL.
Choses nues—in the tone of Victor Hugo's *Choses vues*

Many of these projects became books; some of them remained in the limbo of the imagination. This is a great pity; they were half done.

As for lectures, I talked a great deal about what I called the *common heritage* of our civilization, deriving from Greek wisdom, Roman law and Judeo-Christian mysticism. I tried to show that in maintaining this civilization France could play as great a role as in the past. The universities helped me. My friend William Allen White, the great-hearted journalist who had worked so splendidly for the cause of the Allies, had died in January 1944. But he had previously introduced me to another great journalist, his neighbour Henry Haskell of the *Kansas City Star*—an important meeting for me, because Henry Haskell had me invited for two weeks to the new University of Kansas City. I mention this sojourn among so many others because it was agreeable, fruitful and was to produce a sequel in this story of mine. The president of that university, Clarence Decker, and his wife Mary with whom I stayed, became dear friends of mine, and Deck (this was the president's nickname) asked me to return for a whole semester at the beginning of 1946 to give a course on Balzac and Tolstoy. Uncertain about the future, I accepted.

In August 1944 news of the liberation of Paris reached New York. It was a day of tremendous jubilation not only for us French but for our American friends as well. All of Fifth Avenue was hung with blue, white and red flags. A ceremony was hastily arranged on the Plaza at Rockefeller Center. The French consul-general, Guérin de Beaumont, gave an excellent speech. Lily Pons sang the Marseillaise. My wife wept and I believe I did too.

In France my mother had been set free and taken back to our home in Neuilly. Emilie and Gaston Wolff looked after her with affection, my daughter came to see her almost daily. *Maman* said: 'Now I am going to see my son.' But the captivity had weakened her; to live in a room with others at her age and with her infirmity had been hard; although she had been the admiration of her companions in prison (many told me so) because of her courage and confidence, she left exhausted, at the end of her strength. A few weeks after her return to Neuilly she died of a stroke. Gaston Wolff was at her death bed. We received the news first by cable, then by letter. It was an enormous sorrow to me. She, like my father, had been a being without faults; I owed her my first contact with the poets, with books; I admired her and loved her equally. In my mind I can see her in the shuttered drawing room at Elbeuf, selecting for me from the handsome gilt book-case a Racine, a Victor Hugo, or that volume of *Moralistes français* (La Rochefoucauld, Pascal, La Bruyère, Vauvenargues) which she had received as a prize when she was a young girl. I continued to wish passionately to return to France, but now that she was gone it would no longer be all I had hoped, and my happiness would wear a mourning band.

[323]

My parents-in-law had decided to leave the town house in the Avenue Hoche (this really belonged to my wife, but they had always lived there) and to settle permanently at Essendiéras. They wrote us that our apartment in the Boulevard Maurice Barrès had been plundered. This was an exaggeration, but there was a great deal to be done to make the place habitable. It had to be repainted, new curtains had to be found. Simone wished to go ahead as advance scout and camp in Neuilly in order to undertake the work of rehabilitation; it was agreed that I should join her as soon as I had fulfilled the engagements made for me in America, the last of which was a semester at the University of Kansas City (January–June 1946).

Immediately after the German surrender in May 1945, we had called on the French consul-general, Guérin de Beaumont, and asked for passage for my wife. He had said; 'I'll do all I can, but it will not be easy for some time. The war in the Far East is going on. The only boats that cross the ocean are troop transports or warships. They are run by the Americans and, so far as I know, no reservations have been given to women. You are on very good terms with them. Try. I will give you my support.' Thanks to him, in August Simone obtained a cabin for September aboard the *Vulcania*, an Italian transport captured by the Americans, which was to leave for France loaded with nurses, army doctors and medicine.

As soon as our friends in New York knew that she was returning, they came to beg her to take gifts, clothing and food for their families who lacked everything. Maurice de Rothschild, on his account alone, had sent to our apartment a veritable cargo. Before she knew it Simone had eleven trunks. To get permission to load them required innumerable strategies. Guérin de Beaumont in his providential way helped us. I was unhappy at remaining in America without my wife, but happy to think that she was going to arrange for our life in France, and to imagine the pleasure that our gifts would give to those we loved.

Simone made the trip on a ship with blackout curtains over the portholes. In Le Havre Maurice Pouquet and Emilie and Gaston Wolff were waiting for her. On the Boulevard Maurice Barrès she found our library empty. Immediately her friends began to entertain her; the Mauriacs, the Lacretelles, Edmée de La Rochefoucauld, Pierre Sardou, and twenty others. She would have liked to spend the winter at Essendiéras which was heated, but there was a great lack of lodgings in Paris and unoccupied apartments ran the risk of being requisitioned.

And so Simone camped at Neuilly after a short trip to Périgord to embrace her mother.

In December Georges Duhamel and his wife Blanche announced their arrival in New York. Duhamel was to give a lecture at the French Institute. I offered to put them up since after Simone's departure the room that had served as her office was available. It was Duhamel's first trip to America since he had published the very anti-American *Scènes de la vie future*, and I was informed that a number of journalists were preparing hostile articles. I had enough friends of the press to scotch this campaign and everything went off well. I was happy to show Georges the museums and to take him to concerts so that he might see that the Muses occupy a more important place in the United States than the immigration officials who had made such a bad impression on him. It was a charming visit although Duhamel still had trouble forgiving the Americans for not being French. 'Their English makes me laugh,' he said.

The visit of the Duhamels was a brief and happy interlude for me. How many fine things we saw together; the Corots in the Metropolitan, the Gothic arches of the Cloisters, the unicorn tapestries, in which Blanche Duhamel recognized the symbolic history of France, and that return in the fog from Staten Island to New York, close to the *Vulcania*, the ship on which Simone had sailed and which was now coming back from Europe laden with exuberant soldiers. 'We have had a cubist day,' Duhamel said that evening. A few days before Christmas they embarked from Brooklyn on a small Norwegian vessel, highly varnished, mysterious, Ibsenian. I was sad to lose them but happy to think that I would soon see them again in Paris. All partings at this time had a bitter sweetness.

32

The End of Exile

Time must needs call the tune and man must follow it.

Alain

January 1, 1946: A melancholy awakening. I am alone. On this first day of each year, like Buster Brown I make resolutions: work, work, work. To live in France, in the country as much as possible, where the length of the days is doubled. Except for moments of action, to rise above our difficult time and to see it not as a sharp-edged instrument of moral torture but as an illusion to be described. To forbid myself to suffer for imaginary or temporary woes when so many men are suffering from real ills for which there is no remedy. To be exact and fair in all things . . . But what is the good in writing down resolutions? They must be lived. ·

Around ten o'clock the dear Milhauds came to get me and we lunched in the country at the home of Pierre Claudel. Violaine, grave and sensitive, recited verses by Vigny. Dominique had deciphered a piece Milhaud had written for her: *Bon jour Dominique!* The house of Pierre and Marion is two hours away from New York, isolated from the outer world by woods and fields. How wise to withdraw this way from the city, to be among trees and books and there to raise one's children. The intimate, familial charm of this day.

January 4: The arrival of Gérald whom I have not seen for six years. Emotion and anxiety. How will he be? He sailed on a small French ship, the *Désirade*, which has taken three weeks to make the crossing in foul weather. At the office of the 'Transat' I was told: 'Nine o'clock.' The last time I came to the pier it was with aching heart to see Simone off on her departure for France . . . This morning there are many French people from New York who like me have come to meet their children, relatives or friends. Political adversaries of yesterday look at one another, hesitate, then smile and cordially extend the hand of friendship. A long wait in the shed formerly filled with baggage, but empty today. Finally the ship, astonishingly small, glides up to the pier like the swan in *Lohengrin*. Immediately I see Gérald on the upper deck, searching for me with his eyes. He succeeds in jumping onto the quayside and cries to me over the heads of the American officials: 'Don't wait. The customs will take two hours. I'll join you at your hotel. *Okay?*' I reply: '*Okay.*' O most international of words!

Same evening: He is greatly changed. His mind is more mature. Necessity has made him active. We have come a long way from the spoiled boy, used to being waited on, whom I left in 1940. I had a splendid time showing him New York and enjoying his astonishment, but all seemed familiar to him. He knew America from the screen and the army; he does not feel uprooted here like a stranger. In the evening I got two seats for *State of the Union*, a benevolent political satire. 'The American public laughs,' Duhamel remarked, 'as the people in Europe no longer laugh.' Gérald was greatly amused: 'What good actors!' he said. *And so to bed.*

I hastened to install Gérald in my apartment, for the time of my departure for Kansas City was imminent. Could he afford to stay in that hotel? Perhaps, for I had found him, thanks to Philip Courtney, a position with Coty, and I knew I could give him part of my professor's salary. Life in Kansas City would not be expensive. I knew that my friend, President Clarence Decker, had reserved two rooms at forty dollars a month for me at Epperson House, a bizarre mixture of Norman chalet and feudal château, a building left to the university by some local Mycaenas. Meals at the cafeteria would cost me a dollar. Yes, I could easily help my son.

On January 23, after a brief stopover lecture in St. Louis, I reached Kansas City. Some of my friends in the East were astonished that I had agreed to teach in a very young institution when so many prestigious universities had offered me much better paid posts. But I did not regret it. Friendship was taking me back to that city. Deck and his wife Mary, as I have said, had given me the most affectionate welcome on my other sojourns there. This young, enthusiastic president had the appearance of one of his own students. Around him and his wife lived a group of cultivated men; Henry Haskell, manager of the *Kansas City Star*, a powerful paper and the only one in that area; Ernest Howard, an engineer and builder of great bridges; the painter Thomas Benton;

Professor Craine, a famous Balzacian. Their company was worth more to me than a high salary.

I was to give two courses; the first in the morning on the art of biography; the second, a public course in the evening, on several great writers. One month on Balzac, one month on Tolstoy, one month on Proust, one month on Poe. The course on biography embarrassed me a little. Sixty lessons! I managed it by talking not only about the technique of biography but about that of style; by taking a certain number of biographies as the basis for a study of action; and by asking each of my students to write a long essay on a personage of his own choice. These essays, read, discussed and criticized in class, formed the most effective part of the instruction. At the first meeting I asked them to tell me their choice of subjects. Surprise: none of them wished to write about the great figures of their past history. No Washington, no Jefferson, no Lincoln. But a Roosevelt and a Willkie. Writers: Thomas Wolfe, Dreiser, Emily Dickinson, Hemingway, Walt Whitman, T. S. Eliot, Stevenson, Swift. Painters: Van Gogh, Picasso. Labour leaders and captains of industry. Musicians: Chopin, Beethoven, Schubert, Bach, Tchaikovsky, Gershwin, Debussy.

Forty young men and women had signed up for my course. I have always loved the profession of teacher. To form young minds enchants me. Rarely have I had a group of such quality in my classes. The veterans, to whom the government was giving scholarships, were at the head; the war had taught them to understand men and given them a homespun philosophy; three or four of the young women turned out to be brilliant. All these children of farmers or tradesmen showed an appetite for culture and a vigorous intelligence which gave me great pleasure. As for the public course, although it was held in a large hall people always had to be turned away, despite my incorrigible French accent which made my English rather difficult for an audience accustomed to the twang of the Middle West. Soon all the elite of the city were talking about Balzac, Tolstoy and Proust. From this I came to realize how much could be done for French culture and for culture in general in this country, if twenty Frenchmen who knew English and had a passion for their calling were to undertake a crusade. At the end of the course on Balzac I sketched out the plan for an *American Comedy*, and suggested to my students that one of them might eventually do for the United States in our time what Balzac did for France in his.

[328]

Visitors helped me to endure the long interval before my return. My son Gérald came from New York and was astonished by the beauty of the gardens and the houses. My friends in Kansas City went to a great deal of trouble to make his stay agreeable. Mary Decker gave a dinner in his honour; the Professor of Russian, Soloveitchek, gave a completely Russian meal: bortsch, blinis with caviar. Gérald was becoming attached to America but he did not much like his work at Coty's. His thoughts, like mine, sped across the ocean. Each morning I peered with exquisite anxiety at the letters from France, at the envelopes ornamented with laurel-crowned heads of France, green, violet or red.

I would say to myself as I sorted out my mail: 'What friendship is going to be renewed this morning through a few lines? What appeal will reach me from my country, enveloped in a shroud of mystery? What child, what family, will tell me of the joys given them by a package of clothes or food? Long envelopes edged in blue and red, I know that you bear my wife's regular, crenellated hand and that you will repeat day after day: "Finish up that course and come back to Neuilly." . . . "Come back, everyone is waiting for you," the fine writing of Emile Henriot will say. Little yellow envelopes of rough paper with infantile handwriting, you no doubt come from a school child in Périgord or Normandy' . . . But this morning a green envelope instantly catches my eye. That firm hand without hairstrokes which seems to pierce the paper announces Alain. I hastily open the envelope . . . Joy, joy, tears of joy . . . It is Alain: 'From my heart . . . ' I read and reread those few lines marked by the paw of the old lion. Then the bell sounds: it is time for my course, but on entering the classroom I seem to see on one of the benches a young man 'who resembles me like a brother' and through the windows the notched towers of Rouen which now bear in their side a gaping wound.

One Sunday in April Père Minéry, a Jesuit, came to my room wearing the uniform of a captain of Spahis. He had been a member of Leclerc's division, and he was young and enthusiastic. It gave me pleasure to find in him a Frenchman who continued to feel unswerving confidence in our country. I asked him to take my place next day and talk to my students. In excellent English he described the sufferings of young Frenchmen under the occupation, emphasizing what the best of them had gained by it: a taste for adventure, greater strength of will, association with other social classes. The Deckers gave a tea party for him, the students besieged him with questions: 'You are a combat officer? Does the Church allow that?' 'Of course. All French priests who were able were soldiers.' As he was leaving he told me how much he had delighted in that atmosphere of youth and friendliness.

I loved it too. Toward seven in the evening after a day's work it was delightful to hear a knock at my door and to find a charming girl who would say: 'Professor, are you free this evening?' 'Yes, I think so.' 'Then I invite you to dinner and you can take me to the movies.' But my heart turned toward France. I knew through my wife that our apartment in Paris would be ready in June. Crespin, the publisher in New York who controlled the French rights to those of my works published during the war, had left for Paris to place them. He wrote me that they have been received with enthusiasm. And so it seemed that I had not been entirely forgotten as I had sometimes feared.

The end of the semester was approaching. On the evening of my last public lecture Deck gave a little talk about the role of French culture in the world and about what my my courses had meant for the community. Many of my faithful listeners came to shake my hand and wish me well. 'Good luck! Come back to us!' Then, laden with my heavy volumes of Proust, I returned to Epperson House beneath the vault peopled with stars. The night was mild, calm, happy. 'One day,' I thought, 'I shall long for this lovely spot and these uncomplicated friendships.'

May 31: Examinations. Men and women students come to my office to find out their grades. What pleasure I have had in seeing a number of fine intelligences blossom in the course of these months of work. Darlene Van Biber, a charming girl (who wants to be an actress), says to me:

'You have no idea what you have done for me in opening up this world of Balzac and Proust. All my life will be transformed by it.'

Another: 'One day on the bus I was reading Tolstoy in preparation for your course. An old lady was looking over my shoulder. Suddenly she said to me: "That Rostov family is wonderful, isn't it?" We got to talking about Vera and Natasha and Sonia. She ended by inviting me to come to her house and we have become good friends. Tolstoy performed a miracle.'

I hate departures and separations. Why kill a germ of happiness? Epperson House which during the winter had seemed so lugubrious turned out to be an amiable residence in the light of the sun. I owned nothing; I was responsible for nothing except my courses. A classical library took shape around me, for wherever I may be I surround myself with books. The daily schedule was unvarying. Affections ripened. O reward after long labour! Is it necessary when the harvest is ripe to leave before reaping it? It is necessary; above everything I desire to return to France and live there.

On June 3 I was to take off at six o'clock in a Constellation for New York. Deck and Mary had arisen before dawn to drive me to the airport. They had brought me the text of an editorial which was to be published that day (and was published) in the *Kansas City Star*. Although it may be too laudatory, I am taking the liberty of quoting some sentences from it because they give an understanding of the role I had succeeded in playing in that city and in that section of the country.

MAUROIS IN KANSAS CITY

During these last months France has had an admirable interpreter in Kansas City in the person of André Maurois . . . His role has been to unite the French and to help Americans to understand the genius and the destiny of France. The French Revolution, Chateaubriand wrote, has dug a bloody ditch. One aspect of M. Maurois' mission is to help in filling up that bloody ditch . . . The other aspect of this mission is to show foreigners that France is far from finished; that the torch of European culture which she has so long held aloft has not been extinguished . . . The wisdom of M. Maurois, his delicacy and the grandeur of his feelings have made his lectures unique and stimulating for all his auditors. They have awakened a new understanding of the genius which in spite of temporary eclipse has not ceased to blaze across the centuries in the French nation.

I could not conceive of a finer reward. But life is a dream. Yesterday my students, my work, my courses filled existence. A few hours of flight and already this most recent past was sinking into the pale world of memory.

In New York I found the little world of French residents reunited. The two French papers, *Pour la Victoire* and *France-Amérique* were giving a joint dinner at which I was present. It was in tribute to Jules

Romains who had quite recently been elected to the Académie Française. Simone was to arrive from Paris on June 11. She was coming
simply to make arrangements for our move. In our New York apartment we had accumulated a horrifying quantity of papers, books and
a thousand other objects which would be useful in restoring our home.
She had worked diligently, bringing back from Essendiéras the pictures
she had taken there in 1940 and obtaining part of the furniture from the
Avenue Hoche where her mother no longer wished to live, but much
remained to be done to reassemble the fragments of our life.

TWA airlines had telephoned me to say: 'Seven o'clock at La
Guardia Field.' Naturally I was there by six. Finally the great plane
(a Constellation, *Star of Cairo*) landed and immediately I saw Simone
at one of the windows. Sweet end of anxiety.

For three days while we worked at sorting papers and tying up
bundles we talked endlessly, my wife and I, about what she had seen
and heard in France. She had found my daughter Michelle thin but
very valiant. Emilie and Gaston Wolff were looking after our apartment. Would we have the means to keep it? My confiscated property
had been returned at the time of the Liberation. But the banks had told
Simone that because it had been badly administered its value had fallen
greatly. We no longer had assured means. On the other hand my
books, once more on sale, had resumed their place in all the bookstores.

The sufferings of the French and in particular those of our relatives
and Jewish friends had been infinitely greater than anything that has
been described here. In New York one read articles, saw films, listened
to stories, but the human contact was lacking and the sadly cumulative
effect of daily terrors:

'When I saw families that were so happy when we knew them,' she
told me, 'reduced to a single child and an old man, I was overwhelmed
... The conditions of our life? They will be difficult. Everything is
expensive and the taxes are staggering. Certainly we will not find at
home the kind of life that we could have here. Nevertheless I would
feel happier back there ... There's no reason to be sorry for your
long absence; everyone is unanimous in saying that if you had stayed
in France during the occupation you would have been dead long since.
The Germans came twenty times to search my parents' house in
Périgord to see whether you were hidden there ... But prolonged
absence is dangerous; one ceases to understand. In one month in Paris

[332]

you will learn more than all the books, journals and travellers have told you.'

All that remained was to complete the formalities of departure. TWA had promised me two seats for July 12, but on the evening of the 11th we were thrown into consternation by a big headline in the papers: 'Constellation Crashes.' At Reading, Pennsylvania, six people had been killed . . . Already in the preceding month a motor had fallen from a plane in flight and the left wing had caught fire. Obviously there was a fault in the structure and the danger of fire. Paul-Louis Weiller just a few days before had explained it to us. We think, Simone and I, that it is vain to flee from death, and that it comes in unforeseen ways and that it is not to be dreaded. But at seven o'clock in the morning the radio announces: 'All Constellations grounded for thirty days by government order.' Now here is our eagerly awaited departure in danger of being delayed still further; I phone Trans World Airlines and they confirm the interdiction.

'We are going to try to maintain service with other aircraft, but this will take some days . . . '

The strange situation of the traveller in suspense. He has packed his luggage, said goodbye and suddenly finds his time empty of all engagements. This total freedom ought to be a joy, something one dreams about in overcrowded days. But it comes by surprise and one is not prepared to take advantage of it; like a bird whose cage has been opened and which lingers on the threshold dazzled by liberty, the traveller does not see that the cage with its bars of anxiety is open.

A letter from Georges Lecomte, permanent secretary of the Académie Française: 'My dear friend, I believe my letter will find you still in New York. Before you leave the United States, I want to tell you of my very strong feeling for all the services you have rendered France. I think of the emotion you will certainly feel in arriving beneath a French sky, in landing on the soil of France and in revisiting Paris. My thoughts will be there to greet you.' The Académie is an affectionate and loyal family.

I had hoped to be in Paris by July 14; in the morning to hear the music of the regiments under the trees of the Bois; in the evening to see the couples dancing to the sound of accordions under tricoloured lanterns. *Dis aliter visum.* I had been promised two seats for the 18th. But it is harder to embark on a trip in the time of Hemingway than it was in the time of Montaigne. The last days were consumed in running about for the necessary papers. I had paid all my American taxes up to June 10 and I had the sailing permit. But this morning the travel agency tells me:

'Your departure has been delayed and you must have the receipt stamped again.'

'But this is infernal! You have to stand two or three hours on your feet in that office.'

'It's indispensable.'

I go back to Forty-Second Street; I stand in line once more; all this to be confronted by an amiable elderly man who tells me;

'But I recognize you, my friend . . . It was entirely unnecessary for you to be inconvenienced on account of these few days.'

These absurd last-minute errands remind me of a remark by Gide in his *Journal* about death which is supposed to resemble a departure. This gives me the idea for a story.

Spent the day writing this story *Le Départ*. (It can be found in *Pour piano seul*.)

July 19: Departure yesterday from New York. The Skymaster plane (the *Shamrock*) is smaller than a Constellation but comfortable and steady. Above the waves I read Schopenhauer (*The World as Will and Imagination*); 'Every man is what he is by virtue of his will . . . Man is his own work . . .' Would Schopenhauer be considered an existentialist? No, for he does not believe for a moment in the possibility of engagement. Character is given, immutable; 'We must first learn through experience what we desire. Until we know that, we have no character. Character is the knowledge, as perfect as possible, of our own individuality.' Man, as spectator of himself, versus man, as sculptor of himself . . . *Mon Dieu*, I am on the side of the sculptor.

The airplane sweeps over dreary marshlands; this is Newfoundland. An hour's pause; we spend it in the sun, for despite the season it is not warm . . . Another take-off. Soon nightfall; the lights are extinguished. One does not sleep but one dreams. Tomorrow France. I picture my house in Neuilly, the trees of the Bois, the sky of Périgord with light clouds foretelling rain . . . At dawn land is in sight; it is Ireland, all green under a veil of mist. Inexpressibly European villages; authentic castles. We land close to a pleasant hotel with chintz-covered easy chairs where a classic breakfast is served, porridge and eggs and bacon . . . When the plane takes off for the last time, I cannot get back to my reading. The next descent will be at Paris, the first coast will be the coast of France.

The valley of the Seine; I had thought I could remember it perfectly but these capricious turns, these islands strung out like a string of barges, this river-garden, these innumerable hamlets of the colour of tile and slate, sown over the mosaic of the fields—no, I did not fully know how beautiful all this is. I recognize Mantes as we sweep by, then the plane before descending on Orly crosses a corner of Paris, nobly grey and austere. Orly. From far off I see my daughter Michelle, whose blonde hair gleams in the sun, and from that moment I see nothing else. The time, brief though it is, between the landing and the opening of the cabin door seems to me interminable. At last the landing steps.

The newspaper men are understanding and discreet, recognizing our desire to be alone; they ask the usual questions very quickly. I am struck, just as Jules Romains was on his return, by the extreme kindness of everybody, customs men, porters, photographers. The formalities are completed ten times faster than at La Guardia airport. Already we are driving toward Paris ... the Seine ... the Louvre ... I expected a hundred shocks of pleasure. But I have evoked these images so often over six years that their actual appearance seems to me completely natural. Was it not yesterday that I was gazing thus at the Place de la Concorde?

Neuilly. Here is our house. How often I have asked myself while my train traversed the deserts of Arizona or my plane flew over the Rocky Mountains if I would ever again see through my windows the green waves of the horse chestnut trees in the Bois, the Eiffel Tower drawn in India ink against a sky that Boudin might have painted, and in the haze of the distance the ramparts of Mont Valérien like a Florentine convent. Here, faithful to our appointment, conforming in all respects to their recorded memory, are the scenes so eagerly awaited. This would be one of those miraculous moments when one says to the passing instant: 'O linger still, you are so fair!' If only my mother were here, come to wait for us from her nearby apartment ... I imagine her leaning on her cane, her face shining, her smile mingled with tears.

Those who were with her when she died talked to me about her: 'Poor Madame Ernest! She was so courageous. To give her a chance to escape, the French police told her one evening that the Germans were coming next day to arrest her. She could go into hiding. She refused: "I will not implicate anyone else," she kept saying. She bore up as long as she was a prisoner of the Germans despite her eighty years. She would say: "I want to live to see my son again." And then when she had been freed, emotion was too strong. She survived for a few days, which were happy days, then she fell asleep . . . '

I open my door. In my office the shelves that I had filled through forty years with books lovingly chosen are now empty. Not finding the man, the Gestapo seized the library. Despite myself, my eyes go to Littré's corner, to Alain's, where I kept so many manuscripts of his *Propos*, to Stendhal's. My yellow leather chair is still there. I sit down at my table. This morning friendly hands have laid out paper, the same kind I used to use. Let us to work.

PART FOUR

THE YEARS OF SERENITY

33

The Return

Yet we have gone on living
Living and partly living.

T. S. Eliot

Essendiéras. Summer 1966: I have no sooner written the title of this
fourth part than I begin to worry about its accuracy and my own
prudence. Who could guarantee that my life will end in serenity? To be
sure, I am now so old in years that the game seems over. 'But the years
are like the Alps: hardly has one crossed the first of them when others
are seen rising beyond. Alas, these final and taller mountains are unpeopled, barren and desolate.'

Thus spoke Chateaubriand. He loved to wrap himself in an iridescent mantle of melancholy. I am scarcely willing to have recourse to
this funereal lyricism. Unpeopled? Yes, certainly on these last snowy
summits I will no longer encounter the companions of my youth. My
father and mother repose in the cemetery at Elbeuf on that rocky slope
from which we used to see the high flat roofs of our mills, now just as
dead as those who founded them. What has become of my classmates
from the Lycée Corneille? The last of them, whom I used to see from
time to time at the war correspondents' meetings, has just vanished.
But as long as the earth is alive, new shoots of corn will replace each
year those that the Grim Reaper has just harvested. The friends around
me are still numerous and many of them are young enough to assure
me against the fear of a solitary old age.

Barren, these last mountains? I hope not. The *Vivier* is swarming
with projects. Without doubt I am at the mercy of some illness that
might damage my creative faculties. A burst blood vessel in the brain,
the broken shoulder of a femur, and the chances are that my dreamed-of
works would remain the shadows of books. But since I have thus far
been spared such catastrophes, I breathe the air of the summits
with happiness. The climb has been laborious; the mountaineers are

panting; let us cast a backward glance over the icy regions we have crossed.

1946. My first morning in France. Strong feelings aroused by each rescued object. Emilie and Gaston Wolff who stayed in our apartment during the whole occupation, have had the courage to hide a thousand things. Thanks to them, I recover clothes, ties, shoes, linen. Astonishment after having been for the whole period of my exile a man who literally possessed nothing but what he earned and bought from day to day, at finding himself suddenly the owner of an apartment and a car. (The latter had been hidden through the war at Essendiéras, with wheels removed and concealed in the granary so that the occupants could not use it.)

The Boulevard Maurice-Barrès in the July sunlight has kept its glorious and opulent beauty. The green ocean of trees runs in billows to the steep and distant slopes of Mont Valérien. In the drawing room Simone has arranged the furniture from the Avenue Hoche which her parents left behind. The tall draperies, the Louis Quinze armchairs embroidered with the fables of La Fontaine, the marble busts make a more solemn setting than our modern prewar drawing room. The emptiness of the library stupefies me. So many of the books there preserved so many memories. Where is *L'Ame russe* which Kittel gave me at the end of the sixth form? Where is the Spinoza (*B. D. S. Opera Posthuma*), the precious present from Alain after my Year of Philosophy, which he himself had received from Lagneau? Where are my prizes in the Concours Général, with their gold blocking? And where are the works of my friends, of Valéry adorned with affectionate dedications and drawings, those of Gide, of Mauriac, of Duhamel?

'Do not worry,' my wife says, seeing me run a disconsolate hand along the empty shelves. 'Do not worry, I will collect a new library for you finer than the old one.'

Beginning on this very first day (for she had alerted our friends), there began to arrive complete sets of Mauriac, Emile Henriot, Jules Romains as well as touching gifts from neighbours, from unknown readers who had seen in the papers that I had returned and were offering me their best books to replace those that had been stolen. Valéry, alas, was no longer there to fill the flyleaves in his supple, slanting hand. As a matter of fact, on the day after my arrival the Minister of National Education was to christen the Rue Paul-Valéry, formerly the Villejust, where our friend had lived and which with miraculous appropriateness intercepts the Rue Léonard de Vinci. At nine o'clock in the morning Georges Lecomte telephoned me: 'You *must* be present at the ceremony ... It will be a chance to regain contact with many of our colleagues on your first day here ... They will be so happy to see you again ... Come!'

I went. A platform had been set up. Blue sky with tiny tufts of white. I was astonished by the sweetness of the air and also by the smallness of the houses. After the high cliffs of Rockefeller Center all this part of Paris seemed to me like a work of art in miniature. Here the colours of sky and objects are less vivid than in America. Joy and surprise at seeing so many familiar faces at one time. In a similar crowd in New York I would have known almost no one. Here I encounter the smiling faces of Henri Mondor, Pasteur Vallery-Radot, Emile Henriot, Gérard Bauer, Admiral Lacase, Georges Lecomte, with his flowing beard unchanged. The Prefect of Police, Luizet, comes up to talk to me about our campaign in Corsica. Madame Valéry and her children come from their nearby house. The police are all wearing the red service cord, something new to my eyes.

After the ceremony my wife and I go on foot to my daughter's for lunch. Michelle with great pains has prepared an excellent repast, but to provide these courses, what an amount of shopping and waiting for her! She tells me that Robert Fraenckel, my cousin with whom I worked for fifteen years of my life in the family mill at Elbeuf, one of the men I most looked forward to seeing again and from whom only a few days ago in America I received a long letter, has died suddenly from a heart attack during our return trip. A hostile demiurge seems in relentless pursuit of my affections. My mother dying just after being freed, Robert at the moment when, after six years of separation, I was about to call him; these blows all struck at the most sensitive points.

Robert's widow Olga is in Paris. We spend the afternoon with her. She tells me that Robert was exhausted. A large part of the mill had been burned by the Germans in 1940, then the property confiscated and turned over to an inefficient manager. After the Liberation Robert and his nephews (the sons-in-law of Paul and Victor Fraenckel) tried to operate with a hundred looms, though under immense difficulties. Since many of the buildings in Elbeuf had been destroyed by bombs, several families had to live together. Robert and Olga could occupy only two or three rooms in their own house. 'The works', that all-powerful organism for which my father had lived all his life and I a good part of mine, was only barely alive. I had the feeling of witnessing the last days of someone dear to me and formerly so full of strength.

Thus Sunday passed. On Monday I wanted my first visit to be to Alain. His little house at Vésinet is intact. I find him seated behind a table, an open book before him, infirm, unable to move by himself, but courageous and brilliant. In his timeless way he sweeps the war aside in three sentences and immediately plunges into the text that lies in front of him: *Béatrix* by Balzac. 'A fine book,' he says, 'but toward the end it gets lost in the sands. It's a dangerous thing to turn a novel into a chronicle. The art of story-telling is a block.' Then he shows me my own books in his little library. 'I often re-read *Bernard Quesnay*. I love those silhouettes sketched in a few strokes ... Monsieur Achille! I shall never be able to forget him!' I try to make Alain talk about the political situation. 'Oh! There are millions of Frenchmen,' he tells me, 'who are going about their business as they have always done ... That's what will rebuild France. As for the rest, the orator from the Midi will attend to the business. "France is work; work is France," says the orator from the Midi ... It's a poem sung by a tenor who gives tongue and then waits for perfect harmony ... ' Massive in his blue dressing gown, leaning on his elbows, he gives me tea and Genoa bread. He says he does not like people who put lemon in their tea nor does he like *Colomba* by Mérimée which is on the table. 'Its nothing at all.' Then he talks to me about the administrative letters of Stendhal: 'Admirable!' Two fine hours; I promise to return.

The whole week is spent in reunion with friends. Anne Heurgon invites me to lunch with André Gide and Jean Schlumberger, Michelle with Claude Mauriac, son of François. My daughter shows me some stories she wrote during the war; they have genuine qualities (sharpness, humour, a mixture of satire and poetry). What a joy to recognize her as a writer! At the time of the Liberation Claude had been secretary to General de Gaulle. He had published some remarkable critical essays. After lunch I stroll through the streets of Paris. The pleasure of exploring my favourite haunts: bookstores, publishing offices. I have already visited Lemercier in the Place Victor Hugo, Flammarion, Blaizot, Bérès, Henri Lefèvre and the excellent and erudite Camille Bloch. Having brought a few dollars back with me, I am looking for books to replace those that the occupiers stole. There is a service that is supposed to get back works of art, but they give me little hope. A note was discovered at the time of the Nuremberg trials: 'Maurois library, very valuable, to be sold in Switzerland and Italy.'

The choice of new publishers poses a problem for me. Bernard Grasset, who published my first book and a large number of the others, is no longer at the head of his firm. He has suffered from mental illness and was in trouble at the time of the Liberation, I do not know exactly why. In his office I find a Colonel Manhès, a member of the staff of Marcel-Paul, communist minister of industry. He is affable in manner and offers to put a car at my disposal and to publish any manuscript I entrust to him; only he is not a publisher by profession and I feel ill at ease. I miss Bernard's fantasy; he was insufferable, egocentric, but brimming with charm and life. Besides, as a matter of fact, the publisher who bought my war books brought over from America by Crespin is Flammarion. This gives him a sort of priority. Innumerable representatives of new firms come to see me, eager for texts. The companies have pretty names: *La Jeune Parque*, *Le Bateau Ivre*, *Les Deux Rives*, but I am not well enough acquainted with these new fields to venture into them, except by way of short brochures.

July 25, 1946: This is the first Tuesday since my return, the day on which the Académie Française meets. The Duhamels come to luncheon, and Georges and I go together to the Institute. Here of all the places in the world is the one that has changed least during three centuries. The beautiful Palais Mazarin extends its welcoming wings. One climbs, as formerly and always, by the stairs with a double turn; one leaves one's overcoat in the hall of busts; one signs the register. The attendant says to me: 'Why, Monsieur Maurois! I must add your name ... It's been such a long time ... I had stopped putting you down.' When Victor Hugo returned to the Quai Conti in 1874 for the election of Dumas *fils*, one of the attendants said to him: 'You cannot enter!' Another intervened: 'Look here, this is Monsieur Victor Hugo.' Only five members shook hands with him. I have less genius and more friends.

A certain number of new faces: Robert d'Harcourt, the historian Grousset, the philosopher Leroy, successor to Bergson. I sit beside Jules Romains. This is a session on the dictionary. When I left the Académie in 1939 to go into the army, we had reached the word *agresseur*; after seven years I find we are at the word *ardeur*. At this rate it will take a century to complete a new edition. But what difference? The Académie like the Church takes no count of time. It has made a great impression on me today in its tranquil courtesy. In a time when everything is topsy-turvy, it is a fine and beneficial thing that continuity should be assured by certain institutions. No doubt political passions divide the Académie as they do the rest of France, but exterior forms are respected, and that is a great deal. Ceremonies are the supports of civilizations.

In general, I have been struck since my return by the good humour and tolerance of the Parisians. I remember the political conversations in New York and Algiers which so quickly turned into bitter quarrels. Here there is nothing of the sort. Each seeks information, wants to know what you think and why you think it, but no one replies to arguments with insults. Few men refuse to meet one another. The only newspaper man who wrote a hostile article on my return came to apologize: 'I was misinformed,' he said. As a matter of fact, in my whole life there are few periods of which I am so proud as of the last five years. At the expense of my own obvious interests and convenience, I served France in the manner that seemed to me most effective— and it was. The way I have been welcomed back proves that the French have understood.

One remains speechless before the sorrows of the Jewish families whom the Nazis treated with almost incredible cruelty. Ginette Lazard tells us about the arrest of her brother-in-law, Christian Lazard, a faultless character of great dignity. Arrested by the Germans, he was taken to a camp near Paris. Ginette and Lazard's wife tried to go and see him, but they were not allowed to enter and were only able to catch sight of him at a distance, wrapped in a sleeveless cape; from behind the barbed wire he made a gesture of farewell. He was taken to Germany and when the train was emptied took his place in line, maintaining (this was told me by one of his companions) his sovereign dignity. An officer looked at him and asked:

'You there, how old are you?'

'Sixty-one.'

'Then step out of line . . . Get in that truck.'

'How is this?' Christian Lazard said to his neighbour. 'Is it possible that they are human?'

But for several days his companion in the camp did not see him. Finally he inquired about him.

'What do you mean? He was in the truck? Why then, he is dead. The old go directly to the gas chamber.'

In hearing this story I see again his delicate face with its short moustache, the head of a British nobleman.

July 26, 1946: Today I am sixty-one years old. This is old age, though I do not feel its effects except for a certain relief similar to what one experiences when, watching a bad play, one thinks contentedly: 'There is only one more act.' I work all morning preparing for publication the new edition of my *Histoire d'Angleterre* which Cape (my British publisher) has asked me to bring up to the present time. For luncheon we have Marius Moutet, Minister of Overseas France, an old socialist friend of mine; the Julien Cains, the Jules Romains and my friend Geneviève Tabouis from New York. Joy at seeing Cain again, a great scholar, a great public servant, a pupil of Alain who was deported to Buchenwald. The minister is late in arriving. At this time he is carrying on a difficult negotiation with Ho Chi Minh. 'Reach an agreement,' I tell him. 'In a distant and mysterious affair of this sort surrounded by dangers, the worst of compromises is better than the best of wars.' He shares this view. 'But I am not alone,' he adds.

July 28: And now my Sunday morning visitors are turning up again just as before the war. Yes indeed, the bonds of friendship are quickly renewed. At the same time there is one profound cause of distress: Pierre Brisson refuses to come. This strikes me to the heart. His mother (Yvonne Sarcey) has been my friend since my start in the world of letters. I was one of her favourite and devoted lecturers at the *Annales*. Together with Pierre I was part of the first staff of *Figaro* and I admired his courage. I loved him. It was he who said to me at the time of my first articles against Hitler: 'Go to it! One must take a stand.' In short, he was one of those I counted on most—to protect my children when I was absent and to support me when I was present. But I found him reticent. What had happened?

Two things: one easy to remedy, the other more dangerous. In the first place he had been affected by the slanders carried on the west wind. Nothing was easier than to set him right about this. I asked for an appointment at *Figaro* and brought along my articles from America. 'But the dates?' he inquired.

'You can see them printed there.'

He checked them. The texts were irrefutable and there was no further question. The second problem seemed much more difficult. Here it is: At the time when Léon and Yvonne Cotnareanu, owners of the largest block of shares in *Figaro*, were leaving France they stopped for several days at Essendiéras in Périgord. Forced to flee before the Germans (Léon was Jewish), they had given full legal powers of attorney to my father-in-law, Maurice Pouquet, to represent them both in the Coty business and at *Figaro*. It was an odd idea, but necessity makes its own laws. After their departure numerous negotiations had taken place between Brisson, manager of *Figaro*, and Maurice Pouquet, trustee of Yvonne Cotnareanu's fortune. But with these two difficult characters collisions were inevitable and brutal. Maurice Pouquet maintained that he was defending the interests of the Cotnareanus, Pierre Brisson the honour of his paper. The two men came to hate each other. Inevitably their quarrel placed my wife in a very false position; she did not wish to quarrel with her mother; and I was placed indirectly in the same position. On July 30 Pierre invited us to lunch at a restaurant in the Champs-Elysées along with Jeanne and François Mauriac. And so relations remained cordial, but Pierre's parting words were: 'In this quarrel I am having with Maurice Pouquet, either you must get him to give in or you must drop him.' It was an impossible situation. I felt affection and admiration for Pierre Brisson at a time when I, like him, did not lack grievances against Maurice Pouquet, but I could not ask my wife to break with her own mother.

Next day we left for Essendiéras where we planned to spend two months' vacation. I was driven there by my American publisher Crespin, of the Maison Française in New York. As a foreigner he had a right to petrol coupons. Driving through Orléans saddened me. The centre of the city appeared almost razed. We crossed the Loire on a temporary bridge. For lunch we stopped at La Motte-Beuvron. The dining room of the Hôtel de la Cloche was full. 'There is nothing I can do,' cried the owner. 'Not a single table!' At this moment his wife whispered a few words in his ear. 'Ah! you are Monsieur Maurois, the writer? ... Why, that's different. We can't, after all, refuse you a table at the moment of your return!' And he installed us in his personal apartment. This courtesy warmed my heart. I kept fearing after such a long absence that I would be forgotten, if not by my friends, at least by strangers, but the French know how to be loyal.

We arrived at Essendiéras about six in the evening. As in the old times the whole family came out on the lawn the minute they heard the noise of a motor approaching along the avenue of oak trees. It is delightful to see this beloved setting again: the ancient house covered with Virginia creeper, the hortensia bushes on either side of the door, farther off the red roofs of the tenant farm of Brouillac. Embraces. Eyes a little moist but with joy. In the house nothing is changed: the same tapestries with their sombre verdure, the same wooden sculptures with their archaic faces, the same sideboard of ancient, gracious marquetry. The huge rooms astonish me and also the profusion of paintings, bibelots, miniatures. It is rare in America, except perhaps in Boston, Philadelphia or some old southern mansion, to find such an accumulation of heirlooms, witnesses to past generations. I climb to the second floor and with a sigh of content seat myself at my big worktable from which I see through a large opening in the mass of trees the line of cypresses, the towers of the château, the clock in the steeple at Excideuil and in the distance the long misty valley extending toward Périgueux. This was the scene of my loves and of my best work. I consecrate it anew by writing at this old table my first article of the new life.

The next day is spent in exchanging experiences. I am asked about America, about North Africa, about Corsica. I want to know what has happened here. A number of châteaux nearby (Rastignac, Badefol d'Ans) were burned by the occupiers. The latter came to Essendiéras a number of times to look for me and one day they brought their incendiary equipment. An officer of the Gestapo from Périgueux who spoke perfect French interrogated Roger Menicot, son of the bailiff: 'Maurois is hiding here, isn't he?... You might as well tell me.' All the personnel were lined up against a wall under the muzzles of machine guns. My mother-in-law who has great wit and great presence of mind succeeded (as I have already related) in getting the Gestapo to leave by making fun of their suspicions. 'Search the house, messieurs!... We have nothing here to hide.' But in the barns and stables there were tanks and military trucks hidden by the secret army. For two years everyone lived in terror. But human nature is so constituted that these impressions are, if not effaced, at least cleansed of their painful qualities. We are told these stories with passion but without fright. Nerves have ceased to quiver.

From the first day we resumed our customary rhythm. Up at seven o'clock. At the worktable from eight to twelve-thirty. Luncheon. Then with my wife the walk along the two avenues—departure by the avenue of the oaks, return by that of the chestnuts. Work from four to seven. Dinner. To bed at ten o'clock. 'Solitude is a fine thing when one is at peace with oneself and has a well-defined task.' I have a very well-defined task, which is to finish the *Histoire de France* which I began in the United States. The great consolation that history bestows is to identify the ills of humanity in various epochs and to discover that everything worked out, sooner or later, more or less ill, more or less well. In 1798 Bonaparte found France in the abyss, her money valueless, her citizens with drawn knives; in a few months he restored her. This happened again in 1872—and it will happen again tomorrow.

But there is a great deal to do. Our walks across the fields and pastures show us the extent of the damage. Our lands produce fifty per cent less than in 1939. Why? Because the exhausted fields lack fertilizer, because manpower is lacking and, without those taken prisoner by the Germans, it has been impossible to till the soil; because the ill-nourished cows give less milk and less veal; because the chickens, forced to forage for themselves in the meadows, run about too much, grow thin, and lay their eggs under the bushes where they are lost. Thus impoverishment grows like a snowball.

Simone consoles me by making me listen on the radio every morning to a professor of physical culture who, to an accompaniment of piano and violin, teaches exercises that are so difficult I have very nearly broken a leg trying to do them. But the instruction is pleasant and the musicians are inventive in their improvizations. The final stanza:

> On recommenc'ra demain matin
> Toujours en musique
> La culture physique,
> On recommenc'ra demain matin
> Avec encore un peu plus d'entrain.*

It has become the family leitmotiv: as soon as things go amiss, someone intones, '*On recommenc'ra demain matin . . .*'

* *Approximately:*
> We'll begin again tomorrow
> With the music keeping time—
> Stretch and bend, stretch and bend—
> We'll begin again tomorrow
> With a little bit more vim.

At the end of September we shall return to Paris. We would have preferred to stay in the country where autumn seems likely to be fine, but during this year of my return I must prove myself assiduous at the Académie. In addition we must vote for or against the Constitution and both of us are registered in Neuilly. We have not been able to resolve the conflict between Brisson and Maurice Pouquet during this stay here. Maurice who is in the wrong in this affair shows himself harsh and intransigent; my mother-in-law sides with her husband; my wife does not want to quarrel with her mother at any price. This situation is painful to me, for I am infinitely more attached to Pierre Brisson than to Maurice Pouquet. But I feel myself at one with my wife. A total reconciliation with Pierre will happen some day. It will take a long time and that is a great pity. 'Life is just one damned thing after another,' Colonel Bramble used to say.

34

Back on Course

Our return to Paris in the autumn of 1946 marked the real re-establishment of contact. Our stopover there in July had been too short to permit us to see all our friends. As a matter of course our group of prewar intimates, aside from the absences caused by death, closed ranks around us. Some persons, among them the dearest, had disappeared: Paul Valéry, the Canon Mugnier, Charles Du Bos, Saint-Exupéry, Louis Gillet; but Paul Claudel, François Mauriac, Robert Kemp, Henri Mondor, Emile Henriot and Jules Romains remained our favourites among the men of letters. It will be seen that very soon younger men joined in this fraternity. Our sojourn in America had brought us a new contingent: Darius and Madeleine Milhaud, Fernand Léger, Geneviève Tabouis, Monica de la Salle, Lacour-Gayet, Père Couturier. With the men I had already known before 1939 closer bonds were soon formed. Doctor Delaunay, head of the pathological laboratory at the Institut Pasteur, a great-hearted man and scholar who knew my writings better than I did, helped me to understand the nature of scientific research. Francis Ambrière, who had taken over the management of the *Annales* lectures after the death of Madame Brisson, exercised a beneficent influence on my work. While he was planning his first programme, he asked me to give a series of ten lectures on a writer of my choice; I agreed to the plan, and it will be seen that these courses were the foundation of the second part of my life's work.

Bonds were renewed with the political world as well. The Fourth Republic was taking its first steps. What would it be like? I had the impression that it would resemble the Third Republic like a sister. It was making use of the same people. Herriot was President of the National Assembly; Vincent Auriol was to be President of the Republic. I knew both of them well. Julien Cain, administrator of the Bibliothèque Nationale, was playing the same role that had been his before the war in the corridors of parliamentary life, that of intelligent and disinterested Grey Eminence. His long captivity in Buchenwald had conferred added prestige which he used for the public good. At his home we used to see Léon Blum and Mendès-France. Although the government treated me with kindness and even respect, I could not help feeling anxious at seeing prewar customs springing up again. There were to be unstable coalitions and the frequent fall of ministries. I remembered my programme *Remedies* which I had written out on the jacket of a book on board the boat that took me to Canada. My political prescription had not been followed, and although I was struck by the rapidity with which France rose from her ruins, the future inspired me with grave anxiety. Had we learned nothing from so many misfortunes?

My mother had expressed the desire to be buried beside my father, and so at the end of October I journeyed to Elbeuf to accompany her body. I was naturally much moved at the idea of seeing again the city where I had been born and where I had spent thirty years of my life. I believed I would know every stone and I planned to take the walk from my house to the mill, as I had done daily, then on to Caudebec and Saint-Aubin. On the road from Paris I impatiently awaited the familiar scenes: as we left Saint-Germain, the beautiful village of Ecquevilly, so well nestled in its hollow; the two towers of Notre-Dame de Mantes, vertical strokes faintly sketched in the mist; the shore of Rolleboise and that charming view over the islands of the Seine that had overwhelmed me when I had seen it for the first time from an airplane returning from America.

'I could still tell you the name of every store in Elbeuf,' I said to my wife, 'from the Rue de la Barrière to the Place du Calvaire and the Place du Coq. In the mill I could walk about with my eyes closed; I would recognize the workrooms by the noise of the machines, the odour of grease, of soap, or of wet cloth. From the heights of the cemetery overlooking the city I will show you a hundred chimneys rising into the sky like slender minarets and I could put a name to each one of them.'

Alas, when we arrived at the Place du Calvaire, I could not repress a cry. The centre of the city no longer existed. In place of the expected scene there was nothing but great waste space to be seen. Here and there grass was growing. In the course of my life I had seen many bombed cities. During the 1914 war I had spent months in Ypres, then in the Somme on the scorched earth between Amiens and Abbeville.

[351]

In 1940 I had seen sections of Arras and Lille disappear before my eyes; in 1943 I had known Tunis, Bastia and Naples. Ruins, unhappily, were no new sight for me.

But to see an unknown city crumble evokes a very different feeling from finding that city murdered where each stone is a memory. To every man the house of his childhood, the city of his youth, seem more solid than others. They are implanted in him by so many deep roots that, realizing it would be impossible to tear them from his heart, he cherishes the illusion that it is impossible to wipe them from the earth. To feel oneself lost in one's own city, not to be able to find one's own house, is frightful.

'Here is your mill,' my wife said suddenly.

Ah no, these low buildings at the edge of a desert, they cannot be *the* mill for which we worked so hard and which formerly so gloriously raised its high façades crowned with brightly coloured tile. This court-yard that opens on the city through a yawning wound, is it really the one that was formerly surrounded by workshops bristling with machines, with cases of thread, bales of wool and through which sped numberless trucks loaded with cloth of many colours?

I had to bow to the sad evidence. It was *the* mill. I knew that the Nazis had deliberately set fire to it in 1940, but I had never imagined that the destruction could be so great. However, when I went inside the building, I saw that work was going on as it had before. The looms were beating, the cloth shearers were running, the skids with Fuller's earth went bouncing by. In the storeroom the pieces of cloth, though less numerous, were moving across the table at the same rhythm as before. The employees who received them, the packers who took them away, were old fellow-workers of mine, veterans of 1914–18.

After a private ceremony at my mother's grave in the cemetery of Elbeuf, I went to the cemetery in La Saussaye to meditate and dream in front of Janine's grave. I believed I saw again that face of a Reynolds angel, the white flowers that she used lovingly to arrange in the high vases in her room, her mysterious and melancholy smile. Ah, what would I not have given for five minutes of 'palaver' with her! But under that marble and beneath that pensive willow tree Janine was no more than a phantom. Our best-loved images, those that have meant everything to us, presently recede behind a light but impenetrable haze.

On my return to Paris I lunched at the Mauriacs' with Frances Phipps, widow of the British ambassador who had been so loyal a friend, and dined at Jefferson Caffery's, United States ambassador. The world was taking charge of me. Meanwhile I was beginning to feel ill; chills and fever shook me and I experienced violent pains around my hips. It was shingles, very distressing and very inopportune, for I had just agreed to go to Switzerland and give a number of lectures there. Once more I had given in to my fatal fondness for public speaking. To dominate an audience, to feel that one has its whole attention, to sense that whirlwind of applause all ready to break out at one's first pause and sweep the room, all my life this has been one of my peculiar delights. And so I had put up no resistance to the invitation from Switzerland.

The shingles made movement difficult, and on the day of my departure this was to place me in a ridiculous situation. At the Gare de Lyon I was astounded to find a young woman in my sleeping compartment. She was as astonished as I was. Before the war I had never seen mixed sleeping cars. No doubt the scarcity of berths had brought about this daring innovation. Here was the last chapter of Sterne's *Sentimental Journey*, complicated by my shingles which forced me to request my companion of the night to take the upper berth, to which I was unable to climb. She agreed with good grace and, since she was a very cultivated woman, before wishing each other good night from our superimposed berths we chatted about Shakespeare, Apollinaire, Cézanne and Utrillo while the train rattled through the dark.

Next morning I was happy to see again the familiar scenery of Geneva, the network of curiously angled bridges, the squadrons of swans slowly cruising by, the oblique flight of the gulls and, on the far shore, those noble and solemn façades that remind one of what the quais of Rouen used to be. But Rouen was grey and blue slate; Geneva is ochre and rose. Here is the hotel where in 1924 Briand held me spellbound. I see myself sitting beside him and I hear him saying to me, his voice like a 'cello: 'I shall try everything . . . If the League of Nations does not succeed I shall devise a European Union . . . At all costs a new war must be avoided, Europe could not survive it.' Poor Briand! He was human and wise; the cynics of all parties never forgave him for that. Here is the Parc des Eaux-Vives where for the first time I sat on a bench beside Janine; this for me makes Geneva a memorial pilgrimage.

Geneva, November 16, 1946: Mist on the lake. Swans and gulls.

[353]

Nothing has changed in six years. To be sure, these are not the same swans nor the same gulls as formerly, but what of that? Swans and gulls count here only as supernumeraries in the scene. One can imagine Micromégas after the war casting a glance at the earth from Sirius and saying: 'Nothing has changed. Men are still there. To be sure, they are not the same men, but what of that?' ... It is a question of scale.

Luncheon with Robert de Traz. He has not changed either. Returning to Europe after six years' absence, I expected to behold the Prince de Guermantes' ball and see my friends disguised as ancients. Nothing of the sort. With a few exceptions, I have found Paris little touched by Time. Morale seems to have had more effect than age. Those whom circumstances or their own courage has lifted into the first rank have blossomed; in spite of earlier persecutions, public esteem has given them a renewal of youth. The others, however, who today are under a cloud, some fairly, others unfairly, seem wan and haggard or perhaps flaming with vengeance. I have met more than one Timon of Athens: 'Burn house! Sink Athens! Henceforth hated be of Timon, Man, and all Humanity!' On this subject as on others, Shakespeare has said it all before. As soon as there is a transfer of authority, with triumphs and downfalls, you see the same ingratitude, the same changing of sides, the same desertions, the same rejoicing and despair. The Human Comedy is dateless.

This evening at the hotel after my lecture (huge attendance and very young), before going to sleep I was reading Delacroix's *Journal*. He writes from Nohant where he is living with George Sand: 'We were expecting Balzac who did not come and I am not displeased at that. He is a chatterer who would have disturbed the settled nonchalance in which I love to cradle myself.' To think that one could expect Balzac and then rejoice at his not coming! As early as 1850 Delacroix understands that progress (then a venerated concept) is an accident and can be reversed: 'Tomorrow we may be embracing despotism with the same fervour with which we have set ourselves to become independent of all restraint.' And here is a sentence that, for all its abstract, sentimental tone, could have been written by Stendhal: 'On arriving here I did not experience those impulses of joy or sadness with which this place used to fill me, impulses whose memory was so sweet.' I have the good fortune still to experience strong feelings, and these days in Geneva have awakened the same impressions as before: Geneva is a muted France, of worthy and gracious austerity, a segment of the

eighteenth and nineteenth centuries marvellously preserved. Not every-
thing here is luxury and delight, but there is order and beauty certainly.
Calm? Not so much calm. The people of Geneva love argument and the
Angel of the Bizarre likes to perch on the *Petite Fusterie*.

November 19: A trip. Fir trees. The gentle slopes of the Jura. Who
was it who said: 'Pocket Alps?' Finished Delacroix on the train. At
fifty-nine he is astounded that he is still able to work 'at this advanced
time of life'. He says that no novelist has ever depicted 'the disenchantment, or rather the despair, of mature years and old age.' What
folly is mine! I am a good deal older than he was; I live in more
difficult and truly apocalyptic times; nevertheless I preserve my confidence in some happy issue, I know not what, and in the generosity
of men. What need to throw in the sponge and accept defeat, when
that defeat would also be the defeat of your times?

After two weeks of trains, universities and snow I return to Paris,
my shingles cured, just in time to deposit my vote for Edouard Herriot
in the antique urn at the Académie. My wife has arranged a luncheon
for the '*Herriotistes*': the Duhamels, Pasteur Vallery-Radot and his
wife, the Tharauds, the Romains and Herriot himself.

'I apologize for the luncheon,' my wife says. 'There was nothing to
be found in the market this morning. No fish, no eggs.'

The friendly and animated conversation makes up for the deficiencies
of the menu. Herriot gives an excellent description of his captivity, of
how he was freed by the Russians, and of the Allied air raids on Berlin.

'I re-read all of Balzac,' he said, 'in that air-raid shelter.'

At four-thirty the Académie. Pasteur Vallery-Radot presides, flanked
by Georges Lecomte and Emile Henriot. I am seated between Siegfried
and Monseigneur Grente. Beyond Siegfried, the two Broglie brothers.
There are twenty-six present. A majority, then, is fourteen. According
to rule, the director asks each one to swear that he has not pledged his
vote. Hands rise one after the other as the names are called. There
should be an understanding about the meaning of the word *pledged*.
I recall that Victor Hugo relates in *Choses vues* that Monsieur de Ségur
when asked: 'Have you pledged your vote?' replied to the director:
'No more than you.' The vote is counted. Herriot has twenty-four; the
historian Sagnac two. No blank ballots. Everyone sighs with relief.
The Académie does not like to feel itself sinking into impotence and
incapable of renewal. Another vote: Madelin is named director and I

chancellor. Then with Romains I go to congratulate Herriot. He seems very happy, and so are we.

On the day following this election we once more take to the road for Essendiéras to spend the Christmas and New Year holidays.

December 15, 1946: The woods and fields have put on their winter wraps. From my window the landscape, so leafy last summer, is a bare skeleton. Yellow grass, the colour of dead leaves, covers the fields and hills. The house is full of stacked logs, for it is very cold outside and all the stoves are roaring. We are much better heated here than in Paris. The closer you get to primitive civilization the less vulnerable you are.

For our first Christmas in France since 1939 we have eaten the traditional turkey, the blanched chestnuts, and a Yule log bought at the pastry shop in Excideuil, which has taken on new life for the holidays. The country is being reborn little by little. This Yule log à la crême, which would have been inconceivable three months ago, seems symbolic. In the store windows numerous vanished objects are to be seen again. It is now possible to get a taxi by telephoning. We go to take toys to our neighbours' children. One could not dream of finer Christmas weather. The ground is frozen, the sun warm. The roofs of the tenant farm at Brouillac no longer look red but rather a pale rose, probably through lack of contrast with green trees. The distances are no longer bathed in cerulean mist but emerge from a grey fog. Excideuil, in its valley, makes one think of the city of Ys. And all day long unbroken silence reigns.

I sketch out a novel, *La Vierge de Sunam*. 'Brown Abigail, the virgin of Sunam' who warms the aged bones of King David, haunts me. Is it because I am past sixty and feel a vague need for a bath of youth? Or because it is 'the punishment of those who have loved women too much to love them always?' Perhaps. But this novel 'does not come' easily. The heroine is imaginary, and this is apparent. I possess no brown Abigail and moreover all I want is peace of heart. Well, I must give up this novel and make a different work plan. I do not have so many more years of health. What would I still like to accomplish?

(a) Finish these memoirs. I must accurately state what I did and saw during this war.

(b) Complete the history of France, which will finish up the trilogy: France, England, the United States.

(c) A few more novels about our time, and especially about the period 1939–46, which would allow me to introduce the children of my heroes.

(d) Write out the Tchekhov and the Tolstoy which were almost ready in 1939, and for which my notes have been stolen. And then . . . but will there be anything more?

December 31, 1946: Last day of the year. Our hill is enveloped in such thick fog that one cannot see a hundred yards. Only a few phantoms of trees haunt this mist. Wild boars came last night to root in our fields. No mail. The postman must have lost his way or be taking his ease. The house, which is far from any village and on the summit of a hill, seems suspended in a sphere of vapour.

Let us take stock. The first half of my year was devoted entirely to the courses in Kansas City. I feel the need from time to time to go back to the role of professor which I like so much. Then the return to France. I have found my country less ill than I had been told. The difficulties are great. The lack of food and fuel is lamentable, the parties are excessively divided, but France remains the France I knew. The foundations are sound. Cities and countryside are calm. The Republic goes on and would at need be defended. I hope that it will know how to discipline itself. I am happy to see proven liberals like Herriot and Blum in power. The latter, whom I used to regard with a mixture of sympathy and anxiety, now is in control of the parties and of himself. Respected and accepted, he deserves all this. The old team will give the young men time to develop. *Ça ira.*

January 1, 1947: First New Year's Day in France. An address by Blum on the radio. He asks the country for a great effort to lower prices and thus save the franc. His tone is warm, simple, moving. I admire this man in his old age; suffering has raised him above feuds and dogmas and he is today a truly national figure. I am a little sceptical on the subject of his economic policy. You do not make prices go down by a decree, nor even by an appeal to civic duty. No more than you can make a thermometer drop by appealing to a feverish patient's good sense. Menicot, when he comes to give us his greetings, says of Blum: 'In the past I was not on his side, but I take off my hat to him now . . . One will do all one can to aid him!' The communists in our neighbourhood remain rebellious: 'And our stores of wheat, barley, corn,' they say, 'they'll go down in price too?' I tell them: 'You will gain much more

in security than you will lose . . . You all have bonds, bank notes.
What will be left if the franc falls to zero?' Yvette and Roger Menicot
bring their children with them. These latter will not be upset by a new
France. They will be born with her; they will have made her. Looking
at them, I suddenly feel reassured: 'Youth prophesies by its very
existence, being what is to be.'

Mademoiselle Tourte, the charming girl who teaches English at the
Excideuil Lycée, comes to see me. She tells me that six British airmen,
who were killed in this region during the war, are buried in the village
cemetery where the townspeople have piously tended their graves.
Last summer their families came from England and my friend served
them as interpreter. She was surprised to see the women slip papers,
letters, into the wreaths of flowers they placed on the graves.

'These were letters for the dead . . . A young widow said to me:
"I have written a verse in French for my husband: *Un seul être vous
manque et tout est dépeuplé.'"**

In the evening a second address by Léon Blum. We listen to the
Marseillaise with confidence. Yes, *ça ira.*

* Lacking a single being, your whole world is a void.

35

Intermezzo

During the summer of 1947 I went on a long lecture trip through South
America. Three years earlier while I was in New York I had been
visited by Eugène Rognedov, an impresario of Russian birth but with
an admixture of Spanish blood, an enthusiastic and explosive man who
had said to me: 'Believe me, maître (he pronounced it maîtré), believe
me! You are worshipped in Latin America . . . The women there are
the most beautiful and most loving in the world . . . And the scenery!
And the audiences! Believe me, maîtré, you will not regret it.' Although
he was persuasive and persistent to the point of importunity, I declined.
After my return to France he made fresh attempts. 'Believe me, maîtré
. . . the most beautiful trip of your life!' I ended by saying: 'All right,
I'll go for two months.' As a matter of fact, I was curious about this
country whose youthfulness and freshness of spirit had been extolled
to me once by the philosopher Keyserling.

I was not disappointed. Everywhere, from Brazil to Argentina, from
Chile to Colombia, I found a sincere love of French culture, enormous
auditoriums which were nevertheless too small for the avid public and,
as my lively impresario had said, the most gracious women in the
world. The ineffable Rognedov accompanied me everywhere. All
things considered, I had a certain affection for him. He amused and
irritated me. An organizer by vocation and profession, he organized a
little too much. The president of each South American republic was
summoned by him to give a dinner in my honour—and did so with
good grace. In every city Rognedov held a press conference, took me
to see newspaper publishers, students, supervised my radio appear-
ances. I had imagined a tranquil and solitary journey, infinite time to
read and rest; he made it into a presidential tour. But I came to see
beautiful regions and I formed precious friendships. The Brazilian
Academy elected me a member of their company, and I was solemnly
received by the amiable Roderigo Ottavio. Federico Schmidt, a poet

both massive and charming, who said to me, smiling, 'I am Valéry Larbaud's Barnabooth,' appointed himself my guide and showed me ancient Brazil. I loved to wake up at the Copacabana with the sublime view over the Bay of Rio and its bizarre mountains: Sugarloaf, the Finger of God, the Corcovado; I loved my beautiful listeners who after the lectures would come to ask me keen and difficult questions; I loved the Brazilian *saudade*, that nostalgic melancholy of a people blended from three sad races who suddenly at the time of the Carnival find release in violent festivities; I loved the tropical trees, the giant flowers, the jungle at the gates of the cities. The French Ambassador, Hubert Guérin, brother of the poet Charles Guérin, was efficient and helpful.

In Buenos Aires my friend Vladimir d'Ormesson was the French representative. He had been a member of Lyautey's team and had often recited his chief's verses to me in Morocco at that time. When I arrived in my room at the Hotel Alvear, I found it full of white and red roses. 'We did not know what to do,' my Argentine lecture manager explained to me ingenuously. 'The hero of your novel *Climats* likes only white flowers; the hero of *Terre promise* only red roses. Well then, when in doubt . . .' As in Rio I was to speak in an enormous theatre: the Politeama. In Paris a hall of this size could never have been filled for a simple, brief talk. In Buenos Aires I had to give repeat performances of all my lectures. In that city I knew writers of great talent: Jorge Luis Borges, Eduardo Mallea, Mujica Lainez. The Peronist regime gave the press little liberty; when I talked the stage was surrounded by policemen; my lectures, which were purely literary, gave them no occasion to intervene. I was surprised to see an Argentine film, *Les Verts Paradis*, based on themes from my novel *Terre promise*.

To be candid, I was both astounded and delighted to find that I was so widely read on this distant continent, sometimes better than in France. For the duration of my stay in Argentina my hosts put a car and chauffeur at my disposal. The latter, Antonio, was a *caballero*, proud, faithful, devoted. He looked after me when I was sick, taught me Spanish, provided me with anything I lacked. When I left Buenos Aires after two weeks, I wanted to give him a gratuity, which he had earned a hundredfold. He declined it with courtesy and dignity. 'From a poet,' he told me, 'I could only accept a poem.' I gave him one of my novels with an inscription: 'To Antonio who knows how to do everything and does everything better than anyone else.'

Crossing the high Andes, the airplane glided dangerously between two walls of ice. Rognedov, who was terrified, kept crossing himself desperately during the whole time of these aerial acrobatics. He had heart trouble and the airplanes of that time were not pressurized, and so the poor fellow was in actual danger. Chile conquered me at once. Two enchanting ladies were my guides there: Chavela Edwards (wife of the owner of a big newspaper, the *Mercurio*) and her sister Lala. Santiago, a modern and animated city, stands out against the snowy circle of the Andes. To speak to the students in French was a delight. It is delicious to feel oneself loved, or to believe that one is.

From there I went on to Lima, Peru, that ancient, mysterious, bewitching Spanish city. A Castilian aristocracy lived there in houses like those in Madrid, with wrought-iron balconies covered with red and violet bougainvillea. The most ancient university in either America, San Marcos, very solemnly made me a Doctor *honoris causa*. Jean Supervielle, son of the poet, held the post of cultural attaché at our embassy. The city's entertainments enchanted me; he offered to take me to see more of them in his car and together we went to look for the car in the nearby streets. He could not find it and suddenly he exclaimed, striking his forehead; 'But I had forgotten! I have no car.'

In Lima poetry was to take on more than one guise for me. Above I have told how I tried unsuccessfully to write a novel, *La Vierge de Sunam*, and in it to transpose to our time the story of brown Abigail who warmed King David's last years. Because I could not find a model for the heroine I had given it up. In Lima the virgin of Sunam suddenly appeared without my having done anything to evoke her. The adorable girl who was to be, under the name of Lolita, the central character in *Les Roses de Septembre* is, alas, no longer alive today and I have the right to speak of her with tenderness and *saudade*. I had noticed her at my first press conference at the airport in Lima, in the beginning because of her amazing beauty, and then because she had been an interpreter of rare intelligence between the Peruvian journalists and me. Not only did she speak French but she knew by heart Verlaine, Laforgue, Aragon, and she added profound and enchanting commentaries to my replies.

'But who is that amazing woman?' I asked Rognedov as we left the conference.

'Ah! Maître!' he said with an air of ecstasy. 'She is the most remarkable woman I have ever met. A great actress, very famous here; more cultivated than anyone; a power in the world of politics! A marvel!'

[361]

Then, having the strong instincts of a go-between, he added;
'She told me that you made a great impression. Ah! Maître! If you
wish . . . '

I did not wish anything. I was sixty-two years old; I loved my wife
permanently and exclusively. I was certainly not looking for an adventure. Nevertheless I kept encountering this young woman, whom
I shall call Lolita. She had proposed taking me to see the Périchole
mansion, that curious creole palace in the style of Louis Quinze in
which the columns instead of being of rose marble are of bamboo.
There she had given an inspired performance of *Carrosse du Saint-
Sacrement* for me, playing all the roles herself. Then we had gone
together to the Magdalena Museum, a prodigious collection of pre-
Colombian art where she had led me to admire the woven materials of
the Incas. 'Gauguin's palette,' she said, 'sombre greens and blues,
noble reds.' When we left the museum she went into a little baroque
church close by and knelt down on the stone at the foot of an altar
which was surmounted by a canopy supported on columns of twisted
silver.

'You are a believer?'

'How not?'

For six days I listened to her conversation about religion, the theatre
and poetry, with always increasing admiration. She threw herself into
everything with a simple and sublime passion. She would translate the
finest passages from her favourite Spanish authors, Lope de Vega,
Federico Garcia Lorca, extemporaneously and with an incredible sureness of vocabulary. Then suddenly she would point to a portrait of the
matador Manolete on the wall of her room. He was one of her heroes
and she would describe to me his inimitable style. Through her I
learned to know the Spanish soul, great and noble, disdainful of death,
at once religious and savage. After a reception at the French embassy
she took me into a blessed and mysterious wood where the moonlight
carved out the pale shadows of olive trees. I felt myself outside time,
far from my country, freed from moral constraint and happy as one
can be in a dream, a wholly unreal happiness.

At the end of the week I was to leave for Colombia. Rognedov had
gone ahead to mobilize, as usual, the president of the republic, the
French ambassador (Lecomte-Boynet) and God knows what other
dignitaries! To my great astonishment, at dawn I found Lolita at the
airport. Like me she was leaving for Bogota. My modesty forbade me

to believe that she had decided to make this long trip to follow me; my reason was forced to recognize that no other explanation was possible; my joy triumphed over all other feelings. In Bogota where she was known and admired by everyone (she had often played Claudel and Calderon there) she did not leave me. Supervielle had said to me; 'You'll see, in Colombia people talk more about poetry than about politics.' It was true. Important officials were translating Valéry. Bankers wrote plays in verse. Lolita reigned over this enchanted world. But poor Rognedov, no longer able to drag me to official receptions, exhausted himself in futile rages.

The lofty mountain, Monserrate, dominates the city. On its summit, paradoxical and unexpected, luminous and airy, the white profile of a church. Lolita took me to see the falls of Tequendama. These falls are a living thing. The water does not fall in a sheet as at Niagara. It shoots out liquid rockets in all directions which unravel, grow thinner, ending in sharp points, then die. The water of the falls seems pale yellow; the vapour that rises from the gulf forms a misty fringe of lilac blue. It was of incredible beauty, but to be truthful, when I was with Lolita, everything seemed beautiful. She talked so well of the things she loved. One day we went together to a bullfight, *mano a mano*. Another time she took me across the savannah, a vast plain where the grass is intermixed with rushes, crowned here and there with the tender green of the eucalyptus. These scenes are associated in my mind with the bird song that was her language; 'You are happy, no? . . . *Cómo se dice?*' I knew that in three days, in two days, next day, the enchantment would be only a memory, but I abandoned myself to the pleasures of the Enchanted Island.

I had finally found the virgin of Sunam and I knew it. My last novel would now write itself effortlessly. It would be entitled *Les Roses de Septembre*, in memory of a short poem I had written for Lolita; for the old man, restored for a fortnight to adolescence, was writing lovesick verses to the one he called his *companiera*. If of an evening she talked to me passionately about the *Noces de sang* by Lorca, next morning she received an improvised sonnet:

O grand cheval de l'aube! O douceur de la neige!
J'ignore, Lolita, quel fut ce cavalier,
Mais je sais que jamais je ne vais oublier
Le son de votre voix créant ce sortilège.

[363]

Car vous avez pour moi noué le florilège
De ce Federico qui mourut sans plier
Et vous m'avez décrit, émue jusqu'à crier,
Le lâche assassinat qui fut un sacrilège.

De ces *Noces de sang* tout me demeure obscur.
Quel est ce grand cheval qui ne voulait pas boire?
Quel ce destin neigeux et quelle cette histoire?

Ah! que j'attends le jour où ton visage pur
Dans mon ciel orageux va reprendre sa place,
Aube d'un soleil neuf dont l'absence me glace.*

When we parted at the airport in Bogota we promised each other to meet again some day in Spain. In New York where I spent a week on my return trip, I received long and beautiful letters from her. But as soon as I found myself in Paris once more, I knew that the dream had been a dream, that my only strong, indestructible bonds were in France and that *Les Roses de Septembre*, both novel and reality, would end in a total victory for the wife. As it happened, I wrote something more for the distant Lolita—a rondeau in which I evoked our memories and a ballad with the refrain: '*Mais où sont les nuits de Lima?*' rhyming with '*Où est celle qui me charma?*' (*But where are the nights of Lima? Where is she who charmed me?*)

Where is she who charmed me? In the grave, alas! 'How not?' she would say. Lolita ate nothing, was a chain smoker and drank, as she said, savage liquors. She played *Tessa* (her own character), she danced, she recited Apollinaire. But she lived outside life and made no effort to cling to it. I do not know whether she was still in this world when *Les Roses de Septembre* appeared. Contrary to what was thought and said by numerous critics, this was not an autobiographical novel. In

---

* O great horse in the dawn! O softness of snow! Lolita, I cannot tell who that horseman was, but one thing I know well, that I shall never forget the sound your voice made working that magic spell.

For it was you who twined the wreath for Federico, unyielding in death, and it was you, moved to the point of tears, who portrayed his cowardly murder, itself a sacrilege.

In these *Noces de sang* I find everything obscure. What is this noble horse that would not drink? What is this snowy fate? What does the fable mean?

Oh, how I long for day when your pure face will once more dominate my cloudy skies, dawn of a new sun whose absence turns me cold.

depicting the aging writer, I had found inspiration principally in Anatole France who, in the course of a trip to South America, had fallen in love with an actress; as a model for the hero's wife I had chosen Simone's grandmother, Madame Arman de Caillavet, who had suffered a great deal from that adventure. What was this late novel worth, this my autumn or even my winter rose? I had a certain indulgence, a certain tenderness, for it, but it did not seem to me likely to reach a large public. I was mistaken, and with it I regained the vast audience of *Climats*.

These travels on a new continent, the unhoped-for reception, the delightful *companiera*, all this had an intoxicating effect. It was necessary to put that dream back in the land of dreams and to return to earth. During the journey home I had read a great deal of Montaigne, the only book I had taken with me. 'It is truly profitless for us to get up on stilts, for on stilts we must still walk with our own legs. And on the highest throne in the world we are never seated on anything but our backside . . . ' An excellent text for a sermon to myself; it taught me humility. But as the astonishing Rognedov had predicted before my departure, I had no regrets.

36

The Big Biographies

For fifteen years after *Les Roses de Septembre*, my principal work was a series of big biographies. To tell the truth, I never deliberately decided to devote part of my life to this genre. It happened, as all important things do, first by chance (our decisions are always made by a small majority), then because I became attached to research work in the course of doing it. In my boyhood and adolescence when I had felt such a tremendous desire to write some day, I certainly was not thinking about biographies. How could I have come upon such an idea? In French literature that genre played almost no role at all. There were a few famous books: Voltaire's *Charles XII* (which I do not much like), Chateaubriand's *Vie de Rancé* (which is a confession), the very summary lives that Stendhal wrote, the flat lives by Victor Cousin, the biographies of unknowns scattered through Sainte-Beuve, the heroic lives by Romain Rolland. Each of these works had its merits; not one of them was a biography to suit my taste and heart. In short, there was nothing in France that could have drawn me to these untrodden ways.

In its place I have told how I came to write a life of Shelley in 1924. There followed a Disraeli, a Lyautey, a Chateaubriand, but between each pair of biographies I went back with satisfaction to the novel. Then the war of 1939 swung its axe and severed my career. At the time of my return to France I was getting ready to write a series of novels when, as I have said, Francis Ambrière asked me to give a full-scale lecture course in ten sessions at the *Annales*. A nostalgia for teaching remained one of my lively feelings. A single lecture did not give me the same pleasure. To live with my audience, observing how from lesson to lesson they became more attentive and more numerous, this was the great joy of my sojourn in the American universities. The public that attended the *Annales* unfortunately could not be as young as that, but I thought if I chose a subject that was both close to them and to me I could perhaps attract students. And so I decided to devote that course to Marcel Proust.

It was a success and, after much reworking, a book emerged from it: *À la Recherche de Marcel Proust*. Our friend Suzy Mante-Proust, who had inherited Proust's papers, was generous enough to put at my disposal many unpublished items, Marcel's notebooks, family letters. My wife, who had known Proust well, helped me to understand him. More than ever, during that period, she was an incomparable collaborator. I proposed to write at once a life and a study of his work. There has been a great deal of discussion in our time about the possibility of treating these two subjects together. Proust in his *Contre Sainte-Beuve* maintained that the author of those great books we admire is not the person who loved, suffered and grew old, but a different being who has risen above his individual self and bears no resemblance to it.

Proust criticized Sainte-Beuve for having tried to circumscribe a writer by studying his family history, his peculiarities, his friendships, his correspondence, in short by introducing into literary history the methods of natural science. He scoffed at him for trying to understand Stendhal by questioning Stendhal's friends—Mérimée, Ampère, Jacquemont—instead of simply reading with fervour and intuition the novels Stendhal wrote. In fact a writer, so Proust maintained, is something entirely different from the actual friend about whom people tell stories, often false. In the case of Balzac one can describe his houses, his strange way of dressing, his mistresses, without giving the reader any idea of those moments of ecstasy in which a man of genius, quite different from the commercial traveller of his leisure days, saw ideas advancing in serried ranks, and created Vautrin or Rubempré.

In point of fact it seems to me altogether impossible to dissociate the work and the author. The human being is single. The creature of those moments of ecstasy is also the poor fellow of the sordid moments and the man of everyday life. Proust himself in analysing *Booz endormi* finds the sensuality of the aged Victor Hugo in it; and in commenting on *La Colère de Samson* he finds the rages of Alfred de Vigny. The beauty of biography lies just in this, to show how from an apparently humdrum life a sublime work can burst forth. I have tried to preserve the romantic elements in great lives. What does that mean? The romantic element is the difference between the provisional image of the world and the people in it that every adolescent forms and the more adequate image which life little by little reveals to him. Goethe wrote *Wilhelm*

[367]

Meister's Apprenticeship. That is the romantic subject *par excellence*.
When Proust shows that in his childhood at Combray 'the Guermantes
way' was only a name and when later on he discovered behind this
name a reality quite different from the one he had imagined, he like
Balzac is describing lost illusions, but he finds salvation in a deliberate
illusion that is art.

That is exactly what I have attempted to do in my biographies.
If they have one merit it is to reveal a society, a human group, by slow
degrees as the hero himself discovers them. I want the reader to see the
Balzac family, Tours, Vendôme, as the child Balzac saw them; then I
want us to learn with him about life, women, love, ruin, and the
miseries and grandeurs of being a writer. I want the reader to feel at
times that he is in Balzac's own workroom, possessed of the same rich
memories, at the moment when that blazing fusion occurs from which
emerge *Le Père Goriot* or *Une Fille d'Eve*. If I have succeeded, if the
reader participates a little in the life of Balzac and in the Balzacian
creation, then I have won, then I know I have produced a useful work.

For it is a salutary thing to live with a great man and admire him.
Not like a marble statue, motionless and glacial, but the way he was,
with his strength and his weaknesses, putting the accent on his strength,
for he *is* a great man and if he produced a great work that is because
his strength triumphed over his weaknesses. I know and I admit that
George Sand was a daughter of the earth, subject like us to all temptations, but that did not prevent her, Alain said, from creating Consuelo,
a model for all women. I know and I admit that Victor Hugo is sometimes harsh, sometimes libidinous, and sometimes crude, but that did
not prevent him from creating Bishop Muriel, a sublime Christian.
I know and I admit that Balzac was sometimes ungrateful to Laure de
Berny, forgetful of Zulma Carraud, but that did not keep him from
paying splendid homage to Madame de Mortsauf. A great life proves
to the reader that such reconciliation is possible and it gives him
confidence in himself. That is what I wanted to do.

The success of *Proust* led me to continue on the same course. I had
to choose new models. But the great subjects had all been treated. Yes,
but very rarely in the manner that I liked. For example, I read what had
been written about George Sand. The great work by Madame Karénine
contained, to be sure, most of the essential facts (even though much of
the correspondence that my wife and I owned had not been discovered

until after its publication), but George Sand was not in it. What had she felt? What was the reason for her attitude toward love? What did her strange novel *Lélia* mean? I found some dim light on this subject in Karénine, but it seemed to me that everything still needed to be said, and that it should be shown that far from being a sensual lover George Sand had pursued physical love all her life because she had not found it. This problem would interest innumerable women; these were my auditors and my readers.

In writing about George Sand I had also wanted to comply with one of Alain's wishes. He had loved that great woman and believed that justice had not been done to such novels as *Consuelo*. I thought as he did and I said so to the best of my ability. Unhappily Alain was not destined to read that life, for it was published in 1952, the year after his death. It was also in memory of Alain that I chose a subject for a lecture course—and a hero for a biography—Victor Hugo. There too injustice had been persistent. I had on my heart André Gide's witticism, 'Victor Hugo, alas!'—the reaction of preciosity and cleverness toward genius. Academic criticism (Lemaître, Faguet) had jeered at Victor Hugo's commonplaces. But his stanza bears the commonplaces along on the surge of the rhymes. 'The great theme is that there is no great theme.'

The poet does not need a great subject; the biographer does need a great life. With enough talent, no doubt, one could discover and reveal the grandeur of a humdrum existence. The ordinary life of an ordinary woman gave rise to a beautiful book, *Madame Bovary*. One could conceive of a 'Bovaryian' biography. Unfortunately only great men leave a visible wake for any length of time after their passage. Their letters are saved; the memoirs of the times are monuments raised in their honour. Hugo was a great subject for a thousand reasons: he had been involved from childhood in the history of France; his adolescent love affairs, the failure of his marriage, his long passion for Juliette Drouet, the insatiable old age of that too vigorous octogenarian, all constituted a fine novel; his political and religious ideas merited a study in depth, the relationship between his personal life and his genius was close. Those were three happy years of work and poetry.

After Hugo, wishing to continue to live in an epoch that I had come to know better than our own, I agreed to write *Les Trois Dumas*. The works of Dumas (*père* and *fils*) do not have the same importance as those of Victor Hugo or Proust. I had trouble identifying myself

[369]

with the Dumas for the purpose of understanding them. But I was consoled by being borne along by their verve and their strength. Moreover the secondary characters were familiar to me. George Sand, Victor Hugo, Mademoiselle George, Mademoiselle Mars, and a hundred others reappeared in this story. My wife and I had got to the point, when we were alone, of talking much more about the world of 1840 than about ours. Our friends were named Charles Nodier, Théophile Gautier; Sainte-Beuve inspired us both with interest and with distrust. In order to complete my studies of that period perhaps I should have written a Musset, a Vigny, but while I was hesitating other temptations crossed my path.

One morning in my mail I found a letter from Lady Fleming, widow of the great Scottish scientist who discovered penicillin. 'I would like my husband's life to be written,' she told me, 'and I would like it to be written by you.' I replied that I was honoured by the choice, but that I lacked competence. Sir Alexander Fleming had been an eminent microbiologist. What did I know about that science? The reply was a telegram: 'Am coming.' A few days later Lady Fleming was in Paris. I was charmed by her beauty, by her intelligence and by her devotion to the memory of her husband. She attributed no importance at all to my objections. I was ignorant of microbiology? All I had to do was learn it.

Now a dear friend of mine was Dr. Albert Delaunay at the Institut Pasteur. I went to him for advice; he offered to give me lessons and to follow with me under the microscope the paths Fleming had taken. I knew that Delaunay would be a marvellous teacher and that his explanations would be of luminous clarity. Moreover it seemed to me that to reconstruct the life of a scientific researcher and to understand that other ecstasy which is scientific discovery, would happily complete the studies I had just made in literary creativity. I had always been interested in the sciences; I could not conceive of a twentieth-century man being cultivated if he were totally ignorant of the physics and biology of his time. Now if I had general ideas on these subjects, I had never pursued a scientific enquiry to the end. This opportunity was offered to me; it should be seized.

There followed a period of difficult researches. I worked not only with Lady Fleming and Delaunay but I went to see Professor Florey in England and Professor Chain in Italy, the co-recipients with

Fleming of the Nobel Prize. When I asked Lady Fleming if it would be possible to find a doctor who had been a student with Fleming, she replied: 'Yes, there is Dr. James.' This was the name of a comrade of mine in 1914–18 with whom I had shared a tent in the Flanders mud at the time of Colonel Bramble. The brilliant Dr. James had become, in my book, Dr. O'Grady. 'It's not likely,' I said, 'that this could be *my* Dr. James. That would be too much. Life is not arranged as artistically as that.' But yes, it was indeed my James. In Lady Fleming's small apartment, crowded with souvenirs, he talked to me about Sir Alexander with the same picturesqueness and verve that he had shown when he was discoursing under the tent in the Armentières sector or at Ypres, to the rattle of machine guns and the glare of rockets. Once more in my life Fate had looped the loop.

After Fleming I once more allowed myself to be tempted by a subject that seemed very far from my usual researches. My friend René de Chambrun, one of La Fayette's few descendants, came to tell me that he had discovered in the attic of the Château de La Grange (where his ancestor had lived) a huge collection of family papers, letters, journals, documents; that in these there was the material for a biography that would put La Fayette's life in an entirely new light; that the American publisher with whom he had got in touch had expressed the wish that I write this biography; that he himself agreed; and that consequently he was offering me the opportunity to read and make use of these papers. As in the case of Fleming, my first impulse was to hesitate because 'it was not my period.' My second and correct one was to accompany Chambrun to La Grange and at least to glance over the collection. I was stupefied. The premises had remained practically intact. In La Fayette's desk, his last day's mail remained unopened. The attic contained innumerable boxes full of documents which miraculously had not been spoiled by moisture and which the mice had not destroyed. I began to read a few papers. It was hallucinating. One found oneself transported into the intimacy of a great family of the Ancien Régime, then into that of 'the hero of two worlds'. Most of all I became attached to La Fayette's wife Adrienne. Before that I had known nothing about her; what I learned amazed me.

Adrienne had been literally a saint, all kindness, love, faith. Without a trace of bigotry and indeed with admirable tolerance, she had modelled her life on the image of a heroic and perfect Christian woman. Married while still very young to a courageous man who proved to be a difficult husband partly because of his infidelities and partly because of his rigid political principles, torn between conjugal loyalty and her attachment to the royal family, she had at every moment of her tragic life adopted the most noble and the most generous attitude. She had supported her husband when he tried to take the Revolution in hand and keep it within legal limits; she had supported him when he fell from favour and had joined him in hiding. Later she had shared his seclusion and his defiance of Bonaparte. All this without show, without pride, without jealousy.

I said to my friends the Chambruns: 'Here we have the most lovable of saints. It is *her* life and not that of La Fayette that I would like to write, provided you will give me the opportunity.' It turned out that my choice corresponded with their own secret wish. Both of them had a cult for Adrienne. I shared it. The book was written with tenderness, emotion, respect. In writing it I came to know the superhuman strength of a deep, pure faith. I had often had a foreknowledge, a presentiment, of it. Never had I felt in such intimate intellectual touch with a believer who had lived her faith. This seemed to me very beautiful and I was not the only one to think so, for I received thousands of letters written by women readers who thanked me for having introduced them to Adrienne. The only country where, to my great surprise, the book had no success, was the United States. I had thought that the name La Fayette would be a talisman there. But in the eyes of Americans the hero should have been La Fayette himself. In fact, I showed him as less strong and, to be frank, less great than his wife. This produced disappointment and, in America, the book suffered from it. Nevertheless I am happy to have written it.

Later on it will be seen that I was to return once more to my favourite exercise and write a final biography of a great writer, Balzac. But about that at its proper time. Here I must talk of a different book which was not a biography but a study in gratitude on the writings and philosophy of Alain. Since 1946 I had continued to visit him in his little house in Vésinet as often as I could. I always found him seated at his table, a book open in front of him. To fill his long days of immobility he was re-reading everything he had loved: Balzac, Stendhal, Saint-Simon, Hugo, Sand, Dickens, the *Mémorial*, Marcel Proust. On my arrival he would throw his head back joyously and plunge at once into impromptu commentary on the author he had just been reading.

I would stay a long time. Those were sublime hours. The lightning-struck oak tree retained its beauty. One of my liveliest desires was that justice should be done to my master. I myself, to be sure, and others among the faithful maintained the cult, but the writer, the thinker, whom I held to be one of the greatest of our time (and Valéry, Jean Prévost, Simone Weil had agreed with me about this), merited a universal and lasting glory. However, in that postwar period, there were those who disputed this, some for very obscure political reasons, others because, being philosophers by profession, they could not pardon him for having eschewed their jargon. In the modest degree to which I had some effect on my own readers, I undertook to make known this body of irreplaceable work.

Immediately after my return, I wrote in a long article for *Nouvelles Littéraires*:

I have known few great men; by that I mean men without flaws. One can count them on the fingers of one hand. The philosopher Alain is among them and there is a large number of us who have been his pupils or his readers who know this fact. It is a truth already widely acknowledged and becoming more so: in a hundred years Alain will live in memoirs among the writers of our time not far from Valéry, while many will be forgotten who today naïvely believe their immortality is assured.

In an anonymous article published in 1932 by a pupil in the top form of the Lycée Henri Quatre on *Alain the Teacher*, I read this: 'In his teaching we see a movement of ideas much more important, much more profound, than Bergsonism and without a trace of concern about being original or the leader of a school . . . His is not a secret that can be expressed in three lines; it is a thousand secrets. Here is a ferment of living ideas and at the same time a direct action, optimistic, virile, gay, whose amazing effects every one of his pupils, even the most backward, has felt.'*

Here are the facts. In France there are several thousand men who say with pride, recalling their finest memory, proclaiming their most splendid title: 'I was a pupil of Alain.' Among them was Jean Prévost, whom we so much miss, who would have been one of the thoughtful minds of the new France and who used to proclaim on every occasion

---

* S. de Sacy (no longer anonymous).

how much he owed to his master. As for me, I have said a hundred times that I owe him everything, even some of my misfortunes, for he taught me to set my sights too high. But his thought remains my religion and, what is more, firmly religious.

When I returned from America one of my liveliest desires was to see Alain again. The last text of his I had read, *Les Aventures du coeur*, had the beauty of the earlier ones and affirmed once more his whole un-dogmatic doctrine. I found my master not far from Paris in the retreat he no longer leaves. Old age had detracted nothing from the vigour of his thought. He talked about the eternal, which is the only subject, about Balzac, and about our classes in Rouen. How happy we were in those days, both of us young and setting out each morning on the search for ideas. The master and the pupil are today white-headed. But during that hour I spent with Alain I found again the joys of liberty. Splendid flashes of insight leaped from that strong head bent toward me. I emerged from the little house more confident than ever in the strength of the invisible spirit, sparkling and brilliant.'

The success of this campaign exceeded our hopes. Alain, published by Gallimard in *La Pléiade*, became one of the authors most in demand in that series. Young people read him and found rules for the conduct of life. Statesmen quoted him. With caution and with love I attempted to write a book about him, not, I repeat, a biography but an explanation of Alain's system of morals, politics, aesthetics, metaphysics. This was daring, for Alain had never constructed a system. He preferred, like Montaigne, free and roaming thought. Thus I felt abashed when I brought him my work. I was wrong, for here is the letter he wrote me the following day (December 28, 1949):

My dear Maurois, I have just read *all* of your *Alain*. I have reached a point of admiration which perhaps I shall never attain again; that's why I am making a point of writing you now; for there are things that need to be said . . . Here is my impression. In the thought of Alain there are some exceedingly difficult passages. In advance I said to my-self that with your writer's skill you would each time leap lightly and adroitly over them.

Eh bien! Nothing of the sort. Each time I found, on the contrary, an almost violent attention that forced the passage. Each time I under-stood my own thought better. For example, the passage about the cross in *Les Dieux*. Item, the presence of Socrates, the other, the fellow being. Etc. etc. Actually I have been instructed about myself by reading your *Alain*. As Gabrielle said without hesitation: 'This has been written with love.' Also I discover a point of doctrine, that is, one can only understand what one loves. *Eh bien!* I admit it. I put myself to school, I take lessons in my turn; my fellow being (my other) no doubt owes me that. What is thinking? It is to think like that other. I have succeeded in doing so; I shall not relinquish the knack. *I shall be human.* That is no small thing. But make no mistake, I am no longer capable of self-disparagement. Read one line by me and you will understand my happy immobility. I am not going to review your whole book; to do that I should have to copy it out. What I find admirable is that you have given this pupil who teaches a sort of grave authority not devoid of gaiety. You have penetrated even my style; it's marvellous.

In short, no author was ever read as I have been read by you, my only friend. My other friends have always had a weak point, for example, the objection on which X would never give in. Or the insistence of Y that I should explain some difficult point to him. *Eh diable!* It seems to me that I have explained enough points in my life. In Lagneau's time I never wanted him to be different from what he was. I never raised objections! Instead, in the presence of no matter what other person, I devoted myself to him with fury. The simple fact of comparing oneself to Lagneau was a crime in my eyes. Have I made myself clearly understood?

This document consists of these two pages. And that is all.

Alain

In this world where all things desert us, honour, pleasure, fortune, I find it marvellous and reassuring to create little citadels, permanent and impregnable; these are certain lasting friendships. The citadel I had dedicated from adolescence to my master has never been breached by absence, illness or by new friendships. One of my joys was to arrange for him to receive, a few weeks before his death, the Grand Prix National des Lettres, given then for the first time. I went to Vésinet to bring it to him, accompanied by Jacques Jaujard, Director of Arts and Letters, and Julien Cain.

When he died in 1951, his wife, his friends, his pupils asked me to say, in the cemetery of Père-Lachaise, what all of us thought. I could not, nor did I wish to, refuse, being only too honoured to speak of such a man before such an audience. The ceremony was simple and beautiful. All those who attended venerated his memory. Many former pupils had come from the most distant parts of France. The generations were mixed, the feelings unanimous. I quote part of the speech I delivered before that open tomb because it was in my eyes a momentous instant in my life.

We have come together in this funereal place to honour our master and our friend. The dead cease to be dead when the living piously revive them. 'It is through the living that the dead live again, that they regain consciousness, that they speak,' as Homer strikingly expressed it, 'through the fresh blood that the shades drink, which for a time brings back to them their memory.' Since our adolescence we have been nourished by Alain's thought. The day has come when the shade of Alain must be nourished by our thought. It is because he is present in each one of us that he here enters into eternity.

Everything we loved in him, everything we admired, remains. Our ideas, our writing, our feelings, our acts and even our dreams bear his magisterial stamp. We who are here, this numerous band, have been witnesses of that great life; we will hand on its memory and example to generations who will follow. Socrates is not dead; he lives in Plato. Plato is not dead; he lives in Alain. Alain is not dead; he lives in us.

There are men who only begin to live through death. Alain loved the word *legend*, legend being the thing that needed to be told, the story of an existence after it has been purified by time and forgetting. But the life of our master was already his legend. We always found him equal to our highest expectations of nobility. Always the height of his thought, the beauty of his style, the courage of his decisions exceeded our expectations. 'Lagneau was loved by me,' he said of his own master. Alain was loved by us, with devotion.

We delighted to go, as white-haired disciples, to the house in Vésinet which in our eyes was one of the high places of the spirit, and seat ourselves in the presence of the sage. Old age had been harsh to him. His knotted and stricken limbs refused to serve him. He suffered. But he never complained. His smile of welcome affirmed the complete constancy of his friendship. The aged master, faithful to his Socratic method, would shake the mind of his visitor by some affectionate thrust, and there would burst forth flashes of insight about nature, generated by his poetic genius. The admirable woman who through her care and tenderness made that long torment less painful, would be present, attentive and discreet. Soon illustrious shades would appear, Descartes, Stendhal, Balzac, Auguste Comte. Unforgettable meetings.

Last Sunday when we entered the little room our master's body, emaciated by long fasting, lay on the bed. On his face, forever motionless and modelled by death, there was some faint trace of strong and affectionate malice. For a moment I thought I saw again the young professor, mysterious and full of joy, who nearly fifty years ago came into our classroom at Rouen and wrote on the blackboard, 'One must go to the truth with all one's soul.' I remained for a long time at the foot of that bed. It is natural that meditation should carry us toward the dead who were our models, to seek from them example and advice. What did he ask and what oath should one swear to that great soul?

I think that the oath consists of one word: hope. Alain asks that we have confidence in man, and this leads to respect for his liberties; confidence in our mind to proceed from error to error toward the truth; and confidence in our will to forge a passage amid the forces of this huge universe which itself has no will. He who knows how simultaneously to doubt and to believe, to doubt and to act, to doubt and to will, is saved. This is his message; this is the image that we must keep living in us so that the spirit of Alain will not die. The farewell we address to him is a promise. We swear to be faithful, insofar as we are able, to his lessons and his example.

It will be easier for us, who have been his pupils and his friends, to accomplish this if we are able to maintain among us the beautiful fraternity that unites us around him today. We know that he loved commemorations, in which the great dead guide the living, and that he praised the pious custom of adding a stone to the pyramid over a tomb. To be or not to be, for Alain and for us, the choice must be made. It depends on us that Alain shall continue to be. Today we place the first stone on that monument of the spirit.

He who for half a century had supported, inspired and guided me was no more. It was necessary to continue along the road without that luminous torch. But in fact, just as stars that have been extinct for centuries continue to light us by their rays, Alain, though his body has disappeared beneath the earth and the flowers in Père-Lachaise, has remained my master. His books are always within reach both in the country and in Paris. I constantly reread the *Propos*, *Les Dieux*, *Histoire de mes pensées*. Each time I find in them nourishment constantly renewed, the only nourishment that perfectly suits my mind. Plato, Descartes, Spinoza, Hegel are more accessible to me through Alain. Even with Balzac, Stendhal, Dickens, his insights are invaluable. It is a great destiny to have brought to thousands of young people, some of them his students, others the students of his students, a high and noble image of man.

37

In Search of Time Past

Perhaps the true man can be seen only on ceremonial occasions,
for changing moods are by no means true.
                                                Alain

Bergson and Proust were right in saying that time lived is wholly different from the time of clocks and calendars. When I think of the twenty years that have slipped by since the end of the war, I find only a few instants vividly illuminated. The rest is already plunged in ageless shadow. To reconstruct my life during that period of time I have only my works and certain documents. About the works I have just spoken. The documents remind me that at this time, without desire on my part and sometimes with dread, I often played an official and international role.

One of the dangers of old age is that it tends to engulf one in obligatory functions. When young, one declines obligations cheerfully; in old age with some little reputation, one is required to preside by reason of seniority. It is an honourable but heavy burden. Thus I was for a time president of France-Amérique, then of France-Etats-Unis; president of the Association des Lauréats du Concours Général; president of Amis d'Alain; president (on occasion) of the Institut de France. Minor titles but ones that entailed meetings and speeches. The Académie asked me to be its representative; on Lamennais' centenary I had to rush off to Saint-Malo where a tempestuous wind snatched away the sheets of my speech; on Victor Hugo's centenary I had to speak in the Panthéon before the President of the Republic and the government, while the enthusiastic populace outside assembled and beat against the bronze doors; on the four-hundredth anniversary of Shakespeare I had to officiate at the Sorbonne before thousands of students. I acquitted myself as well as I could in this role of public orator, but I feared it, being still in the depths of my heart timid, provincial and devoted to small groups. For myself I would have preferred a class, a small amphitheatre, a few students. Hugo, Balzac, Shakespeare brought together huge audiences. I acquiesced.

Abroad I also saw my audiences increase. From the start I had had numerous readers in England and America. I kept them, and I still often went to those countries. In 1954 the British writers asked me to open the literary festival at Cheltenham with a speech, in English, on the philosophy of reading. My English had become a bit rusty. At the start of my talk I had trouble mastering my accent. Then I found the public so indulgent that I relaxed. In 1956 at the time of the Congress of PEN Clubs in London, I was asked to propose the toast to the City of London and also to give the closing address after a dinner in the House of Commons. During that trip I saw once more that very gracious and sweet lady whom I had known as Queen of England in my days of misfortune, and who was now Queen Mother.

Other countries had adopted me. Italy asked me to speak in the Roman Capitol. Spain, Yugoslavia, Japan published my complete works. I was translated in the USSR and I received visits in Paris from Soviet writers who talked to me very well about my books. In Germany I had had a vast public before the advent of Nazism. Under Hitler my books had been banned. After the war I found my faithful readers again. I was invited from all sides to go there and give speeches. I hesitated; to be sure, I did not impute to the German people the entire responsibility for the death camps and the brutal follies of the SS. I was convinced that there were many Germans as horrified by that as I was; but the wound remained incompletely healed. Nevertheless when the city of Munich, which had restored its ravishing Cuvelier Theatre, asked me to come and open it with a reading from my works, adding that this choice had a symbolic quality, I thought it would be proper to accept. Franco-German reconciliation was necessary to the peace of Europe. My reception was unbelievable. I could not help thinking, while the ovation went on and on, that a few years before I would not have emerged alive from that fair city. But hearts had changed; the theatre sparkled; a charming young lady, daughter of an anti-Nazi hero, acted as my interpreter and guide. Resentment melted in the warmth of sentiment. Good riddance!

My more sedentary friends asked me: 'Why so many trips?' I made the same reply as Gide at the time when *Les Caves du Vatican* was in rehearsal. He was asked by Roger Martin du Gard: 'Why indulge in this hazardous game? That play adds nothing to your stature.'

Gide replied in the tone of a spoiled child: 'I know it's not very good. But what of that? I am over eighty years old and it amuses me. So there . . .'

My reply would have been the same. 'Why these speeches? Because they amuse me. To try out a new subject on a new public, to improvise, to find hitherto unknown friends in every city, yes, I admit that I love these things. And I believe they are not without their useful effect. Europe has need of agents of liaison. I have been playing that role.'

I did not feel in any way that I had become a personage. In my own eyes I remained the young man of the Lycée Corneille, vulnerable and trembling, avid above all to learn, to read, suddenly inundated with happiness if he discovered a masterpiece, if he heard sublime music or if he witnessed Marivaux or Beaumarchais played by faultless actors. The only hours that now emerge from the silent depths of that time are those brief ecstasies into which I would be thrown by a book, a performance, a conversation. One book: *Les Cahiers* by Paul Valéry; a performance: Hélène Perdrière in Marivaux; a conversation: with Jean Cocteau. As a mark of friendship, he often came to lunch alone with us. I loved his angular features, his frothy hair, his mournful gravity, his childish laughter.

To keep my memory in order, I learned by heart at my advanced age poems by Baudelaire, Verlaine, Mallarmé, Valéry. This was taking measures against moments of solitude and of waiting. To recite Corneille or Molière, to read Stendhal or Balzac, to discover a new intellect, these remained my real pleasures. The official side of my life was something I tolerated; I acquitted myself; it hardly counted in my eyes.

In 1952 my friend and contemporary François Mauriac received the Nobel Prize. I approved the choice and I was very happy about it. Mauriac is a great writer of that fine French line that proceeds by subterranean ways from Bossuet to Rousseau, then from Chateaubriand to Barrès. I published an enthusiastic article: 'He has courageously skirted the precipices with steady foot, proudly sounding his bells in the mists. The zigzag course up the side of the mountain has been long and perilous. Mauriac followed it without flinching. Now he emerges from the haze on the sunlit summit. Those of his generation who have been companions in his career and have followed him as far as the camp before the last stage, sometimes losing sight of him but always filled with wonder at his gifts and always faithful in their affection for him, rejoice at it with all their hearts.'

A distrustful reader, one always alert for a chink in the armour, will no doubt think: 'Wasn't there a certain amount of envy mixed with your joy? Didn't the idea occur to you that you yourself, one of the most widely read writers in the whole world, might have a claim?' Absolutely not. Jealousy is not my strong point and I know my place, a place of which I am proud, but it is not at the top. I not only consider Mauriac but Malraux, Aragon, Montherlant as writers more consistently excellent than I am. My best pages (*Disraeli*, *Alain*, *Climats*, *Choses nues*, certain stories, the end of my *Proust* and that of my *Balzac*, the end of the second part of these Memoirs) perhaps will survive me for a time. For the rest, one will see. Time will be the judge of that.

Recurrent events punctuated my life. Every year a little after Easter we used to go to Monaco to award the Prix du Prince. There was a whole group there that I loved: Duhamel, Henriot, Genevoix, Pagnol, Achard, Géraldy, Dorgelès, Jean Giono, Gérard Bauer, Jacques Chenevière, Carlo Bronne. The principality put us up at the Hôtel de Paris. We used to eat together, and a violinist would stroll around the tables. Each of us would ask for his favourite composer: Schumann, Schubert, Fauré, Granados, Albeniz.

The unvarying procedure was, as soon as the choice had been made, to call the winner by telephone to let him know about his million francs and to invite him to come by air as quickly as possible. Since no candidacy for the prize was allowed, the surprise of the winner was always great. Paul Géraldy phoned to Louise de Vilmorin who had just been designated. She did not understand. 'But who is speaking?' she asked. 'Paul Géraldy.' 'Paul Valéry? He is dead.' She came and she charmed us, as did later Camille Dutourd, chosen on my recommendation, who was accompanied by her husband.

April 11, 1954. Palm Sunday: The meeting in Monaco is ending and I am sorry. Around that immense circular table, recollections, anecdotes and ideas were gaily bandied at random in a fashion that was happy indeed, for unreserved friendship with no arrière-pensée is a strong feeling. And then we were delighted by our prize-winner, Jules Roy. What a prize list this has become! We shall have to take care in the future not to lose altitude!

Gérard Bauer tells the shortest ghost story: 'I ran into Smith, with his widow.' Whereupon Paul Géraldy is reminded of a painter who, showing a portrait of his wife, alive and present, said: 'Portrait of the artist's first wife.' She survived him.

At the Prince's I lunched beside Colette whose beautiful eyes were tired but charming. 'At my age,' she said, 'pleasure consists in not working.' This caused me some uneasy reflections. What the devil shall I do when I am not working any more? But this is not a real problem. I shall be a different person and will find it quite natural.

In Paris on the second Tuesday of each month a luncheon of the *Annales* took place at which ten writers had to select the five best books of the month for foreign readers. I used to call this repast the Magny luncheon in memory of the meetings attended by Flaubert, Gautier, the Goncourts, Renan, and also because Claude-Edmond Magny, a critic who has vanished today, took part. As a matter of fact, it was the Ambrière luncheon. He was the one who founded it and summoned his friends. Alas, of the founders the only survivors (in 1966) are Ambrière, André Billy and myself. I find a note: 'Magny luncheon. Tumultuous and jolly as usual. Today we are surprisingly benevolent. Robert Kemp and Emile Henriot speak well of Faguet, of Lanson . . . Claude-Edmond has a good word for Jules Lemaître. And there is not even time to speak ill of our contemporaries.'

October 6, 1954: Magny luncheon. Conversation about the books of the month, and André Billy laments the naïveté of novelists who feel themselves obliged to appear young by adding to their books a proper proportion of obscenities—of the most monotonous kind.

'You could organize a contest: to write two pages to be inserted in *La Princesse de Clèves* or *La Chartreuse de Parme* to make them modern novels.'

'That's easy: Monsieur de Nemours spreads the beautiful legs of the princess—gently penetrates—et cetera . . .'

'My friends and masters,' Ambrière says in his fine oratorical voice, 'after all, we must continue the discussion of the books of the month. Be serious.'

But he had much trouble in bringing his class to order.

I had never written for the theatre. This may seem surprising because

[383]

in my youth my greatest pleasure was in composing short plays or revues for the amateurs in Elbeuf or for my comrades in the regiment. Besides, in childhood there had been that five-act tragedy in verse about Odette de Champdivers. But chance plays as large a role as vocation. Having begun my literary life with novels and biographies, I found myself solicited by publishers and not by theatrical managers. One can say that Giraudoux and Mauriac had both successfully made the transition from the novel to the theatre. It is true. Only Giraudoux had the good fortune to be initiated by Jouvet, Maurice by Edouard Bourdet. I had had no such honour. That is, up to the day when my friend Pierre Descaves became manager of the Comédie Française, He was making an effort to bring new writers to the stage and he offered me his support.

'You tempt me,' I said. 'I passionately love the theatre and most of all the one of which you are director. But it is a different calling from mine and I know very little about it. It is probably too late to learn. Putting together a play is a quite different matter from constructing a novel.'

'The dialogue in your novels is admirably suited to the stage . . . If you don't want to start by writing a full-length play, give me a one-acter. I need something to extend some bills that are too short. You admire De Musset's curtain-raisers . . . '

'That's just the reason I'd be afraid to venture into a field in which he is inimitable.'

Pierre Descaves with his cordiality and tenacity carried the day. It was not too difficult, for what he was offering me corresponded to very old wishes of mine and evoked vacation time when my mother and my aunts used to take me to see the classics in that great red and gold temple of the Théâtre Français. To be performed in Molière's theatre, what a surprise and what a joy! I promised Descaves to put together a curtain-raiser from one of my stories. It was *Aux innocents les mains pleines*. To tell the truth, I was not entirely satisfied with it. The dialogue was natural, the intrigue well enough contrived; but the subject seemed to me thin, too literary, and the setting lacked picturesqueness. To reassure myself I recalled that Molière in *Les Femmes savantes* had put on the stage mincing ladies of the middle class and men of letters, that the subject of *Un Caprice* was thin too. A voice in me replied: 'Supposing that what you have written were *Un Caprice*, which it isn't, how would you be received by the critics? Probably not

[384]

very well. You are old, you are an Academician, there is bound to be prejudice against you and since your little play will not be a master-piece . . . ' But pleasure won out over discretion.

My 'curtain-raiser' was quickly done. I had to read it to the Com-mittee. These sessions took place in what seemed to me impressive surroundings. One is introduced into the office of the manager with its justly famous tapestries. The Committee meets in the adjoining room. 'I am going back in there,' Descaves tells me. 'Then you will be called. Your place at the table will be marked by a glass of water. You will read and when you have finished you will leave. Then the Committee will deliberate—I shall come back and tell you the result.'

A painful wait. A touch of anguish. I say to myself: 'My voice is sticking in my throat; I am going to read very badly.' Summoned, I see as though in a misty dream the celebrated actors who are my judges. I read without lifting my head so that I cannot perceive any mark of censure or approval . . . When I am through, I bow and leave. In the manager's office I find an amiable secretary who helps me endure the minutes of doubt. I say to her: 'After all, it's only a curtain-raiser; that has no great importance.' In this way I try to persuade myself. After a short deliberation the mysterious door opens and the face of Pierre Descaves appears. He is smiling, and I know before he speaks that all is well. Then he takes me in his arms and gives me the accolade. We are in the theatre, *que diable!*

The Comédie Française spoiled me. I was given as director Jacques Charon, the most various and subtle of comedians. I saw him from the first rehearsal translate my poor lines into movement. A comedy is also a ballet. Charon knew how, by simple and human commentary, to illuminate a word, indicate a proper intonation. As to the cast, it was dazzling: Lise Delamare, Hélène Perdrière. I was astounded that these great actresses were willing to accept such small parts. As soubrette Annie Girardot, at that time quite young and unknown, but who was to become famous. The male lead was Paul Guers. Add to this that the rehearsals took place in the Foyer des Artistes amid the most beautiful paintings, that Mademoiselle Mars, Rachel, Madame Dorval looked down on us from the height of their glory and that Molière himself, in his portrait by Mignard, dominated the scene. This was one of the dreams of my distant youth that had suddenly come true.

During rehearsals we all had a great deal of fun. The word spread. On opening night I hid myself at the very back of the manager's box.

The public was enthusiastic, but it was an audience of friends. I awaited the notices with more anxiety. Robert Kemp proved generous: 'For a long time the Comédie Française has been looking for new plays to piece out some of its productions . . . This time I believe it has hit the bull's eye. *Aux Innocents les mains pleines* is a wholly graceful play of subtle perfidiousness; the anecdote is well knit and the style has quality. The success was definite. One recognized the quality of this theatre.' Paul Gordeaux (*France-Soir*) said: 'Monsieur Maurois has the dramatic rhythm. He knows how to construct a scene; he has style and wit.' Unhappily Jean-Jacques Gautier did not like the play: 'Calling a one-act play a curtain-raiser,' he said, 'is not enough to summon up Musset.' This harsh judgment spoiled my pleasure, but it changed nothing in my friendship for the critic.

All things considered, this playlet did well with the general public. Pierre Descaves was pleased and said to me: 'The Committee would love to see you write a play in three or four acts for the Comédie Française. Have you any subjects?' In my *Vivier* I had kept a dozen in reserve, without hope, for the last twenty years. Descaves asked me to tell him about them, which I did, very badly, for I find it almost impossible to summarize a play or a novel without betraying it. To my great surprise he chose a historical subject, the story of Mrs. Fitz-Herbert who was the mistress of the Prince of Wales, then his wife by a secret marriage, and was abandoned by him when he became George III and married Caroline of Brunswick. This heroine, a favourite of my wife's, had always allured me (she was an anticipation of Adrienne de La Fayette) and the political situation lent itself to effective scenes.

'Perfect!' Descaves said. 'Drop your other work and write the play this summer. It will be produced next winter.'

I allowed myself to be tempted. In the month of July at Essendiéras I finished the four acts. I was pleased with some of the scenes but not with the overall structure. It was agreed that Pierre Descaves and his wife should come in August and listen to a reading. This ceremony which was completely private (there was no one there but my wife and the Descaves) seemed to be an unmistakable success. One member of the Society told me that Descaves had written to him: 'I believe we have got hold of a masterpiece.' And yet . . .

And yet this play (which I had called *La Reine de coeur*) was never destined to see the stage. Here is the reason. When I returned to Paris at the end of September Descaves said to me: 'Before reading it to the

[386]

Committee you must show your manuscript to Jean Meyer and ask his opinion. He is all-powerful; his friends see only through his eyes. I myself can do nothing without his consent.'

'In that case,' I told him, 'it would be better to give up right now. I know Jean Meyer; he has tastes that are not the same as mine; he will hate this play and will prejudice his associates against it in advance.'

Descaves insisted, and I was weak enough to yield. What I had foreseen was exactly what happened. Jean Meyer read my play, came to see me and said: 'It's impossible. This script was not made for the theatre.'

'I would be the first,' I said, 'to admit its imperfections. You are an expert in this business. I ask you: How can it be improved?'

'It can't be improved,' he said. 'It's hopeless.'

After this summary judgment should I give up my right to a reading before the Committee? I thought so. Jean Meyer had certainly announced roundly enough that the piece was unplayable. He was considered (temporarily) to be an oracle. I was going to find myself faced with a wall of preconceived ideas. The unhappy Descaves advised me to hold at least a private reading before certain selected actors. I agreed, but without any illusions. The meeting was held at my apartment. I felt at once that the atmosphere was bad. The faces of those who came were already fixed in a look of rejection. These listeners, whom I loved and admired, who had often shown me their friendship, seemed to be on their guard against any indulgence. This icy atmosphere paralysed me and I read badly, very badly. At the end no one spoke. It was not necessary. Their silent refusal ratified the brutal rejection by Jean Meyer.

And so *La Reine de coeur* was never submitted to the Selection Committee. Is this something to regret? I think not. Such as it was, the play suffered (as I had felt) from serious faults of construction. A good play doctor, an Edouard Bourdet, could have shown me how to remedy them. This work deserved to be done, for the dialogue rang true and the subject was not lacking in grandeur. Circumstances decided otherwise; I bowed, a little regretful for my lost summer's work, but loyal to Alain's rule that regrets are always vain. 'Remind yourself to forget.' In two days I had digested this discomfiture. The sad consequence was that I gave up the theatre for good. To tell the truth, it had been very rash of me to hope that I could begin a career in it at the age of seventy. What a pity! It would have been so nice.

Around 1954 I began to take a more active interest in the elections to the Académie. Till then I had contented myself with voting, without campaigning. One evening Jean Cocteau and I had been dining at the house of a mutual friend in Versailles. After the meal Cocteau took me by the arm and led me into a little parlour. 'I would like to talk to you ... Here's the thing. Probably people have told you that I have no desire to become a member of the Académie Française and that I would even refuse the honour if it were offered because it is not in my line and because it would be a contradiction to my whole life ... *Eh bien,* that's not true. If the Académie would accept me, that would give me enormous pleasure. Contrary to legend, I have always had great respect and even great love for traditions. Nothing seems to me more stupid than to be a conformist of anti-conformism. And then there's something else. I need to feel myself sustained, supported, by a band of friends. You can't imagine to what extent I have been attacked, harassed, hunted. Then judge for yourself. If you think I have a serious chance and if you are willing to support me, I shall present myself.'

I weighed the matter rapidly. For half a century Cocteau had played a great role in France both as poet and as animator; he was famous throughout the world; his titles were impressive. Moreover I hoped (with the assistance of my confrères) to rejuvenate this old establishment and make it as true an image of our times as possible. Cocteau would give us an air of youth. Sartre, Anouilh, Aragon had declined. Cocteau was seeking us; if we did not accept him, we would be behaving badly both toward him and toward our association.

'I will support you,' I told him, 'with all my might.'

I found reliable helpers, Jacques de Lacretelle, Maurice Genevoix, Pierre Benoît. Certain Academicians expressed dismay at Cocteau's past, at his impudence. I went to see them and reassured them. Cocteau himself paid his calls and won over the most refractory by the brilliance of his conversation. He was elected on the first ballot. Léon Bérard, who had been Director of the Académie at the time of Cocteau's predecessor's death, was entitled to welcome Cocteau beneath the Cupola. He came to see me and said: 'I want to talk to you about Cocteau ... I don't know his work at all well. It would be a hard speech for me to write ... For you, on the contrary, it would be a joy to talk about your friend. Do me this kindness.' I was happy to be able to express my friendship publicly. I presided over the meeting of welcome and delivered the address. Cocteau seemed very happy. The crowd on the Quai Conti proved the size of his audience. He loved the prolonged roll of the drum, the guards doing the honours, the presence of queens and poets.

This success was beneficial for our Association, and inspired me with the desire to engage more actively in other elections which I considered important. (René Clair, Henri Troyat, André Chamson, Jean Paulhan, Louis Armand, etc.) I believe that in the course of those ten years the Académie Française reversed its drift toward ultra-conservatism. To-day the Association is liberal, receptive to talent even when it is un-conventional. If certain great names are lacking, that is not its fault, as it was at the time of Balzac. The Association cannot compel recal-citrants. Campaigning for my friends brought rewarding meetings. At the time when I was battling for André Chamson and we were checking over together the probable adversaries and supporters, we came to Paul Claudel. 'I am afraid,' Chamson told me, 'that that intransigent Catholic will not vote for a Huguenot like me.' 'You are going to call on him tomorrow. Talk to him about the Bible. Before that, I will talk to him about you. It will turn out all right.' And indeed on the Wednesday following that visit, Paul Claudel said to me: 'Your friend Chamson came to see me. I liked him very much. He is a fanatic like me . . . and he knows the Book of Job by heart . . I shall vote for him.'

Shortly after that Claudel died. We attended the national obsequies in a body. In Notre-Dame de Paris, chilled by winter, the Academicians shivered in their uniforms. Opposite them the rose window shed a supernatural light blended of bright, rare tones. A giant flag hung from a monumental staff in the centre of the cathedral. The blue and white unrolled in sinuous waves, the red fell in folds over the catafalque. The choir glowed with an iridescence of purple, violet, black and gold. It is a fine thing that the capital of a nation has high places for supreme consecration. Hugo went from the Arc de Triomphe to the Panthéon, as was proper. Foch from Notre-Dame to the Invalides, as was customary. The fact that the ministers of the Republic, believers and nonbelievers, were massed around Claudel in this venerable choir, was a symbol not lacking in grandeur. France was pulling herself together. She would soon feel the need of this more urgently than ever.

38

1958–1962

The ancient mariner said to Neptune during a great storm: 'O God, you will save me if you wish; but I am going to go on holding my tiller straight.'

Montaigne

'It does not require the passage of twenty years,' La Bruyère wrote, 'to see men change their opinion on the most serious matters, those that had seemed to them the most certain and the most assured.' As a republican and a liberal, I believed in all good faith that the Fourth Republic would prove durable, despite its obvious weaknesses, and that I would end my days under that regime. I maintained close relations with President Coty. Before my lecture trips to America, he had often had me come to see him (as Vincent Auriol had formerly done) to inform me about France's foreign policy.

Sometimes he wrote to me. One day I was surprised to see from my window a *Garde national* stop in front of the house and hand a large envelope to the concierge. It was brought to me immediately and proved to be a letter from the President of the Republic. The day before I had published a literary article. 'Your article,' wrote Monsieur Coty, 'has inspired me with the high ambition of pointing out an error (which is perhaps a typo). *Prends l'éloquence et tords lui son cou,** is what I believe Verlaine wrote,' the president went on.

Yes, Verlaine had written 'son cou' and I had quoted inaccurately . . . *et tords lui* le *cou*.

I had been much at fault and Monsieur Coty explained to me with a great deal of relish that this was serious, that the grammatical irregularity constituted the whole dissonant charm of the verse.

'The odd thing is that Paul Reynaud made the same change in this verse. When I pointed it out to him, he took the position that he was right and that poor Verlaine had ruined the syntax. But poetry tran-

* Seize eloquence and wring his neck.

scends grammar. A propos of the relations of poetry to politics, do you know this passage in a letter from Gneisenau to Frederick William of Prussia: "The safety of thrones is founded on poetry."

'Cher Maître, excuse my idle talk and pardon our presumption. Accept my most cordial and, if you will permit me, most affectionate greetings. *René Coty.*'

I confess that I felt very proud that France had a president capable of saying: '*But poetry transcends grammar.*'

Another time he wrote me that he was planning a speech in which he would draw a parallel between the two Andrés, of Rouen and of Le Havre (André Siegfried and André Maurois), 'both sons of a region in which their roots found nourishment and where the winds from abroad have turned them—unlike our beech trees—toward the great horizons beyond the Channel and beyond the Atlantic.' Yes, truly we had a friend of letters as chief of state.

President Coty professed profound respect for General de Gaulle and considered him a final recourse in the event of misfortune. The head of his military establishment, General Caneval, whom I encountered quite often, kept in constant touch with Colombey-les-Deux-Eglises. During the first years of the seven-year term I did not see any source of threats serious enough to endanger the regime. But 1958 presented a very sombre aspect. France did not have enough foreign currency to purchase raw materials. Was our whole industry going to come to a stop? At the same time events in Algeria which I had long considered a distressing guerrilla action, chronic and without issue, took a more active and disquieting turn. Not only did the strength of the FLN partisans remain undiminished but a breach was opening between the French army in Algeria and metropolitan France.

Nothing is more dangerous for a country than to mass its best troops in a distant region. Rome had had experience of this, and more than once a proconsul returning from Africa or Gaul and supported by his legionaries, had dictated his wishes to the Senate. In 1958 France found herself in a similar position, aggravated by the fact that our army, aware of its courage and its strength, felt an imperative need of reassuring itself by a victory. The army had experienced the most tragic defeat in 1940; it had been forced to leave Indo-China after the catastrophe of Dien-Bien-Phu; many of its officers thought it their duty to make good these defeats by holding on victoriously in Africa. In this the army felt itself supported, encouraged, cheered on by the

French in Algeria who were defending a cause that was completely just in their eyes. Had they not been in this country for four or five generations? Had they not transformed through their labour an impoverished area into a storehouse of abundance? And who could make them believe that the French army, equipped and commanded as it was, could not quickly make an end of guerrilla forces?

Suddenly a French revolt broke out in Algeria. The Algerian crowds spontaneously rushed to the Forum, howling down the government in Paris and acclaiming the generals. Many times before they had shown their contempt for the governors of the mother country. Guy Mollet, the Premier, had been greeted by a barrage of tomatoes. In 1958 it was more serious. Some of the generals endorsed the grievances of the Algerian French. Soon the military leaders were threatening their civil superiors and the motherland. Moreover they found allies there. Numerous Frenchmen had suffered from the past capitulations and refused to accept new withdrawals. The day came when Monsieur Pflimlin, the Premier, had neither army nor police force to obey his orders. An appeal from President Coty himself went unheeded. A government that has ceased to have any authority is no longer a government. The hour seemed close at hand when the revolt would transform itself into a military coup d'état. Two circumstances channelled the vast forces that had been set in motion in the direction of General de Gaulle.

Certain loyal Gaullists undertook to inspire the crowds in Algiers and the generals whom they acclaimed with the idea of demanding that the general be returned to power after twelve years of retirement at Colombey. A campaign of the same origin deluged the Elysée with a torrent of letters and petitions all demanding his return. I am not sure the general at that time believed in success. Not that he doubted his right to govern France when she was in peril nor the possibility that he could put an end to the crisis, but he doubted the will of the French. 'They want no part of De Gaulle,' he said. But he had shown in even more tragic moments that he did not need hope in order to act. Persuaded that he could assure the safety of the country, and consulted in advance by secret messengers and by the President of the Republic himself, he declared himself ready to take the formidable situation in hand. At the same time he laid down his conditions: he intended to respect the law, but to pay no heed to party bickerings.

The other element favourable to a renascence of Gaullism was

President Coty's acquiescence, given not in a spirit of resignation but wholeheartedly. Seeing no other solution and having no personal ambition, moreover admiring the general intensely, he would have willingly turned over to him his place as head of the nation. It seemed wise, however, to make this transition in two stages, and the general first became Premier. In order to remain within the framework of republican doctrine the consent of Parliament was necessary. Between De Gaulle and the Assembly relations in 1946 had been strained to the breaking point. In 1958 the general who could be charming when he wanted to be—all the more easily because everyone is grateful when these abrupt characters make themselves for an instant intimate and friendly—conquered Parliament in a single session.

There remained the problem of making the country accept a new constitution, which was indispensable for the new government if it was to assure the stability of established institutions. A referendum had to be arranged. The newspaper *France-Soir* questioned four writers who were considered to have some influence on public opinion, asking them whether they would vote yes or no. I replied: 'I shall vote yes because France needs to be governed, because for a democratic government there must be a majority and because General de Gaulle alone can secure that majority.' I was profoundly convinced of the wisdom of this choice. In that state of chaos no one aside from De Gaulle had prestige great enough to bring the army and the police force to heel. No one aside from De Gaulle had a will strong enough to carry out the reform of our institutions. Formerly I had not approved the methods of the RPF; this time I did not hesitate an instant in giving my reply.

Next day I was visited by a young friend who was influential at that time in Gaullist circles. He said to me: 'It now seems certain to us that the general will have a majority in the referendum, but in the present circumstances it is important for him, if he is to have the necessary authority, that this majority be massive and that the significance of the vote should not be mitigated by abstentions. And so we are going to found a *Front d'Action Civique*, the first object of which will be a fight against abstention; will you assume the presidency? Everyone hopes so. Observe that it's not a question of telling the electors how to vote but simply that they *must* vote.'

'I think as you do at this hour of decision abstention would amount to desertion. Am I qualified to say so? Will I be the one most likely to be listened to? I confess I have no idea.'

'We think so . . . All the necessary means will be put at your disposal. You will have a staff, free access to radio and television and local committees in each *département*.'

I was a little fearful of this mission which was going to take a great deal of time and would alienate some of my friends, but I saw no valid reason to refuse it. The enterprise did not run counter to my ideas. If it succeeded in making the citizens more aware of their duties, it would be very useful. I agreed and gave myself completely to this task. The *Front d'Action Civique* was stimulated not only by me but by Professor Richet and in particular by Ambassador Offroy who supervised its activities most ably. I wrote the texts for posters and numerous articles on the theme: 'Vote Yes or vote No. But vote!' I talked on the radio and on television; I held numerous meetings with our correspondents from the provinces to give them their instructions and to communicate my own confidence.

There is reason to think that we did not do a bad job, for the proportion of voters, rigorously checked by all the parties, was eighty-five per cent which was (and remains) a record in France. General de Gaulle, the winner, wrote me a fine letter in which he thanked me 'for the movement led by you within the framework of the *Front contre l'Abstention*. The voting on September 28 has proved its usefulness and effectiveness.' A few days later a reception was given at the Palais de Chaillot by the Keeper of the Seals, Michel Debré, for the benefit of the charities of the Chancellor's Office. General de Gaulle was present. During the intermission I was in the foyer when the General came up to me: 'Ah! Maurois,' he said to me, 'I'm awfully glad to see you here. I've just re-read your *Chateaubriand*. What a fine book! What a great man!'

The reader, who has seen me in Algiers in 1943, without direct relations with General de Gaulle, will perhaps be amazed both at my devotion and at his affability in 1958. But that reader must bear two things in mind. First of all, I had never ceased, even at the time when I was not in complete agreement with his policy, to have a lively interest in the man, admiration for the writer and respect for the leader. I say this today without flattery (what need have I to flatter?) but through simple loyalty because it is the truth. On his side the general in the depths of his retirement had sent me his Memoirs when they appeared with a cordial inscription. In my turn I had addressed my new books to him and each time he had replied as was his custom in his own hand. I became well accustomed to that slanting, poet's writing.

I shall quote a few sentences from his letters, more or less at random, because I want to show their style and tone: '*Mon cher maître*, I have just read *La Vie de Sir Alexander Fleming* and I admire the extreme skill and depth of your talent which goes to the bottom of the most complex imaginable problem and gives stature to a personage who never wanted to be a personage although that is what he was . . . ' *April 4, 1961.* 'In writing this book, *Adrienne ou la Vie de Madame de La Fayette*, you have done sacrifice this time to a heroine of virtue, devotion and simplicity. Nevertheless I do not think you have ever been more interesting. Accept my thanks and believe, I beg of you, *mon cher maître*, in my strong and lasting devotion . . . ' *May 26, 1963.* '*Mon cher maître, Choses nues*—there is a book truly well born and well named! I admire the fact that all you add to the many character portraits you have drawn of all the people you listened to, is judgments of subtlety and humour, never of malice. And what a talent you have for hitting a person off, even those who are not of your own invention! . . . ' It should be remarked that great men of action are often great writers: Napoleon, Lyautey, Churchill. Their strength impregnates their style.

In 1959 a well-known American agent, Colston Leigh, asked me to make a long lecture trip through the United States the following year. I was to traverse the whole country just as I had done during the war, beginning with the Library of Congress in Washington, going from university to university and from club to club as far as California and returning by way of the Southern states to finish in New York. It was a rash enterprise for a man of seventy-four, but it seemed to me almost as essential as in 1941. The relations between France and the United States were deteriorating. In the Algerian affair Americans had adopted an attitude against 'colonization'. Any Frenchman (even some of those who shared this opinion) was exasperated by these admonitions from across the Atlantic, first of all because the French did not think anyone had a right to meddle in their affairs and also because this 'moral' attitude seemed to them tinged with hypocrisy. After the death of Paul Claudel I had accepted the presidency of the *Société France-Etats-Unis* and I was doing my best in France to help the two countries understand each other. It seemed even more necessary to try the same thing in the United States and to explain the new France.

For a new France existed and I had tried to describe it in a long essay, *La France change de visage*, which Pierre Lazareff had published in *France-Soir*. In American eyes France had long been a charming and obsolete country. Americans loved Paris for the historical and literary memories it evoked, for the freedom of its ways, for the quality of its painting and its theatre. Meanwhile another France was emerging which refused to let the onward march of new techniques pass her by without instantly seeking a place for herself. Industry, commerce, agriculture, all activities in France were trying to put themselves on a level with the great modern nations. We were not always successful but where we had succeeded the result deserved to be described—and recognized.

And so I accepted Colston Leigh's offer and was to find no cause to regret it. I was happy to encounter the students again, the women's colleges, the questions that burst out on every hand at the end of the lecture. Those were two frantic and intoxicating months. Each morning I took a plane; I flew from Washington to Chicago, from Chicago to Los Angeles, from Los Angeles to Houston. Each evening I talked before attentive audiences. Americans love success and they know better than any other people how to bestow it.

This tour had another purpose as well. Before leaving Paris I had promised to write in collaboration with Aragon a *Histoire parallèle des Etats-Unis et de l'URSS*. To be truthful, we did not succeed in establishing a very convincing parallel. But I was happy to have this chance of more frequent meetings with Aragon whose talent I had admired for a long time; and however imperfect our two histories might be, I thought they would be useful. They were to be translated in both countries and would contribute perhaps to peaceful coexistence. During Stalin's time I had had few relations with the USSR. Now my books were widely welcomed there; Russian magazines asked me for articles; my Soviet translators came to see me in Paris; readers wrote to me from Moscow and even from Siberia. I was delighted by these ties with the country of Tolstoy and Tchekhov, of Pushkin and Gorki. Now this *Histoire parallèle* was to contain a section consisting of interviews between Americans and myself, and distinguished Russians and Aragon. My trip facilitated the necessary meetings. I went to see physicists and astronomers, biologists and city planners, historians and artists. I learned a great deal and came to recognize the high level of scientific thought in the United States.

[396]

The New York hotel where we had lived in 1941, the Ritz Tower, had been transformed and the apartments there were only rented by the year; the management, however, was kind enough to let me have one for a month. My wife came from Paris to meet me there at the end of my tour, and we spent several happy weeks meeting again our faithful friends of the times of trouble now become happy times. My wife found great pleasure in revisiting all the little shopkeepers of the neighbourhood who made a fuss over her. Before our departure the Alliance Française and France-Amérique joined to give us a banquet which was attended by five hundred guests and presided over by Ambassador Armand Bérard. France still had an immense store of friendship in the United States; I hoped with all my heart that it would be maintained.

The year 1961 was marked by the most serious illness of my life. I was already feverish when leaving Paris for Périgord in July. As a matter of fact, I had the beginnings of pleurisy, but I did not know it and neglected to look after myself. At Essendiéras we were visited by an American friend, the cultural adviser to the Embassy, and on a day of terrific heat we undertook to show him the Dordogne. In my novel *Climats* I have described the hero of the story, Philippe Marcenat, entering an icy cave in broiling weather; he caught pneumonia and died of it. This was a strange premonition. I tarried with my American guest, perspiring and overheated as I was, in the grotto of the Last Judgment at Brantôme; that evening I felt so ill that my wife begged Dr. de Beaulieu, our physician in Excideuil, to come up to Essendiéras. His diagnosis was pleurisy and double pneumonia.

There followed a period of acute anxiety for my wife. As for me, I was aware of the danger but I was not afraid. The idea of death did not terrify me at all. I thought, like Montaigne: 'And even if this be death itself . . . ' Like Alain as well who had said: 'Death is only an idea.' Meanwhile I did my best, by being calm, to help those who were looking after me so well. Another strange coincidence: I had just written a life of Fleming so that I took a professional interest in Beaulieu's search for the proper antibiotic. Specialists—cardiologist, radiologists—came from Périgueux, from Bergerac. The newspaper *Sud-Ouest* announced that I was gravely ill. The radio spread this news all over France. The foreign press picked it up. I was thought to be dying. A deluge of letters and telegrams arrived in Essendiéras. My Paris doctor, Professor Claude Laroche, although he had been on vacation, rushed to us. He had high praises for the treatment prescribed by Dr. de Beaulieu.

For two weeks the uncertainty persisted. It was still at its height when my wife's mother on the morning of July 14 began to feel ill, lay down on her bed, lost consciousness, and died of a heart attack without regaining consciousness. My poor wife had to go from my sick bed to the church and to the cemetery in the midst of the holiday flags. She had barely returned to Essendiéras when a fire broke out in the kitchen of our house. When the firemen from Excideuil arrived, they said: 'If we don't get control of the fire immediately it would be well to move Monsieur Maurois out ... Once the timbers are weakened the roof will fall in and the whole house will go up in flames.' Very fortunately the firemen performed wonders and it was not necessary to move me. I was so weak that this would have been difficult.

At the end of a month we emerged from that nightmare atmosphere, but although I was out of danger I was exhausted both by the illness and by the huge doses of antibiotics that I had received. To walk and later to go downstairs proved a painful apprenticeship. Nevertheless the impression that stayed with me from this close call was not without a certain sweetness. Doctors and nurses had proved their incomparable devotion and the solicitude shown by so many friends known and unknown seemed to surround my old age with warm affection.

In August I was able to get back to work and I felt myself beginning to live again. 'Do people know what writing is?' Mallarmé asked. 'An ancient and ill-defined but jealous practice in which lies the mysterious meaning of the heart. He who performs it totally entrenches himself.' Yes, the writer entrenches himself and so comes to exist only when in front of the paper 'defended by its whiteness.'

39

Essendiéras

For thirty years Essendiéras had been not *our* home but that of Simone's mother and her husband Maurice Pouquet. We went there as guests and had no voice at all either in the management of the estate or in the maintenance of the house. Life moved at a slow pace. My mother-in-law, aged and weary, hardly ever went out except to take a few steps on the arm of the husband whom she adored in the fullest meaning of the word. She left entirely to him the business of managing her affairs and in this she was mistaken, for he rapidly brought her to ruin. I have spoken a number of times of Maurice Pouquet, an intelligent, appealing and enigmatic man. At times I was beguiled by his charm, at times shocked by his actions. He had held the very best trumps in his hand; proxy administrator of the Mines of Ouenza, president (during the war) of the Coty interests in France, manager of *Figaro*; he had lost everything by intransigence of character and by an odd refusal to adapt his theories to the facts.

After the war he had triumphantly shown us that he owned a large block of stock in Ouenza, the gold mines that he had discovered in Limousin and in a pharmaceutical company, Ostréiode. Ten years later not only was there nothing left of these enterprises but he had squandered the considerable fortune left to my mother-in-law by her first husband. The gold mines disappeared into the mists of the moon. There remained Essendiéras, and that was important. I loved the sweeping landscape of hills and woods, the gaps through which appeared bluish horizons, the tenant farms with their brown roofs, the fields dotted with drowsy cows. In the time of my wife's grandfather the estate had been worked by the tenants. This did not bring in much by way of revenue but it did not cost anything. 'Essendiéras? As good as ready cash,' said the old stockbroker with the curly beard. Maurice Pouquet who had theories about agriculture as well as about everything else suddenly decided that Essendiéras could be made a source of income.

He let the tenants' leases run out or cancelled them and decided to farm the whole area himself. I do not know exactly why this was such a failure. An absentee proprietor who leaves complete authority in the hands of a manager brings on his own ruin, that is a law of nature, and Balzac a long time ago explained it in *Les Paysans*. But Maurice Pouquet lived the year round at Essendiéras, occupied himself actively with farming and breeding and was considered so competent by many of the neighbouring farm owners that they sought his advice. In his defence it could be said that the soil of Périgord is not very rich, that the return per hectare remains well below that obtained by the peasants of Beauce, that the fields, less fertile than those in Normandy, do not allow the cows to produce an equal amount of milk. These factors played a part but also my father-in-law's fatal inclination to experiment with every new and bizarre method that he discovered in some American magazine. Always open to influence from anyone who used a technical vocabulary, he was capable of exchanging a whole herd as the result of a single conversation. Loss through sale and loss through purchase mounted up.

I speak of this without rancour and even without blame, having myself committed equally serious mistakes later on when I busied myself with agriculture, but I have had under my eyes, since his death, Maurice Pouquet's accounts of his management. The losses varied between two and four million francs a year through good years and bad, despite the fact that a large part of the beautiful oak trees, the honour and adornment of the estate, had been felled and sold by him. Naturally he did not inform my wife and me of his miscalculations, but numerous indications showed us that, since the war, Simone's parents were in a dangerous financial situation. The most urgent repairs to the house were postponed. If we asked that at least the roof be mended we were met with the reply: 'Well and good, but you pay.' We agreed to this but not without anxiety, for would Essendiéras ever be ours? Maurice Pouquet had the secret but transparent plan of cutting up the estate 'to make money' and Simone had seen in the office of the notary a big red poster announcing the auction of La Cerise, the best of the tenant farms. Despite our protests, he had already sold Capian, Madame Caillavet's estate which dated from the First Republic, together with the library it contained. He was doubtless counting on selling what remained and moving somewhere else.

The unexpected always happens. The best laid plans collide with the unforeseeable. Much younger than his wife, Maurice Pouquet had every reason to think he would survive her. Methodically he had prepared for that time: a will in his favour placed in his name the furniture, the linen, the silver (although all this obviously came from Simone's grandparents) and he turned into cash everything he was able to sell. Balzac would have made a whole novel out of this ingenious trickery. But death has a way of thwarting all plans. I did not know what suddenly caused the deterioration of health in a man who had been so vigorous. It began with blood poisoning caused by a prick from a gardening tool. This was not enough to explain the frightening emaciation, the premature aging, the sudden deafness. My wife, who went to Essendiéras without me during the winter, was horrified by her father-in-law's condition. Despite her painful grievances against him, she tried to save him by having him taken to the best clinic in Bordeaux. There, after prolonged examination, a cancer of the intestine was diagnosed, so advanced as to be inoperable. Since her mother was too old and too grief-stricken to leave Essendiéras, my wife (with my agreement) decided to find a place to live in Bordeaux and to go daily to see the sick man. He died in November, 1956.

My mother-in-law's sorrow was profound, less so, however, than I should have expected from the death of a husband she had loved so much. It is often said that old people fall back on egoism and no longer have the strength to feel emotions deeply. My mother-in-law talked eloquently about her sorrow, but she bore it well enough. She had never paid any attention to her own affairs and refused to listen to anything about the inheritance. This was just as well, for in her case the assets were nil; Maurice had willed the little that he possessed to his very elderly sisters—which was fair enough. No doubt he had disposed in some occult fashion of the liquid assets if there were any. He left his wife completely ruined, possessing nothing but Essendiéras. She could have sold the estate and thus assured herself of an income, but she refused to make any change in her monotonous and pampered life. Simone, moreover, entertained an almost morbid attachment to this beautiful neighbourhood. She could not conceive of life without the old family mansion, without the trees in the park around which clustered fragments of her girlhood memories. The problem for me was not: 'Should Essendiéras be sold?' but: 'What can be done in order not to be forced to sell Essendiéras?'

I could have reduced the expenses considerably, to be sure, by letting the fields lie fallow and pasturing sheep on them. But on our estate there were a number of families who had lived there always, father and son. Simone since her childhood had been on intimate terms with many of them. There could be no question of abandoning them, much less of forcing them to leave. To give them work it was necessary to farm the land. Naturally I knew nothing about this calling. I was carrying on my own profession, that of writer, to the best of my ability; in my youth I had successfully directed a business enterprise. All that I knew about the earth was what my father-in-law had told me during thirty years, and he had never told me very much. But, having generally succeeded in what I undertook, I had developed a dangerous self-confidence. Formerly when I had taken charge of the mill I had thought: 'This cannot be harder than writing a French composition or a translation into Latin,' and success had proved me right. Why should I not become in my latter days a model farmer, an Olivier de Serres of Périgord? The adventure tempted me. Alas, it was beyond my strength. The situation bore no similarity to that which I had found in 1901 in the family mill, which at that time was sound and prosperous. And even in Elbeuf, as soon as I had become a writer, I had ceased to be a conscientious industrialist; attention and will must be like a sort of laser beam which can be powerfully focused on a single point; as soon as it is split its action becomes irregular and ineffective.

I had experts come to Essendiéras to advise me. They examined the estate accounts and pointed out (as we knew all too well) that expenses were well above income. To reduce the expenses it would have been necessary to dismiss part of the personnel and my wife and I were opposed to this. There remained only one remedy; to increase the receipts. The experts recommended a large investment; huge purchases of fertilizer, rotation of crops, the purchase of Dutch cows to assure a high yield of milk. I pointed out at once that this programme would require expenditures running to a number of millions of francs. I received the traditional reply; 'He who desires the end desires the means.' Forecasts were made out for me. If I bought a hundred pedigreed cows whose grandmothers had produced six thousand litres each per year, then the milk would bring me in so much; in addition, I could sell each year so and so many heifers, and so and so many young bulls. On paper, the profits seemed assured. Was this brilliant future worth tremendous temporary sacrifices? I planted the fields in clover, I bought the cows, piebald Friesians, aristocratic and elegant, which made an enchanting picture on our green fields.

The granddaughters, alas, had not inherited their grandmothers' productive genius. Or was it the climate that did not agree with them? Or the grass of our fields? In any case, the fact remains that they never exceeded the twenty-five hundred or three thousand litres of the humble Norman and Breton cows which had preceded them there. As a matter of fact, I should have expected this. The granddaughter of a great poet is never a great poet. But I was obstinate. I began the experiment with the princesses from Holland all over again, this time with thoroughbred pigs; I built a model piggery, equipped with infrared rays. But despite all this luxury our pigs developed sepulchral coughs. Those that did not die brought a low price. I learned to my cost that the price of pork is as variable as the prices on the stock exchange. As a general rule it falls when one has animals to sell and rises after they are all gone.

Farewell heifer, cow, pig and brood! In vain I threw into the estate everything I earned through my literary labours; the annual losses remained dismaying. One book a year barely sufficed to feed my cows and my pigs. Meanwhile my wife was becoming more and more attached to Essendiéras. Her mother had become, after her husband's death, completely passive, still brilliant in conversation but indifferent to what was going on in the house. My wife now boldly took the initiative. In order to put up our friends, she decorated new rooms, making use of the prodigious resources of that ancient house with its attics full of furniture and draperies. Her parents, who had been very exclusive, had never received any but the lords of the manor of the neighbourhood. Simone took to inviting members of Parliament of all parties, civil servants of the *département*, various priests, our dear friends, and writers from the region. It had been proposed to me that I become mayor of our district, Saint-Médard-d'Excideuil, but this district had an excellent mayor and besides I did not want to become involved in local politics. On the other hand my wife agreed to become municipal councillor and took her duties very seriously as she did everything else. Almost every day some one of her constituents would ask her to intervene at the Prefecture or at some ministry in Paris. She took pleasure in being useful and busied herself with schools, the aged and the orphans.

It is a great and wonderful happiness to be deeply rooted in one corner of the world, to know its remotest footpaths and to feel oneself known by all. In my youth I had had this endearing experience in Elbeuf; I re-acquired it in Dordogne. For our neighbours were not rivals but friends. My wife knew all the children on the estate by name and her liveliest pleasure was to arrange a Christmas tree for them each year. She kept great lists in which she noted the presents she had given so that she could choose different ones the following year. There was no hint of 'paternalism' in this celebration. The parents, whatever their political views, accompanied their children. Equality was absolute. Simone had performed the miracle of being on equally friendly terms with communists, socialists, radicals, Gaullists and with the lords of the manor and with the clergy. Her house was one of the rare places where everyone was willing to meet everyone else.

She had also tried to make Essendiéras, *mutatis mutandis*, a little like the Nohant of George Sand, a meeting place for writers and artists. My work kept me shut up all day in my office; my wife was hardly less occupied. The guests who could accommodate themselves to this sort of life were themselves hard workers. François Mauriac finished at Essendiéras *La Fin de la nuit*, Simon Porche his Memoirs, Jacques Suffel his *Flaubert*, Marcelle Auclair her *Sainte-Thérèse d'Avila*, René Clair a film, Lacour-Gayet his *Histoire du Canada*. Poulenc, Sauguet, Jacques Dupont gave us the pleasure of visiting us for several days. Little by little a younger generation took its place among our intimates. Jean Dutourd, Maurice Druon, Michel Droit, Jean-Jacques Gautier, Maurice and Constance Dumoncel were generous enough not to treat us like crumbling ancestors. The meals were merry, the evenings devoted sometimes to conversation, sometimes to television (if there were a film or a good play), sometimes to music.

August 1959: During this week-end Essendiéras was a place of delight. Summer, pure summer, enveloped us with an Attic sky. We had with us very dear friends. The conversation was endless. We talked in the car while admiring the high plateau of Hautefort or the valley of the Vézère between its broken, black cliffs. We talked at Delsaut's in Saint-Léon, while dining under the arbour. O memorable truffles and mushrooms!

I know of no greater pleasure than conversation between like-minded souls. There must be trust and, as far as possible, no vanity. One must love the same books, or at least the same qualities of style, and one must know more or less the same people. Then Stendhal, Balzac, Proust, Mérimée join in the conversation, and these talkers from beyond the grave enliven the dialogue of the living. Excitement rises, maxims are hammered out: 'Curiosity is the homage that virtue pays to vice.' And the flood of words carries with it enough anecdotes to supply ten novelists.

Jean Dutourd quotes a remark by Léon-Paul Fargue: 'One cannot argue unless one is in agreement, and then only on points of detail.' During these happy days I have felt the truth of this maxim.

September 1959: Jean and Camille Dutourd are here. Work, walks, freedom. In the evening we listen to records. Today Beethoven's Eroica. Never has the Funeral March seemed to me so fine.

'That's what I would like to have played at my funeral,' I say.

'Yes,' says Jean Dutourd, 'so would I. It is death as it should be, with heroism and serenity.'

'As it should be before, during and afterward,' says Camille.

Each of us arranges his funeral programme. My wife prefers the march from *Twilight of the Gods*, which accompanies the laying of Siegfried on the funeral pyre.

'But,' she says with a sigh, 'that requires a whole orchestra! It's not possible in a church. Well then, Fauré's *Requiem* ... '

'What I do *not* want,' says Dutourd, 'is Chopin's Funeral March.'

'Why?' I ask. 'It is beautiful, though no doubt less profound than Beethoven.'

Then, in order to get out of the crypts, we play the next movement.

'The whole landscape of Italy, the entry into Milan, the beautiful plains of Lombardy ... '

'And the young Countess Pietranera who from her window watches Bonaparte's soldiers marching past.'

And now we have Rossini's overtures directed by Toscanini. They dispel the air of melancholy without tearing us away from the charms of Stendhal. The composer, the orchestra, the conductor, what a splendid combination! In earlier days I had heard a rehearsal in Carnegie Hall of these same works with Toscanini on the podium. He was severe, alert, charming, perfect. Italian through and through.

Dutourd quotes a brilliant definition by Paul Valéry of this kind of composition: 'A past composed of fragments of a future.' The opera that is about to come casts backward glimpses of itself.

[405]

Here are examples of the conversation at Essendiéras. With Maurice Druon, Roman ruins, Greek mythology, Nero and Julian the Apostate, with the signs of the zodiac taking first place. My daughter Michelle, herself a great traveller, kept feeding him cues. During the time of the festivals, which are so numerous in Périgord, our guests would go with my wife to Bonneval to see Hugo or Calderon, to Sarlat to see Shakespeare or Molière, to Brantôme to see a performance of classical dancing in the Grotto of the Last Judgment, which had so nearly been my grotto of the last gasp. If we did not have, like George Sand at Nohant, a marionette theatre, our whole province during the summer months was humming with poetry.

But like the violet-coloured storm clouds that come to us from Périgueux borne on the west wind, from far off an oppressive concern was climbing into our clear sky. Could this incomparable life go on? It was dependent on our ability to keep Essendiéras. But the losses of the estate continued to mount. All that was needed was for one of my books not to find the audience which thus far had been faithful, or for me to fall ill so that I could not write, and then it would be impossible to meet these crushing costs. My wife and I had frequent conversations on this painful subject. 'I regret,' she would say, 'not having had the courage to make a clean break at the time of Maurice's death. But there was my mother who paid no attention to anything and who refused to listen . . . And I myself used to wonder whether I would survive such a cruel wrench.'

Nevertheless from year to year we held on, though at great cost, and we were right to hold on, for salvation came, as it always does, in an unexpected way. In 1962 at a luncheon at the Prefecture in Périgueux my wife was seated beside Sylvain Floirat, a native of Périgord who had become one of the greatest French industrial leaders. The son of a postman in the nearby village of Nailhac, educated by a teacher who had been his master just as Alain had been mine, he had through intelligence, capacity for work and boldness made a career that was reminiscent of the American captains of industry. At the time when we met him he was a man of great power, president of Europe No. 1, of Aviation Bréguet, of Engins Matra and a dozen other companies. The government relied on him to renovate great enterprises that were in trouble; *L'Express* nicknamed him 'our national resuscitator'. At the Prefect's table my wife, chatting with her Périgord neighbour who shared her love for the district, told him how much she feared that she might some day have to leave her dear province. Monsieur Floirat expressed concern.

'But madame,' he said, 'one must never be downcast; one must act.'

'We have acted but without results.'

'One must act in a different way; there is always a solution . . . How big is your property?'

'Five hundred hectares, of which two hundred are under cultivation, the rest is underbrush and wasteland.'

'Is your soil good for fruit trees?'

'I have no idea; we have never tried them.'

'Madame, one must try everything. I am going to send specialists to your place who will take samples of the soil and analyse them. If the results are favourable I shall propose a business deal to you. You will contribute your property, I will furnish the capital and we will plant an orchard of apple trees. I already have a pilot orchard not far from you and it is doing well.'

Floirat was a man who, once a plan was conceived, went into action. Within a week samples of soil were taken, analysed and the report was excellent.

'Now,' he said, 'we must act fast. If we want to plant our apple trees at the beginning of 1963, our company must be organized at once.'

He set in motion his staff of lawyers, notaries and friends, and in a few weeks the Société des Plantations d'Essendiéras was formed in which he was the principal stockholder but in which my wife retained a considerable share. Suddenly the estate was invaded by bulldozers and mechanical shovels, the princesses from Holland and the coughing pigs were liquidated; the fields were covered with little sticks which were, I was told, future apple trees. I have trouble in believing it but at this moment as I write, less than four years later, the grounds are covered as far as the eye can see, with espaliered apple trees laden with enormous fruit. Will the growing of these trees prove more profitable than the keeping of cattle? I do not yet know, but my wife has been able to keep her lime trees and her oaks, the morning mists and the blazing sunsets, the enchanting view over the towers of Excideuil and over the valley of the Isle. And better still, all her friends on the estate have their work. That is the important thing.

40

Toward the Dénouement

My lives of Fleming and of Adrienne de La Fayette had been excursions outside literary history. In 1962 I was sharply called to order by Francis Ambrière who had played a tyrannical and tutelary role in my career as a biographer. 'What's all this?' Ambrière said. 'What do you hope to accomplish? What's it all about? People expect the sequel to a fine series of romantic lives and you go off playing truant with Fleming or teaching the catechism with Adrienne! No! A thousand times no! There is a great subject made to order for you; it is Balzac.'

I admitted that I admired Balzac more than any other novelist, that for sixty years I had read and re-read him and, finally, that I had often gone to study the precious Balzac material in the Lovenjoul Library in Chantilly. I confessed also that I had dreamed of writing a life of Balzac, but that I had been prevented from doing so by the certainty that this would cause great distress to Marcel Bouteron, the Pope of the Balzacians and a delightful man who knew all about Balzac and was better qualified than anyone for this immense undertaking. But Bouteron had died without having written that book. I agreed that Ambrière was right and that the moment had come for me to put the capstone on the edifice by a Balzac.

The labour of collecting and sorting out the material seemed frightening. The Balzacians in all countries, but especially in France, form an active, brilliant and passionate band. They have searched out all sources, dug in all directions, studied in minutest detail the lives of the most obscure members of that celestial family. To collect all that had been written about Balzac, to read it and clarify it seemed beyond human strength. Fortunately I could count on my wife, herself an ardent Balzacian familiar with the Lovenjoul archives, and I received as well valuable support from a young woman, assistant professor at the Sorbonne, Madeleine Fargeaud by name, to whom Bouteron had entrusted before his death his card indexes and his archives. Thanks to her, the rarest brochures on obscure points in the life of Balzac reached my worktable at just the moment when I needed them. Little by little the subject became clearer and I glimpsed my essential theme, the relation between Balzac the man and the *Comédie humaine*. For three years I was to lose myself delightedly in that existence at once trivial and sublime. Soon I decided that the first chapter should be entitled 'Tours under Bonaparte', and I left for an assault on the archives at Indre-et-Loire where the astonishing Monsieur Balzac had left numerous traces of his prudently opportunistic career.

On many side issues I found unpublished documents in the splendid collection of autograph manuscripts that my wife had assembled. An indefatigable worker and researcher, she had already procured for me at the time of *Lélia* numerous letters from George Sand, at the time of *Olympio* letters from Victor Hugo to Madame Biard. She had unearthed in Limoges all the papers left by Madame Marbouty, the young woman who in male disguise had accompanied Balzac to Italy and had become (with some necessary retouching) the model for the *Muse du département*. With total self-effacement Simone devoted herself to my work. She deserved all the more credit for this since she could have been if she had wished an excellent writer herself. She had an original style, wit and humour, and enormous erudition. A small book by her on Miss Howard (the English woman who made Napoleon III an emperor of the French) had had a lively success. She had written an excellent description of the friendship between George Sand and Marie Dorval and had reconstructed the story of Vigny's last love affair. Among her papers were manuscripts, well advanced, on new topics. She abandoned everything to help me explore the world of Balzac. Her modesty and her passionate devotion were the only traits of character in which she took justified pride.

It was during the time when I was working on the *Balzac* that I became the horrified but helpless witness to the agony and then the death of the Elbeuf 'Works' to which in earlier days I had devoted my youth and labour. Naturally I could not closely follow the course of events, but from time to time my cousins, who were the managers, kept me informed of the situation. It was deteriorating rapidly. Textile mills were springing up throughout the whole world. The production in France exceeded the demand. People were wearing different clothes and fewer of them. Fewer waistcoats, fewer overcoats. For women (and to some extent even for men) artificial fabrics were replacing wool. One after another almost all the mills in Elbeuf had been forced to close. It is true that our rival during the heroic period, Blin and Blin (the Pascal Boucher of *Bernard Quesnay*), survived. But the difference between the fates of the two mills can be explained by difference of luck during the war and the occupation. The two businesses had been confiscated by the occupiers as being Jewish properties. But Blin and Blin had had the good fortune to see their interests entrusted to a temporary administrator who looked after them honestly, and more important still, they had been largely spared during the bombings. On the other hand, more than half of our mill had been destroyed and our temporary administrator had been very inefficient. That is why, after the Liberation and the Victory, Blin and Blin were able to regain their foreign markets while Fraenckel and Herzog were binding up their wounds as best they could.

The day came when it seemed impossible to go on. The losses were increasing each year. It was to be feared, if we persisted, the business would fall into bankruptcy. This was not a worthy end for that honourable house which was more than a century old. It would be better to shut down, sell the plant and thus put oneself in a position to meet all obligations. The decision was a sad one. When I thought about the sort of visceral attachment that my father, my uncles and my cousins had devoted to that enterprise for so long; when I remembered all the Alsatian and Norman families that from generation to generation had handed on such a noble tradition of work well done; when I pictured the last day, the looms stopped forever, the driving belts motionless, the machines condemned to the scrap heap, my heart broke. If I had believed that by getting back into harness I could have saved the Works, I would have done so, not without a certain pride in thus making the ultimate effort. But it would have been no more than a beau geste, and would have done no good. The mill did not need an aged boss; the young people were competent. The trouble was of long standing and beyond human control. French economy was being transformed. In that ancient wool city new factories were opening up: automobiles, electronics, metal furniture. At least the workmen would have no trouble in finding an opportunity for new employment. This consoled me a little, but it would not have appeased my father's sorrow.

One of the consequences of this *Chute de la Maison Quesnay* was that nothing remained to me or almost nothing of what had seemed between 1914 and 1939 my fortune. Everything was happening as if I had never been anything but a writer. Empires fall to pieces faster than they have grown.

Since the research work on Balzac was demanding because of the need for precision and thus deprived me, as long as I did not feel ready to begin composing the book, of the irreplaceable joy of writing, I allowed myself from time to time, by way of respite, to sketch out a short story. I have always liked this form and soon I had accumulated a large enough number of titles to make a volume: *Pour piano seul*. The reader will perhaps remember my first stories, which I had written while young and then condemned. After sixty years of work my manner of storytelling had hardly changed. It remained simple and direct. Not that I was indifferent to new forms. I greatly admired the stories of Katherine Mansfield and the harsh, quick tales of Hemingway. The experiments of the young French writers in attempting to renovate the novel interested me. Around 1930 I had found diversion in writing a hundred or so pages in the manner of Marcel Proust: *le Côté de Chelsea*. In the same playful fashion I could have amused myself by doing imitations of Robbe-Grillet or Nathalie Sarraute. But my natural way of writing would have returned at a gallop the instant I began to write under my own name.

I did not feel at all as if I were living outside my time. The masters acclaimed by the young writers of the 'new novel' were among those I admired: Marcel Proust, Joyce, Kafka. Surrealism never alarmed me and I was aware of how much it had contributed to a writer like Aragon. I was willing to admit that a shock may be necessary to tear minds away from the monotony of a formula. The fact that Balzac had been a novelist of genius did not imply that every novel had to be Balzacian. As president of the jury of the Bourse del Duca, I had had the prize awarded to Robbe-Grillet, then a beginner; as member of the reading committee of the Comédie Française I voted for Ionesco. This is to show that I was not opposed to experiments. At the same time I distinguished between those that were designed to bring a closer understanding of reality and those that were simply meant to startle. To eliminate from the novel subject, narrative and characters seemed to me vain and dangerous. Neither Proust nor Joyce had done that. *Un Amour de Swann* is a story like that in any traditional novel.

Charlus, Albertine, Swann are characters, as are also Bloom and his wife in *Ulysses*.

It seemed to me legitimate to reject obsolete conventions. Valéry had said: 'I shall never write: "The marquise went out at five o'clock."' Claude Mauriac used this phrase for the ironic title of a novel. In the *Dîner en ville* he suppressed not the characters but their descriptions and their names. It was up to the reader to discover them and to identify the interlocutors by what they said and even more by the undercurrents that ran beneath the spoken sentences. In a general way these new novelists juggled with time and space. Often the reader, dizzied, no longer knew where he was. Present, past and future blended; the settings dissolved into new images like fade-outs in the cinema. The average reader complained: 'Why this disorder? One can no longer understand anything.' The young reader might reply that these brusque transitions, these puzzles in scattered pieces, forced the mind to be attentive, to be on the alert and thus kept it from dozing. The art of the motion picture had long since accustomed the viewer to receiving his ration of romance in short, disjointed sequences.

I kept up frequent contact with the cinema. On various occasions I was asked to preside at the Festival at Cannes. It was tiring and a great sacrifice of time. For two weeks one had to look at two or three films a day. I consented because I found there pictures of countries that I did not know well and also an opportunity to understand a little how those distant peoples felt and loved and also to discover what their favourite artists' subjects were. Nothing interested me more than to observe the wholesome and epic quality of the Soviet films; the eroticism of the Swedes and their symbolic poetry; the realism of the Italians, sometimes comic, sometimes tragic; the humour of the British and their genius for the absurd. I did not always succeed in getting my jury to reach a decision that satisfied my personal taste. One year I tried in vain to secure the Golden Palm for Fellini's *Cabiria*. Sometimes with the help of the young I carried the day. Thus awards were given to a Swedish film, *Miss Julie*; an Italian film, *Miracle in Milan*; a charming and imaginative British film, *The Knack*; and *Un Homme et une femme* by Lelouch. Often I failed and the atmosphere of the Festival would become unbreathable; the audience would assail the jury. I had to take a large measure of responsibility for choices made against my will. I found consolation in the presence there of such charming women as Sophia Loren and Olivia de Havilland. A beautiful face has always

[412]

seemed to me 'the most beautiful of all sights'. This remains as true at eighty as in those distant times when I went into ecstasies over Helen of Troy.

In 1962 I received a letter from the University of Maryland which had formed a daughter institution in Europe: The Army University. There American soldiers could continue their studies. Its headquarters were in Heidelberg. The President offered me a degree of Doctor *honoris causa* and asked me to come and receive it in Heidelberg. The ancient and famous German university, he told me, would put the great *aula* at the disposal of the Americans for the investiture. How could I refuse? And so I went to Heidelberg to receive my doctorate. The ceremony reminded me of those at Oxford and Princeton. The governor of the state of Maryland had come from America. The dean read a long citation, much too laudatory, but from which I will copy out a passage because it expressed, not what I have done, but what I have tried to do.

During half a century of continuous creation, in a world rendered pitiless by the disorders of war and perilous by the discords of peace, André Maurois has always described peoples and nations in his stories, his novels, his courses, his lectures and his essays in a rational manner designed to reconcile them with one another. In particular he has revealed to Anglo-Saxons the Spirit of France and to France and the entire world the Spirit of the Anglo-Saxons.

On the day before the ceremony my hosts had taken me out on the Neckar in an open boat. There I had caught a heavy cold. Feverish and voiceless, I did the best I could with my speech of thanks. The university played Handel and this consoled me.

With England, too, I kept up my connections. This was not always easy. The two countries were too often opposed in politics and econ-omics. The French Chamber of Commerce in London invited me to be the guest of honour at its banquet on the day after the setback in Brussels and the cancellation of Princess Margaret's trip to Paris. I thought: 'The British are hurt, annoyed. The atmosphere will not be good.' To pretend to have the grippe, Asiatic or Dalmatian, as an excuse would have been cowardly. I agreed to give this speech. The toastmaster, a giant clad in red, rapped the table with his gavel. Seated beside me was the Secretary of State for Foreign Affairs. I began: 'When Joseph Chamberlain gave his maiden speech in the House of Commons, he was very brilliant. The eloquence, the precision of language and the assurance of the young orator astonished his colleagues. After the session an old member came up to him: "That was good, Mr. Chamberlain, very good . . . But the House would be grateful to you if you would hesitate . . . occasionally." I assure you that I hesitated a long time before choosing a subject with which I could entertain you this evening without risk . . . ' (Laughter, applause. The game was won.)

The following day I was to give a lecture at Cambridge. I was happy to see again the old college where I had formerly talked about biography under the portrait of Henry VIII. The students gave me tea in their rooms. Cultivated men, they spoke a very pure French. They told me that the Société Française of the university had four hundred members and that Michel Butor had spoken there that afternoon.

'Two lectures in French on the same day? Isn't that too much?'

'You will see. They will both have the same success. For us it's interesting to see two different generations.'

In fact it was necessary that evening to move into a larger amphitheatre. No, nothing had been irremediably spoiled by the misunderstanding in Brussels. I realized that the renewing of a few bonds would suffice to consolidate a precious friendship. From my window I saw the willows, the Gothic towers and the swans gliding over the frigid waters. A huge fire burned on my hearth. This was England.

In France the stage around me was emptying. In that year of 1962 my dear Jean Cocteau had a serious heart attack. It was not his first. We went to see him at the home of Jean Marais. Wearing a white dressing gown, his face thin and very pale, his hair rebellious, he seemed like a shadow that had emerged from one of his films. He was watching television but with the sound turned off, any noise being a dangerous shock for him. This silent spectacle, these ever-changing and unexplained images, combined with Jean's gasping voice, made as strange and beautiful an impression as one of his films. I was not to see him again. It was in England, where I had gone to talk about Tennyson in his native county, that I learned from the newspapers of the death of this man who had been my friend for half a century. I hurried back.

His burial in Milly la Forêt was a poignant and touching ceremony. The October sky seemed like a sky of spring, of a pure, intense blue in which floated miniature white clouds. A bountiful sun flooded the little town. All those who stood around the coffin, covered with tricolour silk and wonderful flowers, were his friends. The square in front of the town hall with its white houses and its flags looked like one of Utrillo's finest paintings. Firemen in copper helmets and school children stood in a circle around the Academicians and the prefects. This mixture of the official and the rustic would have enchanted the Enchanter. In the church the choir from Saint-Eustache sang noble music. Then the cortège entered the chapel decorated by Cocteau, behind which the grave had been dug amid the simples, those medicinal plants which he had chosen as ornaments in his frescoes. Simple too, but beautiful and touching, were the speeches. A few late birds came to perch on the yellowing branches. The poet slept in the calmness of an unforgettable day. We were sad to have lost him, happy to have given him what he would have wished. We wept for a man who had died and we escorted an immortal, not by virtue of that feeble laurel-wreathed immortality that men and titles try in vain to bestow, but by virtue of the authentic and durable immortality that lives in minds and hearts.

Another death saddened me as though it had been a personal loss, that of John Fitzgerald Kennedy, the young president of the United States. I had seen him a short time before in Paris. At the Elysée I had had the opportunity of exchanging a few words with his enchanting wife, who seemed so French. At the luncheon for the press, I had been delighted by the president's toast which had been full of humour, and I told him so. Like Churchill he had style in action as well as in speech. Sometimes he made mistakes but he rectified them generously. I clearly remembered that robust face sown with freckles. Suddenly on a November evening while my wife and I together with René Clair were watching a film at the Centre du Cinéma in the Rue de Lubeck, someone came in and said: 'Kennedy has been assassinated.'

'It's not possible!'

'It's true. The announcement has just been made on the radio.'

'What a misfortune,' I thought. 'We had the good luck to find a strong man at the head of the strongest nation in the world. I believe that in the long run he would have reached an understanding with De Gaulle. The difference in age would have facilitated relations by introducing an element of paternalism and thus mitigating the rigidity. After a bad beginning, Kennedy was beginning to get along with the Russians. And now a bullet directed by some mysterious grievance cuts short all those hopes!'

Nothing takes the place of existence; nothing takes the place of that actual balance in which things great and small have the same importance. The grain of sand in Cromwell's urethra, the bullet in Kennedy's throat. We anxiously question a world we have pictured in our minds; we imagine dialogues between heads of state; we are fearful, we worry, we make plans, we wait for an answer; and he who could perhaps have given the answer dies because an inexplicable plot placed in the hands of an obscure nobody a rifle with telescopic sights and the nobody at once carried his secret into the shadows. 'The woes we fear do not come,' said my friend Jean Rostand. 'Worse ones do.'

4 I

Annus Mirabilis

Alain had said: 'It is needful that old age be honoured.' That is true. Old age is feeble. It has lost the dearest charms of youth: freshness of complexion, ease of movement, the ability to please. It needs consolation and support. Sometimes through the working of institutions it retains power and sometimes, being wholly detached, it exercises power with wisdom. As for me, I have never wished for that. Twice in my life I have had the opportunity of taking that road; at the fork I chose to go the other way. All representative functions bored me; I preferred mediation or some form of action that involved only myself.

Nevertheless at eighty I found myself, not as Disraeli said, 'at the top of the greasy pole', but at an honourable height, far enough up not to have either bitterness or complexes. It will be seen that this eightieth year brought me proofs of affection that were sweet to my heart. Was I going to terminate my life, which could not last much longer, in this atmosphere of warmth and love? The year 1965 has been the one in which I had brought home the fruits of long labour. Fate and men had smiled on me. The curtain should have been rung down on this happy dénouement. But how? Body and mind seem intact; here I am compelled to improvise a sixth act. I do not know what the end of my life will be if it is prolonged beyond the desirable span. As in the days of my adolescence I often think of the ring of Polycrates. What am I to throw to the jealous gods?

In March 1965 my *Balzac* was published, the book to which I had just devoted three years. I was anxious, as is natural. I announced in my preface that this would be my last biography; and so a great deal was at stake. Had I been right in precluding for the future the fine occupation from which I had derived so much pleasure for so long? My reasons seemed to me sound. An important biography demands two or three years of research. Beginning at eighty, the enterprise seems rash. Time is lacking. Moreover could I, after *Balzac*, find another subject that was equal or superior to him? My wife, who cherished a weakness for Vigny, would have liked me to make him the hero of my last book. I could not have worked at that book with the same steady enthusiasm that had inspired me throughout the *Balzac*. And other work was incumbent upon me. Before writing finis to the last page of my life, I had to complete these Memoirs which would preserve a reasonably accurate portrait.

The success of *Balzac* exceeded my hopes. Reviewers in all the papers in every country were gracious enough to say it was my best book. I could not keep from remembering Alain's warning at the time of *Bramble*: 'You will not have this unanimous praise except for your first book and your last.' Public enthusiasm equalled that of the critics. Printing followed printing. No doubt it was due in large part to the immense popularity of Balzac and to the picturesque quality of his life, but I think that my method, which consisted in preserving the romantic aspects of a great life by revealing the world through the eyes of the hero, helped readers to follow me. Professional Balzacians, of whose reactions I had been somewhat afraid, were not annoyed to see an outsider walking in their chosen company, and they were indulgent. Innumerable cordial letters arrived. I quote the beginning of one of them because it suggests an ingenious title (I had called my book *Prométhée ou la Vie de Balzac*); it is from André Malraux:

Mon cher maître et ami, Conversation at the Elysée on the subject of your *Balzac*, which received nothing but praises. This fact is natural enough since each one is grateful to you for bringing benevolence of mind to a period when it is almost unknown and concern for accuracy to a time of dogma.

In addition you have brought to the biography of Balzac an element that, in my eyes, reverses it completely. At first little was said about this, but now, it seems, everyone feels it. By wiping out the traditional picture of a writer-Balzac harried by the debts of the printer-Balzac and by substituting for an 'accident' a predestined and constantly repeated process, you have dissipated the uneasiness that the conventional biography inspired. A cruel title for yours would be *Sisyphus*. It used to be asserted that Balzac battled against a past; you have proved that he was battling against himself.

One can see, furthermore, what a psychoanalyst would make of it.

And also what he would not make of it; part of the biographer's talent consists in the quality of his human experience.

And I add a second because it came from a Balzacian as impassioned as Alain and myself but belonging to a much younger generation. This was Jean Dutourd, an author I greatly admire and love:

Mon cher André, I am completely enraptured by your *Balzac*. It is a work that goes beyond biography; it is, in fact, a successful re-creation and altogether unique. You have treated your subject not as a great biographer (which is the way the publicity posters have it) but as a great novelist. The reader's interest increases as he reads. And at each instant the imprint of the master is apparent—I mean yours and not that of your hero—in the reflections that tell all. For example: 'He had the experience, so dangerous for any artist, of contempt for his art.' That is fine, absolutely worthy of Balzac or Alain, in other words, worthy of the greatest.

The portrait of Balzac that emerges little by little from the book is magisterial. There is not a detail lacking, not a shade. The arrangement of the contours is remarkable and the whole composition of the book is as fine as a painting by Poussin. At the beginning especially the portrait of the Balzac family is a marvel. Not a stroke to do over. Bravo! Father Balzac, his rural love affairs, Laura, Lawrence, the mother, Madame de Berny, grandmother Sallambier, all this is *made* with the strength and brilliance of Balzac himself. A rare thing: the biographer is not 'superior' to his subject; on the contrary, he stands before him, observing him with an eye as piercing, as objective and as just as Balzac's would have been. Henceforth it will be impossible not to put *your Balzac* at the opening of the Complete Works of Balzac. It is their introduction and their lighthouse.

In short, I am very happy and you should be very happy, you too. You have written the work of a man in full possession of his abilities, with a vigour, an amplitude, a sureness of touch which I see hardly anyone else capable of today. A remark by Claudel some time ago impressed me greatly. At eighty-five he maintained that one should still be going forward . . . Thank God you are not eighty-five years old but you marvellously illustrate his thought. In your *Balzac* there is something that goes beyond your other books, a greater depth, a new and mysterious form which is the proof of the youthfulness of your soul. And thus all is very well . . .

[419]

I entitled this chapter *Annus mirabilis* in memory of Byron who gave that name to the year in which the publication of *Childe Harold* suddenly opened the doors of palaces and hearts to the young unknown poet. My case was very different, but the old man rejoiced no less mightily in the indulgence with which his last work was received. Another success, minor and fleeting, added a final touch. Jacques Rueff, the economist and philosopher, had just been elected to the Académie Française. Now André Chamson who, according to the customs of the Company, should have received him, expressed reluctance to deliver the speech. Economic theory frightened him; although an excellent orator, one of the best in the house, he did not feel on familiar ground. Our Permanent Secretary, my dear friend Maurice Genevoix, turned to me and asked if I would assume this task. It represented considerable work, Jacques Rueff having written a great deal and on difficult subjects, but I have always had a perverse taste for what is difficult. I agreed and threw myself heart and soul into the preparation.

I received my reward. Not only was the theme far from boring, but I discovered an absorbing person. Jacques Rueff, while he was still quite young, had been associated with the financial history of France, which in turn is closely connected with the political history. He talked humorously and very well about himself, and I got glimpses of picturesque scenes that furnished material for those 'couplets' so necessary in academic eloquence because by piquancy of style or by the paradox of contrast they relieve the often rather dull tone of the long sessions. When the day of the reception arrived, Rueff had convoked the whole array of his chiefs past and present. Under the Cupola in the first row there were, in addition to Paul Reynaud and Antoine Pinay, Couve de Murville, Christian Fouchet, Peyrefitte and Palewski. It was no longer, as it had been for Cocteau, a gathering of queens but a gathering of ministers. Jacques Rueff was the successor to Jean Cocteau and so I found myself led to an evocation of the latter, with much affectionate sadness, in that same high place where ten years before I had greeted him. I had the good fortune in my remarks, which were sometimes warmly laudatory, sometimes technical and finally sometimes humorous, not to displease that consular audience. I believe that the success of *Balzac* and that of this speech were what led to my selection by the Chief of State and the Council of Ministers to receive on July 14, 1965, the single grand cross of the Légion d'Honneur bestowed on that occasion. Why should I not confess that this gave me pleasure? I know very well, together with Marcus Aurelius and Alain, that a ribbon however wide is never anything but a ribbon; nevertheless this one is associated with great historical memories. As a child I had admired it when it was spread across the breast of Sadi Carnot, President of the Republic. As for me, it brought to mind my parents who would have been so happy and the awarding of prizes in Rouen, in the Courtyard of the Great, under the red and white striped tent.

Meanwhile time went by as I moved from task to task, and by degrees I became a sort of patriarch of letters together with my friends François Mauriac and Jules Romains. I did not notice it happening; my heart remained young, almost naïve; I still often had the feeling of living the *Illusions perdues*. Actually one never stops losing illusions and acquiring new ones. I considered myself a beginner in every task that remained to be done, and suddenly, if I turned around, I saw behind me that long line of volumes. It gave me vertigo. I could easily have said (the sentence is from Aragon): 'How much I still resemble myself; is it possible I have dreamed all the rest?'

I had not dreamed. In 1965 the press reminded me that I had been born on July 26, 1885, that I was about to be eighty years old, with fifty years of literary life behind me, and that it was customary to celebrate this anniversary. My friends in Paris did not fail to do so and then, when we had gone to spend the summer at Essendiéras, various communes in the Dordogne made me an honorary citizen. And so for a month I went from speech to speech and I could not help thinking of a reply made by Marshal Joffre. Immediately after the war of 1914–18 the communes of the Marne had celebrated the anniversary of the victory and had asked the Académie Française to send a representative to the ceremony. Naturally Marshal Joffre was designated. The following year when the anniversary came again, the Académie was asked once more to send one of its members. Again with a unanimous motion the company turned toward Joffre. He lifted his arms in fury and boredom: 'Oh no!' he said, 'we're not going to fight that Battle of the Marne all over again every year!' In the last speech I delivered, at the Prefecture of Périgueux, I told this story and then added: 'I am touched by your kindness but nevertheless happy to think that this ceremony is the last and that henceforth I am not going to be eighty years old every year.' In fact, the turn now came for my juniors by a few months. Jules Romains was fêted in Saint-Julien-Septeuil, Mauriac in Bordeaux and then both in Paris with deserved enthusiasm.

As for me, I was to find myself once more at the centre of a final ceremony. General Catroux, Grand Chancellor of the Légion d'Honneur, came himself to Essendiéras to bestow the Grand Cross. It was a very intimate ceremony and company: our charming Prefect, Jean Taulelle; Monseigneur Louis, Bishop of Périgueux; the deputy from the Dordogne; Maurice Druon; Michel Droit; and also the mayors of the district, the staff from the orchard and my family. General Catroux, tall and slim, astonishingly young, gave an affectionate impromptu address:

You are about to receive the highest distinction of our national order, the honour of the Grand Cross of the Légion d'Honneur, as recompense and celebration of all your merits and all your talents which are known not only by those here but in the whole of France and, I can say this without exaggeration, in the whole world. For your works have been translated in all countries. It would be appropriate to discuss these titles and these accomplishments, but I am a soldier unfamiliar with things of the spirit, action being my calling . . .

Well then, not finding material myself, I must borrow a passage from you: 'Most men fight against their shadows. The first duty is to be a will; that is the only way to be a man.' Ah, that is fine. To be a man, to be a will, that is the course in life you have chosen. You are loyal to France. It is because the French recognize France in your works, because strangers find it there too, that the whole world has read them.

You have served France, *cher maître*, in letters and at arms. I believe I am serving as interpreter for General de Gaulle as well—indeed, I am sure of it since he has told me—when I tell you what joy he felt in rewarding one of the masters of French literature and of French thought.

The Prefect thanked the Grand Chancellor for having done Périgord the honour of coming in person to Essendiéras: 'This province is happy today to link in equal gratitude and affection the recipient and the sponsor.' Thus ended the last chapter of the jubilee.

I was happy to retire into the shadow.

The advance preparations for the presidential election were already beginning. My decision had been made: I would vote for General de Gaulle. Why? Because the stabilization of our institutions had produced happy results; because, without everything being for the best in the best of all possible worlds, our country was enjoying relative prosperity; because I did not see anyone who could do more. I would have preferred more flexibility in our relations with the United States. If many of my friends (Mauriac, Julien Cain, Druon, Dutourd, Michel Droit) were ardent Gaullists, others (Paul Reynaud, Jules Romains, Edouard Bonnefous) had thrown themselves into the opposition. I listened to heated conversations and predictions:

'It is not working,' said the opponents, 'not at all. The middle class is disturbed by the slackness of the exchange, the farmers by the failure of the Common Market . . . In foreign politics, our allies side with America first of all. Her incredible prosperity dazzles them.'

'A completely artificial prosperity,' replied the other party. 'Private and public debts there are immense. The gold reserves of the United States are melting away before your eyes.'

'Gold is not wealth. The true capital of a country is youth, its scientific research, its army and its industrial plant. If gold were the only criterion, the whole capitalist system would be dependent on a revolution in South Africa.'

'Why can't the opposition at least agree on a serious candidate?'

'Because France is not like that . . . You will never make a member of the MRP vote for a lay socialist, nor a Maurrassien for Lecanuet.'

Often the evenings at Essendiéras were transformed into political forums; sparks flew, but before we separated for the night, friendship had the last say.

On the radio we followed a brilliant debate between Debré and Mendès-France. They hurled unverifiable figures at each other's heads. Mendès criticized the government for stabilization: 'Each time you people of the Right get into power, you plunge the country into deflation . . . Look at Poincaré, Pinay, Giscard d'Estaing . . . '

'Certainly. Every time you people of the Left get into power, you behave like demagogues and later we have to make good your mistakes. Your follies require our acts of penance . . . What's more, we are not the Right.'

In Dordogne it seemed clear that Mitterand would win. I barely knew him; the voters did not know him at all; but in this radical and socialistic *département* they acted by hereditary reflex. Moreover the farmers were discontented because they had trouble earning a livelihood. They held the government responsible. The role of the opposition is easy; it promises without acting. If it gets into power it has to keep its promises and this is where everything goes awry.

The day of the election arrived. My wife and I went to vote in the little town hall of Saint-Médard-d'Excideuil. Then in the evening we returned to the village to be present at the count. The watchers opened the ballots and handed them to the Mayor who announced: 'Mitterand ... De Gaulle ... Mitterand ... Mitterand ... De Gaulle ... Lecanuet ...' The faces of those present revealed their views. All the voters seated on the benches of the town hall knew that I had voted for De Gaulle; I had said so in the press. They respected my freedom as I respected theirs. There was no comment. If the whole of France voted like the Dordogne, a second ballot seemed certain, but we were south of the Loire; the north and east could change everything. As soon as the result of the commune was announced we went back to Essendiéras to follow on television the results in the nation at large. I love these election evenings, which are as exciting as horse races. By midnight the need for a second ballot was confirmed. We returned to Paris and then came back for the second round. This time the result was positive.

Life resumed its course. Eighty years! A great age and one that I hardly expected to attain when at eighteen an army doctor had said to me: 'No, I cannot take you; you are too delicate.' Like so many frail men I have endured. Why? Partly because a life of unremitting work imposed a severe discipline. Most of all because Alain taught me the duty of being happy. I received hard blows like everyone else; I made haste to forget them. Nevertheless my body shows signs of wear. I used to love long strolls; now all walking tires me. I loved conversation; I still enjoy it in a small group of friends, but if the group grows too large I have trouble hearing. In short, the hour of arrival has come. One must fasten the seat belt—and apply the brakes.

But to apply the brakes is not so easy, even at the end of the trip. I am still asked to do a thousand tasks. Raymond Gérôme the director begged me to adapt a one-act play by Bernard Shaw, *Don Juan in Hell*, a section of *Man and Superman* which I had liked so much at the beginning of the century when I had seen it in London in company with Florence, the beautiful English girl whom I used to take boating on the Thames. The text was difficult; I admired it too much to refuse. A popular success seemed unlikely, despite the excellence of the actors. Shaw's paradoxes about Heaven and Hell were better suited to an Anglo-Saxon audience acquainted with the Bible than to Catholic or free-thinking Frenchmen. I seemed condemned to fleeting relations with the theatre. Nevertheless the play was performed a hundred times. An honourable number but not a triumph.

In 1966 Albin Michel, who had published a series of *Lettres ouvertes* to which Jules Romains, Maurice Garçon, Robert Escarpit had already contributed texts, asked me to compose a *Lettre à une jeune femme*. I preferred to compose a *Lettre à un jeune homme* which allowed me, not to give advice to youth (which had not asked me for it) but to present the experience of a long life. I did not think that this little volume could find a large public, especially among the young. To my great surprise, fifty thousand copies were sold in three months; face-to-face interviews with students were arranged on television and radio. Everything went perfectly. Some of them criticized me for an excess of wisdom. I praised such criticisms and reminded them of Alain's remark: 'Whoever is not an anarchist at twenty will not have enough energy at thirty to be a fire-chief.' Actually my young interlocutors were not anarchists at all; they simply shared furiously in the passions and pleasures of their time.

The *Lettre* had tossed me back into an active life: round-tables, colloquiums, speeches. I did not regret it. In old age most of all it is necessary to live each minute. Let death find us on horseback or planting cabbages—that is approximately what Montaigne said—'among games, festivals, jokes, common and popular amusements and music and amorous verses.' Each age has its preferences; games and festivals no longer interested me very much, but the little screen took me to common and popular amusements. I remained 'in the swim' and I enjoyed it.

42

Old Captain Death . . .

How right I had been, alas, when I wrote the title of this fourth and last part, to consider it a rash and imprudent choice: *Years of Serenity*. After the blaze of happiness in 1965–66, I dreaded the vicissitudes of life's flame and I thought once more about the ring of Polycrates. Yes, I had been right, miserably so. Suddenly in a few days serenity becomes anguish. My wife falls ill and wastes away in frightening fashion. Why? The best doctors had no explanation. She was greatly overtired. Her demanding and too scrupulous conscience, which she brought to bear in all her activities, had undermined her. Copying my tiny hand-writing through the whole length of the enormous manuscript of *Balzac* had strained her eyes; hurrying about performing services for her innumerable protégés had overtaxed her strength. Exhausted, frightened at no longer being able to read, she fell into a woeful de-pression. The idea of food filled her with horror. She had loved to see her friends, to receive them, to go to their homes; now she desired solitude, silence. Formerly so active, she now spent hours at a time in front of the television, hiding her poor eyes with her hand. X-rays, analyses, revealed nothing. I was in despair and thought only of her recovery and, while waiting for that, of distracting her from the mys-terious illness that was causing her to pine away.

Thus the first part of the year 1967 passed, interrupted only by a short trip I had to make to England. I had promised a long time before to give the Zaharoff Lecture at Oxford University. Professor Seznec, an old friend, had invited me to be his guest at All Souls College, an admirable institution unique in the world. Housed in an ancient build-ing of honey-coloured stone, there live fifty fellows—scholars, scien-tists, economists—of whom nothing is required except that they shall be cultivated and subtle and that they shall observe the traditions of the college. There are no students there; it is so richly endowed that the life, monastic in some respects, is delightful as well, without ostenta-

tion, in good taste. Lawns everywhere, generosity, poetry and humour
... That is the eternal Oxford. Once more I was overcome by the
strange and powerful spell of England. I saw again the charming
Frances Phipps who summoned up the happy days of the past. But I
could not tarry. On the day after my lecture I took wing again. My
wife was waiting for me at Orly, fragile, emaciated, but happy to be
reunited.

We left for Essendiéras on June 20. Our plan was to spend the
summer there and then in October I was to go to the United States to
give a quite original lecture series. A year earlier I had received from the
National Laboratory at Brookhaven an invitation to deliver the Pegram
Lectures before an audience of physicists, chemists and biologists.
Until then these lectures had been given only by famous scientists such
as Oppenheimer. I replied that I was a layman, curious about the
sciences but ignorant and hence unworthy to talk before such a group.
Nevertheless the correspondence continued and we reached agreement
on a fine subject: *Illusions*. Three or four lectures that would be entitled *Illusions of the Senses*, *Illusions of the Feelings*, *Illusions of Science*,
Intentional Illusions or The Fine Arts. I had worked on them all winter
with great pleasure. This kind of reflection led me back to Alain's
classes. During our three months at Essendiéras I polished my text
with care, at the same time working on a little book which had been
suggested to me by a young publisher, Roger Maria, and which amused
me.

This was the theme: in 1927 I had published, in a small printing, a
pamphlet entitled *Le Chapitre suivant* in which I had sketched out by
anticipation the history of the world from 1927 to 1967. Roger Maria
said to me: 'Many of your predictions were true, others were not. I
propose to reprint the text, adding first a self-criticism in which you
will explain your ideas about the possibility of predicting history;
secondly, a history of the planet from 1967 to 2007.' I was tempted,
but I asked to do the second part in two forms; hypothesis A, optimistic, and hypothesis B, pessimistic, which would end with an atomic
war and the annihilation of our civilization.

This little book was almost finished when my trip to America and
my work were put in question by troubles with my health. They did
not seem serious but when, on advice of my friend Dr. de Beaulieu,
I went to consult a specialist in Périgueux, the latter told me after his
examination that an operation was necessary and urgent. It was an

unlooked-for thunderbolt. The years of serenity were transforming themselves more and more into years of calamity.

For myself I am not afraid. I have been operated on before; I know that you suffer a little, that you bear it, and that then you are happy at having eliminated a peril. But I dread the shock.

Index

Académie Française, 161, 165, 193–7, 205–7, 264, 333, 343–4, 349, 355, 379, 385, 388–9, 420
Achard, Marcel, 382
'Alain', 31–40, 43, 55, 57–8, 60–1, 64–6, 70, 71, 119, 121, 126, 131–2, 138–9, 158, 160, 187, 188–9, 197, 215, 329, 336, 340, 342, 345, 368–9, 372–8, 379, 387, 417, 418–19, 421, 424–5, 427
Alain, 374–5, 382
Alexander, General, 317
Alleaume, Abbé, 23, 58, 150
Alphand, Hervé, 309
Altmayer, General, 242
Ambrière, Francis, 350, 366, 383, 408
American Comedy, An, 328
Ame russe, L', 19, 340
Amour de Swann, L', 411
Ampère, 367
Anacreon, 34
Andersen, Hans, 10
Angell, Norman, 267–9
Angers, David d', 205, 218
Annales, 245, 350, 366, 383
Anouilh, Jean, 388
Apollinaire, Guillaume, 353, 364
Apprentice Years, The, 213
Aragon, Louis, 382, 388, 396, 411, 421
Ariel, 131–2, 161, 164, 166, 169
Aristotle, 31
Armand, Louis, 389
Army University, The, 413
Art de vivre, Un, 262
Asmodée, 209
Aspects of Biography, 168
Aspects of the Novel, 168
Asser, General, 104–7, 109–10, 113, 128
Association des Lauréats du Concours Général, 379
Athalie, 20
Attlee, Clement, 193

Auclair, Marcel, 404
Audra, 246
Augier, 22
Aumale, Christian d', 307
Auriol, Vincent, 350, 390
Aus Innocents les mains pleines, 386
Aventures du coeur, Les, 374

Bach, 72, 328
Badoglio, Marshal, 312
Baldwin, Stanley, 192–3
Balzac, Honoré de, 10, 33, 34, 36, 53, 57, 65, 126, 165, 175, 188, 290, 322, 323, 328, 330, 342, 354–5, 367–8, 372, 374, 377–80, 381, 389, 405, 408–11, 418–19 and see *Prométhée*
Barbedienne, 52, 89, 152
Bardini, Jerôme, 191
Bargeton, de, 246
Baring, Maurice, 128–9, 151, 261, 265
Barker, Granville, 277, 291
Barrès, Maurice, 23, 31, 150, 181, 184, 227, 381
Barrès, Philippe, 184
Bartet, Julia, 29
Barthou, 193–4
Baudelaire, Charles, 29, 77, 124, 322
Bauer, Gérard, 382–3
Baumeister, Loulou, 81–3, 86
Beaconsfield, Lord, 288
Béatrix, 342
Beaulieu, Dr de, 397–8, 427
Beaumarchais, 81, 381
Beaumont, Guérin de, 323–4
Beaumont, Pauline de, 194
Becque, 41
Bédier, Joseph, 196
Beecham, Sir Thomas, 291
Beethoven, 72, 153, 292, 328, 405
Beith, General, 238
Bellé, René, 292

[429]

Belloc, Hilaire, 128
Bennet, Arnold, 143, 157, 164
Benoît, Pierre, 388
Benton, Thomas, 327
Bérard, Léon, 388
Bergson, Henri, 31, 139, 192, 196, 198, 343, 373, 379
Berle, Adolf, 275
Bernard Quesnay, 13, 51, 122, 150, 154, 187–8, 217, 322, 342, 410
Bernhardt, Sarah, 29
Bernheim, 44
Bernstein, Henri, 196
Berr, Georges, 29
Berthon, 81
Bertrand, Louis, 196, 264
Béthouart, General, 296, 298–300, 305, 307, 315, 320
Beynet, General, 320
Biard, Mme, 409
Billotte, General, 241
Billy, André, 383
Blanchard, General, 241
Blaque-Belair, Lieutenant, 138, 147, 155
Blin, André, 94, 97
Blin (Family), 13, 25, 61
Blin (Firm), 53, 55, 64, 122, 410
Blount, Air Vice-Marshal, 242
Blum, Léon, 177, 192
Blum, Louis, 351, 356–8
Boelle, Colonel, 47
Bonnet, Georges, 202
Bonnet, Henri, 305
Bos, Charles du, 124–6, 131, 133–6, 138, 151, 154, 155, 158, 208–9, 350
Bos, Zézette du, 124, 136
Bossuet, 47, 206, 214, 381
Boucher de Perthes, 120
Boudin, 184, 335
Bougrain, General, 241
Bourdet, Edouard, 384, 387
Bourget, Paul, 23, 73
Boulé, 44, 46, 61, 92, 97
Bouteron, Marcel, 408
Bovary, Madame, 23
Boyer, Charles, 285
Brantôme, 152
Brazilian Academy, The, 359
Bret, Captain, 254–5
Breteuil, Jacques de, 106
Breynat, Lieutenant, 44
Briand, Aristide, 159, 177, 353
Brière, 282

Brisson, Mme Adolphe, 161, 350
Brisson, Pierre, 209, 285, 346, 349
Broglie brothers, 355
Bronne, Carlo, 382
Brontë sisters, 88, 185
Browning, Robert, 135, 322
Brownrig, Colonel, 231
Brunetière, Ferdinand, 19, 61
Brüning, 17
Bruyère, Jean de la, 77, 390
Buckle, 164
Bullitt, William, 244
Buloz, 161
Bussmann, Bertha, 16–17
Butler, Nicholas Murray, 290
Butor, Michel, 414
Byng, Lord, 128
Byron, 171
Byron, Lord, 77, 143, 150, 162, 169–71, 199, 207, 420
Byron, Lady, 170
Byron, The Last Phase, 170

Cadogan, Peter, 199
Caffery, Jefferson, 353
Caillavet, Françoise de, 143, 155, 171–3, 197
Caillavet, Gaston de, 140–1
Caillavet, Simone de, *see* Maurois, Simone
Caillavet, Mme Arman de, 140
Cailloux, Colonel, 231, 247
Cain, Julien, 345, 350, 375, 423
Calderon, 406
Cambon, Roger, 260, 264
Candide, 34
Canet, Louis, 31
Caneval, General, 391
Cape, Jonathan, 345
Cardes, Colonel de, 230–1
Cartier, Pierre, 275
Casadesus, Robert, 294
Castéja, Commandant de, 110
Castellane, Captain Georges de, 214, 264
Catroux, General, 285, 306, 308, 422
Causeries du lundi, 23
Caves du Vatican, Les, 380
Cercle de famille, Le, 186–8, 193, 217
Cellier, Comandant, 147
Cendrars, Blaise, 238
Cézanne, 353
Chabaud-Latour, 105
Chain, Professor, 370
Chambe, General, 305, 308

Chamberlain, Austen, 128, 177
Chamberlain, Joseph, 414
Chamberlain, Neville, 200–1
Chambrun, General de, 146–7, 371
Chambrun, Captain de, 235, 278
Champdivers, Odette de, 384
Chamson, André, 389
Chants du soldat, Les, 8
Chaplin, Charles, 161
Chapman, Percy, 174
Chapuisat, 289
Chardigny, General, 225–7
Chardonne, Jacques, 144
Charon, Jacques, 385
Charpentier, 17–18, 100
Chartier, Emile, see 'Alain'
Chartreuse de Parme, La, 37, 62, 188
Chateaubriand, 143, 144, 156, 193–5, 213,
    268, 339, 366, 381, 394
Chateaubriand, 193–5
Chaumeix, 196
Chaworth, Mary, 169
Chenevière, 382
Chénier, André, 29
Chérets, The, 71
Chesterfield, Lord, 183
Cheval et le faune, Le, 101
Chevalier, Maurice, 234
Chevrillon, André, 207
Childe Harold, 420
Chopin, 72, 328
Choquette, Robert, 274
Choses nues, 160, 192, 264
Churchill, Winston, 102, 202, 260, 261–3,
    275, 284, 293, 395, 415
Chute de la Maison Quesnay, 410
Clair, René, 389, 404, 415
Clark, General, 296, 316
Claudel, Paul, 35, 119, 151, 216, 290, 297,
    298, 307, 319, 326, 350, 363, 389, 395,
    419
Clayburg, Alma, 282
Clerk, Sir George, 192
Clemenceau, Georges, 49, 106, 112, 117,
    159, 299
Clermont-Tonnère, Captain de, 304–6,
    308
Clews, Henry, 136
Climats, 10, 23, 165–8, 186–9, 217, 360,
    365, 397
Cobb, Irvin, 391
Cocteau, Jean, 381, 388, 414–15, 420–1
Coindreau, Maurice, 174, 294

Colefax, 130, 177
Colère de Samson, La, 367
Colette, 383
Colomba, 343
Colonel Bramble, 3, 109–12, 119, 121, 126,
    128, 131, 145, 161, 164, 183, 217, 236,
    240, 314, 349, 371, 418
Colonna, Commander, 311
Colonne, 72
Comédie Française, La, 29, 384–6, 411
Comédie humaine, La, 34, 409
Comte, Auguste, 33, 35, 36, 57, 65, 377
Conan Doyle, Arthur, 9
Constant, Benjamin, 208, 322
Consulat et L'Empire, Le, 9
Consuelo, 35, 369
Contre Sainte-Beuve, 367
Cooper, Lady Diana, 128, 255–6, 266
Cooper, Duff, 128, 255–6, 266
Coquelin, 29
Corap, General, 243–4
Corbin, Charles, 183, 257, 260, 262
Corneille, Pierre, 19, 26, 28, 32, 193, 205,
    218, 381
Côté de Chelsea, Le, 411
Cotnareanu, 274, 346
Coty, President, 390–3, 399
Courbet, Admiral, 105
Courcel, Lieutenant de, 262
Courier, Paul-Louis, 34
Courtney, Philip, 327
Cousin, Victor, 366
Couturier, Père, 350
Cowan, Arthur, 280
Coward, Noel, 226
Craine, Professor, 328
Crane, Mrs Murray, 275
Crawshaw, Captain, 254
Creed, H-.J, 227
Crespin, 330, 346
Custine, Delphine de, 194
Curzon, Lord, 177

Daladier, 209, 244
Daniel-Rops, Henri, 263
Danrit, Captain, 10, 42
Daphne Adeane, 129–30
Darlan, Admiral, 296, 299, 303
Darlu, 31
Daudet, Alphonse, 19, 292
Dautry, Raoul, 242–3
David-Weill, Pierre, 297
Davis, John W., 293

Davray, H. D., 164
Debré, Michel, 394, 423
Debussy, 322, 328
Decker, Clarence, 323, 327, 329–31
Decker, Mary, 327, 329, 331
Delacroix, 354–5
Delamare, Lise, 385
Delorme, 294
Demanche, 46
Denis, Monsieur, 69–70
Denny, 317
Dépêche de Rouen, 61
Député de Pont de L'Eure, Le, 289
Déracinées, 57
Dernière Classe, La, 19
Dernière Histoire du monde, La, 59
Déroulède, 8
Descartes, René, 29, 31, 35, 38, 377, 378
Descaves, Lucien, 112
Descaves, Pierre, 384–6
Desfours, 26–7
Desjardins, Anne, 124–6, 138, 158, 207, 306–8, 316, 342
Desjardins, Paul, 123–4, 158
Desjardins, Mme, 124–5
Devinck, General, 305, 310, 313, 316
Dialogues sur le commandement, 138–9, 155
Dickens, Charles, 37, 58, 88, 124, 162, 188, 235, 372, 378
Dickinson, Emily, 328
Dieux, Les, 375, 378
Dillon, Clarence, 275
Dillon, Douglas, 275
Dîner en ville, 412
Disraeli, Benjamin, 46, 150–1, 165, 197, 207, 417
Disraeli, 161, 164, 336, 366
Dorgelès, Roland, 382
Dormeuils, The, 71
Douglas, 106, 113
Doumer, Paul, 189–90
Doumie, Jacques, 198
Doumie, René, 161–2, 186–7, 193, 194, 195, 198–9
Dreiser, Theodore, 161, 328
'Dreyfus, Affaire', 27, 49, 63, 151
Droit, Michel, 404, 422, 423
Druon, Maurice, 404–5, 406, 422, 423
Duhamel, Blanche, 207
Duhamel, Georges, 194, 325, 326, 340, 355, 382
Dumas, Père, 369–70
Dumas, Fils, 341, 343, 369–70

Dumas, Professor, 144
Dumoncel, Maurice and Constant, 404
Dumur, Louis, 164
Duncannon, Lord, 306
Dupont, Jacques, 404
Dupré, Fr, 72
Dupré, Monsieur, 16, 205
Dupré, Marcel, 16
Durfort, Countess de, 194
Durozoy, Captain, 148, 306
Dutourd, Camille, 382
Dutourd, Jean, 404–5, 419, 423

Edwards, Chavela, 361
Edwards, Lala, 361
Eisenhower, General, 303, 310, 317, 318
Eliot, T. S., 328, 339
Elizabeth, Queen Mother, 179, 257–9
Equipes Sociales, 178
Ernle, Lord, 170
Escarpit, Robert, 425
Esperey, Marshal Franchet d', 195–6
Estaing, Giscard d', 423

Fagalde, General, 242
Fargeaud, Madeleine, 408–9
Farrère, Claude, 189
Father and Son, 24
Fauré, 136, 144, 382, 405
Fayard, Jean, 230
Fayolle, Marshal, 139
Fels, André de, 304
Fels, Christian de, 304
Fels, Martha de, 207, 304
Figaro, Le, 200, 209–10, 276, 345, 346, 399
Fille d'Eve, Une, 368
Fille de Madame Angot, La, 8
First Hundred Thousand, The, 102, 238
Fisher, H. A. L., 192
Fisher, Admiral Sir William, 182
Flaubert, Gustave, 20, 23, 175, 292, 383
Fleming, Sir Alexander, 370–1, 395, 397, 408
Fleming, Lady, 370–1
Flers, Robert de, 139–40, 152, 155–6, 165
Floirat, Sylvain, 406–7
Florey, Professor, 370
Foch, Marshal, 9, 229, 299, 389
Follies, 66
Fontaine, Jean de la, 29
Forster, E. M., 168
Fouchet, Christian, 420
Fraenckel, Adolphe, 9–10, 14, 51

Fraenckel, André, 89, 91, 98, 110, 117, 278
Fraenckel-Blin, 13–14, 51–2
Fraenckel, Caroline, 9
Fraenckel, Eulalie, 14
Fraenckel, Henry, 8, 9, 14, 25, 40, 51–3, 65, 69, 84, 88, 121
Fraenckel, Marie, 9–10
Fraenckel, Olga, 341
Fraenckel, Paul, 14–15, 51–3, 60
Fraenckel, Robert, 61, 89, 91, 123, 341
Fraenckel, The Uncles, 6, 10, 14–15, 38, 51–2, 57, 65, 68, 69–71, 77, 83, 117, 410
Français et Allemands, 5
France-Amérique, 331, 379
France-Etats-Unis, 379, 395
France-Soir, 386, 393, 396
France, Anatole, 23, 28, 34, 88, 111, 140, 142–3, 153–4, 175, 193, 364
Francis Ferdinand, Archduke, 90
Franck, César, 199
François-Poncet, 298
Fraser, Lieutenant-Colonel, 227
Fritz, 54
Front d'Action Critique, 393–4
Frossard, 244–5
Fry, Roger, 123, 126
Furse, General, 102

Gallimard, 374
Gambetta, Léon, 6
Gambiez, General, 310
Gamelin, General, 202, 232–3, 244, 245, 262
Garçon, Maurice, 425
Gard, Roger Martin du, 123, 125, 126, 155, 156, 189, 194, 214, 218, 380
Garric, Robert, 178
Gaucher caporal, 59
Gaulle, General Charles de, 262–5, 286, 290, 296, 299–300, 303, 316, 317, 391–5, 415–16, 422, 423–5
Gauss, Dean, 174
Gautier, Théophile, 383, 386, 404
Genevoix, Maurice, 388, 420
George V, King, 106–7
George, Mlle, 370
Georges-Picot, 308
Géraldy, Paul, 382–3
Géraud, Henri, 267
Germinal, 56
Gérome, Raymond, 424
Gevel, Claude, 73

Gide, André, 36, 88, 123–7, 138, 155, 194, 218, 284, 297, 306–8, 334, 340, 342, 369, 380–1
Gillet, Louis, 186, 194, 198, 218, 283–4, 350
Gillot, Colonel, 230
Gilson, Etienne, 44
Giono, Jean, 382
Girardot, Annie, 385
Giraud, General, 229, 242, 245, 296, 298, 303, 305, 313, 316–17
Giraudeau, Lieutenant, 44
Giraudoux, Jean, 144, 190–1, 211, 212, 225, 226–7, 384
Goethe, Wolfgang, 129, 156, 208, 216, 367
Goering, 240, 266
Goering, Captain, 284
Gogol, 19
Goncourts, The, 383
Gone With the Wind, 287
Gordeaux, Paul, 386
Gordon, Major, 228, 230, 254
Gorguloff, 189
Gort, General, 228–33, 235, 245, 249, 254, 277
Gosse, Sir Edmund, 24, 131–2, 165
Grammar of Science, 57
Grand Prix National des Lettres, 375
Granier, Jeanne, 152
Grant, Captain, 230, 245–6
Grasset, Bernard, 110–12, 121, 139–41, 144, 164, 343
Green, Julien, 230, 289
Grente, Mgr, 355
Greville, Mrs., 130, 257
Grothuysen, 125
Grousset, 343
Guérin, Charles, 360
Guérin, Hubert, 360
Guermantes, Prince de, 205
Guerre de demain, La, 10
Guers, Paul, 385
Gunther, General, 316

Haig, Field Marshal, 113
Halévy, David, 112
Halifax, Lord, 183, 286
Handel, George Frederic, 136, 144, 413
Hankey, Sir Maurice, 183
Hanotaux, Gabriel, 144, 155–6
Harcourt, Robert d', 343
Hardinge, Sir Alex, 257–8
Harlé, 46

Harper, 275
Harris, Frank, 165
Haskell, Henry, 323, 327
Hausse et la baisse, Le, 123, 150
Haviland, Olivia de, 412
Hay, Ian, 102, 238
Hazard, Paul, 196, 284
Hegel, 31, 34, 378
Heine, Heinrich, 143
Helmotz, 57
Hémelot, General, 230
Hemingway, Ernest, 328, 333, 411
Henderson, Sir Arthur, 183
Henri Brulard, 35
Henri-Robert, 140
Henriot, Emile, 145–6, 190, 191, 340–1, 350, 355, 357, 382–3
Hermant, Abel, 112, 196
Hermant, Captain Max, 249–50
Herriot, 148, 177, 192, 301, 350, 355
Herzog, Ernest, (the author's father), 6–8, 11, 13–15, 22, 30, 51–2, 55, 66, 68–70, 78, 82–5, 88–9, 149–50, 342, 410
Herzog, Edmond, 14, 15, 38, 51–3, 69, 70, 90
Herzog, Germaine, 82
Herzog, Mme (the author's mother), 7–8, 10, 11, 12, 16, 22, 24, 29, 82–5, 205, 218, 263, 283, 307–8, 323, 335–6, 351
Herzog, Marguerite, 10, 24
Herzog, Pierre, 89, 91, 97, 113, 117, 278
Heures latines, Les, 142
Heurgon, Anne, 218
Heusch, General, 146
Hibben, 174, 176
Histoire d'Angleterre, 182, 192, 345
Histoire de France, 9, 23
Histoire de mes pensées, 378
Hitler, 200–1, 211–12, 229, 234, 235, 261–262, 264, 269, 276, 289, 295, 311, 380
Hoare, Sir Samuel, 183
Ho Chi Minh, 345
Holmes, Oliver Wendell, 282
Homer, 34, 376
Hoover, Herbert, 204
Hore-Belisha, 202, 239
Howard, Ernest, 327
Hugo, Victor, 8, 22, 28, 29, 35, 188, 193, 194, 290, 323, 343, 367, 369–70, 372, 379, 389, 406, 409
Hugo, Victor, 322, 348
Huguet, General, 94
Hull, Cordell, 299

Humbert, General, 313
Huysmans, J-K., 20
Hyde, James Hazen, 161

Imitation of Christ, The, 33
Institut du bonheur, L', 187
Intermezzo, 143
Isler, Lieutenant, 44
Istel, 297

Jaloux, Edmond, 123, 125, 144, 194, 195
Jaloux, Germaine, 144
James, Dr., 101, 371
James, Edwin, 297, 299
Janssen, General, 242
Jaujard, Jacques, 375
Jaurès, 63
Jenner, Colonel, 130, 137, 184
Joffre, Marshal, 421
John, Augustus, 184
Johnson, Dr., 102
Jour, Le, 286
Jouvet, Louis, 384
Joxe, General, 303
Joyce, James, 411
Juin, General, 296, 316–17

Kafka, Franz, 411
Kansas City Star, The, 323, 326, 331
Kansas University, 323, 326–31, 357
Kant, 35, 70
Karenine, Mme, 368
Keats, John, 133
Kemp, Robert, 350, 383, 386
Kennedy, J. F., 415–16
Kernan, Tom, 300
Kessel, Joseph, 227
Keyserling, 359
Kim, 36
King Lear, 287
Kipling, Rudyard, 35, 46, 57–8, 60, 104, 111, 112, 130, 162, 183
Kittel, 18–20, 26, 40, 292, 340
Kling, Dr., 319, 321
Knox College, 288
Koszul, 164
Kreisler, 101

Labiche, 22
Lacaze, Admiral, 144, 196
Lacour-Gayet, Robert, 290, 350, 404
Lacretelle, Jacques de, 388
La Fayette, 371–2

La Fayette, Adrienne de, 371–2, 386, 395, 408
Lagneau, 340, 376
Lamartine, Alphonse de, 22, 322
Lammenais, F. de, 379
Lamont, Mrs., 276
Lamoureux, 72
Langevin, 240–1
Lantelme, 152
Laroche, 225, 398
Latour, Colonel Boyer de, 314
Laurencie, General de la, 242
Lavallière, Eve, 152
Lawrence, Dr., 241
Lazard, Christian, 344
Lazard, Ginette, 344
Lazareff, 226
Leahy, Admiral, 295
Léautaud, Paul, 164, 165
Lebrun, President, 234, 273
Lecanuet, 423
Leclerc, 329
Lecomte, Georges, 196, 264, 333, 341, 355
Lecomte-Boynet, 362
Leconte, Marie, 152
Leduc, Dr., 104
Lefèvre, 239, 246
Léger, Alexis, 267
Léger, Fernand, 292, 297, 350
Legouis, 164
Legrix, Jean, 44, 46–7, 87, 94, 95, 97
Lehanneur, 40, 314
Leigh, Colston, 395, 396
Lélia, 369, 409
Lelong, General, 254
Lemaigre-Dubreuil, 298, 306
Lemaître, Jules, 193, 369
Lemoine, Abbé, 134
Leroy, 20, 343
Level, 297
Lherminier, Commander, 311
Little Lord Fauntleroy, 17
Littré, 336
Livy, 29
Lloyd, Lord, 253
Lolita, 363–6
Lorca, Federico Garcia, 362
Loren, Sophia, 412
Lorey, Eustache de, 106
Lovat, Lady, 128
Lovelace, Lady, 169–70
Lovenjoul Library, The, 408

Lowell, John Jr., 287
Lowell Institute, 273
Lowell Lectures, The, 250, 281–2
Luce, Clair, 280
Ludendorff, 111
Luizet, 314, 316, 341
Lyautey, Marshal, 49, 112, 145–6, 178–80, 207, 366, 395
Lyautey, Olga, 87
Lyautey, Pierre, 148, 230
Lycée Corneille, 22, 381
Lys dans la vallée, Le, 34, 62
Lys rouge, Le, 73

MacAnulty, Lizzy, 17
MacCarthy, Desmond, 128, 168, 171, 182, 259, 261, 267
MacDonald, Ishbel, 190
MacDonald, Ramsay, 177, 190
MacFarlane, General Mason, 238, 245
Mackenzie, Winifred, 135
Macmillan, Harold, 299
Madame Bovary, 187, 369
Madelin, Louis, 192, 196
Maeterlincks, The, 276
Magli, General, 314
Magny, Claude-Edmond, 383
Maille, 63
Mal-aimés, Les, 209
Mallarmé, S., 133, 261, 322, 381, 398
Malraux, André, 226, 382, 418
Man and Superman, 424
Mandel, 192
Mann, Thomas, 276
Manolete, 362
Manon, 80
Mansfield, Katharine, 133, 211
Marais, Jean, 414
Marboutier, Mme, 409
Margaret, Princess, 414
Maria, Roger, 427
Marivaux, 41, 205, 381
Marquand, John, 282
Mars, ou la guerre jugée, 131
Marsh, Mrs. John, 287
Martel, Henriette de, 207
Martel, Thierry de, 251–2
Martin, Henri, 9–10, 14
Martin, General Henri, 306, 313, 314
Marx, Karl, 57, 250
Maryland, University of, 413
Mast, General, 305

Mathematical Demonstration according to Kant, Leibniz and the Modern Mathematicians, 40
Maupassant, Guy de, 20, 23, 60
Maupin, Mlle de, 23
Mauriac, Claude, 342, 412
Mauriac, François, 3, 144, 194, 195, 209, 230, 340, 342, 346, 350, 352, 381–2, 384, 404, 421, 423
Mauriac, Jeanne, 207, 209, 346, 352
Maurois, Gérald, 132, 157, 172, 196, 218, 237, 250, 284, 309, 326–9
Maurois, Janine (the author's first wife), 73–97, 101, 103, 105, 108–9, 112–13, 123–4, 126, 132, 134–7, 140, 143–4, 150–1, 184, 352
Maurois, Michelle, 132, 137–9, 196, 332, 335, 339, 341, 342, 406
Maurois, Olivier, 132, 157, 172, 196, 218, 308, 315–16
Maurois, Simone (the author's second wife), 139–45, 151–9, 167, 170–3, 174–5, 184–6, 195, 196, 218, 223, 227, 236–7, 243, 245, 247–53, 254, 259, 272–5, 283, 289–91, 294–6, 300, 304, 305–8, 314, 317–19, 324–5, 326, 332, 339–43, 346–9, 351–2, 354–6, 362, 370, 397–407, 424, 426–8
Mendès-France, Pierre, 351, 423
Médecin de campagne, Le, 34
Medlicott, Colonel, 248, 251
Melchior, Lauritz, 291
Menicot, Roger, 347, 357–8
Memoirs, 213, 224, 289, 382
Mémoires d'outre tombe, 35, 197, 198
Mémorial de Saint-Hélène, 22, 34
Mérimée, Prosper, 28, 124, 143, 342, 367, 405
Meyer, Eugene, 275
Meyer, Jean, 387
Michel, Albin, 425
Michelet, Jules, 23
Milhaud, Darius, 292, 295, 297, 326, 350
Milhaud, Madeleine, 292, 295, 297, 326, 350
Mill on the Floss, The, 142
Millerand, 148
Mill, Pierre, 112
Mills College, 3, 214, 217, 291–2, 294–5
Minéry, Père, 329
Misérables, Les, 36, 188
Mitterand, Edgar, 423–5
Molière, 81, 381, 384, 406

Mollet, Guy, 392
Mondor, Henri, 341, 350
Monkton, Sir Walter, 255
Monsabert, General de, 306
Montaigne, Michel de, 28, 152, 224, 272, 334, 374, 397, 425
Montherlant, Henri de, 382
Monypenny, 164
Moore, Colonel, 96, 97–9
Moore, Tom, 170
Morand, Paul, 144
Morize, André, 211, 227, 285
Mortimer, Raymond, 259, 261
Mouchel, 20–1, 40, 56, 63–5
Moulin, Captain, 44–5, 47
Mounet-Sully, 29, 207
Mountbatten, Lord, 310
Moutet, Marius, 345
Mousquetaires au couvent, Les, 8
Mozart, 133
Mugnier, Abbé, 129, 144, 155–6, 160, 173, 193, 350
Mun, Captain de, 110
Munster, Lord, 228, 230
Murphy, Bob, 296, 298, 299, 306
Murville, M. Couve de, 420
Muse du département, 409
Musset, Alfred de, 22, 28, 41, 370, 384, 386
Mussolini, 261, 312
Musters, The, 169

Napoleon Bonaparte, 232, 395, 409
Napoleon III, 409
New York Times, 294, 297, 304
Ni ange, ni bête, 121, 131, 132
Nicolay, Christian de, 307
Nicolson, Harold, 128, 170, 225–6, 259, 265
Noailles, Anna de, 144
Noailles, Nathalie de, 194
Now with the Morning Star, 300
Nouvelles Littéraires, 373
Nuffield, Lord, 229

Ochs, Eugene, 297
Oedipus Rex, 207
O'Hare MacCormick, Anne, 299
Oiseaux de feu, Les, 189
Oliver Twist, 172
Olympio, 409
Orano, Signora Paola, 143
Ormesson, Vladimir d', 148, 360

Otage, L', 216
Ottavio, Roderigo, 359
Oxford, Lady, 130

Paganon, 190
Painlevé, 177
Palewski, 420
Pareto, Vilfredo, 57
Paris, Gaston, 124
Parsifal, 319
Patapoufs et Filifers, 172
Paulus, Mlle, 16
Pauvres Gens, Les, 8
Paysans, Les, 400
Peake, Charles, 255, 313
Peat, Harold, 204
Pegram Lectures, The, 427
PEN Club, 205, 320, 380
Perdrière, Hélène, 381, 385
Père Goriot, Le, 187, 368
Perrault, Charles, 10
Pesquidoux, Joseph de, 194
Pétain, Marshal, 139, 195, 259, 263–4, 276,
    278–80, 283, 284, 295–6
Petit Lycée (Elbeuf), 22, 27
Petits Soldats russes, Les, 23, 41, 74, 136,
    214
Pétry, Captain, 48
Peyerhimhoff, Simon de, 230
Peyrefitte, Roger, 420
Pezés, The, 71
Pflimlin, 392
Phipps, Sir Eric, 200, 226–7, 257, 259, 261
Phipps, Lady, 200, 207, 259, 265, 352, 427
Pichon, 28
Pilot, Commander, 307, 320–1
Pinay, 420, 423
Pink Library, 10
Plato, 31–2, 34–5, 38, 138, 377–8
Poe, Edgar Alan, 328
Poeymirau, 179
Poincaré, Henri, 57, 106–7, 144, 158–9,
    177–8, 212, 423
Poletti, 276
Polk, 279–80, 301
Pons, Lily, 323
Pontigny, 205
Porché, François, 198
Porché, Simon, 404
Porges, Michel, 307
Poulenc, Francis, 404
Poumier, Commander, 230, 235, 247
Pouquet, Maître Antoine-Chéri, 152, 155

Pouquet, Mme, 144, 151–2, 325, 347–9,
    398–402
Pouquet, Maurice, 155–6, 314, 325, 346–9,
    399–402
Pouquet, Pierre, 156
Pour la victoire, 331
Pour piano seul, 411
Poussin, 419
Prévost, Jean, 166
Prévost, Marcel, 23, 373
Principes de Guerre, Les, 9
Prioux, General, 242
Prix du Prince, 382–3
Prométhée ou la vie de Balzac, 224, 405,
    409–11, 418–19, 420
Proust, Marcel, 31, 124, 140–3, 152, 158,
    160, 166, 328, 330, 367–9, 372, 378, 405,
    411
Puck of Pook's Hill, 130
Punch, 128
Pushkin, 19
Puthomme, Captain, 230, 247

Queen of Spades, 19
Queen Victoria, 169

Rabelais, François, 28
Rabier, 39
Rabouilleuse, 53
Race blonde, La, 189
Racine, Jean, 28, 193
Réau, Mlle Cécile, 292
Recherche de Marcel Proust, A la, 367–8
Reclus, 23
Reinhardt, President, 192, 295
Rembrandt, 11
Renan, Ernest, 28, 138, 194, 383
Renoir, 126
Republic (Plato), 138
Retz, Cardinal de, 35, 214, 303
Revue des deux mondes, 161, 186
Revue de Paris, 166
Reynaud, Paul, 242, 244, 253, 259, 260,
    273, 390, 420, 423
Reynolds, Colonel, 227–8
Richet, Georges, 102
Ridel, Captain, 95–6, 98–100, 102
Rimbaud, Arthur, 322
Ring of Polycrates, 18
Ringeisen, 47
Ritleng, Mme, 16
Robbe-Grillet, Alain, 411
Robineau, 26–7

Rochefoucauld, La, 323
Rochefoucauld, Edmée de la, 207
Roehrich, Pastor, 7, 23, 25, 58, 236
Rognedov, Eugène, 359, 361–2, 363
Roi Primerose, Le, 140
Roland, Romain, 88, 292, 366
Romains, Jules, 276, 289, 290, 332, 335, 340, 343, 345, 355, 421, 423, 425
Romier, Lucien, 209, 213
Roosevelt, F. D., 203, 204–5, 262, 275, 276, 279–81, 293, 301, 328
Roses de Septembre, Les, 361, 363–6
Rostand, Jean, 416
Rothschild, Maurice de, 324
Rouchard, Louis, 285
Rouchaud, 290, 297
Rouen-Lycée, 25–31, 36–8, 47, 59, 205, 218, 289
Rouge et le noir, Le, 37
Rougier, Louis, 284
Rousseau, J-J., 3, 183, 193, 381
Rozier, Etienne Burin des, 284
Rueff, Jacques, 420
Runcimans, The, 190
Russell, Lord, 182

Sacams, Sergeant-Major, 46
Sainte-Beuve, 23, 62, 366, 367, 370
Saint-Exupéry, 284, 289, 290, 295, 304–6, 350
Saint-Privat, 6, 57
Saint-Simon, 34, 57, 214, 303, 372
Salisbury, Lord, 162
Salle, Monica de la, 350
Sand, George, 36, 354, 368–70, 372, 404, 406, 409
San Marcos University, 361
Sarcey, Yvonne, 345
Sardou, Victorien, 152
Sarraut brothers, 177
Sarraute, Nathalie, 411
Sartre, Jean-Paul, 388
Saturnin, 117–18
Sauguet, 404
Saumur, Ecole de, 138
Scènes de la vie, 325
Schiffer, Colonel, 249–50
Schlumberger, Jean, 123, 218, 342
Schmidt, Federico, 360
Schmitt, Bertrand, 290, 322
Schubert, 328
Schumann, 72
Seaman, Owen, 128

Sentimental Journey, 353
Seznec, Professor, 426
Shakespeare, 79, 132, 145, 146, 156, 162, 193, 207, 236, 287, 353, 379–80
Shaw, G. B., 66, 321
Sheehan, Vincent, 276
Shelley, 119–21, 126–7, 131–3, 143, 164, 166, 169, 366
Shelley, Mary, 156
Siegfried, André, 161, 355, 391
Smoke, 74
Socrates, 32, 35
Soir des siècles, Le, 289
Soloveitchek, 329
Sorel, Julien, 33
Souday, Paul, 144
Soupault, Philippe, 307
Spinoza, 31, 34, 35, 41, 340, 378
Staël, Anne de, 77
Stalin, 396
Stalky, 46
Stanhope, Lord, 183
Steinhardt, Lawrence, 244
Stendhal, 34, 42, 57, 60, 62, 121, 168, 175, 292, 336, 342, 354, 366, 367, 372, 377–8, 405
Sterne, Laurence, 353
Stevenson, R. L., 328
Stirling, Colonel, 182
Storrs, Ronald, 129
Strachey, Lytton, 123, 135, 169
Stravinsky, 12
Suze, 59
Swift, 328
Swinburne, 132
Szymkiewicz, Count Constantin, 74
Szymkiewicz, Janine, *see* Maurois, Janine
Szymkiewicz, Jean de, 76

Tabouis, Geneviève, 286, 350
Tacitus, 34, 40
Taine, H., 23, 57, 194
Tardieu, 189, 192
Tartuffe, 284
Taulelle, Jean, 422
Temps retrouvé, 14
Tennyson, 415
Terre promise, 289, 321, 360
Texcier, 28
Tharaud, Jérôme, 196, 227, 355
Thelma, 17
Thesiger, General, 99, 102
Thiers, 9

Thomas, 306
Thompson, Dorothy, 244
Thomson, Sir Joseph, 168–9
Thousand and One Nights, The, 214
Times, The, 257
Timon of Athens, 287, 300, 354
Tolstoy, 19, 57, 124, 214, 323, 328, 330, 357, 396
Toscanini, 405
Tourte, Mlle, 358
Tractatus politicus, 143
Tragedy in France, 276, 306
Traz, Robert de, 123, 354
Treasure Island, 17
Trevelyan, 169
Trocquer, Le, 320–1
Trois Dumas, Les, 369
Twain, Mark, 161
Tyrell, Lord, 177, 183

Ulysses, 412
Ursin, Mlle, 53
Ursin, Père, 53–4, 63

Valéry, Paul, 35, 139–40, 144, 150, 194, 261, 322, 340, 350, 363, 373, 381, 382, 405, 412
Valette, 164–5
Vallery-Radot, Pasteur, 341, 355
Van Biber, Darlene, 330
Van Gogh, 328
Vansittart, Sir Robert, 183, 184
Varley, Miss, 152
Vase étrusque, Le, 143
Vaudoyer, Jean-Louis, 144
Vauvenargues, 323
Vega, Lope de, 362
Verlaine, 29, 322, 381, 390
Verne, Jules, 10, 161
Veronese, 150
Victoria, Queen, 159, 162, 169, 258
Vie de Sir Alexander Fleming, La, 395, 408
Vienot, Pierre, 147
Vierge de Sunam, La, 356, 361
Vieux Colombier, 161
Vigny, Alfred de, 22, 42, 326, 367, 370, 418

Villon, François, 28
Vilmorin, Louise de, 382
Virgil, 28
Vogüé, Félix de, 148
Voltaire, 34, 125, 183, 193, 366
Voltaire, 230
Volupté, 62
Voruz, General, 230–1

Wagner, Richard, 144, 153, 322
Wake, Major, 106
Walpole, Horace, 161
War and Peace, 41, 57, 74
Warre, Colonel, 105, 113
Washington, George, 328
Washington Post, 275
Watteau, 205
Weil, Simone, 373
Weiller, Paul-Louis, 333
Welch, Brigadier-General, 104–6, 113
Wells, H. G., 164, 276
Werther, 129
Weygand, General, 144, 249, 295–6, 298
White, William Allen, 280, 322
Whitman, Walt, 328
Wigram, Ralph, 190
Wilhelm Meister's Apprenticeship, 368
Willkie, 280–1, 328
Wilson, Woodrow, 160, 276
Wilson, Lady, 128
Winterton, Lord, 259
Witasse, de, 147, 306
Wolf, 59
Wolfe, Thomas, 328
Wolff, Emilie and Gaston, 174, 323, 324, 332, 340
Woog, Raymond, 105, 109, 110
Wordsworth, 133
World as Will and Imagination, The, 334

Years of Misfortune, The, 213

Zaharoff Lecture, The, 426
'Zoilus', 166
Zola, Emile, 56
Zweig, Stefan, 276